WITHDRAWN

"Army Recruits being led from the station in Berlin in 1909 to the barracks, by non-commissioned officers."

1900

The Generation
Before the Great War

Also by *Edward R. Tannenbaum*

THE NEW FRANCE
THE ACTION FRANÇAISE: Die-hard Reactionaries in Twentieth-Century
  France
EUROPEAN CIVILIZATION SINCE THE MIDDLE AGES
A HISTORY OF WORLD CIVILIZATIONS
THE FASCIST EXPERIENCE: Italian Society and Culture, 1922–1945
MODERN ITALY: A Topical History Since 1861, with Emiliana P. Noether

1900

The Generation
Before the Great War

Edward R. Tannenbaum

ANCHOR PRESS/DOUBLEDAY

GARDEN CITY, NEW YORK   *1976*

ILLUSTRATION CREDITS

Courtesy, Documentation Française, Photothèque, p. 6; courtesy, Georges Sirot and the Estate of H. C. White, p. 15; courtesy, Manchester Public Libraries, pp. 22–23; courtesy, Bildarchiv Preussischer Kulturbesitz, p. 26; courtesy, Osterreichischenation-albibliothek, Bildarchiv, pp. 42–43; courtesy, Staatl. Museen Preussischer Kulturbesitz. Nationalgalerie Berlin West. Foto: Anders, p. 58; courtesy, Cultural Services of the French Embassy, p. 97; courtesy, Osterreichischenationalbibliothek, Bildarchiv, p. 101; courtesy, Osterreichischenationalbibliothek, Bildarchiv, p. 105; courtesy, Radio Times, Hulton Picture Library, p. 109; courtesy, Manchester Public Libraries, pp. 112–113; courtesy, Documentation Française, Photothèque, pp. 126–127; courtesy, Radio Times, Hulton Picture Library, p. 143; courtesy, Hans Rauschning, Fackeltrager-Verlag, p. 147; courtesy, Osterreichischenationalbibliothek, Bildarchiv, p. 162; courtesy, Basic Books—Photograph "Competition in Camp" (1913) from *Young Germany: A History of the Youth Movement*, by Walter Z. Laqueur, copyright © Walter Z. Laqueur 1962, Basic Books, Inc., Publishers, New York, pp. 180–181; courtesy, Aberdeen University Library, G. W. Wilson Collection, pp. 194–195; courtesy, Bildarchiv Preussischer Kulturbesitz, p. 197; courtesy, Radio Times, Hulton Picture Library, p. 200; courtesy, Osterreichischenationalbibliothek, Bildarchiv, p. 202; courtesy, Radio Times, Hulton Picture Library, pp. 204–205; courtesy, Museum of Modern Art/Film Stills Archive, p. 221; courtesy, Conservatoire National des Arts et Metiers, p. 223; courtesy, Museum of Modern Art/Film Stills Archive, p. 224; courtesy, Museum of Modern Art/Film Stills Archive, p. 227; courtesy, Claude Bellanger, Directeur Général, *Le Parisien Libéré*, p. 230; courtesy, Osterreichischenationalbibliothek, Bildarchiv, p. 245; courtesy, Elvehjem Art Center *Dispersal of the Striking Workers*, by Markova, Gift of Joseph E. Davies, Elvehjem Art Center, University of Wisconsin-Madison, p. 287; courtesy, Radio Times, Hulton Picture Library, pp. 308–309; courtesy, Osterreichischenationalbibliothek, Bildarchiv, pp. 312–313; courtesy, Radio Times, Hulton Picture Library, p. 330; courtesy, Swedish Information Service, p. 366; courtesy, Collection, Museum of Modern Art, New York. Mathew T. Mellon Fund, p. 368; courtesy, Chanticleer Press, Inc., p. 370; courtesy, German Information Center, p. 372; courtesy, Museum of Modern Art, New York. Katherine S. Dreier Bequest, p. 373; courtesy, Collection, Museum of Modern Art, New York, p. 374; courtesy, Kunstmuseum Basel, p. 387; courtesy, Metropolitan Museum of Art, The Alfred Stieglitz Collection, 1949, p. 389; courtesy, Collection, Museum of Modern Art, New York, Hillman Periodicals Fund, p. 395; courtesy, Collection, Museum of Modern Art, New York. Acquired through Lillie P. Bliss Bequest, p. 397; courtesy, Belgian National Tourist Office, p. 399; courtesy, Museo Civico di Como, p. 403.

Library of Congress Cataloging in Publication Data

Tannenbaum, Edward R
   1900, the generation before the Great War.

   Includes bibliographical references and index.
   1. Europe—Social conditions. I. Title.
HN373.T33   309.1'4'0288
ISBN: 0-385-00431-1
Library of Congress Catalog Card Number 76–18369

CONTENTS

940.2
T166n

LIST OF
ILLUSTRATIONS

PREFACE

This comparative study of European society and culture in the period 1890–1914 is based on twenty years of research and teaching. In 1973 it was supported by a travel grant from the Research Council of the Graduate School of Arts and Science of New York University; in 1975 its completion was made possible by a Senior Fellowship from the National Endowment for the Humanities. The footnotes at the end of the book contain my sources for specific points as well as an up-to-date selection of specialized studies to help the reader probe further into those topics that interest him or her. Whenever possible the titles of these sources and studies are of editions currently available in English. Thus, instead of citing Max Weber's *Wirtschaft und Gesellschaft*, I cite its most recent English translation, *Economy and Society;* instead of Marcel Proust's *À la recherche du temps perdu*, the reader is referred to *Remembrance of Things Past*. In the text itself all titles of books are given in English with the date of first publication or, in a few cases, of completion. Thus, "Franz Kafka, *The Trial* (1914)" tells the reader that this novel was written in 1914, even though it was first published (posthumously) in 1925 in German and translated into English ten years later.

I wish to acknowledge the assistance given to me by the staffs of the following libraries and museums: the British Museum, the Bibliothèque Nationale, the New York Public Library, and the Tamiment collection on labor history of the New York University Library. In London I found many contemporary documents on religion in the Dr. George Williams Library and on feminism in the Fawcett Library. In Paris the curators of the Musée des Art Décoratifs and the Musée des Arts et Traditions Populaires were particularly helpful. I also want to thank the Department of Film of the Museum of Modern Art in New York for allowing me to view the motion pictures described in Chapter 6.

Although I alone am responsible for any errors of fact or interpretation in this book, I want to express my gratitude to those colleagues and friends who read parts of the manuscript. Roger Shattuck, of the University of Virginia, prompted me to rethink a number of points in Chapter 10; Hans A. Schmitt, also of the University of Virginia, made several important suggestions regarding Chapter 9; Raymond Grew, of the University of Michigan, did the same for Chapters 5 and 6. At New York University, William L. Blackwell helped me with certain Russian sources and with the complex theme of modernization. Other NYU colleagues who read sections dealing with their respective fields are: Isidor Chein (psychology), Eliot L. Freidson and Dennis H. Wrong (sociology), Brian L. Fennelly (music), and Robert H. Rosenblum (fine arts).

New York City
March 1976

1900

*The Generation
Before the Great War*

Detail from photograph of an English telephone exchange at the turn of the century, pp. 112–13.

INTRODUCTION:
Modernization and Its Discontents

The years 1890–1914 have been viewed with nostalgia as the *belle époque*—a time when life was leisurely, people were considerate, goods and services had real quality. How different from today's modern civilization, which has mobilized, homogenized, and computerized us to the point where our identities are reducible to zebra numbers. Technological rationalization makes undistorted rational communication itself increasingly difficult—as anyone knows who has tried to correct an error in his credit-card billing. It is no wonder that modernization has acquired a bad name in some circles.

But modernization has been going on for a long time, and what was the *belle époque* for some people was not so for others. What exactly *is* modernization? A discussion of this term will be found in the Appendix on Modernization, but, in short, it refers to the long-term transformation of societies by industrialization, urbanization, bureaucratization, and the extension of social mobility and political participation. Europeans were the first to accept modern ways of mastering their environment and earning their living, but they resented having to change their social and political arrangements and the cultural forms that gave meaning to their lives. This resentment was one source of discontent. Another was the impatience of those people who had been repressed under the old arrangements and who felt that these were not changing fast enough.

People feel at home only in their own society and culture. Society comprises the political, economic, and social structures within which their behavior takes place. Its arrangements of status, power, and identity define the real contingencies with which this behavior must deal. Culture gives people their view of reality. It includes what they know and how they know and express it, as well as their values and standards of behavior. Each culture has its own orientations to political, social, and economic action. And each culture has a common structure of feeling, "a way of responding to a particular world which in practice is not felt as one way among others—a conscious 'way'—but is, in experience, the only way possible."[1]

Modernization brought changes in economic, political, and social structures which tore people away from their familiar worlds and thrust them into situations in which they had to cope with competing moral orientations based on unfamiliar views of reality. In these new situations most people tried to cling to the standards they had learned in their own culture, but social conflict arose when these standards were no longer able to resist "the domination of one moral orientation over others."[2] Consequently people became more and more self-conscious about their occupational, sexual, and class status, their nationality, and their place in the power structure. And their new outlook became increasingly secular, materialistic, and self-centered.

This book examines these social and cultural responses to modernization in Europe beginning around 1890. By then economic and political concentration, electricity, railroads, steamships, cheap daily newspapers, and compulsory education began to affect the daily lives of millions of Europeans in most countries. After 1890 new mass movements intensified their efforts to mobilize the discontents of different categories of people uprooted from their traditional communities and cultural patterns. And during the years 1890 to 1914 outstanding critical thinkers and avant-garde artists set forth new views of reality which reflected their heightened awareness of the changes brought about by all aspects of modernization.

Many of the discontents of this pivotal period in European history were clearly not caused by social change and the emerging technological-bureaucratic civilization. The decline of religious influence in the late nineteenth century stemmed at least as much from the withdrawal of support and respect from religious institutions on moral or political grounds as from a decline in belief based on scientific analysis. In art, music, and literature the neoromantics were moved by feelings of alienation that often resembled those of their predecessors as far back as Rousseau. Resentment over traditional social injustices was widespread in the preindustrial sectors of the economy wherever these still existed. Nevertheless, many discontents in the 1890's and early 1900's were provoked by those forces of modernization which changed people's lives with unprecedented speed.

This study is limited to the ways in which people coped or refused to cope with these forces. It focuses on their perceptions, attitudes, and expectations and the kinds of behavior these prompted. German aristocrats often responded differently from British aristocrats, and there were regional and generational variations within each of these groups; yet there were also important similarities based on common interests and class biases. The same was true for other social groups in all European countries. Each nation and each social group had its own cultural heritage. There was no one type of worker, peasant, or bourgeois, but there were national types of each. And in certain situations the typical attitudes and behavior of each were based more on class than national cultural norms. This pattern appeared in such diverse areas as industrial relations, treatment of social inferiors, education, the arts, and fashions in dress and grooming.

Between 1890 and 1914 modernization helped to make people both more nationalistic and more international-minded than they had ever been. Never before had Europeans been able to travel more freely from one country to another, owing to the railroad and the steamship. Yet never before had national consciousness been so strong, owing to mass circulation newspapers, universal military training, and the patriotic feelings instilled by compulsory elementary schools. Silent films from France, Italy, and the United States were gaining an international audience on the eve of the most nationalistic war in history. Socialist workers and their leaders were especially torn between their feeling of solidarity with their comrades in other countries and their feeling of loyalty to their own.

The outbreak of the First World War makes a logical stopping point, for it subjected Europeans to unprecedented forms of mass mobilization by the state itself. Many features of the postwar years had their origins before 1914: movies, radio, air travel, modern art, attacks on bourgeois moral values, the emancipation of women. But the tone of European life, except in isolated rural areas, was markedly different from what it had been in the prewar era. (As one popular song asked: "How ya gonna keep 'em down on the farm after they've seen Paree?") Europe's aristocrats lost most of their remaining influence; the comradeship of the trenches was perpetuated in militant veterans' organizations; "totalitarian" regimes ruled by plebeian dictators took root in Russia, Italy, and, eventually, Germany.

Another example of a permanent change caused by the war was new attitudes toward prices and wages. During the hundred years preceding 1914 the currencies of most countries had been backed by gold and seemed to have stable values. This perception gave people with savings and fixed incomes a feeling of security. Prices had fluctuated, to be sure, but they had gone down as often as they had gone up. In fact, during the first part of our period it was lower prices that increased the workers' purchasing power more than any nominal increase in their wages, whereas from 1906 or so until the war their income leveled off as prices rose. The war itself brought pressures toward inflation which have never ceased (except during the world depression of the 1930's).* Before the war employers regarded wages as a fixed cost; since its end they have viewed them as a marginal cost because of the apparent irreversibility of wage and price increases.

Since this book is a synthesis, it is based on both primary sources and specialized scholarly studies; for some topics I have also relied on the works of creative artists and thinkers of the period. The arts can reveal and embody the effects of a whole lived experience in a community at a specific time. Literary and dramatic writers in particular draw on a total structure of feeling in ways not available in other contemporary documents. But they often distort certain aspects of life for their own aesthetic or ideological purposes, so that their portrayals of political and economic behavior, class antagonisms, or sexual attitudes must be used with caution. When creative writers and intellectuals turn consciously to social and cultural criticism, what they say can sometimes tell us more about *them* than about the reality they claim to expose. A major conceit of many such critics is to be able to say "we knew." Like the original Cassandra—but without her gift of prescience—they see themselves as impotent prophets in an alien world. This kind of response and those of all other social groups are what this book is about.

* Although the rate of inflation has varied among different countries in recent years, pre-1914 wages and prices cited in this book should be multiplied by twelve to obtain their approximate equivalents in the late 1970's in the United States and most Western European countries and by ten for West Germany and Berlin.

The first trains on the Paris Métro.

CHAPTER 1

MODERNIZATION REACHES THE MASSES

At seven-thirty on the morning of January 29, 1901, one thousand employees of the Paris subway system went on strike. In a cafe where some of the strikers gathered the following conversation might have taken place between the ticket-puncher Jacques Laval and the motorman Louis Martin.* They had just met.

JACQUES: Did you see the article in *Le Petit Parisien* calling us privileged workers who behave like spoiled children?

LOUIS: What do you expect from that bourgeois rag? If we're so privileged, how come the company fired forty-three of our comrades without notice and without compensation? That's what started the strike, isn't it?

JACQUES: It's hard for me to think of people I don't even know as com-

* This imaginary conversation is based in part on events and attitudes reported in Roger H. Guerrand, *Mémoires du Métro* (Paris: La Table Ronde, 1961), pp. 138–53. In early 1901 the morning daily *Le Petit Parisien* had a circulation of close to one million.

rades. Where I come from your comrades are the guys you grew up with.

LOUIS: I'm a native Parisian but I noticed your Auvergne accent. Where exactly do you come from?

JACQUES: A village you probably never heard of. My father has a tiny farm there, but I didn't feel like hanging around to inherit it. Besides, I didn't want to be a farmer anyway.

LOUIS: What did you want to be?

JACQUES: Well, it sounds childish now, but you know the picture book *La Tour de France par deux enfants . . . ?*

LOUIS: Every school kid in France has read it. More bourgeois propaganda.

JACQUES: Anyway, it made me want to be a railroad man, so I could travel all over the country like the two kids in the story.

LOUIS: So why are you working on the Métro? You don't see anything of France under the streets of Paris.

JACQUES: When I left home at eighteen I couldn't find a job on the railroad. I worked as an office boy in Clermont-Ferrand for two years, did my three years of military service, and came to Paris in '96. I did see a lot of the city as a bus conductor, but I got laid off in July of last year. Luckily that was just when they were opening the first Métro line.

LOUIS: So how do you like riding in those crowded cars? I prefer being by myself in my motorman's cab.

JACQUES: No offense intended, but I find Parisians too cold, too rude, and too smart-alecky. At first I tried to be friendly with the passengers, but they couldn't care less about me or about each other. The shopgirls think they're ladies, and the construction workers think they're Don Juans. I just don't think it's right, pinching a woman's bottom just because the car is packed.

LOUIS: But do you think it's right that our female comrades make ninety francs a month while we make a hundred fifty?

JACQUES: There you go with "comrades" again. Are you a socialist? Of course women should earn less than men. They don't have families to support. Ninety francs is plenty to supplement a husband's income.

LOUIS: What if a woman has no husband?

JACQUES: So much the worse for her. She can always become a servant in some rich man's home. That's what many of the girls from my village have done. By coincidence I married a girl who worked as a parlor maid in the home of Édouard Empain, the head of the board of directors of the Métro company. She says he's a very liberal gentleman.

LOUIS: The "liberalism" of those "gentlemen" stops short of recognizing the new union we formed last night.

JACQUES: But they did say we were free to join any union we liked.

LOUIS: Their idea of a union is an organization to keep us under their thumbs. The workers have to use their unions to get rid of those dirty capitalists and run things in the interest of the people.

JACQUES: Is that socialism?

LOUIS: No, that's revolutionary syndicalism.

JACQUES: It sounds more like anarchism to me. How can we have law and order without a strong state? And how can France protect herself against her enemies without a strong army?

LOUIS: We·French workers have no foreign enemies. Our enemies are right here at home. The state and the army are tools of the capitalists.

JACQUES: I don't mix much in politics. I'm just a simple country boy.

LOUIS: How can you say that? You left your village ten years ago.

JACQUES: I just don't want to argue politics with you, "comrade." Let's have another drink and talk about the next big bicycle race. Who do you think will win?

Ordinary people like Jacques and Louis were being affected by modernization in every aspect of their lives—from their jobs and leisure-time activities to the value system of their society. (See Appendix on Modernization.)

ECONOMIC GROWTH AND RISING STANDARDS OF LIVING

The most noticeable effect of modernization in the 1890's was the growing amount of goods and services available to masses of people in northwestern Europe and the urbanized regions of Central Europe and northern Italy. Only the unfortunate few were not appreciably better off in a material sense in 1895 than they had been twenty years earlier. During those two decades the purchasing power of the British working classes had increased 40 per cent; in Germany the figure was 22 per cent. Even in Italy, where real per capita income was one third that of Britain and one half that of Germany, a skilled worker in Milan spent less than 10 per cent of his earnings on wheat products for a family of four in the late 1890's. (To be sure, his wife had to spend a good deal of time haggling with fruit and vegetable vendors in order to provide some variety in the family's highly farinaceous diet.) People ate better, wore better clothes, and had better health care, more schools, and cheaper entertainment than ever before. This improvement was due in part to cheap food prices during the agricultural depression of that period, which allowed people to spend a greater portion of their income on other things. But it was fundamentally the result of the fact that, during most of the nineteenth century, industrialization had increased productivity as well as production faster than demand. Thus the prices of manufactured products, as well as food, remained relatively low, despite rising labor costs.

Between 1880 and 1913 world manufacturing production increased three times as much as world population, the volume of commodities entering into world trade two and one half times as much.[1] These rates of increase had never been equaled before nor have they since. In 1913, approximately 36 per cent of the world's manufacturing production was in the United States, 36 per cent in Germany, the United Kingdom, and France, and most of the rest was in other European countries. In Europe the rate of increase was highest in the newer industrial states: Germany, Russia, and Italy. But since the last two started from a much lower base, their total production was smaller than their growth rates suggest. In the older industrial areas, especially Great Britain, the process by which the economic base and society itself were becoming more complex and diversified did much to offset the relatively slower rate of increase in manufacturing per capita. Advances in technology made possible an immense expansion in the newer light industries, while cheaper distribution methods and rising standards of living stimulated the production of consumer goods such as soap, chocolate, processed foods, and cheap newspapers. In the most advanced societies there was also a great increase in the number of people employed in the service sector of the economy: transportation, department and chain stores, banking, communication, and professional occupations—particularly teaching and the civil service.

Increasing world trade affected almost everyone in agriculture and industry. Despite the tariffs imposed by many countries in the late nineteenth century, lower transportation costs on steamships and railroads helped cause the price of wheat in Europe to fall by half between 1871 and 1895. This fall hurt masses of marginal peasants and it accelerated their emigration to the cities and overseas. As competition for foreign markets for manufactured goods grew, domestic markets acquired increasing importance. The population of all advanced countries except France continued to grow rapidly during the 1890's and early 1900's, but national income grew even faster. Hence more and more people had more money to spend for manufactured goods as against food, for conveniences as against necessities. (Today these indicators of a rising standard of living are called "discretionary income.")

As people's living standards rose, so did their aspirations. Hence, by the turn of the century, many ordinary Europeans began to feel frustrated as their increased purchasing power stimulated rising prices. This inflation was reinforced by new gold production in South Africa and Alaska. It was also reinforced by the demand for the goods and services made available by new technological developments: electric power and motors, organic chemistry and synthetics, the internal combustion engine and automotive devices, precision manufacture and assembly-line production. These innovations had possibilities for increasing productivity which might have yielded a further decline in prices. But before these possibilities could be exploited the First World War sparked an inflation that has made demand stay ahead of supply throughout most of the twentieth century. Once initiated, the rising level of aspirations of Europe's masses was to remain a permanent feature of the process of modernization.

Modernization is dependent upon industrialization but is not assured by it. In our period, for example, Russian industrial output probably increased about 5 per cent per year or over 3 per cent per head of population. This growth rate was not exceptionally high in comparison with other countries, though it was somewhat higher in relation to the rate of population increase than in Germany and the United States. Yet despite the growth of industry in Russia, the gap between its per capita income and that of the advanced countries of the West may not have appreciably narrowed and in some ways may even have widened. The reason was that the growth of Russia's total national income was still largely determined by the forces of agriculture. By 1914 two thirds of the economically active population was still engaged in agriculture and almost half of the total national income was derived from it. The majority of Russian peasants bought few manufactured goods, and there was no way (before the Soviet period) to get investment capital from their meager incomes. As long as this situation persisted, the industrial enclave in Russia was bound to remain small and its progress impeded by a limited home market and inadequate supplies of domestic capital.

Although aggregate wealth mounted faster than total population between 1890 and 1914 in all countries, it was distributed in different ways, depending upon their level of industrialization. In Great Britain the amount of aggregate wealth that went into new capital investments increased more slowly than the amount that was received as real income per person. At the other extreme, in Russia, where heavy investment was still required in the basic equipment of an industrial society, real income grew at a slower rate, though to a greater extent than ever before. The result was that, between 1890 and 1914, real income was sacrificed to capital investment in Russia, as it had been during the first half of the nineteenth century in Great Britain. But by the early 1900's Russian workers, influenced by the gains of Western European labor by then, were unwilling to accept the wages and conditions of work which British workers had accepted when their country was in its early stage of industrialization. Their rising aspirations made them more militant in their demands for higher wages and better working conditions.

France and Germany provide a good comparison of how national aggregate wealth was distributed to two advanced countries. By the 1890's Germany had forged ahead of France in economic growth and was investing more heavily in new capital equipment in the electrical and chemical industries. Consequently, while Germany's aggregate national wealth grew at a faster rate than that of France (even after adjusting for her greater population growth), real income per head in France remained somewhat higher than in Germany until 1914 (partly because of her smaller population growth, to be sure). This seems to have been true even for French industrial workers, who had a slightly higher standard of living than German workers.

In agriculture, too, people began to aspire to a higher standard of living in Western and Central Europe. The agricultural depression of the late nineteenth century posed a special challenge to peasants who were getting used to buying and selling more as railroads opened up new markets. They were also learning more about the outside world from their schools and newspapers. Not only did many wage earners and marginal peasants leave for the cities, but those farmers who remained had to find new ways to get out of debt and increase their income.

In France many farmers began to rent threshing and reaping machines for grain, to clear new land for planting, and to switch to more profitable commercial crops. When phylloxera decimated the southern vineyards in 1907, the winegrowers, unlike their parents in the face of this disease a generation earlier, organized unions and mass demonstrations to force the government to help them out of the crisis so that they could return to the standard of living to which they had become accustomed. By 1910 a labor shortage had developed in other parts of rural France, thus forcing the average annual wage for farm workers up from 450 to 600 francs, with food, since the beginning of the century.

A similar situation appeared in Germany and Switzerland during the immediate prewar years, but the greatest transformation in agriculture had already occurred in Denmark. During the 1880's and 1890's Danish farmers had profited from the opportunity of turning cheap grain into livestock products. These were increasingly in demand as standards of living rose, and they found a ready market in Great Britain. Through a highly developed co-operative system Danish farmers had also built an integrated and efficient structure of production, processing, distribution, and marketing. In addition to making Denmark a great agricultural exporter in the twentieth century, this foundation enabled agriculture to make an indispensable contribution to the nation's over-all economic growth.[2]

Danish farmers were also among the best-educated in Europe. By 1913 there were over 8,000 students in the country's 60 folk high schools and 22 agricultural schools. The folk high schools aimed at giving an insight into the problems of life, rather than at purely vocational instruction. Denmark's rural population enjoyed a high standard of living, its property was more evenly distributed than elsewhere, and its co-operative and educational movements were creating "a fellowship in the quest of the joys and values of human life, which, irrespective of class and profession, family and income, unite[d] all."[3]

At the beginning of this century the health care available to working-class Europeans was improving, though still limited by today's standards. The friendly societies and trade unions to which a minority of wage earners belonged sometimes paid for a doctor or a hospital bed, as well as issuing sick pay. If their wives or children became ill, however, they had to turn to the charity wards of voluntary hospitals and public clinics. In some countries the public health authorities were beginning to hire practical nurses to visit women and children at home, and almost every district had a licensed doctor who treated the poor. Unfortunately, the stigma attached to consulting a "poor man's doctor" made many who had no other alternative go without any medical help at all. But, except for such people, most Western Europeans were healthier and lived longer than ever before. Improvements in sanitation and the control of a number of children's diseases helped to lower infant death rates. In England and Wales infant mortality reached its peak of 163 per 1,000 in 1898–99 and declined rapidly thereafter; by 1905 it was down to 128; in 1910, 105.

In other European countries the decline in death rates lagged far behind those of England and Wales, primarily because of greater overcrowding in housing. Between 1895 and 1905 the average death rate per thousand declined 4.6 per cent in Manchester, 3.6 per cent in Liverpool, and 2.6 per cent in London, whereas in Paris the decline was 1.8 per cent, in Vienna 1 per cent, in Berlin and St. Petersburg 0.6 per cent; in Rome the rate *increased* by 1.5 per cent. At the turn of the century only 8.2 per cent of the population of England and Wales lived in overcrowded housing (more than two persons per room), while the corresponding figure for Scotland was 50.6 per cent. Overcrowding was particulary severe in the newer industrial cities of Germany. Breslau had 49.9 per cent overcrowded and Chemnitz had 36.5 per cent, along with the highest infant mortality in Saxony. Death rates for adults were highest in the overcrowded cities and lowest in rural areas. According to a contemporary urban historian:

> while 426 out of 1000 men born in Prussia survive to the age of 50 years, only 318 native Berliners reach the same age . . . while the mean age at death is 42 years and 2 months in France, it is but 28 years and 19 days in Paris . . . while the average duration of life in the rural population of the Netherlands is 38.12 years, in the urban population it is only 30–31 years.[4]

A man who was born in the English countryside and stayed there might expect to live almost fifty-two years, whereas the average Manchester-born man died at twenty-eight.

Still, after 1900 material improvements accelerated in Europe's great cities. Electric lighting made the streets safer and pleasanter at night, and an increasing number of dwellings had running water. Bicycles and electric streetcars allowed working people in Vienna to visit suburban woods on Sundays. Badly housed Parisians could spend their leisure time in outdoor cafes or the new movie palaces that appeared around 1910. Londoners of all classes flocked to public sporting events in massive new stadiums. Middle-class Berliners could consume half a dozen oysters and a glass of German champagne for forty cents at Kempinski's restaurant. In the *belle époque* all but the poorest slum-dwellers sang popular songs about their capital city, asserting that life was sweeter there than anywhere else. There was much discontent in Europe's great cities, as we shall see, but it was based more on rising aspirations than on deteriorating material conditions.

POPULATION CHANGES AND MIGRATION

The total population of Europe, including Russia, increased from 370 million in 1890 to 480 million in 1914, or at the rate of about one per cent

Paris 1900 Exposition.

a year. This growth was remarkable in view of declining birth rates and the loss of close to 30 million people through emigration overseas. It occurred because the crude death rate (per thousand disregarding age and sex distribution) fell faster than the crude birth rate, though the latter fell at a somewhat slower rate in Germany and Russia than in Western Europe. The fall in the death rate resulted from developments already mentioned: an increase in the food supply, better sanitation and hygiene, and generally higher standards of living.

Family planning is one of the most widespread effects of modernization. People in most traditional societies do not ordinarily limit the number of children they produce. Their fertility rate—the average number of live births for women of child-bearing age—is determined almost entirely by natural forces. This was no longer so in Western Europe by the late nineteenth century. By then, except in Ireland, fertility declined because of the spread of birth control. And it was through the persistent use of birth control that family size dropped to an average of five to six by 1900. France had been the first country in which birth control (and abortion) had been widely used; between 1830 and 1910 its crude birth rate had declined from 30 to 20 per 1,000 people. Beginning in the 1880's the same decline occurred in forty years in Sweden and Switzerland, and in thirty years in Belgium, Denmark, and Great Britain. Yet Spain still had a crude birth rate of 33.8 per thousand in 1900, a death rate of 28.8 per thousand, and a life expectancy of less than thirty-five years. Demographically as well as economically Spain resembled the rest of Southern and Eastern Europe in its low level of modernization.

The middle classes were usually the first to limit the size of their families in order to maintain their social status in the face of expanding general opportunities. Already by the late 1870's middle-class British families began to sense a serious gap between their aspirations and their standard of living. As their opportunities for spending money multiplied their life style became more expensive. Equally important, they now came to regard secondary and university education as means for achieving or simply maintaining social status as the state provided more free education for the masses. Until the 1902 Education Act most professional people in Britain had found the local grammar schools (public high schools) reasonably adequate for their own children. But one of the unanticipated consequences of this act (which provided a ladder for lower-class children from the elementary to the grammar school) was to raise their aspirations for their sons, whom they now tried to send to costly "public schools" (private secondary schools). In order to be able

to afford this education and to maintain their standard of living they consciously limited the numbers of their children even further. The lower-
middle classes, particularly white-collar employees, soon began to emulate this kind of family planning for the same reason. (Although most
working-class Englishmen balked at using contraceptives with their wives
until the depression of the 1930's, by the end of the nineteenth century,
in England, France, and Germany, a growing number of emancipated
working-class women learned how to abort themselves. After 1880 in
most parts of Europe the fertility rate among unmarried women declined
along with that of married women, apparently because of the spread of
knowledge of contraception and abortion.)[5]

Besides the middle classes, many peasant proprietors had begun to practice family planning during the nineteenth century, especially in France
and Ireland. In France they used birth control in the hope of having only
one son to inherit their small holdings, which would no longer be economically viable if divided. Irish peasant proprietors used late marriage,
rather than birth control, to limit the size of their families. The famine of
the late 1840's left a disproportionate number of survivors in those classes
that traditionally married late and were unaccustomed to subdividing
their holdings. And the surviving laborers and tenants, who previously
had little to lose from early marriage, began to adopt similar norms. "The
Irish farmer behaved as a rational economic man, and, after the wave of
famine evictions ebbed, it was he, not the landlord, who drove his children and the labourers off the land."[6]

Demographic changes will be discussed in more detail in Chapter 3, but
the varying effects of modernization on different types of regions
should be noted here. Not all rural areas had high fertility rates and not
all cities had low ones. And the fact that at the end of the nineteenth century the rate of population growth was much higher in Germany than in
France hid regional variations based on local resources and on occupational and sociological differences. The unmodernized rural areas of western Brittany had a fertility rate as high as that of similar areas in East
Prussia and Pomerania. Nor was there uniformity of demographic experience in the urban areas of the two countries. "The great administrative
and trading cities were typically places of low fertility and high mortality, whereas the coalfield industrial areas experienced high . . . fertility
rates and a much more moderate mortality than the great cities."[7] This
was as true in the Nord department of France as in the Ruhr, in Berlin as
in Paris.

Migration within a given country or overseas was caused as much by dissatisfaction with a traditional existence as by economic conditions. It was the most—and sometimes the only—accessible way for an individual to satisfy new needs, to improve his situation, or, less frequently, to keep himself and his family at its customary economic level, which changing structures threatened to lower. Both individuals and groups emigrated more readily from villages and small towns in which the disorganization of the old social structure had been going on for some time and contacts with the outside world were relatively numerous.

Nowhere was this truer than in Ireland, where almost every family had a relative working in Liverpool, Boston, or New York. An Irish agricultural laborer told an inquirer in 1894: "I don't like the work on the land. It is very laborious and does not lead to anything. I have seen men who have worked all their lives as badly off as at the beginning." Yet in Ireland average weekly agricultural wages had risen from seven shillings in 1870 to eleven shillings in 1914. Thus thousands of Irish emigrants were influenced more by "a revolution in their subjective mentalities than in the objective realities of their standard of living."[8]

Modernization also changed the outlook of farm workers on the great estates of eastern Prussia. Hundreds of thousands of them left for the cities or the United States in order to get away from the patriarchal, almost feudal, social structure of that region. In a novel first published in 1893 a worker living in miserable conditions in Berlin answers his former master who wants to take him back:

> You and your sort are amazed that we run away. You gentlemen are responsible for it. We shall vote as the lord wants; we shall read what the lord permits; we shall keep our mouth shut about the suppression of the people; we shall stoop under the regimen of the Mister administration—no, times are too progressive for it; we are independent men. One has too much honor to allow one's self to be treated like cattle.[9]

Mass emigration was a function of modernization, which gave people the freedom, desire, and means to move. The means—railroads, steamships, telegraphs, and travel agencies—were part of the over-all process of economic modernization which broke up the self-contained existence of preindustrial society. They gave the potential emigrant the freedom to move more easily and cheaply in search of a better life. Economic modernization widened his horizons and gave him the desire to move away from contracting opportunities at home, especially in overpopulated rural areas. It also increased the possibility for social mobility, of which migration was a major aspect.

Emigration overseas reached its peak between 1890 and 1914. The United Kingdom (including Ireland) lost around 7 million people; Italy lost over 5 million; Spain lost almost 3 million; Austria-Hungary and Russia (including the Polish provinces) lost almost 2 million each. British emigrants went primarily to Australia, New Zealand, and Canada; Spaniards almost exclusively to Latin America, particularly Argentina. The Italians were equally divided between South and North America, while most of the Irish and Eastern Europeans went to North America. The bulk of the emigrants from the Russian Empire were Poles and Jews.* Some of the Jews stopped for a few months or years in Germany or England before joining the masses of Eastern and Southern Europeans packed in the holds of the great ocean liners bound for the United States.

But the main European population movement was from the countryside to the cities and from one town to another in a single country.

URBANIZATION

A town differs from a village in that its primary function is non-agricultural. It may be an administrative, commercial, or industrial center, whereas a village consists primarily of peasants and people who have administrative and commercial dealings with peasants. This is true no matter how large the village is; in southern Italy and parts of western Russia and Poland there were villages of over 10,000 inhabitants. A city is a large town, but it has a more diverse economic and social structure than most towns.

These distinctions are important, for the rapid urbanization of Europe in the late nineteenth century was not solely a function of industrialization. London and Paris were the only cities with over a million inhabitants before 1880 and remained among the fastest growing cities for several decades thereafter, yet neither was a center of modern industry. Manufacturing in London and Paris was mainly of the preindustrial craft types: clothing, household goods, printing, luxury items. Indeed a number of Europe's capital cities—Rome, Vienna, Budapest, Madrid—did not develop heavy industry until after the turn of the century, if at all. Berlin and St. Petersburg were exceptional in this respect, and their industries,

* Although few Russians went overseas, between 1900 and 1914 alone three and one half million of them migrated eastward beyond the Urals in a movement comparable to the settlement of the North American West (except that many more came back).

like those of other older cities, were located in their recently annexed inner suburbs. On the other hand, dozens of new towns and cities were dominated by industry in the English Midlands, the Rhineland and Westphalia in Germany, and the border area between France and Belgium. (The Westphalian town of Gelsenkirchen grew tenfold between 1871 and 1910, from 16,023 to 169,513.) Mining, heavy industry, and engineering predominated over textiles and other older industries in promoting the rapid growth of cities.

In 1815 less than 2 per cent of all Europeans lived in cities over 100,000; by 1910 the figure was 15 per cent. Already by 1901, 35 per cent of the population of Great Britain lived in cities over 100,000; by 1910 the figure was 21.3 per cent in Germany. In our period the most rapid urbanization was in Germany, which in 1880 had 14 cities over 100,000 and 48 in 1913. This dramatic increase was mainly the result of immigration and the regrouping of localities, particularly in the Ruhr area, whose status was changed because of their population growth. Between 1882 and 1907 the large German towns gained 8.5 million inhabitants, the small- and medium-sized towns, 8.4 million; in contrast, the rural population decreased by 0.4 million.[10]

Rapid urbanization, though linked with industrialization, was more directly a by-product of over-all population growth. Between 1870 and 1910 the population in Great Britain grew from 26.1 million to 40.8 million, in Germany from 40.8 million to 64.9 million, in Russia from 85.5 million to 139 million. Except in Great Britain, where by the turn of the century the urban population came near to reproducing itself, most of the growth in Europe's cities before the war was caused by emigration from rural areas and smaller towns. Migration played the largest role in the growth of French, Italian, and Russian cities, a somewhat lesser role in the German and Scandinavian, and the smallest role in the English cities.

The rapid growth in the size and number of cities created new service occupations for their feeding, lighting, cleaning, and policing, thus offering increased chances for employment outside of industry and mining for emigrants from overcrowded rural areas. Thus the significance of urbanization was not only the growth of the towns and cities themselves but their assimilation of so many rural people. The absolute number of Europeans dependent on agriculture for a livelihood did not begin to fall until the past two decades, but by the late nineteenth century the tendency for people to accumulate in a relatively few densely populated and highly urbanized regions had already begun to alter the patterns of earlier centuries.

All this mobility, both horizontal (geographical) and vertical, had a number of side effects. In 1890–91 less than 72 per cent of the total population of England and Wales resided in the county of birth; in Prussia those dwelling in the district of birth were 70 per cent, in Saxony only 69 per cent. In most countries the age structure of the urban population differed from that of the national population in having a greater proportion of productive adults and smaller shares of retired people and dependent children. Except in Russia and Serbia there were also more women than men in the cities. The profoundest effect of immigration to the cities was the adjustments the newcomers had to make to unfamiliar surroundings. In 1890–91 in Berlin some 80 per cent of the male labor force between the ages of thirty and sixty had been born outside the capital. Including the children of newcomers, the proportion of native Londoners was 65 per cent, of native Berliners 42.3 per cent, of native Parisians only 36.9 per cent.

As urban areas grew, their structures changed drastically. Nearly every large European city had an old central core dating back to medieval times and surrounded by a wall. During the nineteenth century these walls were demolished in Paris (1845), Berlin (1850), and Vienna (1857), and replaced by a ring of boulevards and railways. But until the development of the electric tram in the 1890's most people lived within walking distance of where they worked. Most worked in shops, small factories, banks, and other commercial and light manufacturing establishments. They lived in overcrowded tenements, while the wealthy lived in town houses or on the lower floors of the more fashionable apartment buildings. (Some poor people lived on their upper floors until the installation of elevators, beginning in the 1890's, made them more expensive.) As larger factories were built in the old inner suburbs, workers moved there into new tenements. Then, with the advent of the electric tram, office employees began moving out to new dormitory suburbs and commuting to downtown areas, which became increasingly commercial and administrative, with fewer and fewer residents.

Prague was a typical example of changing urban structure. In 1914, 400,000 people lived inside the area once surrounded by the old walls (demolished in 1878) and another 200,000 lived outside this area. There was a decrease both in the proportion of built-up land and in the density of population on it as one moved outward from the older residential dis-

The inauguration of the first electric streetcars in Manchester, England, 1900.

tricts. The proportion of children increased outward from the center in all socioeconomic groups. But the percentage of domestic servants was lower in the suburbs, where the residents tended to be younger and poorer than in the city. Working-class people constituted 50 to 70 per cent of the residents in the industrial periphery and one third in the central districts.

Beginning in our period the old and new rings of suburbs were gradually annexed to the central cities, and some of them became more densely populated. Meanwhile, still newer areas were developed, fanning out from the cities along rivers, railways, and canals—some industrial, some residential. These communities had separate governments, and city zoning regulations did not apply. By 1914 Paris had 2,800,000 inhabitants within the city limits and over 4 million with the adjacent suburbs; Berlin had just over 2 million and just under 4 million with its suburbs. London, which annexed its residential suburbs earlier, had close to 7.5 million inhabitants.

By the 1890's large cities had already become giant polluted bedlams. Because of the increasing amount of dirt in the air servants and housewives spent a major part of the day cleaning house. The clatter of horse carts in constricted streets was so deafening that straw had to be put outside sick people's homes to muffle the noise. In London's Strand the layer of horse droppings was said to be as much as six inches deep before the crossing sweepers removed it. And the smells of these droppings, combined with those of coal-burning fireplaces and stoves, factories, breweries, stale food, and undeodorized people, were ubiquitous. No wonder the middle classes began to move to picturesque garden suburbs. Yet the heads of suburban households still worked in the city and its influence on their lives was inescapable.

Urbanization required of European society not only adaptations to changed circumstances or a new environment:

> but a fundamental restructuring of attitudes, the acquiring of new social techniques, the acceptance of new codes of discipline, the pursuit of new opportunities. . . . The adjustment proceeded at a different rate for different groups, and it involved the absorption of new knowledge not merely by the young but by whole classes. The process was literally that of acculturation to an urban way of life.[11]

For many working-class city dwellers the neighborhood tavern was the most supportive setting in which they could make the adaptations and play the new roles required by this process.

The larger cities were really agglomerations of distinct, segregated neighborhoods. London was the most extreme example: Bethnal Green in the East End was a world apart from Golders Green in the north or Mayfair or Chelsea in the west. But there were great differences in class, and often ethnic, composition in the residential districts of all major cities. Vienna was the most varied ethnically as the capital of a multinational empire, but Budapest and Warsaw had large Jewish quarters, and Liverpool and Manchester had large Irish districts.

The different classes became increasingly segregated culturally as well as economically and socially. In the great cities working-class people never went to the shops and theaters in the central district, which were frequented almost exclusively by the upper and middle classes. Each working-class neighborhood had its own shops, taverns, and places of amusement. Even its language differed from that of the middle classes. The residents spoke with the local accent, often combined with the slang of the neighborhood's predominant occupation. There was more community feeling in neighborhoods with the same ethnic background or common working-class occupation than in lower-middle- and middle-class neighborhoods. The commercial center of the city was completely impersonal; everyone was a stranger there. Large cities have always been impersonal, but in our period they seemed especially so to the hordes of new immigrants.

The new social and economic structures of the cities brought new social antagonisms as well as isolation and anonymity. Social mobility and social antagonism were inherent in the urbanization process, and their parallel development reflected both the instability of the new structures and the will to change them.[12] But the flexibility and adaptability of these new structures left them more open to change and offered the individual more ways for improving his social status than ever before in history.

Critics who bemoaned the new urban-industrial society and culture and contrasted it with the stability and warmth of rural life misunderstood both what the latter was like and the fact that it too was changing. Without the safety valve of emigration Europe's overcrowded rural areas would not have been nearly as stable as they seemed to be at the time. The high degree of integration within the family and the village community went along with a good deal of fragmentation within these simpler social units. Many emigrants came to prefer the anonymity and freedom of the city to the "proud and cruel publicity" of life in their native village. A group of Pomeranian farm workers coming into Berlin by train for the first time responded to the city in the following way:

The Berlin elevated electric railroad, c. 1903.

We had been told about its true wonders, its vastness, its skyscrapers, its fabulous illuminated streets. Now we can see a growing number of lights from the railroad station. We take turns sticking our heads out of the train window and look ahead toward the capital's sea of lights. . . . There must be more lights flashing by us right here than there are in all of Hither Pomerania![13]

Not only did the glamour of the great cities attract simple rural people like these but the increasingly dominant urban society and culture were also beginning to have their effects even among those who remained behind.

Urban newspapers, advertising, and traveling salesmen helped to disseminate modern ideas and products throughout each nation. As early as the 1880's an English observer of small-town life had noted how "the place which thirty years ago was only the medium of distribution for local products in the locality itself, is now a kind of petty emporium of empire, the headquarters of whose business no longer lie within the boundaries of the borough, but are in London."[14] In 1902 the London *Daily Mail*, founded six years earlier, carried its first full-page advertisement—for Mellin's Food. Since this mass-circulation daily was distributed throughout the country its ideas and advertisements had an important standardizing effect. In Ireland, whose population declined from 5.8 million in 1861 to 4.4 million by 1911, the number of traveling salesmen, superseding local peddlers, rose from 500 to 4,500.[15] In France itinerant craftsmen had been spreading advanced political ideas from the cities to the smaller towns for a long time. In the late nineteenth century, as rural areas developed closer ties with urban markets, they also became affected by the ideas of these towns. In the department of Gironde the district capital of La Réole, taking its cue from Bordeaux, had begun to register left-wing electoral majorities in the early 1870's, and this pattern spread to the countryside during the next thirty years. The effect of newspapers on rural and small-town political opinion did not necessarily make new converts, but it did help to reinforce the outlook of the faithful.[16]

EDUCATION AND LITERACY

Modernization in our period began to bring not only structural differentiation but also a greater degree of differentiation of roles than in traditional society, especially the roles of women and children. Except among the well-to-do, where it was usually delegated to nurses and governesses, child rearing was not viewed as an exclusive activity requiring rationally applied techniques by mothers. For the lower classes it was one task among many ascribed to women the majority of whom spent much of their time working at other tasks, some of which also supplemented the family income. In contrast, the middle and upper classes saw childhood as a status requiring special attention and direction. While they tried to teach their children acceptable standards of behavior from early infancy, the lower classes, both rural and urban, continued to view childhood as a not fully human state of existence and made no systematic effort to socialize their preschool-age children. But by the 1890's the middle-class proponents of modernization were trying to take young mothers out of the labor market and were redefining their roles as child rearers and homemakers.* They were also redefining the role of children, not only by requiring all of them to go to elementary school but also by educating their future mothers in child rearing and homemaking while *they* were in school.

The modernizers wanted to domesticate and "civilize" all people and all aspects of life. In those countries of northwestern Europe where industrialization was most advanced, wage earners were well accustomed to the discipline and uniformity required by their jobs and to being enclosed in factories and offices and regulated by the time clock. By the end of the nineteenth century the leaders of these countries also wanted to regulate the private lives of the masses as well. They viewed the urban workers as a separate species with two varieties: wild and domesticated. Their goal, through all the media at their disposal, was to domesticate the "wild ones."

In France at the turn of the century one such medium was *The Young Homemaker,* a widely used textbook in girls' elementary schools. It tells the story of the "conversion" of Madame Perrin, a "wild" (traditionally reared and hence "uncivilized") young working-class mother, by Louise Raimbaud, who is from the same class but who is already "domesticated." Madame Perrin wastes money buying food at the delicatessen instead of cooking cheaper, more nourishing meals at home. She is a sloppy housekeeper, and both she and her infant are dirty. Louise is just the opposite. She is orderly; she keeps everything in its place in little labeled boxes; she teaches her little girl the principles of hygiene that she herself had learned as a servant in the household of Dr. Lambert twelve years earlier. One day she decides to take Madame Perrin in hand and help her to become a better homemaker and mother.

> I am going to tell you how I manage to bring up my little Marie. When she wakes up, around six o'clock, I take her out of her crib, I take off the diaper she dirtied during the night . . . and I put her in her little bed. She then leaves me alone for an hour or two. I use this time to clean the house; around eight o'clock I give her her daily bath, leaving her in the tub for five minutes . . . and after her first feeding . . . I put her back in bed. She goes back into a good sound sleep. I take advantage of this sleep to go out as quickly as possible and do my shopping. Around 10 o'clock the baby wakes up again. I take her in my arms for a moment to enjoy myself with her and then put her back into her bed.[17]

* Only in the past few decades has this process been reversed with labor-saving devices for the home, day-care centers, and a broadening of the definition of women's capabilities for self-fulfillment.

What Madame Perrin eventually learns is not a few isolated tips but a habit of regulating and rationalizing her over-all behavior. Just as the bath must last only five minutes, so the affection she gives her infant must also be carefully measured. The author of *The Young Homemaker*, through Louise, tries to rid the girls who are in danger of becoming future Madame Perrins of the benighted popular prejudices they pick up in their own homes. In addition to the impact of the schools the health of the children was improved by the introduction of pasteurization and the spread of other new techniques of hygiene by doctors. These "civilizing" influences undoubtedly helped to bring about a dramatic drop in the French infant mortality rate from 174 per 1,000 in 1890 to 111 in 1910.[18]

Thus the purpose of Europe's free, compulsory elementary schools was not only instruction in "the three R's" but also the formation of healthy, decent human beings, according to the standards of the modern-minded upper and middle classes. These schools were designed to integrate the preindustrial and industrial masses into the new national political, social, and economic structures that modernization had brought into existence. In much of Germany, where public education had a long tradition, they were also supposed to counteract socialist influence on the urban workers. In Great Britain, where public education came later, it was supposed to "debarbarize" the unruly and rootless urban masses; as Her Majesty's Inspector for London put it, "if it were not for her five hundred elementary schools London would be overrun by a horde of young savages." In all countries the ruling circles used compulsory elementary education to impose their values on the rest of the population.

In the early twentieth century Europe's ruling circles continued to use the public elementary schools to "debarbarize" the first generations of children from "culturally deprived" backgrounds, despite the efforts of educational reformers to give pupils more general culture, more vocational training, and more opportunities to develop their potentialities beyond what was needed for learning by rote and passing examinations. Nineteenth-century bourgeois notions of obedience continued to be instilled everywhere. At best, "spare the rod and spoil the child" gave way to more discriminating procedures, like the following recommendation from Sonnenschein's *Cyclopaedia:*

> Boxing the ears or blows on the head of any description are inadvisable, and even dangerous. So likewise are blows on the front of the chest or abdomen. The best site for corporal punishment is the region of the seat, and a flexible cane should be used, not a hard, rigid rod.[19]

English children were also indoctrinated with the same virtues of self-

help, industry, and perseverance demanded of their parents and grandparents by Samuel Smiles. According to one commentator, in order to
acquire these virtues, "the pupil must become accustomed to work requiring *patient investigation,* and he should have fostered in him *indifference
to drudgery.*"[20] In the liberal states of Western Europe boys and girls
were taught their civil rights and duties and given instruction in social
problems. But, according to a textbook used in French normal schools in
the early 1900's, teachers were warned not to speak too much of rights,
which the children would tend to exaggerate. Instead, they should be
told:

> My good thirteen-year-old lad, your tasks are to learn your trade, to
> obey your parents and your bosses . . . to cast your ballot without
> self-interest, to perform your military service with modesty and sin-
> cerity, to work hard, raise children, and keep your pledged word.[21]

The aspirations of elementary school teachers to professional status
made some of them support movements for educational reform. Their
low salaries and their exclusion from secondary and higher education
kept them near the bottom of the lower-middle class. Nevertheless, theirs
was the main genteel occupation that allowed young people to move out
of the lower classes. (By the early 1900's Prussia, France, and England
each had over 100,000 elementary-school teachers.) Although most
teachers everywhere continued to perform as they were told to by the
state authorities, some of the more thoughtful ones wanted to help their
pupils become something more than well-behaved, patriotic drudges.

In the early 1900's the new teachers' unions, associations, and periodicals tried to overcome conservative social forces by backing the efforts of
bourgeois reformers to make elementary education "closer to life" in an
age of expanding opportunities and technological progress. The "New
Education" movement in England mirrored the uncertainties of the
changing society outside the classroom. It offered conflicting proposals
such as manual training, instruction in science, bringing out the child's
natural powers, developing a many-sided interest, moral uplift, physical
fitness. Thus, though the old ways were collapsing, the concerned
teachers had not found their new mission by 1914.[22] In Prussia, on the
other hand, there was a greater discrepancy between the social ideals
taught in the public elementary schools (*Volksschule*) and contemporary
reality than in any other modern country. By the turn of the twentieth
century there were 7 million pupils in these schools, and their graduates,
who were exclusively from the lower and lower-middle classes, remem-

bered mainly memorizing Bible verses and lessons in patriotism. Many of the teachers were committed to popular enlightenment but felt betrayed by the conservative rulers who thwarted their educational efforts and their social and professional aspirations.[23] According to the *Paedogogische Zeitung,* these conservatives

> think of the school as a gift graciously given to the proletariat. They consider the *Volksschule* budget in the same breath as the poor relief budget, and they, like all other "better" people, keep their own children out of the *Volksschule.*[24]

Secularization was another goal of compulsory elementary education. In France and Italy it was specifically instituted in an effort to reduce the influence on public life of the Roman Catholic Church, which was hostile to the political regimes of these countries. Rivalry between the Church of England and the Nonconformists complicated the problem of who would control the English schools until 1870, when the Forster Education Act put them under national control. Still, only in 1881 was attendance at a state or private elementary school made compulsory in England and Wales, and only in 1891 were the state schools made free. In most of Europe state inspectors saw to it that uniform standards and curricula were observed in the "voluntary" or denominational schools. Thus state control reduced the influence of the churches everywhere. In France and Italy instruction in religion was no longer required, though it was taught in some Italian communes until the national government took over the main responsibility for financing all elementary schools in 1911.

Like other aspects of modernization, compulsory elementary education acquired a national structure. In a world of nation-states only such a structure could produce full-fledged citizens and patriots. Local communities lacked both the interest and the resources to do this. In a pinch they might be able to bear the cost of building and maintaining a school and pay the teacher's salary. But they could not pay for the whole machinery required to train him or her and their successors. It was the state-operated normal schools that indoctrinated each nation's future teachers in the values of the dominant classes and made them into enthusiastic propagandists for these values, particularly orderliness, cleanliness, and patriotism.

Patriotism was stressed in the elementary schools in all countries but most intensively in France and Germany. Hence, elementary education reinforced the growing nationalism of the prewar generation. In Russia, where the first program for compulsory elementary education was not instituted until 1908, patriotism (loyalty and devotion to one's fatherland) also developed late, and nationalism (belief in the primacy of one's own nation and hostility to foreign nations) was mainly restricted to the nationalities within the Russian Empire, such as Ukrainians versus Jews, Poles, and Great Russians, and Latvians versus Great Russians and Germans. Education alone was not enough to make a nation of patriots. Nevertheless, only a person who had learned to read and write could grasp the full meaning of patriotism.

Literacy was the minimal requirement for full citizenship in a modern society, and only a nationwide educational structure could help the masses achieve it. A few countries with such educational structures had a high level of literacy before they were industrialized: in 1850, 90 per cent of the adults in Sweden were already literate; in Scotland and Prussia, 80 per cent.[25] England and France achieved 90 per cent literacy among adults by 1890, but the rate by then was less than 50 per cent in Italy and only a little over 25 per cent in Russia. Before 1914 a large share of the work in industry could still be performed by illiterates, though a certain level of technological competence was probably needed as well for full citizenship. And only a literate person could really claim and exercise his rights and attain an acceptable standard of living. Thus the degree of political modernization in most countries depended as much on their proportion of literate citizens as on their level of industrialization.

Receptiveness to industrialization in turn depended upon the level of literacy in different regions and countries. This was as important as the extent to which markets served as channels for both production and consumption. Literate people tended to adapt more readily than illiterates to the changes brought by social and political modernization. In our period both mass literacy and a certain amount of technical training became increasingly necessary for modernizing societies to keep abreast of the advancing technology.

Schools were supposed to mobilize human resources for the needs of modern society, though much vocational and technical training was still acquired on the job. The main advantages of well-run elementary school systems were the foundation they could provide for more advanced work and their ability to stimulate and facilitate mobility and thereby help select talent to fit society's needs. In practice these advantages were not fully exploited in most European countries before the First World War. The overwhelming majority of pupils in Europe's public elementary schools finished their formal education by age eleven. Those who continued thereafter went to vocational schools or normal schools, both of which were considered extensions of the elementary track. In order to get their children into a real secondary school (public as well as private) the parents had to pay and the children had to have spent three to five years studying in private preparatory schools in order to qualify for admission. (Secondary and higher education changed little during our period, and their conservative influences will be discussed later.)

Despite their failures in facilitating mobility and selecting talent, Europe's elementary schools had influenced their pupils in a number of ways. Most of them continued to speak their local dialect for the rest of their lives, but their teachers had made them feel that doing so was backward. They had learned to handle their national language and been exposed to new attitudes that helped many of them adapt themselves to the forces of modernization. Rural pupils had become aware of a broader society beyond their native villages. This awareness was combined with feelings of patriotism in the over 8 million Frenchmen who had read *Le Tour de la France par deux enfants; devoir et patrie* in school by 1905. In every country school children in rural areas and small towns had acquired secondhand images of urban values and life in large cities from their illustrated textbooks. Their successful conditioning in bourgeois values obviously varied from one individual to another, and many remained sloppy, lazy, dirty, and irresponsible as adults. But they had at least been shown how to become acceptable employees and citizens in the eyes of the middle and upper classes, and a small but growing number of them were furthering their education into their mid-teens.

The social mobilization of young men on the Continent was completed during their term of military service, beginning around age twenty. In Russia, Italy, and other countries with high illiteracy rates many recruits learned how to read for the first time. (In Russia the literacy rate among military recruits increased from 22 per cent in 1880 to 68 per cent in 1913.)[26] Basic training in military camps was simpler than it is today, but it did try to instill hygiene, discipline, and obedience to authority. Young men who had never seen a flush toilet learned how to use it from a printed manual. Drilling for hours, like sitting still in the classroom when they were children, conditioned these men to the requirements of modern work discipline. And penalties for breaches of discipline in school and in the army prepared them for similar penalties on the job. They were lectured constantly about their duties to their unit, the army, and the nation. This kind of indoctrination also conditioned them to work effectively in large-scale organizations in civilian life. The military habits they were taught undoubtedly wore off once they left the army, but not the patriotism. They rarely forgot who their national enemies were or their duty to die for the fatherland if this was necessary to prevent its defeat in a war.

MASS ORGANIZATIONS

Armies were the oldest form of mass organization. Before the nineteenth century only they were capable of mobilizing large numbers of strangers on a permanent basis and with a consciously delimited function. Otherwise the structures of traditional societies were communal and relatively unspecialized. In most of them people who knew one another worked together, lived together, and shared common religious and cultural norms. The peasant villager and the noble landlord moved in different worlds and sometimes spoke different languages, yet they knew exactly what kind of behavior to expect from each other. Once initiated, one was not merely a voluntary member of a priesthood or a guild; one was integrated into a closed community which looked after all of one's interests for life.

By the turn of the century the uprooting of masses of people and the growing differentiation of urban social structures made it increasingly difficult for a person to define himself in terms of a fixed social position in a small community. On the one hand he was gradually made conscious of sharing the culture of his entire nation. On the other hand, as he moved (or was forced) into a new social group, he began to seek a new identity through the life style and structure of feeling of its members. In traditional societies one's place in the social structure determined one's identity; the culture of one's social group—its life style and structure of feeling—had served as unconscious supports for one's ascribed status. In modern societies, the more flexible the social structure became and the more opportunities there were for mobility, the more one's culture became the only means of knowing who one was and what one's group interests were.

Consciousness of new group interests usually preceded their mobilization in organizations. Working-class consciousness and the political parties and trade unions that tried to mobilize it affected the largest number of people. But the labor movement was not the only example of the general trend toward the mobilization of the masses. "Large groups of people . . . were being uprooted, moved into cities, thrust into new occupations that their fathers and grandfathers had never dreamed of, threatened and tempted in ways they had never been threatened and tempted before, and organized by men who aspired to be their ideological guides."[27] In addition to the working-class movement this upheaval made ethnic minorities, women, young people, teachers, and writers become conscious of new group interests and join organizations to defend them.

Political parties were the loosest and most heterogeneous mass organizations that developed around 1900. As the role of the central governments expanded, old and new interest groups sought to influence the making and administration of policy. In Great Britain, France, and Italy —the major countries in which parliamentary rule was most effective— all the parties except those claiming to be the exclusive champions of labor tried to be national rather than class parties, though, in effect, they tended to promote middle-class interests. Partly to attract votes, partly to salve their consciences, and partly to co-opt workers from the more militant labor organizations the ruling middle-class liberals in these countries sponsored a certain amount of progressive legislation. But most European blue-collar workers were suspicious of social reform from above and hostile to any interference in their lives by the state, whether in the form of compulsory education, inoculation, restrictions on overtime work, or national insurance programs. Those who supported the socialist parties on the Continent and the Labour Party in Great Britain viewed them more as defenders of their existing way of life than as agents of change. The leaders of these parties were usually more revolutionary than the rank-and-file. The German Socialist Party had a wide network of social and cultural auxiliary groups which tried to foster a self-contained working-class subculture for their rank-and-file members, thus providing them with a kind of negative integration vis-à-vis the national society. Most other political parties were little more than electoral coalitions of fairly diverse interest groups.

The development of trade unionism as a means of defending the interests of the working class as a whole began in our period. Until the 1880's the only labor unions were those of the skilled craftsmen in printing, textiles, and the building and mechanical trades. These craft unions concerned themselves mainly with mutual insurance and self-help against the hazards of accidents, sickness, and death and only occasionally used strikes to reinforce collective bargaining with their employers. Their members looked upon themselves as a labor elite and showed little interest in other unions and none in the working class as a whole. It was the new, industry-wide unions of unskilled and semiskilled workers that developed after the late 1880's that became mass organizations with a strong class consciousness.

Industrial unionism began with a series of long and bitter strikes by the hitherto unorganized Belgian miners and glass workers in 1886, the London dock workers and Ruhr coal miners in 1889, and the French woodcutters in 1891 and 1892. The success of these strikes gave the workers involved a new feeling of solidarity. But despite the efforts of some of their leaders to give the new industrial unions—and especially their national confederations—an ideological orientation, the rank-and-file members remained primarily concerned with their specific grievances. In this respect they resembled the members of the older craft unions. What was new about the industrial unions was their large size and their tendency toward violence, a tendency that was aggravated by the violent methods of strikebreaking used by employers and the police.

Feelings of solidarity during strikes reinforced the class consciousness that unskilled and semiskilled blue-collar workers were developing in response to their working and living conditions. Mechanization, division of labor, and physical isolation from their employers prevented these workers from acquiring the informal personal networks and sense of achievement in their work which sustained the skilled craftsmen. In addition to their low wages and insecurity from unemployment their crowding together in segregated urban tenements made them acutely aware of their proletarian status.

Although the trade unions enrolled many new members in the early 1900's, the movement did not achieve complete solidarity of organization or purpose anywhere. Between 1900 and 1913 trade-union membership rose from 2 million to 4 million in Great Britain, from 850,000 to 3 million in Germany, and from 250,000 to 1 million in France. Not only was the majority of wage earners not organized at all anywhere, but the unions themselves were also divided over tactics and ideological orientation in most countries. After 1906 (when Parliament reversed the Taff Vale decision of 1901 making unions liable for employers' losses during strikes), the British unions dedicated themselves to industrial action and parliamentary politics as the two main ways of seeking social justice for labor. Most of them rejected the syndicalist notion of political strikes and the Marxist belief in class warfare. On the Continent, however, there were separate federations of syndicalist, Socialist, and Catholic unions. Individually, skilled workers were often more radical in politics than the unskilled, partly because they were more literate and thus more open to new ideas and partly because they felt more threatened by mechanization and the standardization of products. Yet their unions continued to avoid politics and to shun solidarity with the unskilled.

Solidarity with workers in foreign countries was even more difficult to achieve. On a few occasions, most notably the general strike in Russia in 1905, Western European workers demonstrated their solidarity with their comrades abroad. But they could be extremely hostile to foreign workers who threatened their own standard of living. German coal miners resented the "imported" Polish workers in the Ruhr; British workers viewed the introduction of Chinese coolies in South Africa as closing an avenue of emigration for them.

The trade unions were a long way from being as powerful as they are today. White-collar employees were not organized at all, except for schoolteachers and postal workers in a few countries. On the eve of the First World War only 25 per cent of all wage earners in Great Britain belonged to trade unions, only 20 per cent in Germany, only 12 per cent in France, and less than 10 per cent in Italy. The closed shop did not exist even in the most heavily organized industries. Exclusive representation in collective bargaining in specific occupations was an advantage still to be won, not an assumed right, as it is now. Until it was won, trade-union leaders were in no position to demand such things as paid vacations, company pension plans, and worker participation in policy decisions.

In the beginning, however, the mobilization of millions of blue-collar workers in trade unions was an unsettling innovation for everyone concerned. Not only did it raise the class consciousness of the workers themselves but it also frightened the employers and the middle and upper classes. Gone were the days when workers rioted only when their misery became intolerable. Now they had become more sophisticated and were striking in times of relative abundance. No longer resigned to a marginal existence, they were beginning to demand better conditions of life. Most of them did not want to overthrow the capitalist order, but the radical rhetoric of some of their leaders, plus the violence and magnitude of some of their strikes, created the impression of revolutionary unrest. In order to defuse this, governments not only passed welfare legislation but also initiated imperialist wars. This "social imperialism" was certainly a factor in Britain's war against the Boers in 1899–1902, in Russia's war against Japan in 1904–5, and in Italy's war against Turkey over Libya in 1911–12.

With few exceptions—the Orange Order in Ulster, the German

Workers Party in Austria and Bohemia, the Jewish Bund in Russian Poland—nationalism had a very limited working-class following until the outbreak of the First World War. Nationalist leaders mobilized thousands, not millions, of people in any particular country, and their followers were predominantly lower-middle class. Still, these nationalist movements were examples of the way modernization could drive masses of strangers into organizations for the defense of a newly defined interest. This kind of mobilization had originated a century earlier, during the wars generated by the French Revolution, and it had reappeared periodically in a number of countries. By the early 1900's it was more widespread and continuous than ever before. The nationalist organizations of subject peoples like the Irish, Czechs, and Poles had their own leagues, newspapers, and political parties. In France, Germany, and Italy nationalist organizations tried to influence government policy-making directly.

Although some intellectuals turned to nationalist organizations to express their feelings of alienation and isolation, other artists and writers founded new aesthetic movements. These movements were small and had little if any formal organization, but the fact that such people felt the need to band together at all was unprecedented in most countries. In their own way the Cubists, Expressionists, and Futurists tried to give new modes of expression to modern civilization through their works. They also published manifestoes and periodicals and organized their own art exhibitions. And famous writers like George Bernard Shaw, Anatole France, and Maxim Gorky helped to popularize the notion that intellectuals as a class should serve socialism and other left-wing causes. Since the Bolshevik Revolution the Communist parties of the world have transformed this notion into a dogma.

Modernization also stimulated the growth of feminist movements. Before our period women had never been mobilized into organizations to advance their interests as women. A few pioneers had campaigned for the vote, higher education, and birth control, but they had received little public support. By the early 1900's, however, "the woman question" was becoming a *cause célèbre* in much of Western Europe and North America. Women's organizations lobbied actively for feminist causes in their own countries and participated in their own international congresses. The suffragettes in England were especially raucous in their tactics, but in a quieter way feminist organizations in Germany and Scandinavia promoted the cause of equal opportunity and the interests of unwed mothers and other victims of traditional prejudice.

The mobilization of youth was based on the radically modern idea that teen-agers and even nine- to ten-year-olds were real people with their own interests. Since most children were still forced to work by the time they were fourteen, only those from middle-class families seemed to need their own subculture outside the adult-controlled schools they attended. The German Youth Movement was the outstanding example of self-mobilization by middle-class high-school students. Not only did this movement oppose the authoritarian family and school structure, but it also rejected materialism and urban values in general in favor of hiking, folk singing and dancing, and intimate comradeship. In England a group of concerned adults organized the Boy Scouts to give younger middle-class city boys a taste for outdoor living while at the same time instilling in them the virtues of service, regimentation, and patriotism.

As we examine the various effects of modernization, we must be constantly aware of the fact that these did not occur with the same chronological rhythms even in the same place. Attitudes, perceptions, and expectations interpret experience and thereby help shape behavior, but they are often out of tune with one another with respect to different kinds of activity. Powerful cultural continuities and adaptations went on shaping the behavior of diverse social groups even in periods of rapid economic and social change. Men and women bred in village cultures differed greatly from urban craftsmen in the culture and work habits they brought to the factory. Modernization put great strains on the family and the traditional social structure, yet despite many changes they managed to survive.

CHAPTER 2

HOLDING OUT

Those classes and social groups most threatened by modernization tried hardest to defend their traditional ways. Aristocratic influence was waning everywhere in the face of aggressive commoners in politics and big business. Yet noblemen continued to hold many prestigious posts, and Europe's exclusive secondary schools—along with a number of popular novelists and operetta librettists—glorified aristocratic values such as physical prowess, charm and good manners, contempt for money-making, emphasis on the aesthetic dimension of life, and a sense of responsibility for the less fortunate. The established churches had few defenders outside their own ranks and they condemned everything from public education and socialism to the bicycle, ballroom dancing, and motion pictures for declining church attendance. Among ordinary people the peasants and independent craftsmen were the most threatened by economic progress. Some simply went away; others turned to revolutionary radicalism. In this chapter we will look at those who tried to preserve their traditional outlook and standards of behavior.

In Vienna, which produced so many revolutionary movements in the arts and thought, the court of Emperor Francis Joseph was an outstanding example of holding out against modernization and change in any form. The fact that Queen Mary refused to use the telephone had little effect on life in Great Britain, but Francis Joseph's insistence on retaining oil lamps and eighteenth-century plumbing in his palace symbolized the court's determination to uphold the status quo in every way possible. In his contempt for the achievement orientation of urban—especially Jewish —liberalism the octogenarian Hapsburg monarch was encouraged by the nobility and much of the lower-middle class. Austrians of all classes supported his resistance to the national aspirations of his subject peoples.

In every country the mentalities of specific social groups—their ways of perceiving and responding to the world—often survived economic and social changes in their members' lives. This "lag" demonstrated the growing importance of culture as the basis for defining one's identity as social structures became more highly differentiated. Before the impact of modernization was widely felt, nobles, priests, peasants, and craftsmen took their culture for granted and were not conscious of having a particular mentality. They simply thought and did what was expected of them. But once other social groups began to assert their own mentalities and to question traditional distinctions, the older orders became consciously defensive. When some of their members found themselves uprooted, declassed, or ignored, they clung tenaciously to a mentality and a life style which were sometimes all they had left in their efforts to put off strangers and upstarts. Pre-1914 Europe was full of nobles trying to maintain their social exclusiveness in genteel poverty, of clergymen still assuming the right to interfere in civil affairs, of peasants recalling village customs and beliefs far from home, of craftsmen refusing to behave like ordinary factory workers away from the job.

ARISTOCRATS

At the turn of the century the aristocracy was generally defined as the hereditary nobility. In Great Britain, where only the first-born son got a heritable title and the family's landed property, this social class also included "leisured gentlefolk," most of whom were descended from noble families. (Winston Churchill, born in Blenheim Palace, was the son of Lord Randolph Churchill, the younger brother of the eighth Duke of Marlborough.) Although feudalism—the rule of the landed nobility—was long dead in Europe, members of this class still dominated high society and the upper ranks of the army, the established churches, the foreign service, and, in Central Europe, the state bureaucracy. These people were

A Viennese society lady and her guards officer escort at the races, 1910.

still aristocrats in the literal sense. But they remained an exclusive class because of their noble birth and their common culture rather than their vestiges of power.

Everybody in the aristocracy knew his own place in it and who ranked above and below him. Among the 650 British peers in 1900 the Duke of Fife (who was made a peer in 1889) was Number 27, and the Marquess of Winchester (whose line was founded in 1551) was Number 28. The *Almanach de Gotha*, published annually, included a directory of the princely and ducal families of Western and Central Europe. It listed French families whose legal status and privileges had been swept away in 1789 and German families that had lost their territories and functions when Napoleon I had "mediatized" them in the course of dismembering the Holy Roman Empire fifteen years later. The German counts were listed separately in the *Taschenbuch der Gräflichen Häuser;* the English aristocracy was divided between Burke's *Dictionary of the Peerage and Baronetage* and *Landed Gentry; Tout Paris* included nonprincely and nonducal French noble families as well as wealthy and distinguished commoners. But most aristocrats had little need for such directories. They knew who was to the manner born and who belonged to their world, which they called *the world* in France, Spain, and Italy and Society in Britain and Germany.

Aristocrats were the most cosmopolitan class in Europe. Although many of them loyally served their own country, they considered nationalism vulgar. In the 1937 French film *Grand Illusion* Pierre Fresnay played a French nobleman who, during the First World War, was a prisoner in a camp run by a German nobleman played by Eric von Stroheim. The French and German noblemen had much more in common than the French nobleman had with a plebeian French officer played by Jean Gabin. Fresnay and Von Stroheim knew of one another's prewar sporting activities, exchanged anecdotes about mutual acquaintances, and displayed no national animosity toward one another. Indeed Von Stroheim found it extremely painful to have to shoot Fresnay when the latter finally decided that it was his duty to help his fellow officers in an escape plan. Parvenu nobles and the country gentry were less cosmopolitan than the higher ranks of the old French and German nobility, which were sometimes related by family ties. When the war came, the sons of these families were to die fighting for their respective countries while their older members lamented losing touch with their relatives across the border.

The responses of Europe's aristocrats to modernization varied, but they can be divided into several fairly distinct sets. Set number one refused to have anything to do with the modern world and tried to live in haughty isolation from it. In her memoirs Elizabeth de Gramont, Duchesse de Clermont-Tonnerre, gives this description of the household of the Prince Duc de Bauffremont-Courtenay, a typical family of the Faubourg Saint-Germain:

> The Prince-Duc Eugène had married a fifteen-year-old Spanish Infanta, Maria Osorio de Moscoso y Borbon, duquesa de Atrisco, marquesa de Leganez, doubly a grandee of the first class. He brought her to France and handed her over to his mother; she lived under the latter's wing, never left her during forty solid years and died a week after she did. . . . When I used to call at 87, Rue de Grenelle to see my great-aunt de Bauffremont, Noémie d'Aubuson La Feuillade, she would be wearing white gloves and sitting up very stiffly, with her daughter-in-law by her side, each in a vast Louis XIV arm-chair. Once or twice a week, they were at home to their relatives, to a few neighbors who were vassals of a sort, and to the clergy of Sainte-Clotilde's.[1]

Each country had aristocrats of this kind as well as lesser nobles clinging to their old-fashioned mentality in dingy apartments or run-down country houses. The sons of impoverished lesser nobles might make a career of the army, but the daughters often could not find husbands of their own class and divided their time between their needlework and the local church.

The "smart" set within the wealthy aristocracy was more up-to-date. Princess Metternich in Vienna, the Duchesse de Rohan in Paris, and Lady Warwick in London organized the grandest functions in high society and patronized the leading men of literature, music, art, and politics. Aristocrats of this type were much sought after and reported on in the press because of their worldliness, their superficial brilliance, and their seemingly advanced ideas. Some of them even began to open their salons to distinguished Jews, a practice much deplored by members of set number one. The Comtesse de Chabrillan's elaborate Persian ball was the outstanding event of the Paris social season in 1912. Her plans included the following:

> Don Luis Ferdinand, Infante of Spain, will be naked, Nattie de Lucinge is marvellous in a sword-dance, Emma d'Arenberg will come on an elephant, Boni de Castellane will wear a Turkish costume that belonged to his ancestor who was Louis XV's ambassador to Con-

stantinople. Henri de Mun will be stunning as a Persian archer, the Baronne de Brimont will make a delightful houri, Comte Louis de Blacas in a turban is as handsome as a Bagdad youth and Suzanne de Montesquiou is a living miniature with her oval face outlined by veils.[2]

Set number three consisted mainly of young male nobles who spent their bachelor years (and sometimes beyond) cavorting with members of the lower classes. In Theodor Fontane's novel *Trials and Tribulations* (*Irrungen Wirrungen*, 1887) Baron Botho von Reinäcker, a young officer stationed in Berlin, has an affair with Lena Nimptsch, the daughter of a washerwoman, but abandons her after his marriage to a young aristocratic lady from his home province. Every aristocratic Austrian youth had his *süsses Madel,* who might be a shopgirl, a typist, or a dressmaker's employee. In Great Britain many nobles devoted their youthful years to hunting, racing, shooting, and other forms of sport. Although vaguely aware that certain political movements threatened to deprive them of some of their fun, they found the jockeys, bookies, valets, and grooms with whom they associated contented with their lot. But their patronage of these people was a distorted form of *noblesse oblige.* These young rakes had few ties left with the cottagers on their parents' estates, and they gave no thought to the plight of the industrial workers. There was nothing new about their frivolity, but their snobbish slumming was new for a class that had always been able to assume the deference of others without testing it.

Despite their different life styles most aristocrats shared the same basic mentality. An aristocrat did not pick up his change or run for cover. He behaved as if his birth and leisure made him superior but never argued the point. By the early 1900's conspicuous consumption increasingly took the place of lost legal privileges as a mark of class distinction; even the most reactionary aristocrats kept as many servants and automobiles as they could afford—sometimes more. Aristocrats might occasionally marry for money but never work for it. If they worked at all it was because they wanted to, not because they had to. They could serve the state in certain traditional capacities, and a few became scientists and scholars. But to become a doctor or a lawyer was unsuitable and to go into trade disgraceful. A number of wealthy nobles held shares in industrial firms and, in Great Britain, some of their younger sons were taking executive positions in insurance companies and banks. The ideal, however, remained cultivated leisure.

The aesthetic view of objects and behavior—traditional among leisured aristocrats since the Renaissance—resisted the modern push toward rationalization and functionalism. According to this view, not only works of art but buildings, household items, and interpersonal relations must be experienced aesthetically, that is, in terms of their form and style rather than their function. Not all aristocrats used this standard in their daily lives, but they all accepted its legitimacy. It was as much a part of being to the manner born as honor, *noblesse oblige*, and elaborate politeness.

In Great Britain, Germany, Austria-Hungary, and Russia aristocrats still played a prominent role in national and local government. A number of prime ministers and foreign ministers of these countries were from established noble families. Despite reforms in local government aristocrats still exerted a strong influence as justices of the peace in England and dominated the district administrations and councils of Russia and East-Elbian Prussia. Even in great metropolises like London, Paris, and Vienna the willingness of middle-class businessmen by default to leave much of the governing to landed or rural interests allowed representatives of these provincial interests to control the way these cities were run.[3] Until the Parliament Reform Act of 1911, which gave salaries to M.P.s, there was a disproportionate number of aristocrats in the British House of Commons. In Germany the Junkers dominated the lower as well as the upper chamber of the Prussian Diet because of an electoral system that gave one third of the votes to the property-owning classes. (In 1913, 22 per cent of the deputies in the lower chamber were nobles and other large landowners.) The Conservative Party—the "party of the Junkers"—was influential not only in Prussia but also in the Federal Council (Bundesrat) of the German Empire, in which Prussia had two-thirds of the votes.*

Prussia also made the most concerted effort to reinforce the predominance of the aristocratic mentality in its civil and military administrations.[4] In this way its leaders hoped to combine premodern values with modern skills while at the same time preventing social heterogeneity from generating challenges to the authoritarian political structure. In the 1890's State Minister Robert von Puttkamer purged the civil service of liberal

* The German Empire had a federal structure, with four kingdoms—Prussia, Bavaria, Saxony, and Württemberg—and a number of principalities. Its lower house of parliament (Reichstag) was elected by universal manhood suffrage; its upper house (Bundesrat) represented the states of the federation, and Prussia's three-class voting system favored the Conservatives there as in Prussia itself. The German Emperor (Kaiser) was also the King of Prussia, but Prussia and the Empire each had its own government.

elements and made certain that its key officials would be aristocrats or commoners recruited from student organizations in which the sons of the Junker aristocracy set the tone. (See Chapter 4.) The army officer corps also continued to stress the importance of noble birth in order to maintain political reliability in the face of rapid social modernization. Thus, although the percentage of nonnoble officers increased from 66 in 1895 to 70 in 1913, 52 per cent of the officers with the rank of colonel and above had titles on the eve of the war. Naval officers were recruited mainly from the middle classes, but their training, and subsequently their own aspirations, led them to adopt values and practices little different from those of their more aristocratic army counterparts.

Russia's service nobility, created by Peter the Great in 1722, did not have as much prestige and status among Europe's aristocrats as the nobility of Great Britain, France, Spain, Italy, and Central Europe. (The only Russian names in the *Almanach de Gotha* were of members of the imperial family.) Yet Russian nobles were a privileged order, with clear advantages over the rest of the population in taxation (until 1906), higher education, and entrance and advancement in the state bureaucracy, the armed forces, and the foreign service. In 1885, the centennial of Catherine II's Charter of the Nobility, an imperial "manifesto" stated emphatically that "Russian nobles should keep their leading position in the conduct of war, affairs of local administration, and courts . . ." A few years later the right to be granted hereditary nobility automatically once one had reached the highest ranks of the civil service was discontinued. And hereditary nobles in the army officer corps decreased from a majority in the late 1860's to little more than 10 per cent by 1914. Nevertheless, Peter the Great's Table of Ranks continued to set the standard by which a person's social status was measured in the civil service. The fiction that the officer corps was still composed of "nobles" was maintained by granting "personal" (nonhereditary) noble status to all commoners on becoming lieutenants and hereditary nobility on reaching the rank of colonel.ᴰ

Even though the majority of the officer corps in most countries were not of noble birth by the turn of the century, the values and standards of behavior of army officers everywhere were still those of the traditional nobility*: honor, duty, loyalty, courage, and responsibility for the men under their command. Those young men who had not already acquired

---

* Even in the United States at the beginning of the Second World War a newly commissioned officer was automatically expected to behave like a gentleman and was given a manual of the rules of etiquette, including the correct uses of calling cards. For example, the shopkeeper's son who became a lieuten-

these virtues at home soon learned them in military academies and from their fellow officers. In Austria-Hungary all officers were entitled to presentation at the imperial court, and, like the aristocracy, they addressed one another as "*Du.*" Dueling had spread to other social groups in some places (journalists and politicians frequently called each other out at dawn in Paris), but this feudal norm for settling issues of honor was mainly restricted to military officers. In all countries officers were forbidden to associate socially with enlisted men, who were physically segregated in theaters, race tracks, and other places frequented by the upper classes. The civilian authorities upheld these rules. It was they, not the military, who posted signs banning "dogs, common people, and enlisted men" from the more fashionable public gardens of St. Petersburg.

In England the aristocracy and its allies in the established church, the Tory party, and Society continued to think of themselves as the ruling class even after the Liberal electoral victory in 1906. Much did remain unaltered on the surface, with the younger sons of the landed nobility entrenched in the army, the diplomatic corps, and the imperial civil services, especially in India. But the peerage had been opened increasingly to persons connected with commerce and industry. After 1885 such persons —including some members of the gentry and nobility who had increased their fortunes in these activities—represented over 30 per cent of all newly created peers, as opposed to around 10 per cent previously.[6] Aristocrats who had traditionally disdained money were now becoming ever more concerned with it. Some of the old landowning nobility began to regard their estates as unprofitable investments to be sold rather than the traditional base that had inspired their aristocratic values. Thus the apparently stable Edwardian society was actually undergoing a social revolution in which the landed interest was quietly liquidating itself. The First World War merely deferred this process[7] whereby an aristocracy of landowners was changed into an aristocracy of business and professional talents.

This change was not uniquely British—it was paralleled to some extent in Sweden and Belgium—but it was the exception among Europe's aristocrats. Most of them tried to hold out until the end. The end came most abruptly with the revolutions in Eastern and Central Europe between 1917 and 1919, but it was already approaching everywhere during the prewar decades.

---

ant was told that, when he wished to inform an acquaintance that he was leaving town, he should write "P.P.C." (*pour prendre congé*) in the lower left-hand corner of his social calling card.

CHURCHES

Like the aristocracy the clergy were fighting a rear-guard action against modernization, but their lower ranks were dwindling in proportion to the total population in many places. Not only did declining church attendance lessen the demand for their services, but their supply was being reduced by a growing number of alternative careers. Until 1871 a man had to be ordained in the Church of England in order to teach at Oxford or Cambridge. In 1899, at age twenty, Joseph Stalin left the Russian Orthodox seminary at Tiflis to become a professional revolutionary (which he continued to list as his "occupation" for the rest of his life). In earlier times a pastoral career, and the education and modest income that went with it, had often been the only alternative to manual labor for many youths. With fewer timeservers and opportunists among them, the men of the cloth after 1890 were probably more dedicated than their predecessors. But their public influence continued to decline even more than that of the aristocracy.

Since organized religion serves a variety of social and cultural purposes for different individuals and groups—and even whole societies—there is no one explanation for the declining influence of churches in our period. Modernization alone cannot be blamed. Industrialization and urbanization certainly created conditions in which traditional religion seemed increasingly irrelevant. But many rural regions of Spain and France were already dechristianized before these processes began. Secularization has also been a major component of modernization, but this term denotes rather than explains the declining influence of religion. Besides, there were predominantly secular societies in premodern times, such as ancient Rome and China throughout most of its history. What we can say is that modernization in all its aspects created secular concerns which most organized churches either refused to deal with or condemned outright. Calvinism and Judaism seemed compatible with capitalist enterprise and, at certain times in the remote past, even political rebellion. But by our period their ministers and rabbis were often more restrictive than the Catholic, Anglican, and Lutheran clergy in the kinds of nonreligious thoughts and behavior they would permit.

Clericalism was the most notorious example of a traditional mentality holding out against modernization. Few clergymen of any faith would admit that religion was restricted to spiritual concerns. Its thou-shalts and thou-shalt-nots were designed to regulate all aspects of human behavior. A good Catholic risked excommunication if he wrote forbidden books or, in some countries, if he voted for proscribed political parties. A good Anglican could not remarry once divorced. A good Lutheran was not supposed to attend plays or operas that took liberties with religion, authority, or the family. A good Jew was prohibited from conducting a business transaction on the sabbath unless not doing so would immediately make him go bankrupt. Aside from private and public morals clergymen and clerical-minded laymen believed that their church should see to it that the schools, the legal system, and even the state itself fostered a truly religious community. It was easier for clergymen to regulate people's lives in rural Scotland and Holland or an East European *shtetl* than in large cities. But their more basic problem was that most of Europe's modernizing political leaders were uncompromisingly anticlerical.

The Roman Catholic Church made the fewest concessions in its struggle against anticlericalism and the modern state in general. In 1864 Pope Pius IX had set the tone with his *Syllabus of Errors*, which declared that the Church was a complete and perfect society, the final authority in everything, independent of and superior to all governments, with the exclusive right to educate and the power to use force if necessary. The last article of the *Syllabus* concluded by warning that it was an error to believe that "the Roman pontiff can and ought to reconcile himself or compromise with progress, liberalism, and modern civilization." Although modified in practice, this mentality was to persist in the Vatican for almost one hundred years. After 1870 it alienated not only the liberal leaders in France and Italy but also the conservative Chancellor Otto von Bismarck in the new German Empire. Indeed it was Bismarck who persecuted Catholics most openly in his *Kulturkampf*, in which he demanded unconditional loyalty to the state and its ideals from bishops and priests as well as laymen.

Because of their preoccupation with political and constitutional issues the Vatican and many bishops found it difficult to cope with the economic, social, and intellectual transformations brought by modernization. They seemed to feel that the anticlericalism of the state was more dangerous for the faith of their flocks than the exploitation of workers by heartless employers. In 1891, in his encyclical *Rerum Novarum*, Pope Leo XIII sought to combat "new things" like materialism, capitalism, and socialism with an updated version of medieval charity and class harmony. He also opposed modernism, a movement among both Catholic and Protestant theologians, which tried to replace traditional biblical exegesis with scientific techniques. Modernist theologians also seemed to call into question the traditional political and economic attitudes of Catholicism, and they and their movement were finally condemned in 1907 by Pope Pius X in his encyclical *Pascendi*.

The churches recognized that modern society had more uncontrollable effects on their traditional influence than modern thought. In his Lenten message for 1911 Bishop Gouraud of Vannes thanked God that the urban vices that led young people into lives of licentiousness and crime had so far spared "our Catholic Brittany" but warned his flock to be on guard against their spread. Families could prevent it by restoring their patriarchal character "with a respect that used to give the word of a father the authority and force of a true priest."[8] This was an extremely reactionary position for the early twentieth century. More typical was that of Bishop Cézérac of Cahors, who, in his Lenten message of 1914, urged all families to use the diocesan catechism in the religious education of their children while at the same time warning them that the modern hygiene taught in state school textbooks like *The Young Homemaker* "enfeebled the body as well as the mind."[9] In the 1890's even the progressive Lutheran pastor Paul Göhre, who was to join the German Socialist Party ten years later, complained that the "unrest of the new social order" undermined the religious education given in the family and the schools.[10]

Because most clergymen refused to relinquish their traditional authority over private morals, they tended to condemn all forms of behavior that escaped their control. Some Catholic priests denied absolution to unmarried village girls who refused to give up ballroom dancing (which the girls considered innocent) while granting it to them for fornication (which the girls still admitted was sinful). Rabbis had little difficulty in prohibiting drunkenness, since most Jews avoided it as a Gentile vice. But clergymen of all faiths denounced the tavern, partly because it sold alcohol, partly because it allowed members of their flocks to congregate away from their control, and partly because it was a refuge where local people could meet outsiders who might have a dangerous and pernicious influence. The French priest who blamed the bicycle for enabling his parishioners to go on Sunday outings instead of attending church services apparently forgot that those people who had wanted to had always found ways of enjoying themselves in their free time.

In Edwardian England clergymen led and patronized far more organizations to preserve Victorian morality than there had been in Queen Victoria's time. On April 4, 1908, the following announcement appeared in the *Times:*

We believe that the time is ripe for more energetic action on the part
of all religious and philanthropic communities to raise the standard of
social and personal purity. Not only in London, but in all great cities
and towns, there is an inevitable demoralisation that can only be
arrested and replaced by a higher tone through combined action. For
this object the forward movement of the National Social Purity Crusade has been inaugurated, and we desire to commend to all who
realise the gravity of the issue, both the crusade and its director, the
Rev. James Marchant, who has already rendered to this cause most
efficient service both by voice and pen.

By 1910 there were so many such organizations in London alone that
they organized themselves as the Conference of Representatives of Lon-
don Societies Interested in Public Morality. They included the Church of
England Men's Society, the Social Purity Alliance, the Friends' Purity
Committee, the Young Men's Christian Association, the Alliance of
Honour, the Society for the Rescue of Young Women and Children, the
London Female Preventive and Reformatory Institution, the Church
Army, the White Cross League, the Salvation Army, the London Council
for the Promotion of Public Morality, the National Vigilance Associa-
tion, and the Southwark Diocesan Association for the Care of Friendless
Girls.

Protestant fundamentalism also had a new upsurge in late Victorian
and Edwardian England. Each Sunday 10,000 people crowded into London's City Temple to hear the spellbinding ministers who preached there.
In his sermon on April 25, 1890, the Baptist minister Charles Haddon
Spurgeon said:

In twenty years' time, some of us may probably find great amusement in the serious scientific teaching of the present hour, even as we
do now in the systems of the last century. It may happen that in a
little time, the doctrines of evolution will be the standing jest of
Schoolboys. The like is true of the modern divinity which bows its
knee in blind idolatry of so-called science. . . . Possibly they [non-
Baptists] will call us bigots or hard-shells, or even idiots; but this
also signifies little if our names are written in heaven.[11]

Reginald J. Campbell, the Congregationalist preacher who succeeded
Spurgeon in the early 1900's, made his audience believe that the Kingdom
of Heaven was not only attainable but almost at hand.

Then the angelic man who had brought them to these heights became
confused, confessed his error, and left them, as the War came upon

them and swept away the old Europe. When the great let-downs of
the world are recounted, a special word will need to be said for the
pre-War congregation at London's City Temple.[12]

With a handful of exceptions those clergymen who recognized social
injustice as a moral issue refused to condemn its structural causes. As part
of the established order the churches opposed any efforts to change it,
particularly by open revolt, no matter how morally just the cause of the
rebels might be. The report of the 1897 Lambeth Conference on industrial relations said that the Church of England could not take sides in
labor-management disputes or on the issue of collective or individual
ownership of the means of production. At most, Anglican laymen could
form committees to study social and industrial problems from a Christian
point of view. The report of the 1908 Lambeth Conference went so far
as to recommend that the church stress the responsibilities of employers
to pay "the living wage" "for conscience' sake."[13]

In Italy and France (after 1905) the Roman Catholic Church was a
pressure group outside the established order, while the state churches in
other countries had been reduced to mainly ceremonial functions in public life. Their efforts at censorship were no longer enforced by the civil
authorities in most places, and their control over education was being increasingly challenged by the new generation of lay teachers. Religious instruction, oriented toward traditional piety, did not help most people to
cope with the modern world. Encouraged by Pope Leo XIII's *Rerum
Novarum*, some Catholic laymen organized Christian trade unions in
France, Italy, Germany, and Belgium while others undertook various
forms of social work. But these laymen and the priests who inspired them
were small minorities. The majority of Catholics, Anglicans, and
Lutherans neither expected nor wanted their church leaders to interfere
in government policy-making or social conflicts. These leaders in turn
looked to their parishioners to control the morals of their children and,
according to Bishop Dubillard of Chambéry, to keep watch on the "so-
called neutral" state schools in France and to counteract "their nefarious
influence on our children and our families."[14] The Russian Orthodox
Church, though administered by a state-appointed layman, was less effective than most in making religion more than a purely spiritual matter.

REACTIONARY INTELLECTUALS AND MANDARINS

Konstantin Petrovich Pobedonostsev (1827–1907) was one of the most uncompromising intellectual defenders of traditional values and norms. After having been successively a literary writer and a professor of law at Moscow University he served from 1880 until 1905 as Procurator of the Holy Synod (the lay head of the Russian Orthodox Church) and chief adviser to Tsars Alexander III and Nicholas II. In these posts Pobedonostsev exercised an enormous influence in Russian affairs. Although he had little use for the nobles and thought that talented commoners like himself could better bolster autocratic rule, he viewed modernizing influences from the West with disdain. He opposed everything from secular education to freedom of the press, from the reform of the army to concessions to Jews and other religious and ethnic minorities. All these things, according to him, were undermining the very foundations of traditional Russian society by making the whole younger generation permanently discontented because it could not realize its bloated expectations.

> In ancient times the number of restful and contented persons was greater, for men expected less of life, were satisfied with less, and did not hasten to extend their sphere of life. Each was held to his place and to his work by a sentiment of duty associated with them. The humble watched the lives of the rich and idle, and thinking, "This is not for us," resigned themselves to the impossible. Now this impossibility has become possible and attainable in the imaginations of all. The private soldier aspires to the dignity of the general. . . . The illiterate journalist becomes the celebrated littérateur and publicist . . . the ignorant, inexperienced youth becomes a . . . judge, and administrator. . . . But the honors of most are quickly dissipated in dust, and the worthlessness of their owners exposed. Meantime their vanity has swollen to unnatural limits, their pretensions and needs have grown beyond measure.[15]

Pobedonostsev's cure for this "malady of our time" was to rescind all reforms and strengthen the influence of the state church on the family and in education and civil affairs.

Whereas Pobedonostsev was a devout Christian, the reactionary French publicist and littérateur Charles Maurras (1868–1952) flaunted his own atheism. (He once told a pious colleague: "With your religion you have dirtied the world in a most bizarre way for eighteen hundred years.")[16] Maurras was a clerical only because he was an authoritarian and a traditionalist. Like Pobedonostsev, he believed that there should be as little social mobility as possible in order to avoid competition for status, which destroys respect for authority and weakens the established order. He also shared Pobedonostsev's hatred for the Third Republic and all it stood for. In fact he spent most of his life preaching its overthrow as the leader of the Action Française, the outstanding movement of the radical right in France in the early 1900's. Maurras was the champion of those Frenchmen who felt insecure in the modern, impersonal political and economic structures that had developed by then. The traditional society he wanted to restore was an idealized version of the Middle Ages. The king would be the true father of his subjects; the church would imbue them with discipline and obedience to authority and revive the family as the basic social unit. Maurras also wanted to dismantle France's centralized bureaucracy and restore the privileges and hereditary power of the feudal nobility.

Maurras's determination to combine his reactionary ideology with nationalism and anti-Semitism stemmed directly from the Dreyfus Affair and the responses of other French intellectuals to it. In the late 1890's the possibility that Captain Alfred Dreyfus, a Jewish staff officer, had been unjustly convicted by the army of espionage divided the nation's intellectuals into two opposing camps. Those with a democratic, anticlerical mentality joined the League for the Defense of the Rights of Man. Founded by the novelist Anatole France in protest against the conviction of the novelist Émile Zola for libel against the army, this league demanded that both Zola and Dreyfus be vindicated. To counteract its influence and to prove that there were as many intellectuals on the right as on the left, Maurras and his associates—including the novelist Maurice Barrès and the literary critic Jules Lemaître—organized the League of the French Fatherland. It championed "the ideas, the morals, and the traditions of the French Fatherland" as embodied in the army, which it placed above the cause of justice for an individual, particularly a Jew. Most of the intellectuals who joined this league were not as reactionary as Maurras, but they disliked the democratic ideals of the Third Republic almost as much as he did. They viewed these ideals as merely an excuse for lowering all established standards in modern society. This was particularly true of the majority of the members of the French Academy—that bastion of traditional literary standards—and they too joined the League of the French Fatherland.

These French literary mandarins had their counterparts in other countries and other areas of high culture. (The antitraditional artists and thinkers against whom they held out will be discussed in Chapters 7 and 10.) Everywhere the men who ran the academies of art, architecture, and music, as well as most critics and professors of literature, staunchly preserved traditional standards and condemned the liberating effects of modernization on aesthetic expression. This marriage of mentality and role was understandable in museum curators, but it was also evident among the organizers of annual exhibitions of contemporary art, who refused to show any paintings that challenged accepted conventions. Eduard Hanslick, professor of music at the University of Vienna, champion of Brahms, and founder of modern music criticism, called Wagner's operas aberrations both as music and as drama. According to Hanslick, Wagner's concentration on tone painting and decoration flouted the basic rule of composition, which is to articulate themes according to "certain elementary laws, which govern both the human organism and the phenomena of sound."[17]

The artistic establishment, official policy, and public taste were in general agreement that art should express the ideals of society and give it spiritual nourishment. They favored the heroic, the allegorical, and the historical, as in the massive monument to Germania, near Rüdesheim on the Rhine, and the one to Victor Emmanuel II in Rome. Nobility of feeling was perceived not only in Bouguereau's amply proportioned nymphs but also in the penned sheep awaiting slaughter in Auguste Frédéric A. Schenck's *The Last Hour*. Hans Makart (1840–84) shaped the taste of a whole generation of Vienna's upper-middle class with his grandiose historical paintings and friezes. His biographer, Emil Pirchan, describes his first major frieze as follows:

> With allegory upon allegory of Art and Science, Labor and Industry, Agriculture, Astronomy, Chemistry, and so forth, Makart covered the walls in the style of the old Venetians. Like a dark-glowing transparent tapestry, which at the same time shimmers and glitters in every color, the *chiaroscuro* of the painting encompasses the entire room, which has come to be a monument of the Viennese style of grand display.[18]

In his later years even a major painter like Adolf Menzel (1815–1905) devoted himself increasingly to glorifying the German imperial court and the aristocrats who attended its official functions. His realistic style heightened the illusion that this world was unaffected by the dynamic changes wrought by modernization in Germany and which he himself had vividly depicted in *The Rolling Mill* in 1875.

No European country developed an official mandarin class, as in old China, but the kind of humanistic education that produced such an elite gained its greatest prestige at the turn of the century. Unlike the aristocracy and the clergy the professors in Europe's universities and exclusive

Adolf Menzel, *Court Supper-Ball*, Berlin high society.

secondary schools had no traditional claim to public power. Their
influence had been negligible before the nineteenth century. It grew with
the increasing regulation of society by the state at a time when the traditional aristocracy could not, or would not, provide all the necessary
leaders and administrators and when the emerging capitalist elite was too
absorbed in making money to fill the gap. (As in the case of John D.
Rockefeller and his grandsons in the United States, it usually took three
generations for business tycoons to occupy themselves with politics and
public service.) In England the dons and public school masters found a
new mission in educating the nation's leaders; in Germany the professors
tried to fashion themselves into a kind of mandarin elite. Europe's universities turned out lawyers, doctors, and engineers, to be sure. But these

professional men were still expected to have had the classical humanistic education that came closer in the *belle époque* to providing something like a substitute for the nobility of birth than at any time before or since.

The implications of a modern, pluralistic society became apparent first in mid-Victorian England, and it was there that academic humanists tried most assiduously to reform higher and secondary education in ways that would strengthen their position in the changing social structure. Until then the dons in the colleges at Oxford and Cambridge had been privileged parasites with time on their hands. Some of them had supplemented their income by coaching students preparing for their comprehensive examinations, but this activity was not as personally rewarding as teaching. Taking their cue from men like Thomas Arnold, the reforming headmaster of Rugby, a number of dons sought a new redeeming ethic, purpose, and status in more active teaching and in molding the character of their students.[19] In the late 1860's these dons began to play an active role in student life. They encouraged undergraduates to come to their rooms for serious or informal conversation; they gave teas and dinners at which they introduced the older and younger members of their college to one another; they shared—or pretended to share—their students' interests in athletic activities in order to gain their confidence and attention. In these ways they hoped not only to reaffirm their own authority and importance in the confusion of political and social change but also to create men of sufficient character to influence the direction of change.

According to the new dons, the direction of change should be away from the degeneration, philistinism, and thirst for gain which they thought were weakening the English character. Reminiscing in the early 1900's, one of them wrote: "It was the man who read hard, the man who rowed hard, and let me add, the man who did both, whom I and my contemporaries admired."[20] By disdaining business and academic subjects (including modern languages) that might be useful to it the dons hoped to retain their new status as part of the intellectual elite. Like John Stuart Mill, they believed that a man's occupation was unimportant as long as he was capable and cultivated and devoted to the ideals of duty and service. Businessmen continued to distrust the humanistic education their sons received at Oxford and Cambridge, but the sons themselves often chose professional careers more in harmony with its values, particularly in the civil service. After the turn of the century a growing number of employers became convinced that a university man was a superior candidate for a job even in business. Thus, through their own efforts and the outlook instilled in their students, the English dons helped to preserve in the nation's new elites virtues that the traditional aristocracy seemed to be losing.

On the Continent university and secondary-school teachers were more interested in maintaining their status within the intellectual bourgeoisie than in influencing the direction of social and political change. Unlike their English counterparts they all insisted on being called "professor" and in having as little personal contact with their students as possible. They were more willing to prepare students for civil service examinations (in part at least because they themselves were under the jurisdiction of state bureaucracies), but they were more adamant in resisting modifications in the classical liberal arts curriculum in the secondary schools. Nor did they concern themselves much with improving the character of their nation's future leaders. Unlike the English public-school teachers, the French *lycée* professors were unwilling and unable to improve their social status by making themselves more useful in the eyes of the modern-minded bourgeoisie.[21] Like their counterparts in other countries, especially Italy, they clung to a fixed classical tradition in the face of modernization. In higher education the professors at France's École Normale Supérieure could bask in the reflected glory of the outstanding political and cultural leaders who had studied under them. But it was in Germany that university professors in the humanities and social sciences were most successful in raising their own social status by their learning and imposing their ideal of cultivation on the nation's ruling circles.

These German mandarins came closest to achieving their ideals in the *belle époque*. While their colleagues in the natural sciences and advanced engineering schools (*Technische Hochschulen*) aided the process of modernization more actively than anywhere else in Europe,* they themselves avoided any contacts with industry or commerce. According to them, cultivation and learning for their own sake were the noblest spiritual goals of mankind. As such they should be generously supported by the state, with no expectation of immediate practical returns and no interference in academic freedom.[22] Yet the mandarins depended on the state to give official sanction to their system of qualifying examinations and to

---

* Even the scientists shared the cultural discontent of other critics regarding excessive specialization in modern research and the demand that their discoveries have immediate practical application. At the annual meetings of the Society of German Natural Scientists they reminded one another of their commitment to the unity of intellectual culture as a whole as well as the unity of science.

bolster their prestigious social position. And the Kaiser did expect them to supply him with loyal and capable civil servants and an ideological defense of his regime. Those professors who were also civil servants themselves were especially jealous of their titles. Recalling her student days at the turn of the century at the University of Leipzig, the Russian revolutionary Angelica Balabanoff cites the following example:

> I was halted in the midst of a desperate plea that a doctor be sent to a student who was dangerously ill because I had omitted one of the three titles of the physician.
> "You mean *Geheimrat* Professor Doctor X, do you not?" interrupted the professor.[23]

If a professor was too liberal in his political views, he could be brought into tow. In 1899 Hans Delbrück of the University of Berlin was fined for writing an article criticizing the Germanization policy of the new governor of Schleswig-Holstein, but he quickly redeemed himself by supporting the government's naval expansion program at a large public meeting. For this service not only was his fine remitted, but Delbrück was also decorated with the Prussian Order of the Red Eagle (Third Class).[24]

There was a significant minority of modern-minded scholar-professors like Delbrück, Max Weber, and Friedrich Meinecke, but the majority of the German mandarins tolerated the illiberal aspects of the political regime, approved the traditional stratification of society, and shared the ruling classes' fear and hatred of socialism. Like many other members of Germany's cultivated elite they were ready to back the Junkers and Conservatives in resisting any effort in the direction of parliamentary or social reform. And like reactionary intellectuals and mandarins everywhere they prided themselves on their disdain for the materialism and vulgarity of modern civilization.[25]

PEASANTS

Professors and intellectuals are poles apart from peasants in mentality and life style. Even Karl Marx spoke of "the idiocy of rural life." In the generation before the war some intellectuals who opposed modernization tried to idealize the simplicity, vigor, and innocence of peasants and, particularly in Russia, to view them as the true "people." But neither Count Leo Tolstoy nor the more plebeian intellectuals who championed peasant interests could shed their own culture and fit into the peasant way of life. Peasants could abandon it and become modern farmers, but no one who was not already a peasant could become one.

In their inarticulate way Europe's peasants clung to their traditional cultures as stubbornly as any mandarin, bishop, or aristocrat, but they were not intrinsically resistant to change over long periods of time. Recent studies[26] have shown that preindustrial peasant societies in different regions were altered in a number of ways. From the late Middle Ages through the seventeenth century changes in land tenure and in the kinds of people who owned land modified the social structure in many places. The introduction of the potato in the eighteenth century changed people's eating habits from Ireland to Russia. In the last third of the nineteenth century the railroad opened rural areas to distant markets, and a money economy and threshing machines relieved millions of Western European peasants of the time-consuming task of separating the wheat from the chaff by hand. Yet all these innovations were absorbed into existing cultural patterns without transforming the basic mentalities of the peasants involved. As one old French peasant said at the turn of the century: "For things having to do with culture I was not one of those people who like to seize on novelties. . . . But when I could be persuaded of the superiority of a tool I used it without hesitation."[27]

Traditional peasant social structures varied considerably throughout Europe and within individual countries and regions. By the early 1890's the small independent proprietor and tenant farmer were becoming rarities in England, whereas in France these types comprised 70 per cent of all males actively engaged in agriculture, and this group accounted for 45 per cent of the total economically active population. In both countries some of these small farmers lived on separate farms while others lived in villages. In southern Spain, southern Italy, and Prussia east of the Elbe the bulk of the peasants owned no land and worked for big landowners as day laborers. Their systems of social organization were accordingly different from those of England and France. In Russia, where the peasants had been emancipated only since 1861, most of them lived in village communities that still controlled much of their economic life and were legally responsible for their obligations to the central government, particularly taxes and redemption payments for land purchased from the local landowners. Although individual Russian families farmed designated plots of land, in most of the country the land itself was owned by the communes. In contrast, many German, Austrian, Czech, Hungarian, and Polish peasants had family property and the kind of mentality that went with it.

The peasants in these different countries all had social and cultural norms that clearly distinguished them from city dwellers. One could see the difference in their very faces. Yet there were major differences in the ways in which French peasant-proprietors, Italian day laborers, and Russian muzhiks lived, worked, and dealt with one another.

None of these traditional peasant societies was static; they only seemed so as the gap between them and the modernizing towns widened in the late nineteenth and early twentieth centuries. In general terms, the role of the patriarchal head of the household, the status of women, and the practice of marrying within the village community had not changed appreciably for centuries. But there had often been cases of upward and downward social mobility among the households. From the mid-nineteenth century onward many rural people who had worked part time or full time in various craft industries, particularly textiles, were being deprived of their livelihood by factory production and forced to emigrate to the cities or overseas. As a result, some peasant villages were becoming more exclusively agricultural than they had ever been. The place of Christianity and its associated festivities in their lives varied widely from one locality to another. In some they were still central, in others they had declined, and in many remote regions they had never been more than a veneer for pagan rites.

The picturesque folk "costumes" associated with European peasants by city dwellers had often been introduced only in the late eighteenth or early nineteenth centuries and were usually worn only on special occasions. Thus the fact that these costumes began to disappear in our period was not as crucial a sign of the disintegration of traditional society and culture as many ethnologists claim they were. The anthropologists and rural sociologists are more convincing in arguing that traditional structures and mentalities may persist after the abandonment of most outward forms of folk culture. In some instances even these structures and mentalities could be modified without losing their inner coherence.

A study of the Rhineland village of Neyl, which in 1883 had already been annexed by the city of Cologne, shows how a peasant society could survive by absorbing "the technological and social changes necessary to preserve its cultural identity."[28] In the years prior to the First World War, Neyl had about forty-five families whose holdings produced enough income for them to remain engaged exclusively in agricultural

A "proper" Hungarian peasant family, near Pécs, c. 1890.

pursuits. But though their techniques were modern, they retained their traditional aversion to speculative investment of labor and capital in a single cash crop, which is a basic trait of a truly modern farmer. Their level of aspiration also remained low and was usually unrelated to their substantial incomes. When they brought their produce to the city market, they found among the lower classes there a common universe of discourse, with the same dialect and similar folk beliefs, attitudes, and values. Thus there was cultural continuity, rather than polarity, between the urban descendants of city peasants from the preindustrial era and the peasants of Neyl. But in their own village they preserved other peasant traits as well. Although they did not wear peasant "costumes," both the men and the women usually wore wooden clogs while working. They still married mainly other villagers and favored folk medicine despite the opposition of the local doctor. Their recreation remained almost entirely centered in the village, which had fourteen taverns, three of them with dance halls. Even the poorer villagers who had given up farming for factory work continued to live like peasants. "Their clothes, dwellings, and food habits were virtually indistinguishable from those of the full-time farmers. Acceptance of wages was the price they had to pay for the continuity of their way of life."[29]

Neyl and other communities like it illustrate the diversity of peasant responses to modernization. We have already noted how many Danish peasants were becoming modern capitalist farmers. This change was also occurring in England, the Netherlands, and parts of France and Switzerland. But the majority of Europe's peasants preserved their image of themselves as socially and culturally unique without, however, developing a modern class consciousness.

Traditional peasants tended to think of themselves as the main type of humanity, "the people," and of other groups as "unnatural" minorities. Rural southern Italians sometimes used the word "Christian" for strangers from other regions who were still recognizably peasants, but they lumped urban Italians and people from other countries together as "foreigners." During the early 1870's Russian peasants had stoned the radical university students of the To-the-People Movement (Narodniks) and turned them over to the police. In 1905 they rose spontaneously—and separately from the urban workers and professional people—in a revolution that forced the tsarist regime to deal with their long-term grievances. The Stolypin Reforms of 1906–10 were actually designed to break up the revolutionary class potential of the Russian peasants by transforming them in stages into Western European capitalist farmers (kulaks). But these reforms were unable to forestall the greatest peasant uprising in European history in the summer of 1917. Like it, almost all the peasant upheavals in the late nineteenth and early twentieth centuries aimed at restoring the traditional peasant world under better economic conditions, not at transforming the peasants into a modern social class forced to compete in a pluralistic national society.

Before the war most peasants in Eastern and Southern Europe lived together in villages, worked their fields co-operatively, and blamed the forces of modernization for their seething discontents: poverty, taxes, the increasing dearth of land and work, compulsory elementary education, forced military service. As we shall see later, their revolutionary impulses could occasionally be diverted into nationalist channels, but their basic outlook was antimodern.

In Western and Northern Europe many peasants were able to retain their autonomy as households and communities within the larger economy and society surrounding them, but this autonomy was only relative, whether they lived on individual farms or in villages. Outsiders could move in, local people could leave, marriages could be made outside the community's limits. Economic contacts with the outside world increased and the national culture penetrated and influenced the local culture. In addition, the local power holders had to deal with and often submit to outside powers. Thus, in our period, peasant communities throughout Europe were always subordinate to national societies.

In the late nineteenth century the decline in grain prices and the ruination of viticulture made many otherwise individualistic French peasants join lobbies and trade associations to force the government to protect them with tariffs and to help them in times of economic hardship. In this way many of them seemed to be developing a kind of class consciousness which their propagandists denied by talking about social peace and condemning class conflict.[30] These propagandists also tried to substitute the word "farmer" for "peasant," thus conveying the idea of an economic interest group rather than a traditional "estate" with pejorative connotations. But these farmers' organizations were led by the larger landowners and attracted only the more prosperous smaller farmers. The tenants and day laborers, insofar as they developed any political consciousness at all, were more susceptible to socialist and syndicalist propaganda. Thus there was no possibility of a united peasant class. In fact, the conservative farmers' groups and the militant socialist and syndicalist leaders were almost as far apart as their counterparts in industry. These divisions and conflicts within the French agricultural population became more frantic as modernization made increasing inroads on traditional peasant society.

The traditional family, rather than class consciousness, was the main bulwark of peasant values and norms. This kind of family was really a household, including all people (except servants) who ate at the same table and shared the same hearth. Sometimes it was restricted to blood relations and their spouses; sometimes it included associates with no blood ties. What held it together was the patrimony—usually land, livestock, and personal property—in which all members had some stake. This patrimony and the alliances that could be formed based on it facilitated upward social mobility. A peasant household with a large enough patrimony could sometimes contract a marriage into a family of local notables and thus gain access to a broader social order and its culture.[31]

In discussing the functions and influence of the traditional peasant family we must therefore set aside our notions of what a family means today. Although usually restricted to a married couple and their dependent children, the term is now used so loosely that it can include a particularly close friend or a pet. The fact that parents and children live under the same roof does little to prevent each individual from having a separate, more meaningful life among his peers outside the home, and it rarely involves an inherited patrimony in which each member has a lifelong stake. In contrast, the traditional household was relatively self-contained, both socially and as an economic unit, particularly among landholding peasants.

In northwestern Europe such peasant households participated in the social and cultural life of their parish and sometimes worked with other households in specific activities such as harvesting and, by the 1890's, marketing the community's products. But it was the household, rather than the local community, that gave the most meaning and purpose to the lives of its members. As long as the household remained a viable unit, it could adopt new material techniques, abandon age-old customs, and even reclaim individual members who had gone away to work or do their military service. It was often strong enough to cope successfully with persistent outside influences such as the church, the primary schools, and the armed forces. Its relations with the larger economy—even when these forced them to abandon one form of agriculture for another—did not basically alter the way it functioned as long as it was able to survive and keep its patrimony.

The function and influence of the traditional peasant household were far more pervasive than those of the most closely knit modern family. The household dictated the economic role of every man, woman, and child under its control to an extent inconceivable today. It left little room for personal feelings, especially in the choice of marriage partners. Bachelors were not allowed to have incomes of their own; those who worked away from the household had to turn their wages over to it without spending anything not given to them by their mothers. The will of the head of the household was the law for all its members. In our own time practically everyone expresses his opinions—albeit manipulated by the mass media and peer groups—on the most diverse questions. In a traditional peasant household it rarely occurred to anyone to have an independent opinion, let alone to express it. People responded to situations in preordained ways, guided mainly by local custom and the good of the household as defined by its head. Anyone who rebelled either left voluntarily or was forced to do so. But the more usual reason for someone leaving was that the patrimony simply could not support him or her.

By the 1890's the traditional household and the peasant community of which it was a part sometimes broke down where the age distribution became too lopsided to sustain the existing order. As long as only the "surplus" young adults sought their economic opportunities elsewhere, this order survived. It began to collapse when there were too few young men to do the necessary work and too few young women to provide wives for them. Then outsiders had to be brought in for both purposes, and beyond a certain threshold of numbers these outsiders could no longer be absorbed into the local households, which consequently disintegrated or were transformed.

In other cases the local peasant community could and often did persist as long as its autonomy with regard to the outside world allowed it to make collective decisions and thus maintain its system of power. Peasant communities of this type involved a maximum of one or two thousand people.* Everyone knew everyone else. They dealt with one another face to face, and their social relations did not need to be mediated by outside institutions—except for litigation in the courts. In such communities one had only to see two people together in a certain place, at a certain time, in a certain season in order to know what they were doing. Any unexpected person or action immediately brought forth comments and discussions to find out the explanation.

Such a strict and personal level of social regulation had to be based on a shared code of precise and limited patterns of behavior known by and

* Interpersonal relations could also work with a larger number of people if the families, clienteles, and social strata and categories involved made it possible to recognize immediately the social status of an individual.

applicable to everyone in the community. All members of the community shared the same view of the world and the same system of values. Their cultural homogeneity was reinforced by their local dialect, which often differed substantially from the language of the larger society of which they were nominally a part.

A few marginal people could deviate from the acceptable behavior of a peasant community only because its members recognized them as marginal and as having their own standards. Foreign agricultural workers such as Poles in eastern Prussia and Italians in southern France lived completely separate lives from the native villagers. In those East European villages with heavy concentrations of long-time Jewish residents the Russian and Polish peasants could not avoid having business dealings with them but condemned them on both religious and racial grounds.* In most countries even Christian day laborers from the same locality were often rejected socially because of their unstable or nonexistent family life. And each village had its drunks, idiots, and eccentric old women.

Each community in a culturally homogeneous rural region had its own group character, recognized by its own members and those in the neighboring communities. But the fact that its members all shared certain personality traits did not preclude differences among them. Aside from individual differences people played different roles according to their age and sex. The greater the degree of social stratification, the more pronounced were the peculiar character traits of the different groups: craftsmen, laborers, small and large farmers, notables. And each family had its distinctive traits and temperament, which its neighbors constantly drew attention to and commented on. The more culturally homogeneous the community, the greater was the significance attached to small differences.

Often these differences were perceived as gradations of conformity and deviance with regard to the dominant norms. A peasant family might pride itself on having no children in domestic service while recognizing the fact that others had to. Family A could disapprove of someone in family B for reading newspapers but receive him socially as long as he

---

* Their priests were especially scandalized by the alleged sensuality of the Jews. As one Polish priest wrote at the turn of the century: "The Jews have this peculiarity that they teach the appreciation of the body and of sexual relations. They bring into the mental horizon of the Polish peasant girl the erotic element . . . which is unknown to the soul of the Polish peasant and so different from the severe Christian view upon the body and sexual functions." Quoted in William Isaac Thomas and Florian Znaniecki, *The Polish Peasant in Europe and America*, 2 vols. (New York: Dover, 1958), 2, p. 1243.

did not flaunt his superior knowledge. Young men could engage in drunken brawls provided that they did not use knives. A peasant land-owner could become rich by local standards and even send his son to high school, but as long as he did not reject the basic norms for behavior in his community, it accepted him as someone who had risen socially without having become "bourgeois."

Thus, even before they were touched by modernization, traditional peasant communities were not static units in which nothing happened or nothing changed. Cultural homogeneity combined with social diversity allowed fairly inflexible structures to provide a full and satisfying social life for most of their members. The tendency toward greater diversity and hierarchy in peasant communities was so pervasive that those with a strong egalitarian mentality devised special mechanisms to offset it. The most famous example, recognized by law in 1893, was the periodic redis-tribution of land by the Russian peasant communes according to the number of consumers in a household or some similar egalitarian norm. Yet even this practice could not eliminate the divisions between large, middle, and small landholders, which persisted until the forced collec-tivization of the early 1930's. In many Protestant countries, including England, the order of pews in the local churches expressed the villagers' view of the hierarchy in their society and their place in it. As recently as the early 1950's in the Calvinist village of Atány two young Hungarian women quarreled in the following way: "After all, I married better than you, as I was led into the first pew and you into the second only."[32]

Cultural homogeneity did not exclude social diversity within a particu-lar community, but each one consciously differentiated itself from neigh-boring communities sharing the same culture. This parochial mentality reinforced its members' feelings of identity as individuals and as a com-munity. In this way it facilitated the internal regulation of the commu-nity. Rules of hospitality toward strangers were designed both to forestall threats to the community's collective identity and to show its members how they wished to see themselves and be perceived by others. Parochialism was sometimes carried to extremes, as in the case of the resi-dents of two rival parishes of the same village in southern Italy who claimed that they could not understand each other's dialects. Although their divided loyalties were based primarily on endogamous kin ties, they chose to believe that the residents of the other parish, including their dia-lect, had a different ethnic origin.[33]

Although the peasant culture of any particular region remained relatively self-contained, it was those rural people with enough land to support themselves who were most able to preserve this culture against outside influences. Agricultural day laborers, especially in the latifundia of southern Italy and southwestern Spain, were not really peasants; they were rather a rural proletariat. They shared some of the prejudices and standards of behavior of the peasants among whom they lived, but they lacked the attachment to the land of those peasants who farmed the same plots year after year. The permanent farm hands and servants were closer to the peasant outlook than the day laborers were.

Among the major countries Russia had by far the largest number of landholding peasants, and their traditional society and culture were altered least by modernization. In 1897, 84.2 per cent of the inhabitants of the European part of Russia (over 80 million people) were peasants, and this percentage did not decline appreciably during the next three decades. Russia's peasants were legally a separate "social estate" and were so designated on their identity cards. Some of those who migrated to the cities resented their continuing obligations to their commune. And some of the richer ones who stayed home no longer wanted to go along with the commune's control over local affairs, particularly the periodic land distributions. But for the majority the relatively closed and self-perpetuating households and communes constituted a world apart from that of the townsmen, whose social structure resembled that of Western capitalist societies in many ways. Russian peasants identified themselves less with national values than most others, and their attitudes toward justice were in flagrant opposition to the national legal code. In their own communal courts the personalities of those on trial and the social implications of the judgment outweighed legal precedent or objective circumstances. The decisions of these courts "were determined by overriding concern for the interest of communal cohesion; the satisfaction of the minimum needs of every family and the maintenance of good neighborhood relations were valued more highly than impartiality."[34]

At the other end of Europe, Ireland presented a quite different picture. Whereas the total population of the Russian Empire grew by 70 per cent between 1890 and 1911, in Ireland it *declined* by over 5 per cent because of a higher rate of emigration than any other country. The amount of land available to individual families increased appreciably in Ireland, whereas in Russia it decreased drastically. As a result, while peasant living standards declined in Russia they rose in Ireland. Since the bulk of the Irish emigrants were landless people, the class balance in the rural areas swung sharply in favor of peasant proprietors, particularly those with fairly large holdings.[35] In 1911 the literacy rate in Ireland was also considerably higher (88 per cent) than in Russia (39 per cent). All these improvements in Ireland affected even the remote fishing community on Great Blasket Island, off the southwest coast. In his autobiography one resident of this community emphasized its increased prosperity. In 1910, for example, when he was twelve years old, his father gave him ten shillings to spend in a nearby mainland town on the occasion of the local canoe races[36]; that was a lot of money at a time when the average weekly wage of an English industrial worker was only thirty shillings. Yet, despite their contacts with the outside world through their relatives in America, the fishermen of Great Blasket Island retained much of their traditional folk culture and used the Irish language almost exclusively, even in their schools.

Europe's traditional peasants held onto their oldest culture traits longer than those they had acquired most recently. Household articles, decoration, and dress, which reached their peak of development in many places in the eighteenth and early nineteenth centuries, were the first to go. Certain farm implements, dances, and rites dated back to pre-Christian times and lasted the longest. Thought patterns and the customs dictated by them resisted outside contacts longer than attitudes toward material things. Belief in folk medicine and its practitioners was one example. Local people had confidence in their healers and considered attacks against them, usually by outsiders, as attacks on their collective structure of feeling.[37] The same was true for anyone casting doubt on a community's shared popular wisdom. Rural people (and first-generation emigrants in cities, as we shall see in the next chapter) often seemed modern in their outward daily behavior while retaining much of their traditional mentality in their private lives and thoughts.

Studies of rural France in the early 1900's confirm these generalizations. According to 3,310 responses in 1944 to a questionnaire* sent to all rural communes regarding the pre-1914 period, almost 90 per cent of the peasants had already begun to use threshing machines during the last third of the nineteenth century, but none of them had electricity until after the First World War. Before the war 95 per cent of all French peasants still wore wooden clogs at work and on certain festive occasions; 38 per cent practiced a ceremonial invocation of the local patron saint of livestock and 34.2 per cent for the local patron saint of the vineyards. In

---

* I derived my figures from the original responses in the archives of the Musée des Arts et Traditions Populaires in Paris. These have never been published, nor, according to the archivist, tabulated systematically.

Postcard of a dairy farm near Cherbourg, France, early 1900's.

a number of communities the wheelwrights, potters, and makers of wooden clogs also had ceremonies for their patron saints. In 37 per cent of the communes responding the young men celebrated May Night by placing bouquets of leaves on the windows, doors, or roofs of all girls eligible for marriage; 32 per cent still gathered and kept until the next harvest a bouquet of the cereal crop harvested each fall. Thirty per cent still had a charivari for remarriages of older people, who had to pay off the revelers. On the eve (June 23) of St. John's Day, 27.5 per cent still lit bonfires. The celebration of May Night, the bonfires on St. John's Eve, and the charivari had never existed in some communities, so that the percentage of "survivals" where it had existed was a good deal higher than the national average. In any case, all these rites were very ancient and obviously pagan. In contrast, a number of domestic items—handmade roofing tiles, baking ovens for homemade bread, beds enclosed by panels —were rare by 1914. Finally, as one would expect, the percentages for all these items were highest in communities furthest away from large cities and modern industrial regions.

CRAFTSMEN AND WORKERS

Traditional peasant societies had always been able to rely on local coopers, potters, wheelwrights, cabinetmakers, saddlers, and blacksmiths to fulfill their needs. Then, when the diffusion of new technology put many of these craftsmen out of business, they tended to leave their villages and seek other kinds of work in the cities or overseas. As this happened many villages became more rural while at the same time increasing their contacts with the national society. But the introduction of new technology was not the only reason for the plight of rural craftsmen. In some cases—like that of the stonemasons in Italy—they emigrated because they did not have enough work to allow them to maintain their traditional social position in their village.

In the cities as well as the villages many craftsmen found it increasingly difficult to resist the forces of modernization. Proud of their skills, their independence, and the social status that had traditionally gone with these, they were extremely reluctant to be declassed into the proletariat by working for wages. The son of a German master tailor recalled his father's pride in refusing to be treated by the local doctor for the poor when he was on his deathbed. "What would people say?" the old man asked his distraught wife, if she should summon this doctor whom everyone called an exploiter of the poor *(Armenschinder)*.[38] But the son had no other choice than to become a traveling artisan who hired himself out for short jobs and then moved on to the next town.

The saddest effect of modernization on craftsmen was the growing aversion for this occupation by their sons. Like that of farmer, it came to be disdained as urban values began to transform villages close to big cities. In his semiautobiographical novel, *Der junge Tobias*, Karl Scheffler, a famous art critic, recalls how, in the 1880's, his hero's father, a house painter, had already found himself a stranger in his own urbanized village and in the numerous cities in which he tried to ply his trade. At the end of the book the hero tries to console his father for his failure in life. The cities of Europe and the New World hosted many such men, who had been taught to believe in the traditional worth of a skilled trade and then found themselves on the margins of modern society.

The hand weavers had suffered their agony of being replaced by machines over half a century before our period, but other types of skilled craftsmen in manufacturing were now experiencing similar feelings of degradation. Not only were there more machines but also new types of machines to take the place of their traditional dexterity and versatility.

"The turner used to do not only turning, but boring, reamering, milling, screw-cutting, and drilling; these other operations came to be given over each to a special machine tool, and at the same time, in turning itself, the marking out of the work, the setting of speed and feed, and the grinding of tools, were transferred to specialists."[39] These "specialists," however, were unskilled "machine men"; even women and boys could do this kind of work. Another development that degraded the skilled craftsman in industry was the increased demand for precision and the standardization that went with it. In the past, when two parts did not fit together exactly, the fitter knew how to file them to make them fit. Now automatic machines were turning out less variable products, and his skill was less needed. Since the parts fitted to start with, a mere assembler could put them together. This change was carried furthest in the manufacture of new products such as the sewing machine, the bicycle, the automobile, and electrical equipment. There the more exact adjustments of the old workmanship were no longer demanded. A semiskilled machine tender could use a gauge to see if parts were within the limits of the prescribed tolerances and then pass them along the assembly line.

In Great Britain and on the Continent some of the most militant labor leaders were embittered craftsmen who had felt degraded by these technological and organizational innovations. Along with Marxist and revolutionary syndicalist theoreticians they helped to nurture the myth of a revolutionary working class organizing and conditioning itself to overthrow the capitalist order and replace it with a newer, more modern one administered by the proletariat. In the early 1900's the first great nationwide strikes in France, Italy, Great Britain, and especially Russia in 1905 gave additional plausibility to this myth, as we shall see in Chapter 8. The most militant and revolutionary blue-collar workers, then as now, were those who felt most threatened by automation and, particularly in Russia and Spain, those who had recently come into industry from a rural setting.

Before 1914, however, the majority of blue-collar workers were still holding out against attempts by trade unionists to mobilize them. This was true even in Great Britain, where the labor movement was larger and older than anywhere else but where many union members resented the increasingly impersonal, bureaucratic character of their national federations.[40] In France, where large factories and automation were still rare, the mentality of the individualistic craftsman remained strong, and there was greater resistance to mobilization by the unions than in Britain. French workers had a more revolutionary tradition than British workers, but they were less willing to pay regular union dues. In Italy, except for the skilled workers of the industrial regions of the north, most workers were too poor, ignorant, and fearful of reprisals from their employers to join trade unions. And the political orientation of many Italian labor leaders made it especially difficult for them to attract workers who were traditionally more fatalistic and deferential than those in Northern Europe.

In Germany, despite its important Social Democratic subculture, a 1912 opinion poll[41] indicated widespread indifference toward political and social change among the 2,085 miners, 966 textile workers, and 1,631 metallurgical workers questioned. Although we have no way of knowing how representative these samples were, the answers seem to give a reasonable approximation of the wishes and goals of German blue-collar workers. When asked what they thought about on the job, 42.8 per cent of the miners replied "nothing," as compared with 14.8 per cent of the textile workers and 13.3 per cent of the metallurgical workers. Only 5.1 per cent of the miners thought about union and political matters, as compared with 18.5 per cent of the textile workers and 12.8 per cent of the metallurgical workers. When asked what their main wishes in life were, 21.7 per cent of the miners said "none," as compared with 2.7 per cent of the textile workers and 3.8 per cent of the metallurgical workers. Only 4.1 per cent of the miners wished "to settle accounts with the capitalists," as compared with 7.7 per cent of the textile workers and 8 per cent of the metallurgical workers. Twelve and a half per cent of the miners wished for the arrival of "the state of the future," as compared with 10.3 per cent of the metallurgical workers and only 3.3. per cent of the textile workers. On the other hand, almost 34 per cent of the textile workers wished "to die soon," as compared with 12 per cent of the metallurgical workers and only 1.5 per cent of the miners. (The rest of the wishes concerned higher wages, being able to eat one's fill, a better life for the workers' children, and more human dignity in their own lives.)

In this survey, unaccounted-for extraneous variables certainly played their part. The indifference of the miners can be attributed to the fact that their work was too long and strenuous to allow them to think about anything beyond their personal needs. And surely the textile workers who wanted to die soon must have been older than the average worker. Yet overall this survey shows German workers in three of the biggest industries as skeptical of the possibility of social improvement through mass organizations.

By the outbreak of the First World War a large number of blue-collar workers in the most modern regions had never known any other kind of existence than that of the factory or mining town. Great Britain had the largest proportion of second- and third-generation workers of this type, but in Belgium, France, and Germany as well many blue-collar workers had few ties left with the rural world. These workers were cynical about a society that segregated them socially and gave them a disproportionately small share of the fruits of their labor. A minority of them wanted to believe that a political revolution would create a better world for them. But the majority were suspicious of any efforts to change their customary routines by their union leaders, their employers, or the state itself. Changes from these quarters might just as easily make their condition worse as better. These workers certainly aspired to a modestly higher material standard of living. But they had "little expectation of social improvement being engineered by political means, and none at all of the 'Welfare State' as we know it."[42] Although their fear of change was based on different perceptions, it resembled that of the traditional peasants and craftsmen. The optimism of the *belle époque* regarding modernization was restricted to the "happy few" among the middle classes.

CHAPTER 3

LEAVING HOME

Modernization made people more mobile. Europeans had been moving into cities and migrating overseas for a long time, but the proportion that did both increased markedly in the 1890's. By then more and more of these people also moved into new occupations in the rapidly developing industrial and service sectors of the economy. But, once settled in their new homes and occupations, they found it more difficult to move up the social ladder. This last type of mobility was usually possible only among their children. Thus, both overseas and in the cities of Europe, it was the second generation—better educated and more effectively socialized to its new environment—that took advantage of whatever opportunities there were for vertical social mobility.

These opportunities varied from country to country and from region to region, not only according to the economic structure but also the political, social, and cultural setting. Although the information available for comparative evaluations is spotty, there was more social mobility in the United States than in Europe.[1] The obvious reason was that the United States had a more open and pluralistic society than any European country. But some regions and cities in Europe offered more opportunities for mobility than others. Swedish society was more open than Hungarian or Polish society because it had no tradition of legal estates or serfdom. Within Sweden the growth of the iron and lumber industries in the north allowed rural people to move into new occupations without going far from home. Throughout Europe there was a wider range of occupations in the service sector of the economy in large cities than in mining and mill towns.

TYPES OF EMIGRANTS AND THEIR MOTIVES

The migration of millions of Europeans from their homes was a function of the modernization of different parts of the world between the 1840's and the 1930's. Population growth gave the initial "push." As dietary and medical advances reduced death rates without a compensating reduction in birth rates, the surplus rural young people whom local labor markets could not absorb became ready to move. But they were unable to do so until communications, markets, commerce, and capital began to erode the traditional economy and encourage greater mobility. "Overseas migration was only one, though the most important, result of a revolutionary increase in social mobility which had the effect of creating large numbers prepared to travel in search of jobs."[2] This movement occurred first in northwestern Europe, particularly Ireland and Scandinavia, and last in Southern and Eastern Europe, particularly Italy, Spain, and Poland before 1914 and Yugoslavia and Greece after the First World War.

Meanwhile, as new job opportunities developed in their home countries, fewer people from these countries emigrated abroad. With the exception of the United Kingdom this development also occurred first in northwestern Europe and reached its full force in Germany by the 1890's. Not only did real wages increase in the late nineteenth century, but the growing number of white-collar occupations also made urban life more attractive in much of Western and Central Europe. And urbanization tended to reduce the birth rate, thus easing population pressure. Thus, the great overseas migration of the nineteenth and early twentieth centuries was a function of population growth and industrialization in Europe. It "occurred in a transitional phase of European development between the break-down of the old rural societies and the onset of modern industrialism."[3]

Economic motives alone did not determine the decision to leave home. This decision was often sparked by the "push" of poor economic opportunities at home and the "pull" of good ones somewhere else. But, except in rare cases where the alternative was starvation, it was made only by people with the predisposition to emigrate for other reasons, such as unwillingness to conform to local standards or a desire to improve their status or to satisfy new needs.

Few people left a highly stable local society, no matter how poor they were. An extreme example was the southeastern region of the Netherlands, with its small family farms, its religious and political conservatism, and its strong family and community ties. Even though this region (and the Netherlands as a whole) had the highest rate of population growth in northwestern Europe and chronic rural underemployment, hardly any of its inhabitants emigrated. In Italy the peasants of Sardinia were even poorer than those of Sicily, yet Sardinian emigration was negligible, whereas Sicily had one of the highest emigration rates in Europe beginning in the late 1890's. The main reason was that, unlike Sicily, Sardinia's social structure was untouched by the market economy and untroubled by threats to the status quo. (On the uprising of the Sicilian *fasci* in 1893, see Chapter 8.)

The people of Sicily were a prime example of the tendency to emigrate out of frustration in an unstable social situation. This was especially true in the western third of the island, where members of the Mafia had been increasing their role as intermediaries between the absentee noble landlords and the local population. Their arbitrary and violent methods replaced the decaying "feudal" order, yet the local law enforcement agencies could offer little protection against their "protection." In any case, most Sicilians had no attachment to the national government that these agencies represented, and they particularly resented its efforts to tax them and take their young men into the army. Many of them felt powerless to preserve or improve their status. In a highly status-conscious environment they could no longer bear their poverty and their forced submissiveness to a political and social order that they perceived as illegitimate. The desire to return home with money to improve one's status was certainly strong. Even so, the percentage of emigrants applying to local registries for reinstatement after residence abroad declined in Sicily from 22 in 1908–9 to 11 in 1912–13.[4] (The comparable figures for Italy as a whole were 24 and 13.) Thus in Sicily, as elsewhere, emigration was often a response to an unstable social situation where certain rigidities threatened inherited status or impending advancement.

This kind of situation was created by modernization and people's responses to it. Marginal peasants and craftsmen most threatened by modernization in such a situation provided the largest number of migrants. But the desire to move was not restricted to these two groups. Individuals from all classes became restless: the English construction engineer who emigrated to Australia to build railroads, the Sicilian nobleman who left his rural estate for Palermo to avoid paying the local hearth tax, the Norwegian small-town publisher's son who sought a more democratic political environment in San Francisco, the Silesian postman's daughter who became an elementary-school teacher in a coal-mining town in the Ruhr, the textile operatives from Italy who worked the looms of Belgium and France, the Jewish tailors from Russian Poland who fled with their entire families because of religious persecution as well as the dwindling demand for their skills.

It is impossible to document and tabulate the individual motives of the 30 million Europeans who emigrated abroad between 1890 and 1914 and the 60 million who moved into the urban and industrial areas of their own country. Yet sufficient evidence exists to place many of these people into certain major groups.

The largest single group of people on the move was male agricultural laborers. During the immediate prewar years close to half a million Italians worked on farms in Argentina from November until May, while about 600,000 Poles worked in eastern and central Germany during the European farming season. Like Mexican migrant farm workers in the United States today, they worked and lived in their own temporary "colonies" and had virtually no contact with the society and culture of the host country. Underemployment at home forced them to seek work wherever they could find it, and wherever they went they worked harder for less pay than the natives. In Germany, for example, the Polish workers accelerated the migration of the native farm workers to the towns.

Despite its early industrialization and urbanization, parts of England still had a considerable surplus of native agricultural laborers. Between 1881 and the outbreak of the war almost 700,000 of them, including their families, emigrated to Canada, Australia, and New Zealand. Many were helped with funds from the National Agricultural Union. But the Union could do little to improve the lot of those who stayed in England; they were as poorly paid and overworked as ever. The Yorkshire farm workers had all left the land to work in the factories and mills, so the local farmers advertised for boys in Suffolk, where—according to the reminiscences of Leonard Thompson, a retired farm worker born in 1897—"things were desperate" in the early 1900's.

> I was getting 9s. a week for a seventy-five-hour week in a cowshed. I had four hours off a week, from 10–2 on a Sunday. So I went to Yorkshire. . . . It was the first time I had been away from home. I lived in a little old room on the farm with two other boys and was

told that I would get . . . 5*s.* a week, but also my food and keep. . . .
I came [back] to Suffolk with eight golden sovereigns in my hand
and felt a millionaire. I returned to my old farm at Akenfield for 11*s.*
a week, but I was unsettled. When the farmer stopped my pay because it was raining and we couldn't thrash, I said to my seventeen-
year-old mate, 'Bugger him. We'll go off and join the army.' It was
March 4th 1914.[5]

Another major type was the rural or small-town young woman in her
late teens who moved to a large city to work as a servant. If her father
was a farmer or a craftsman, he usually had no employment for her and
no dowry to give her for a husband. If she had been reared in an orphan-
age, she was often trained specifically for domestic service. In either case
her background and education limited her aspirations to a position that
provided food and lodging and a little pocket money. She expected to
spend her working life as a servant and, if she was lucky, to marry another servant. Since the norms and values of her status were fairly rigid,
she did not have to make independent decisions or cope with unfamiliar
situations. By 1914, 6 to 7 per cent of the total population of London,
Paris, Berlin, and Vienna consisted of female servants "from the country." Although alternative kinds of unskilled jobs in light industry were
beginning to diminish the supply by then, only after the war did it decline drastically.

The lure of America attracted some poor country girls who did not
want to be servants. This was particularly true in Ireland, as is evident in
the following excerpt from a letter written on January 18, 1891, by Julia
Lough, a twenty-year-old seamstress in Winsted, Connecticut, to her
younger sister.

> I am getting along splendid and likes my work it seems like a new
> life. I will soon have a trade and be more independint[*sic*]. . . . I
> am very glad I made the change. . . . You know it was always what
> I wanted so I have reached my highest ambition.[6]

Most young people who left home to learn and practice a trade did so
within their own country. Having a trade was considered a step upward
from the ranks of the unskilled, but they had to be careful to choose one
that was not being displaced by machine-made products, particularly
clothing and many household items. A butcher or a plumber had a better
future than a candlestick maker or a seamstress. Julia Lough might have
been lucky enough to become a private dressmaker to the rich ladies of
Winsted, Connecticut, but most seamstresses worked as sweated labor in
New York, Paris, and other clothing manufacturing centers.

Women replaced men in some trades—tailoring, chain making, cheap jewelry, press stamping—where the processes of the craft were broken up, but the better-paying skilled trades were restricted to men and highly unionized, especially in Germany and Great Britain. Once apprenticed, a young artisan could usually move from low-wage to high-wage areas; the building trades in Europe's largest cities came to rely heavily on such immigration. The local branches of many craft unions provided lodgings, employment services, and relief to any newcomer with a membership card. Until they became saddled with a wife and family, many young artisans were therefore able to rove from one town to another before settling down in one place.[7] But many ununionized traditional craftsmen, like the father in *Der junge Tobias*, were never able to better themselves, wherever they moved.

Another major type of internal migration consisted of peasants trying to better themselves by working in industry. In the small mining town of Carmaux, in southern France, one investigator found that the most important motive of such migrants was higher wages, followed by more regular work on a yearly basis, insurance against accidents and illness, and the possibility of a pension.[8] These peasant migrants maintained their ties with the land, hoping to save their wages to purchase more land, build a new house, or perhaps provide a daughter with a better dowry. Most of them continued to grow their own food on nearby plots of land. Peasants who worked in larger industrial and mining centers had fewer contacts with their home villages, particularly in Eastern Europe. In Moscow the majority of male peasant factory workers led quite different lives from the miners of Carmaux. They slept in barracks in the city and visited their families in their villages only during brief vacation periods. Yet the money they sent home provided their families with a better existence than would otherwise have been possible.

Mobility in the rural areas of some countries was stimulated by sums sent home from emigrants to the cities and overseas. In Hungary new opportunities for acquiring parcels of land from large estates almost equaled those in the period after the abolition of serfdom; between 1890 and 1914 2.84 million acres were bought by small holders without any state intervention.[9] Many of these small holders thus moved up the social ladder in the course of a few years. Money earned by Polish emigrants and seasonal workers in Germany helped to create several million new small holders back home.[10]

But money from emigrants was not always necessary to stimulate the growth in the number of small- and medium-size farms. The exodus of agricultural laborers and marginal farmers from several regions of France enabled those farmers who remained to enlarge their own holdings. In the province of Lorraine a new class of proprietors of 50-acre farms was beginning to form, and a few farms grew to 250 acres.[11] This transformation occurred without the help of remittances from those who had gone to the cities. In Ireland too, little of the money sent home by emigrants to the United States was used to buy land, but 40 per cent of all their remittances took the form of prepaid passage tickets for new emigrants.[12]

Indirectly, however, money from emigrants helped to launch the greatest revolution in the history of modern Ireland—the abolition of the old landlordism and the transformation of the majority of the rural population into peasant proprietors. This process began in the early 1880's, when a total of one million dollars was sent to the Irish National Land League. The League's agitation against the landlords prompted the British government to initiate a series of state-aided land purchase acts, especially the Wyndham Act of 1903. By then most of the nonproprietors had left rural Ireland or were on the verge of leaving, often with financial aid from their American relatives.

The most attractive new opportunities for rural and small-town young people willing to move to the cities were in the lower ranks of the public services. An elementary-school diploma was often enough to qualify a young man or woman for a job in the national postal service or a low-level clerical position in some other government agency. Most police forces also recruited a large number of men from rural areas. The fastest-growing public service occupation was elementary-school teaching. In most countries the graduates of a nearby normal school could return to their home town to teach, but in France and Italy many were transferred periodically to different posts in their province and sometimes to other parts of the country. The male teachers in France often served as secretaries to the mayors, but otherwise they and their female colleagues lived in a circumscribed world, with few friends or ties in the community.[13] Although their case was an extreme example of rootlessness, like other civil servants from small towns and villages they were willing to leave home in order to raise their social status.

EMIGRATION ABROAD

By the 1890's the varying pace of modernization in different parts of the world brought changes in earlier patterns of European emigration abroad. During the nineteenth century large numbers of Scandinavians and Germans had emigrated to the prairie homesteads of the United States, but as this country became more urbanized and industrialized, the later emigrants tended to move to its mines, factories, and cities. Some Swedes still came to Minnesota to farm, and large numbers of North Italians still worked in the wheat fields during the Argentine summer. "But, by and large, the great migrations after 1890 were from farm to factory, from village to city, whether this meant from Iowa to Chicago, Silesia to Pittsburgh or Piedmont to Buenos Aires."[14] After 1900 a high percentage of skilled, professional, and entrepreneurial Britishers emigrated because of the slowing down of the rate of economic growth at home, particularly in industry. In contrast, Germany's economy grew fast enough to absorb such people as well as migrants from rural areas. Thus the annual number of German emigrants overseas dwindled from over 200,000 in the 1880's to around 30,000 in the immediate prewar years. In Norway and Sweden the introduction of universal suffrage and the growth of the trade-union movement undoubtedly reduced the number of young radicals who emigrated in order to find a less rigid political and social order.

In northwestern Europe emigration remained high only from the United Kingdom, where it reached an annual average of 464,000 in the years 1911 through 1913. By the early 1890's about half of those who came from Scotland, Wales, and England were skilled workers. After the turn of the century nearly one fifth of the English emigrants were professional people and entrepreneurs, and the proportion of Scottish emigrants of this class was even higher. The proportion of skilled and professional Irish who emigrated overseas also increased to about 25 per cent during the early 1900's. By then many unskilled Irish preferred working in Britain to emigrating to the United States.[15]

British emigrants moved increasingly to the English-speaking areas of the Empire rather than to the United States. Of the 174,000 emigrants who went overseas annually in the 1890's, 65.5 per cent went to the United States and 28.2 per cent to these other areas. But in the immediate prewar years, of the 464,000 who left the United Kingdom annually, only 26.5 per cent went to the United States, whereas 40.7 per cent went to Canada, 18.3 per cent to Australia and New Zealand, and 6.1 per cent to South Africa.[16] The majority of the professional and entrepreneurial British emigrants went to these areas because they were beginning to industrialize. The United States, whose industrialization had begun earlier, was already producing its own professional and entrepreneurial personnel, many of whom were the sons of earlier British immigrants.

The greatest change in the generation before the war was the decline of the "old" emigration from northwestern Europe and the increase of the "new" emigration from Southern and Eastern Europe. In 1890 approximately 60 per cent of European emigrants to the United States were of the "old" type and approximately 40 per cent the "new." By 1913 only 20 per cent was of the "old" type and 80 per cent was "new" emigration. Of the one and one half million emigrants to all parts of the world in that year, over one million were from Southern and Eastern Europe. Almost all of the over 300,000 from Austria-Hungary and the Balkans and the over 200,000 from the Russian Empire (especially Poland) went to the United States. Most of the over 200,000 from Spain and Portugal went to Latin America. The 400,000 Italians were divided about equally between North and South America. Foreign-born Italians comprised 11.7 per cent of the total population of Argentina, and first- and second-generation Italians amounted to one third of the population of the Brazilian state of São Paulo, where they dominated the urban building trades and the profession of architecture. (There were also nearly half a million Italians in France—about one third of the Italian-born population in the United States.) Like other immigrants to the United States by the early 1900's, most Italians worked in the cities.

The experiences of these millions of "new" emigrants varied widely, and there is no way of covering the full range. Many rural emigrants moved to the New World in groups, with their entire families, to "colonies" such as the Polish one in Paraná, in Brazil, or the Norwegian one in Wisconsin. The following three life stories are merely examples of certain types of individual male emigrants.

Pasquale Corvo (pseud.) left his native Corleone, in western Sicily, for the United States in 1906, when he was fifteen years old.[17] From the age of twelve he had worked in the fields with his father as a laborer for twenty cents a day. He had only attended elementary school for four years, but he was a bright lad and never lost his ability to read and write. When his uncle in New York sent him a steamship ticket he was eager to leave Corleone. Although he was at first overawed by the noise and congestion of the city, he soon managed to feel at home with his uncle's family and friends on Mulberry Street, in Little Italy. He felt less comfortable working as a bootblack in the Wall Street district (in Corleone this was considered a degrading occupation even for a teen-ager), although he sometimes earned as much as three or four dollars a week. Within a year Pasquale was able to buy a pushcart and peddle fruit in his own neighborhood. At nineteen he returned to Corleone to see his dying mother and settle down, but he could not find a steady job. So he returned to New York six months later to work in the restaurant his uncle had just opened.

By the time the war broke out in Europe, Pasquale improved his prospects considerably. He learned how to cook, buy meat and produce, and keep account books. After the war he was to open his own restaurant, obtain his citizenship papers, and raise eight children, one of whom was to become a New York state assemblyman.

This kind of success story was one of the stereotyped dreams of Europe's "huddled masses." The other dream was to make one's fortune in America and return home in triumph—or at least with enough savings to live better than one's neighbors. Insofar as the more capable and ambitious people emigrated overseas, these dreams often came true. But many people who left home were unable to organize their lives toward personal advancement. The life stories of most of these "losers" remain in oblivion, but the following two are fully documented.

Wladek Wiszniewski was born in 1886 in the village of Lubotyń, in Russian Poland.[18] His parents were still peasants culturally; during his childhood his father ran the local tavern and also kept poultry and livestock. But Lubotyń was not a true peasant village, that is, a community of equals, despite differences of wealth, with a large degree of autonomy in internal matters. Instead it resembled other manorial villages in Poland, Hungary, and East Prussia (and western Sicily before the noble landlords moved to Palermo), where the inhabitants were more or less dependent upon the noble landlord. Their main ambition, usually frustrated, was to climb a rung or two in the local social hierarchy. Consequently they had no feeling of solidarity with their equals and remained indifferent to their hostility when they enjoyed the favor of someone above them. Wladek preserved this attitude both in Lubotyń and throughout his wanderings during the early 1900's. It reflected the breakdown of traditional norms, both among the villagers and between them and the local nobility, whose younger members treated them as merely lower-class outsiders rather than as individuals for whom they felt some responsibility.

There were no traditional community or family ties to hold Wladek in his native village, so, like his older brothers, he left in his early teens to learn a trade in a large town. But, unlike them, he was never content to stay in one place. He worked as a journeyman baker in a number of towns throughout Poland, always losing his job after a few months for one reason or another. He also had an abortive apprenticeship as a surgeon's assistant. Then, when he was seventeen, he worked as a farm laborer in East Prussia. From there he went to Berlin and worked as a gardener for two months. Still restless and unable to find a suitable position as a baker, he joined the Russian army and was stationed in the Caucasus. In 1906 he left the army and wandered around Poland again. He worked as a constable (security guard) for a year and then for his parents, who had opened a bakery of their own.

Finally, in 1913, Wladek could no longer face his failures and decided to emigrate to Chicago, where his sister lived. His parting words to his family vividly expressed his bitterness.

> My dear ones! I regret much to leave my whole family and I don't know whether I shall come back and see anybody of my family, but I prefer to die there far away, even in misery, rather than remain here the laughing-stock of my family. . . . You . . . were ashamed of me when I was in Lódź. Wait, don't interrupt me. . . . I was ashamed of myself. But this is past. Then I was a constable and I have letters in which I was laughed at. But this is also past, and with your help I put some roubles aside and established a bakery in company with my parents. Now, after two years of my labor and of my endeavors, what is left for me? Either to go again tramping or to marry 'even a goat if she has money.' For my parents don't care. They tell me that I have spent this money long ago in drinking, eating and smoking; they simply drive me away from my own property. And this is not enough! They compromise me before girls whom I like in order that I may be refused, for they like it as it is now; they have a journeyman in me and treat me as such.[19]

Wladek lived with his sister in Chicago for a year, until he got married. There too he could not find steady work as a baker, and his last job was in the stockyards at nine dollars a week. His autobiography ends in the spring of 1915. He was out of work, unable to support his wife and child, in debt to his sister, and still blaming bad luck and other people for his failures. Here are his final words.

> From time to time we see my sister and brother-in-law. Brother-in-law sometimes tries to comfort us, but sister . . . always says something painful to my wife. . . . Thus I have improved my lot in this America which our immigrants adore![20]

Wladek had never been adequately controlled by traditional norms and had not yet learned, at age twenty-nine, to organize his life in new ways.

J.S. was born in 1899 in the small town of San Andrés, about twenty-five miles northeast of Barcelona, Spain. (Although his life as an emigrant did not begin until 1927, the editor of his autobiography says that it was similar to earlier ones.)[21] He was the ninth child in a poor, pious family. His father was a day laborer in a vineyard, and his mother did sewing at home for a small underwear manufacturer. Like Pasquale and Wladek, J.S. went to elementary school, but he was already forced to work for a few pennies before and after school at the age of five. The inhabitants of San Andrés were a bit further removed from their peasant roots than those of Lubotyń or Corleone, but their mentality was more dominated by traditional Catholic norms. In any case, J.S. always felt like a greenhorn during his rare visits to Barcelona, and Buenos Aires later on.

Although completely different from Wladek in personality and character, J.S. had a similar life in many ways. He was sober, frugal, pious, and wanted nothing better than to settle down in his home town and raise a family. Yet, from the moment he was apprenticed to a local carpenter at age eleven, he was in and out of work. At twenty he began four years of military service, mostly in North Africa, but this experience did not alter his outlook. Like Wladek, he remained a "loner," with no class consciousness and no community ties. At twenty-four, while working again as a carpenter, he lost his job because he had joined a Catholic union, whereas his employer thought he should have joined the Republican union. When the Catholic union stopped paying him unemployment relief after one month, J.S. said he had learned "a great lesson."

> I learned that a poor man in need must not take any [ideological] position; he must always be on the side of the strongest, whoever that may be; he must take care of himself and support his immediate family and renounce ideas and reflections. . . . Nobody concerns himself with the poor. . . . From now on I will never trust anyone and will always try to take care of myself.[22]

A year later J.S. got married, but he had to live with his in-laws because he could not afford his own house and the independence that would go with it. After two years of this life he decided to go to Argentina, where a relative of his mother-in-law promised him a good job as a carpenter. J.S. hoped to work there until he had enough money to send for his wife and child. But his brother told the editor of his autobiography that his wife and mother-in-law had helped him to make the arrangements and pay his travel expenses in order not to have him around anymore.

J.S. roved about Argentina for ten years, first as a carpenter, then as a photographer, before settling down in a small town near the Brazilian border. He lived there with a woman until she died over twenty years later. Meanwhile his health had deteriorated and so had his photography business. When he found himself alone, he asked the Spanish government to repatriate him. But back in his home town he was still poor and alone.

Whether failures or successes, most immigrants from peasant backgrounds showed little interest in the culture and society of their host country. Most of the "new" immigrants in the Americas made no comments about life there in their letters to the Old Country. Their peasant mentality gave them no standards for evaluating foreign ways. They dealt with foreigners only when they had to and clung to the only culture they knew. This was easier to do for Pasquale in New York's Little Italy and for Wladek in a Polish neighborhood in Chicago than for J.S. in the little Argentine town of Urquiza, the majority of whose inhabitants were of Russian and Polish origin. Their common language was Spanish, to be sure, but J.S. never thought of himself as an Argentine and it never occurred to him to become a naturalized citizen.* It was the children of those immigrants who stayed permanently who were absorbed in the "melting pots" of the New World.

INTERNAL MIGRATION AND ITS EFFECTS

It was usually easier for a European migrant to become assimilated in an urban or industrial area of his own country than in New York, Chicago, or Buenos Aires, but the degree of adaptation and assimilation varied widely. A peasant had more difficulty than a factory worker moving from one town to another. A formerly self-employed person was less willing to accept orders from a boss than someone who had always worked for others. The better-educated found it easier to move to a higher position in a strange place than the less-educated. (It was harder to adjust to a lower position, but this has always been so.) And, in general, women and children seem to have been more adaptable than men.

We can best understand the impact of geographical and occupational mobility on Europeans in the 1890's and early 1900's by contrasting it with the experience of their parents and grandparents instead of our own. Today the proportion of Americans and Europeans involved with both

* In 1914 only 1.4 per cent of the foreigners in Argentina became naturalized, whereas in the United States the figure was 41.5 per cent. This disparity was due mainly to the fact that, unlike their situation in the United States, foreign residents in Argentina could vote, teach in the public schools, and hold local—though not national—office.

types of mobility is about the same as it was then, but the *kinds* of people involved tend to be more ambitious and more highly qualified. In those days the majority consisted of poor individuals who were underemployed or who had lost their jobs, rather than established persons lured away by better offers. And the problems of adjustment are far less serious now. Not only are we more accustomed to changing jobs and relocating, but also our national cultures have become so standardized that we can maintain our usual life style almost anywhere in our own country. Seventy or eighty years ago the proportion of Europeans who left home or moved into new occupations was growing rapidly, and the proportion doing so for the first time was much greater than it is today. Their parents and grandparents rarely got used to the idea, and they gave them little guidance in coping with their new surroundings.

The most important over-all effect of internal migration was a pronounced change in the distribution of population in the more modern countries. In England, which was the most industrialized and urbanized country in 1841, the rural districts sank from 38.8 per cent of the total population to 19.3 per cent in 1911, while the coal-mining districts rose from 8.3 to 14.8 per cent and the towns from 52.9 to 66 per cent.[23] In Germany the proportion of the population in towns and mining districts rose even faster during the much shorter period of the 1890's and early 1900's. The same was true for the influx of immigrants from outside the country, with large numbers of Irish in Liverpool and Manchester and Poles in the coal-mining districts of the Ruhr. Between 1900 and 1910 even in relatively backward Hungary one seventh of the agricultural population moved to the towns. The population of Budapest grew from 500,000 to 1,100,000 between 1890 and 1910, and that of the nine next largest Hungarian cities almost doubled during the same period. Although the total population growth of France was the smallest of any major country, certain regions attracted a high percentage of migrants. At the end of the nineteenth century over 50 per cent of the inhabitants of greater Paris had been born in other parts of the country. This was also true in Montpellier and the province of Bas-Languedoc (the coastal plain west of the Rhône). Almost half of the new migrants to this province were rude mountain people from the north.

The arrival of these outsiders initiated a basic transformation in the kinds of people who lived in Bas-Languedoc.[24] The mountain people came in groups and lived and married among themselves. An investigation in the town of Pézenas showed that 95 per cent of the immigrants between 1900 and 1910 married other mountain people. There were numerous street fights between gangs of immigrants and natives; each gang had its own rites and symbols and operated out of different gambling halls. This cultural clash prompted many of the natives to leave. By 1900, 103,787 people born in the *départements* (counties) of Gard and Hérault had already moved out of the province, one quarter of them to Marseilles and one quarter to Paris. In the mining region of Alès many of the Protestant managers welcomed the replacement of the local Protestant workers, who tended to be radical or socialist, with Catholic mountain people, who were more willing to accept their paternalistic methods. There was also a growing influx of Spaniards after the 1890's in Bas-Languedoc. By the end of the war half of the inhabitants of the city of Nîmes were from Spain.[25]

Internal migration also changed the age and sex distribution in different regions. The overwhelming majority of migrants from the country to the city were between fifteen and thirty-five years old. Thus there was a disproportionate number of older people in many rural areas. Where this was the case the birth rate declined even though the fertility rate among women of child-bearing age did not. In the more modern countries, particularly England and Sweden, more young women left the rural areas than young men, thus contributing further to the declining birth rate in those areas. (Also, birth control was already in wide use in rural Sweden.)[26] In Southern and Eastern Europe more men migrated than women, thus allowing the rural population to continue growing rapidly.

While the effect of internal migration on birth rates and population growth in rural areas varied considerably in different parts of Europe, it was fairly uniform in large coal-field industrial regions and in great commercial and administrative cities everywhere. Leaving aside the increase due to immigration, the population of the English Midlands, the Ruhr industrial region, and the industrial area of the Nord and Pas-de-Calais *départements* in northern France would have tended to increase three times faster than the population of London, Berlin, or Paris.[27] In London the native-born population could not reproduce itself before 1910; in Paris and Berlin it could not do so until long after the war. The fact that these three cities did grow at about the same rate as the three industrial regions was due entirely to heavy immigration.

The impact of immigration in an industrial area becomes especially clear when we project the growth of a given population and then compare it with the population count of a later census. For example, the population of the Ruhr industrial town of Barmen—excluding newcomers and applying the rate of population growth for Germany as a whole between 1871 and 1910—would have risen from 75,074 to 115,924, whereas it actually rose to 169,214. This difference of 53,290 was more than three times the increase of 16,555 that came from immigration alone.[28] It is explained by the fact that there were proportionately more young adults among the immigrants than among the native born and that they had more children per capita.

Internal migration was not a one-way street from rural districts to urban and industrial areas. People also moved from overpopulated to underpopulated rural districts. The most spectacular example was the movement of three and one half million peasants from European Russia to Siberia, but there were smaller-scale movements of this kind in France.[29] People also moved from a city to its suburbs; this was particularly true of London (which also lost many emigrants to the British Empire during the early 1900's). After 1900 there was more migration *between* different cities and different industrial towns than to cities from the countryside in much of Western and Central Europe.

But the degree of mobility and that of the gain through immigration were independent of each other. Whereas in London the net gain in population through immigration was higher than the rate of population turnover, the opposite was true in many industrial cities of the Ruhr and the Rhineland.[30] Turnover was particularly high in cities with a diversified economic structure, where the only jobs open to most newcomers were those rejected by the native inhabitants and where competition for these jobs among the immigrants was particularly ruthless. Wladek, for example, spent only two months in Berlin; others like him left after a few years. Casual laborers, roving artisans, and the less favored individuals in certain services (entertainers, waiters, errand boys, prostitutes, etc.) moved in and out of cities without appearing in the census figures for ten-year periods. There are no readily available estimates of the decennial turnover rate for most European cities, but in many of them it may have approached the 40 to 60 per cent range for most cities in the United States.[31] In other words, for every 100 immigrants to a city in 1890, 40 to 60 may have left by 1900.

In much of Southern and Eastern Europe internal migration, as well as emigration abroad, was higher among peasants with small holdings than among day laborers.[32] Economic motives predominated among such peasants in Russia and Serbia. Unable to support their families from their work in industry or farming alone, they engaged in both pursuits, moving from town to village with the seasons. On the eve of the First World War this was true of 46 per cent of the printers in Moscow, and the proportion was higher in smaller Russian towns and less skilled trades. In those regions of southern Italy and southern Spain where large estates prevailed the polarization of classes provided a setting for a militant labor movement. By holding out the hope of rectifying social injustice this movement gave the day laborers an alternative to emigration. In Hungary and Poland there was no such hope, and the laborers moved away at a higher rate than the small holders.

Although social injustice remained almost everywhere, geographical and occupational mobility helped create a modern social structure in northwestern Europe and Germany. Government statistics for the years 1895 and 1907 show that this structure was fully formed in Germany by the first decade of the twentieth century.[33] The greatest change was in the countryside, where the mass exodus of native agricultural workers created a shortage of rural labor and a shift in the ratio of upper and middle to lower agrarian classes from 1:1.45 to 1:1.35. In the urban areas the ratio of self-employed to wage-earning workers in industry and handicrafts shifted from 1:4.1 to 1:6. The shift was even greater from self-employed to salaried people among the middle classes. The percentage of working-class Germans in industry increased from 44.4 to 45.1 in towns over 100,000 and from 47.4 to 51.7 in towns with 2,000 to 100,000 inhabitants. But the rate of increase among white-collar employees in industry was much greater: 2.9 to 5.6 in towns over 100,000 and 2.2 to 4.2 in towns with 2,000 to 100,000 inhabitants. Since most of these employees were in the lower ranks of the middle class, and since the percentage of rural workers declined, the over-all distribution among the upper, middle, and lower classes remained fairly constant.

THE UPROOTED AND THE CITIES

The experiences of newcomers in towns and cities varied according to whether they were rich or poor, transient or permanent, alone or with their families, of native or foreign ethnic origin.

Great capitals like London, Paris, Berlin, and Vienna had been attracting people from the upper and middle classes for a long time; this attraction became particularly strong in Eastern Europe in the late nineteenth century after the emancipation of the serfs. By 1900, 48 per cent of the Russian nobility had moved to the cities, especially St. Petersburg and Moscow. The percentage of Hungarian gentry that had moved to Budapest was considerably higher. Some of the Russian nobles continued to live on the incomes of their estates or to serve as officials in the imperial government. But others, like the majority of the now landless Hungarian gentry, embarked on new ways of life. A few rich Russian nobles became industrialists; a larger number went into the professions or municipal administration in other large Russian cities.[34] Even more than these newly urbanized Russian nobles the gentry in Budapest clung to their aristocratic attitudes, despite their essentially middle-class occupations. A typical member of the Hungarian gentry made more money as the assistant manager of a bank than from the estate his father had sold after the emancipation eliminated its unpaid work force. But he resented having to work with middle-class commoners, especially if they were Jews. In the professions of law and medicine the main competitors of the gentry and middle classes were Magyarized Jews from the non-Magyar-speaking provinces. In Budapest and particularly Vienna recently assimilated middle-class Jews were becoming major consumers and producers of the urban elite culture.

At the bottom of society were the vagrants and paupers, who constituted 2 to 3 per cent of the urban population in England and France and as much as 10 per cent in some of the large cities of Eastern and Southern Europe, particularly Naples. As always, a significant proportion of these people were outsiders, but this proportion grew drastically in some places. In the eight largest cities in Scotland the number of male paupers increased over 50 per cent between 1894 and 1904, the number of female paupers over 30 per cent.[35] Since the total number of paupers in Scotland rose from 96,671 in 1895 to 110,491 in 1905 (hardly more than 15 per cent), we may assume that there was a tremendous influx of paupers into its cities during this short period.

Applying for poor relief in those days was not like "going on welfare" today. At least one third of those receiving such relief were in workhouses (called poorhouses in the United States), and those on "outrelief" were given only as much money in a year as an American welfare recipient receives in a month today.[36] Of the paupers who flocked to the cities at the turn of the century, those who qualified for relief at all were "the deserving poor"—people too old, too young, or too unfit to work. The others had to shift for themselves.

These immigrant paupers swelled the ranks of what Marx called the *Lumpenproletariat* (literally proletariat in rags), which included casual laborers, street hawkers, drifters, prostitutes, and petty criminals. During much of the nineteenth century the middle and upper classes called these people the "dangerous class." Mid-Victorian London had an underworld

Aristide Bruant, a poster by Toulouse-Lautrec.

"that stretched from the teeming desperation of the slum warrens to the fleshpots of Haymarket, whose channels of communication linked city to city and reached out to the migrant population of the countryside."[37] Though sentimentalized in fictional characters like Oliver Twist and Mack-the-Knife, people in this underworld were individuals without marketable skills trying to survive as best they could.

But by the 1870's the Victorian underworld was being viewed as less menacing as a result of slum clearance, improved police control, and alternative careers for its bolder and more resourceful potential leaders. (Except for the *camorra* in Naples, organized crime as we think of it today was unknown in European cities before the First World War.)

> The young bully-boy who outraged decent citizens as a navvy becomes, if he is shrewd as well as tough, a foreman overseer, and ends up a respected citizen with polished boots and a silver watchchain. The lad sharpened on the streets into a budding magsman realises that the distant gold rush is likely to provide far fatter pickings than Epsom Downs. The bright foundling learns his letters in the workhouse school and dreams of the power and status driving a locomotive or policing a beat may bring him.[38]

During the 1890's the French singer-poet Aristide Bruant expressed some of the feelings of the social outcasts at the bottom of Parisian society. In his song "*À la Vilette*" a young woman laments the loss of her sweetheart, a handsome young *apache* (street bully and part-time petty criminal) named Toto Laripette. Toto never knew his parents and had been on his own since childhood. Like many of his kind, he ends up in prison before he is twenty. The last time his girl friend sees him he is lying, stripped to the waist, under the knife of the guillotine.

In his play *The Lower Depths* (1902) Maxim Gorky vividly dramatized the way of life of the *Lumpenproletariat* of the Khitrov Market district in Moscow when it was becoming a skid row in the early 1900's, but until then this district had served as a labor pool for new arrivals from the countryside. Many European cities had open-air markets that served this same purpose. Each morning able-bodied men without regular jobs assembled there in the hope of finding work for the day. Many were newly arrived from the countryside; some were unskilled farm workers, others had worked as painters, saddlers, blacksmiths, carpenters, and in similar trades for which there was little full-time work in industry. In many ways these "disposable" people resembled the "underclass" of the "ethnic poor" in the United States and northwestern Europe today.

By the turn of the century, however, this European "underclass" was becoming more proletarian than *Lumpen*. Some young women from the country still drifted into prostitution after a few years of working as servants or barmaids and seeing their hopes for marriage or even a permanent liaison shattered by a series of increasingly transient lovers. But many more of these young women worked as sweated labor in light industry. Many young male immigrants remained in the ranks of the casual laborers, but an increasing proportion of them found more regular employment as street cleaners, waiters and busboys, menial workers in public facilities (parks, hospitals, railroad stations, government buildings), and operatives in large factories.

The life styles of these newcomers varied from city to city and depended upon the amount and kinds of work available. Even those who lacked marketable skills were less likely than earlier immigrants to adopt the street culture of the older "dangerous class." And those who were skilled found difficulty accepting the outlook of the existing working class, particularly toward unionization. Both skilled and unskilled workers, especially unmarried men, tended to be more transient than workers born in the city. In each new town they spent their nonworking hours in flophouses, taverns, and labor pools. Thus their life style lacked the social and cultural reinforcement available to the already urbanized working class. (See Chapter 4.)

"Flophouse" is an old American slang term for a cheap lodginghouse with single rooms or dormitories in which transient casual laborers "flopped" into bed at night. Although practically extinct today, this institution was of major importance during the 1890's and early 1900's in many European as well as American cities. In Hamburg a municipally run lodginghouse with 350 beds was used by 4,858 men in 1894, 15,359 in 1898, and 29,820 in 1902.[39] Other lodginghouses in Hamburg were run by Catholic and Protestant organizations. Every major city in Western and Central Europe had such lodginghouses. (One of their famous former "guests" was Adolf Hitler during part of his stay in Vienna.) Milan had its Albergo Popolare, and London's Newington Butts, with 1,015 beds, was part of the Rowton Houses chain, similar to the Mills Houses chain in the United States. The YMCA and YWCA chains and the cheap residence halls for unmarried female wage earners were more respectable than these flophouses, and the traditional boardinghouses, with an average of seven or eight "guests," catered to more settled working people, including white-collar employees.

None of these houses was a home in any sense. They epitomized the lack of family and community ties in cities in a period when there were more uprooted Europeans than ever before or since. One might exchange small talk with fellow lodgers in the dining hall or some cheap nearby restaurant and find a bit of forced fellowship in the local tavern, but one was mostly alone. Even a worker who had a room in the home of a working-class family was treated as an outsider and forced to eat his meals and find his companionship elsewhere.

The practice of taking in lodgers or subtenants was widespread. In 1910, in Vienna, out of 476,000 dwellings, 110,000, or 23 per cent, had one or the other.[40] Since most of the dwellings in Viennese working-class districts were two- and three-room apartments in tenements, they had more lodgers than subtenants, and the lodgers often slept in the same room with persons of the opposite sex. In the district of Ottakring, with 178,000 inhabitants in 1910, only 4 persons in 100 had a room of their own.[41] Only by letting a bed to a stranger could many Viennese working-class families pay the rent, which averaged 15 per cent of the family income. This percentage was above the European average, though rents in other fast-growing capital cities, like Berlin and Budapest, were also high. In most industrial towns rent was 10 per cent of a working-class family's income. Even so, many of these families took in lodgers.

Uprooting had the most extreme consequences in the largest Russian cities. In Moscow most male factory workers lived in barracks; in St. Petersburg 85 per cent of all working men and women roomed by themselves, whether they were single or married.[42] Furthermore, only 48 per cent of all adult males in St. Petersburg were married, and only 18 per cent of *them* lived with their families. In most cases their families still lived in their native village. *That* was where home was. Their visits there and their relative isolation from the urban-born working class helped them to preserve their peasant mentality to a far greater extent than newcomers to the cities of Western and Central Europe.

Peasant immigrants also preserved their peasant mentality in cities like Belgrade and Budapest. In an autobiographical novel the Hungarian writer Gyula Illyés recalls how his grandfather had offered his father enough money to open an inn in the village of his *puszta* (manorial estate) if he gave up his efforts to find a career in the capital.

> At first my father visited us every month, then later every Saturday. He found life in Budapest more and more distasteful. He passed his examinations, but now his plan was to find a better job on one of the pusztas. Grandfather's message stimulated him. Why should not he too choose an easier life?[43]

A working-class tenement in the Ottakring district, Vienna.

Unlike Illyés's father, Nikolai Chikildeyev, in Anton Chekhov's story *Peasants* (1897), did not return to his native village with his wife and daughter for an easier life but because he was too sick to work any longer as a waiter in Moscow. And instead of being welcomed with a loan from his grandfather he was resented by his old mother for bringing another set of mouths to feed. Chekhov's story, based on an actual occurrence in his own village, is famous for its unsentimental portrayal of the squalor, meanness, and hopelessness of peasant life at the end of the nineteenth century in much of Russia. It also illustrates the way in which peasant boys were recruited for menial work in the city. "All the lads of Zhukovo who could read and write were packed off to Moscow and hired out as bellboys or waiters (just as the lads on the other side of the river all apprenticed to bakers)."[44] Nikolai had been taken to Moscow when he was eleven and given a situation by a fellow villager, Ivan Makarych, who worked in the Hermitage Garden restaurant. But on his return Nikolai says that Ivan, now an older man, was working out of town and earning less. No one had heard from him for a long time, and he had long ceased to send any money home to his relatives. When Nikolai dies, his wife Olga, who had been taken to Moscow at the age of eight, returns there to resume her work as a chambermaid. She has lost contact with her own village, and Nikolai's family refuses to keep her and her daughter.

In England it was easier for most migrants to maintain some contacts with their families and friends even when they could not afford to return home for long or permanently.[45] Many were close to their native village, and even those who migrated long distances did so in stages, so that they could visit their village friends who had remained in the town they had recently left. These village friends often lived in a particular neighborhood, thus providing a better urban base from which to become assimilated than the village itself. In 1899, when young William Denny moved from his village in Suffolk to Burton to work in the Bass ale brewery, he lived with his mates in lodgings and spent all of his free time with them.[46] Although he returned home permanently after four seasons, many of his friends stayed in Burton and became citified.

Most rural migrants in England were agricultural workers and craftsmen (the small yeoman farmers having almost disappeared), but elsewhere the children of marginal small farmers left with no intention of returning. This was particularly true of those in the southwestern French cities of Toulouse and Bordeaux, which were full of emigrants whose Gascon and Languedoc dialects still resounded in the streets and workshops but who aspired to full-fledged membership in the urban community for themselves and their children. They still lived in little houses surrounded by a garden that reminded them of the countryside where they had been born. They woke up to the crowing of the cock, and their wives kept a few chickens and rabbits. They also had a vine arbor and raised their own vegetables, but they had abandoned the fields forever.[47]

One of the most disorienting effects of leaving home was the need to adopt new speech patterns. The dialects brought to Toulouse and Bordeaux by rural immigrants helped these people to preserve their image of themselves and to find familiar words for phenomena that were strange to them. As some of the phenomena became familiar through frequent contact, such people began to use nondialect words for them: electricity, labor union, pasteurized milk, etc. The problem of learning new speech patterns is greater the greater the difference between the dialect of the immigrants and the language spoken in the city. Gascon is closer to standard French than Sicilian is to standard Italian or to the dialects of Italian cities on the mainland. Thus a Sicilian immigrant to Naples, Rome, or Milan had to learn to use not only the standard Italian he had studied as a second language in elementary school but also the dialect of the city— or even the neighborhood—in which he settled, if he wanted to become assimilated. In most cases only the children born in the new environment felt completely at home with its speech patterns and the values, attitudes, and perceptions these expressed.

Rural dialects were also being modified by the dialects of nearby industrial towns. Those village people who worked in such towns brought back new words and especially new pronunciations which they and their children adopted. (Older villagers and others with no contact with the town were little affected.) In many larger villages, particularly in Germany, certain clubs, trade unions, and political parties helped to reinforce the new speech patterns among those villagers who had frequent contact with the town.[48] Thus former peasants learned urban lower-class speech patterns that gave them different perceptions from their traditional ones. But these new perceptions were still lower-class, not middle-class or "national."

The spread of national languages and cultures into rural areas was the result of the over-all changes brought by modernization. Some young men returning from their military service brought new ideas and new speech patterns with them. New agricultural techniques made the vocabulary of the old techniques obsolete. Officials, merchants, and other local representatives of the towns and the central government challenged the traditional ruling class and the established distribution of influence in the villages. In response to this reorientation of power many villagers found it in their interest to be on familiar terms with the national language and culture of the new ruling class rather than to treat them as "foreign" subjects learned in school.

In places where the old culture and dialect were strong these people became bilingual and bicultural. This was true in much of Germany, Italy, Spain, France south of the Loire River, and even small countries like Norway and Switzerland.* Indeed, some of the more extensive regional dialects had a thriving literature; Luigi Pirandello wrote several of his early stories and plays in Sicilian, and Allen Clarke, an English spokesman for socialist causes, wrote stories in Lancashire dialect.

Traditionally dialects had reinforced local feelings of community, but by the beginning of this century these feelings were based on false premises in Europe's great cities. Cockney separated the residents of the East End from other Londoners without uniting them among themselves. All classes of people in Vienna could speak the dialect of that city when they had to. (Even the *Schönbrunnerdeutsch* spoken by members of the imperial family was a refinement of it.) Toward foreigners it represented a defense, while against North Germans it guaranteed insularity. Yet educated Viennese frequently spoke High German among themselves. There was no intermediate form of speech—no "national" language—that allowed social contact among different segments of the local population, let alone with other Austrians and German-speaking foreigners.

THE URBAN CONSCIOUSNESS AND ITS CRITICS

One of the severest strains on newcomers in the open and heterogeneous cities of the turn of the century was the need to become self-conscious about the diverse roles they were forced to play in them. In their villages and small towns they had learned to play different roles in their families, in church, in the local tavern, and in their infrequent contacts with the local bourgeoisie and gentry. But that kind of role-playing had been unself-conscious. One was always comfortable in one's role be-

* To this day Norwegians and German-speaking Swiss in all classes use their traditional dialect at home and in their informal contacts and the official language in the schools, the mass media, and most public discussions.

Michaelerplatz, Vienna, showing Adolf Loos's Goldman and Salatsch building (1910).

cause the settings were familiar and limited in number and the responses of other people were predictable. In the cities a man or woman had to act the part of a different character as he or she moved from one setting to another. Individuals had to be able to watch themselves behave so that they could improvise and adapt their role-playing to the responses of people they did not know—in factories and offices, union halls, clubs, sporting arenas, and other public places. This kind of ability could make living in the city more rewarding and interesting than in small communities. It also gave city dwellers a large measure of personal freedom. But the characters who did not become self-conscious about their role-playing were crushed by the harshness and complexity of urban life.

Another aspect of the urban consciousness was learning not to react openly to all the stimuli outside oneself. Anyone who tried to do so would go mad. Not only did one have to be able to shut out many sights and sounds, but one also had to know how to size up strangers in order not to get involved with them. City-bred people develop these abilities at an early age, but for a newcomer the simple act of walking on a busy sidewalk (let alone driving in traffic) can be overwhelming until he learns the rules of avoiding bumping into other people and of not being distracted by everything that is going on around him. The urban consciousness demands a continual turning in on the self for nourishment in the face of countless extraneous stimuli.

But this kind of self-consciousness, though necessary for survival in cities (and more recently in suburbs as well), has produced some of the most nagging discontents in the modern world. The mass media have spread self-consciousness to the lower classes, but it began as a middle-class phenomenon in the late nineteenth century. According to the art historian Meyer Schapiro, the shift of the settings of bourgeois sociability from community, family, and church to the boulevard, cafe, and resort brought a "consciousness of individual freedom [that] involved more and more an estrangement from older ties; and those imaginative members of the middle class who accepted the forms of freedom but lacked the economic means to attain them, were spiritually torn by a sense of isolation in an anonymous mass."[49]

Self-consciousness differs from self-awareness. The self-conscious person is preoccupied with his relations with other people and institutions. How must I behave in order to please my boss, lover, friends? If I attend the right school, own the right car, and have the right tastes, I will acquire a higher position or at least maintain the one I now have. Who can control me and whom can I control? The self-aware person is mainly concerned with understanding his own motives and feelings so that he may function as effectively as his strengths and weaknesses will allow. His perceptions are not distorted by envy, snobbery, resentment, and frustration, as the self-conscious person's so often are. Class consciousness and national consciousness have also altered people's perceptions, but they have often operated as integrating forces to bring people closer together in large, impersonal organizations. Self-consciousness, on the contrary, tends to make individuals feel isolated.

Among the many intellectuals and literary writers who reacted against modern self-consciousness Leo Tolstoy was outstanding. Already in *War and Peace* (1862–69), in a scene in a French prison camp, he has Count

Pierre Bezuhov reflect that, the more self-consciously one strives toward personal fulfillment, the further one strays from the path to true happiness and inner harmony. Pierre had thrown himself into philanthropy, freemasonry, wine, the dissipations of Society, heroic feats of self-sacrifice, his romantic love for Natasha, his project for killing Napoleon. All his thoughts and efforts had failed him. Then, as a prisoner of war, without a thought of his own, he gains peace and harmony within himself simply through having witnessed the horror of the execution of a teen-age boy, through the hardships of the prison camp, and through his relationship with Platon Karataev, a simple peasant who loves everybody and lives from one day to the next. Karataev was not conscious of the meaning of his life as something personal and separate from the world around him. "It had meaning only as part of a whole, of which he was at all times conscious."

But this idealization of the unself-conscious peasant, which Tolstoy was to carry to extremes during our period, was itself a self-conscious conceit. As a later would-be populist intellectual, Cesare Pavese, was forced to admit: "One cannot go to the people; one is already part of the people. Otherwise it is useless." The sociologist Reinhard Bendix has noted that "the idea of unlimited creativity by 'the individual' or 'the people' is as much a chimera as is that of a womb-like security and warmth in human relations attributed to a bygone age. These are projections of intellectuals with a civilization that induces in them an intense ambivalence between elitism and populism."[50]

Negative responses to the urban consciousness included other versions of agrarian romanticism besides Tolstoy's. Lamenting the way in which big cities dissolved rural family bonds, the German Protestant pastor Ludwig Heitmann compared these "shapeless giants" to "vacuum cleaners, which swallow up men, organic cultural forms, and raw materials with irresistible mechanical force, in order to spit them out again, ground down, pressed into a new mold, and stamped with a factory trade mark."[51] Reactionary nationalists like Charles Maurras in Paris and Georg von Schönerer in Vienna constantly berated life in these great capitals not only because it made people self-centered but also because it was so cosmopolitan. According to them, only "natives" with rural roots could preserve their national heritage from being hopelessly corrupted by the Jews and other "foreigners" in these cities. As we shall see in Chapter 9, people like Maurras and Schönerer viewed the city as a symbol for everything they hated in modern civilization. Most socialists held a more favorable view of urban values and attitudes and modernization in general, but this was not the case with Robert Blatchford's *"Merrie England"* (1894), by far the most successful piece of popular socialist propaganda published in Britain. Blatchford's view was nostalgic. "Merrie England" would be free from great cities and large-scale industry; it would return to a decentralized order of more or less self-contained communities in a predominantly agricultural economy.

By the late nineteenth century nostalgia for such a society was utopian for two reasons. First of all, country living was changing not only because of pressures from the city but also because rural capitalism and population mobility had already transformed the agrarian social structure and peasant attitudes in many places. Thomas Hardy dramatized the relation between "the changing nature of country living . . . and one or more characters who have become in some degree separated from it yet who remain by some tie of family inescapably involved"[52] in his novels *Tess of the D'Urbervilles* (1891) and *Jude the Obscure* (1896). Hardy also dealt with the second reason that made nostalgia for traditional country living utopian: the self-consciousness of the returning "native." Once one has learned what living in a city (or in Jude's case a university) means, one cannot go back to a world of unself-conscious role-playing based on unexamined beliefs and values. One now knows that these are subject to challenge and change.

Many highly educated people who had lost their rural ties still felt ambivalent about the city as their home. They enjoyed the personal freedom, stimulating social life, and concentration of high culture available in Europe's great capitals. Yet periodically they felt the need to "get away from it all"—to a country house, a resort, or a friend's or relative's home in a smaller community. Then the novelty gave way to boredom and they longed to get back to their normal lives in the city. For them, leaving home was a temporary escape from the strains imposed by the urban consciousness rather than an attempt to return to another, simpler home. They resembled Sigmund Freud and other Viennese thinkers who claimed that their city was impossible to live in and impossible to live away from.

A larger number of city dwellers adopted the compromise solution of moving to the suburbs in order to escape from the undesirable aspects of the city. The upper classes retained their town houses in London and other capital cities well into the twentieth century. But by the mid-nineteenth century the upper-middle classes were moving out of the industrial cities of the English Midlands to suburban estates within commuting distance by railroad or private carriage. After 1861 the villages of Acton

Traffic at Piccadilly Circus, London, 1910. The automobile is already becoming dominant.

and Ealing became middle-class residential suburbs of outer London, and by the 1880's some middle-class residents of large cities in Central Europe were moving to similar villages. In Acton the open, pleasant, and freely planned neighborhood of Springfield Park and the "garden suburb" of Bedford Park were especially appealing to the middle classes.[53] Ealing retained its late-Victorian middle-class character more successfully than Acton, which attracted London's commercial and government employees in the 1890's and had a number of frankly working-class districts by the immediate prewar years. By the 1890's Berlin and other large Central European cities also had their middle-class dormitory suburbs, complete with thatched-roof stations on the commuting railroad lines.

This kind of migration away from the central cities marked the beginning of the disintegration of their openness and diversity. The middle classes were fleeing not only the noise, congestion, and pollution but also the lower classes. Father caught only fleeting glimpses of slum districts from his train window on his way to and from his office downtown; Mother and the children rarely left the balmy oasis of their suburban home. The fashionable boulevards and theater districts of Paris, Vienna, and other great cities were still crowded with well-dressed people on the eve of the First World War. (The police kept them "off limits" to the lower classes, aside from a few street entertainers and an occasional beggar.) But municipal reformers and land developers, under the guise of urban renewal, were already resettling some slum dwellers in suburban colonies. Thus the middle-class suburbs began to lose their immutability. "To flight had been added pursuit."[54]

WOMEN AND CHILDREN

In traditional societies women and children usually stayed at home. They had certain domestic chores, and they often helped the men in the fields at harvest time, but they rarely earned independent incomes away from the family patrimony. Among the urban poor in our period the traditional view of children as a source of family income died hard, but now the children had to be sent out into the anonymous city during the day to earn their pennies. In the cities, as in the countryside, poor parents resented and resisted compulsory elementary education because it interfered with their children's labor.* Working-class women who had someone, usually a grandmother, to mind their small children and cook the meals also began to leave home during the day to work for regular wages. Often they just wanted to get out of the house, like the one who said to Mrs. Ramsay MacDonald: "D'yer think I could stop at 'ome all dye and mind the blessed byby—it 'ud give me the bloomin' 'ump!"[55] This woman earned 10 shillings a week in a jam factory and paid her mother 5 shillings to feed and mind the baby.

Most middle- and upper-class women and children remained homebound. In the Mediterranean area women of all classes were not allowed by their menfolk to leave the house unaccompanied except to go to

---

* Some poor parents sent their children to school at three, saying they were five, so that they could finish and go to work two years earlier than the law allowed.

church or do the marketing. Even in England many upper-class young women might reach marriageable age without ever having left their homes unaccompanied, if only by a maid.[56] Unmarried middle-class women could move about more freely in most of Western and Central Europe, but they were expected to stay with their parents until they found a husband rather than work and live away from home. The following exchange between the protagonist in H. G. Wells's novel *Ann Veronica* (1909) and her mother was typical:

"Then I suppose when I have graduated I am to come home?"

"It seems the natural course."

"And do nothing?"

"There are plenty of things a girl can find to do at home."

Yet during the early 1900's a growing proportion of unmarried middle-class and especially lower-middle-class women were leaving home during the day to work in the rapidly growing service sector of the economy. In Germany they did much of the routine office work, particularly in the larger firms.[57] In Britain the percentage of female clerks rose from eight in 1890 to thirty-two in 1911.[58] The female typist became the symbol of the lower-middle-class working woman almost everywhere. The other main occupation for such women was elementary-school teaching, where they outnumbered men by two or three to one in the most advanced countries.

Before the time of large-scale industrialization many lower-class boys had been apprenticed away from home at age eleven or twelve, and many teen-age sons of tenant farmers and agricultural laborers had been forced to work and live on neighboring farms, where they had no home life at all. These conditions persisted into the early 1900's in many parts of Southern and Eastern Europe, but they were disappearing in north-western and Central Europe. There the institution of compulsory education and child-labor laws prevented children up to a certain age from working at all. Children could have spent more time at home than in the past, but, except on Sundays, this did not usually happen. When they were not in school they were usually playing in the streets without supervision.

In the early 1890's one observer of a working-class neighborhood in Berlin counted 218 children in a byway surrounded by two dozen houses.

> The smallest ones were sitting or sliding all over the sidewalk, so that a person had to be careful not to step on a little hand or foot. The most popular pastime of the older boys was playing ball in the street.

An English telephone exchange at the turn of the century.

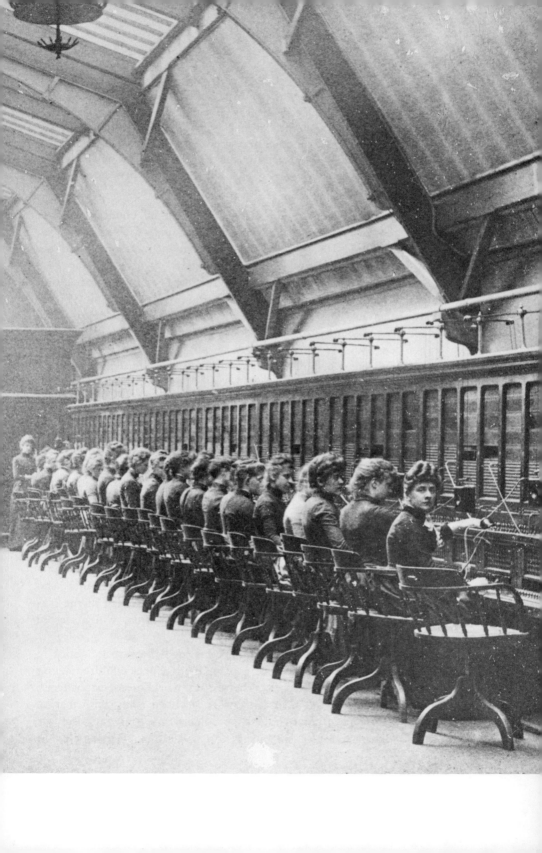

Sitting on the curb the five- to eight-year-old girls played school, and the boys of the same age did this in another place. The difference was that the boy who played "teacher" got his main enjoyment from beating his "pupils," and the "lesson" usually ended in a free-for-all. . . . The boys were amazingly proficient in making noises of all kinds. . . . The older ones stood together in a group and shouted and screamed until their faces turned red from the effort; then they suddenly dispersed.[59]

In contrast, upper- and middle-class children in all countries had to stay in the house when they were not at school. They were carefully supervised and attended to by some servant. Periodically they visited the homes of other children to play, and many were taken to dancing class once a week. But they were carefully sheltered from all corrupting influences, whether from working-class children or from the adult world.

In Edwardian England particularly, the children's quarters in middle- and upper-class homes were often cocoons of innocence. There the child was either "cossetted as a plaything for its putative innocence, or laden, as in many high-minded intellectual families, with the burden of creating a new, clear-eyed, uncorrupted world because [the child] itself reared in a new, clear-eyed, uncorrupted freedom among beautiful thoughts and beautiful things."[60] In 1904 this idyllic vision of childhood reached its apotheosis with James M. Barrie's creation of Peter Pan, the boy who chose never to grow up so he would not have to face the repulsiveness of adult life.

Although the Peter Pan ideal had no meaning among the poor, the middle class in most advanced countries tried to improve the lot of "disadvantaged" children. They favored compulsory elementary education as a means of "civilizing" these children, but they also wanted them to be better treated by their parents. During the 1890's and early 1900's Britain, France, Germany, and other advanced countries passed laws punishing acts of cruelty to children and taking them away from parents who neglected them. Each advanced country also had its equivalent of the National Society for the Prevention of Cruelty to Children, which alerted the authorities regarding such abuses.

But these kinds of public intervention, plus high illegitimacy ratios in many large cities, resulted in more orphans and pauper children living away from their families than ever before—in workhouses, orphanages, and other "institutions." Nonmarital fertility declined along with marital fertility in all European countries except Bulgaria and Ireland.[61] But the *ratio* of illegitimate to legitimate births increased in many large cities. In

1900–2, 24.5 per cent of all live births in greater Paris were illegitimate; in 1909–10 the ratio was 20.7 in Berlin.[62] The ratios were even higher in Vienna, Prague, and Budapest. In France the number of children, both legitimate and illegitimate, receiving public assistance away from their own homes rose from 72,170 in 1877 to 120,344 in 1905 to 223,591 in 1912.[63] England and Wales had one of the lowest ratios of illegitimate births in Europe, yet, in 1913, 73,783 pauper children, both legitimate and illegitimate, received indoor relief.[64] Of these, 47,467 were in various public institutions, 18,110 in private orphanages and industrial schools certified by the Poor Law Board, and only 8,206 in workhouses, as compared with 22,982 twelve years earlier.

Children reared in orphan "homes," particularly girls, felt the stigma attached to them and were ashamed to admit that they had been in one. In many countries girls in such "homes" were trained for domestic service and boys for the industrial labor force. And during the early 1900's many English slum children were "taken from the streets, the workhouses, the temporary shelters, and detained either in industrial schools, reformatories, workhouse homes, or privately conducted institutions (Catholic Emigration Society and Church of England Waifs and Strays Society) until sufficiently trained to be sent to Canada.[65]

The proportion of homeless orphans in some advanced countries was higher in our period than ever before or since. In earlier times a child who had lost its parents was usually taken into the home of a close relative, but this practice declined, especially among the lower classes in large cities. Another reason was that the state began taking slum children away from their "evil" surroundings and "bad" parents and training them to become useful citizens in industrial schools and—the name tells all—reform schools. In Britain parents were forced to contribute to their maintenance and education, though parents in most Continental countries did not have to do so. In any case, the number of orphans was enormous. There were 720,858 of them in Germany in 1907.[66] Forty-five per cent of all French children had lost at least one parent by the time they were in their teens, and France had 660 orphanages run by religious orders, not counting public asylums or local church-run "homes" that did not take children from outside the locality.[67]

Thus a significant proportion of the children who grew up in Western and Central Europe had no family life at all, and the "homes" they were reared in were public or religious institutions. Sponsored and administered by the middle classes, these institutions were designed to take orphan and slum children off the streets and mold them into law-abiding adults and good workers. This process of socialization seems to have been more successful with girls than with boys. One observer in Manchester commented:

> It may happen that a boy kept in a "home," largely freed from the ordinary temptations of the every-day family life as lived in a working-class district, falls an easy victim to outside temptations when he eventually has to leave the "home" which has hitherto shielded him from them.[68]

During the early 1900's many middle-class reformers suggested boarding children in foster homes with respectable families as a better alternative. This practice was tried on a limited scale in England, but it did not become prevalent anywhere until after the First World War.

Illegitimate children fared worse than any others. Unmarried lower-class women had been boarding their children out to wet nurses in the countryside or in peasant homes in their native villages if they had migrated to the city. But around 1900 the commonest way of disposing of unwanted babies in Germany was to give them to an *Engelmacherin* who, for a price, killed them (made "angels" of them), usually with morphine or alcohol.[69]

CHAPTER 4

CLASS AGAINST CLASS

> It's the same the 'ole world over,
> It's the poor what gets the blame,
> While the rich get's all the pleasure.
> Now ain't that a bloomin' shame?

This English music-hall refrain was meant to express a fact of life, but the poor saw less justification for it in modern class societies than their forefathers had in traditional societies. An increasing number of lower-class poor people also became conscious of another fact of life: as long as the rich had the power, the situation would not change. Indeed it was being reinforced in much of Western and Central Europe by the growth of the middle classes and their determination to retain or improve their status within the existing social structure.

Class conflict is endemic in a class society. People who bring varying kinds of property and talent into the economic market have opposing interests. This opposition of interests is chronic, and the perception of it is reinforced periodically by open struggles. The fact that each class often has its own subculture within the larger society also helps to bring about and maintain different types of class consciousness.[1]

Today the majority of people in the most highly modernized parts of the world no longer perceive their society as a class system. In both the United States and the Soviet Union the official image is one of "nonegalitarian classlessness." According to this image, each individual, regardless of origin, is presumed to have an equal opportunity of reaching the highest levels in the occupational structure, provided that he has the appropriate capacities. Some outside observers, however, define the reality in the Soviet Union and the other state socialist societies of Eastern Europe quite differently. They say that there is a "new class" at the top, composed of people whose special privileges and economic advantages are based on the monopoly of power exercised by the Communist Party in political and economic life. In the United States many sociologists have rejected the concept of class and defined American society in terms of "stratification" based on income or occupation. In Western Europe some leading sociologists argue that the class system of what they call "post-capitalist society" is dominated by managers or technocrats. Thus, before examining the class system and the conflicts within it during the 1890's and early 1900's in Europe, we must make clear what we are dealing with.

CLASSES AND CLASS CONSCIOUSNESS

Classes are the largest, most comprehensive groups of individuals in a society and are defined by their relationships with each other. Although classes are formally open, class divisions reflect differential privileges and discriminations concerned with wealth, power, educational opportunities, and access to certain occupations. An individual's class status is relatively permanent, and people from different classes do not usually associate with one another socially.

Even within the same class social intercourse between strangers is impersonally defined and more formal than among members of social groups with clearer boundaries and with cultural links based on a common religious affiliation, ethnic origin, or occupation. By the 1890's most Western and Central European Jews were becoming assimilated into the class systems of their respective countries (see Chapter 9), but they still felt closer to other Jews in their class than to the non-Jews in it. The army officer corps in Germany and the higher civil servants in Germany, Austria-Hungary, and Russia had already become distinctive and exclusive social groups by then. And professional people such as lawyers, physicians, and university professors were also trying to achieve this status. In Great Britain the peers of the realm retained the privilege of immunity from criminal prosecution outside the House of Lords. Still, a British peer and a German general were part of the upper class, just as most medical doctors in most countries belonged to the middle class.

Modern capitalist society tends to produce a basic three-class system. The upper class owns large shares of property in the means of production. The middle class includes small property owners, but modernization reduces the proportion of these people and increases the proportion of those with highly developed professional and technical qualifications. These people are middle-class because their qualifications allow them to bargain in the market for economic returns other than income: security of employment, prospects for career advancement, superior working conditions, and a wide range of perquisites and fringe benefits. The lower, or working, class consists of those people who bring to the market only their manual labor power.

No particular capitalist society has ever exemplified this oversimplified model in every respect. In the late nineteenth century the upper class in Southern and Eastern Europe still contained many aristocratic landowners; this was also true in parts of Central Europe right up to 1914. At that time the middle class in northwestern Europe included a larger proportion of small property owners and entrepreneurs than it does today and a smaller proportion of professional and technical experts. Today, in Western Europe, North America, and Japan, many skilled manual workers have achieved a degree of job security and fringe benefits formerly accessible only to the middle class. But these workers remain lower-class in their conditions of work and their lack of middle-class prospects for career advancement.

In modern capitalist societies the very basis for the existence of classes has been the divergence between the formally open character of economic opportunities and the differential life-chances that a capitalist economy actually creates. An individual's place in the class system is not determined by inherited position guaranteed by law or custom, as membership in the traditional estates and social groups of Europe was. Yet even in the United States today a young person with wealth or highly developed qualifications obviously has a better life-chance than someone without either of these advantages. In Europe at the turn of the century the class system was less open than it is today. And a person's ability to move from one class to another was limited not only by his marketable economic capacities but also by other factors which translated economic relationships into social structures.

Three noneconomic factors have been crucial in determining the ways in which class relationships are structured everywhere. The first was the way in which industrial technology created a different work environment for manual and nonmanual workers and separated them physically. This effect of the technological division of labor overlapped with the different chances for upward mobility of these two groups. It was also strengthened by a second factor: the authority system in the enterprise in which they worked. There were always some administrative workers whose function was to enforce commands to which the manual workers were subject. Thus the two groups were separated in this connection as well. Differential authority in the enterprise also reinforced the structuring of class relationships at the top, where the middle-class managers were subject to the commands of the upper-class owners. (This relationship has been modified, though not destroyed, by the tendency for ownership and control to become separated in large corporations.)[2]

The third factor that has influenced the structuring of class relationships involves different patterns of consumption of goods and services. In this respect the upper, middle, and working classes have been clearly distinguishable. Not only have their patterns of consumption differed but these have also been consolidated by the physical segregation of the three classes in different communities and neighborhoods. In major urban areas middle-class neighborhoods included many homeowners, whereas working-class neighborhoods consisted mainly of renters. This difference was based not only on the lower income of the workers but also on their general lack of access to housing mortgages. The most homogeneous working-class communities—in consumption patterns and over-all outlook—were isolated towns with one industry. This was particularly true of coal mining, and miners at the turn of the century were close to the archetype of the "proletarian worker" with a distinct working-class culture.

The factors that structure class relationships have also been affected by the different sociopolitical settings in which they operated, both before and since 1914. In France, unlike most Western countries, the functional and physical separation of white-collar from blue-collar workers did not prevent these two groups from co-operating closely in the labor movement, from the founding of the CGT. (Confédération Générale du

Travail) in 1895. The landowning aristocracy was a much less significant component of the upper class in Sweden than in Germany, where imitating its ethos and patterns of consumption was the major means by which rich industrialists and financiers could gain acceptance into that class. Since 1914 world wars and revolutions—rather than any of the factors discussed so far—have ended the power of the traditional landowning elites in Central and Eastern Europe and brought state socialism to much of that area.

Landowning elites have not been the only status group to influence the structuring of class relationships. A status group consciously evaluates the honor or prestige of its common pattern of consumption relative to others and derives its coherence from this kind of comparison.[3] Just as certain wealthy commoners tried to raise their status by imitating aristocratic standards of honor and prestige, so most white-collar employees tried to raise theirs by adopting the attitudes, beliefs, and life style of the petty bourgeoisie of small property owners and entrepreneurs, with their high evaluation of cleanliness, sobriety, lace curtains, and a piano in the parlor. When members of a subordinate nationality or race are heavily concentrated in the lowest-paid and most marginal kinds of employment, their status group may be called an underclass. Since the late nineteenth century the more regularly employed workers, as well as the middle and upper classes, have all made the most negative evaluation of the underclass wherever it has existed.

The actual relations between people from different classes reflected not only their respective perceptions and evaluations of one another but also of the class system itself. Until the First World War aristocrats continued to view it as hierarchical, with themselves at the top. Many urban workers perceived it as dichotomous, with themselves as "us" and everyone from white-collar employees to cabinet ministers as "them." Other workers, however, still believed in a hierarchy of classes and were deferential toward their "betters." The middle classes tended to see the class system more as a series of strata. Although there were wide variations in their perceptions of themselves and their relations with the upper class, they all looked down on manual workers and peasants. Peasants were the least class-conscious people vis-à-vis the larger society and, strictly speaking, they were not a class at all. Within their local communities they recognized different strata among themselves and evaluated the nonrural people in their villages as "bourgeois," by which they meant having urban, hence foreign, ways. But the effects of leaving home were already forcing many peasants to recognize the national class system in which they found themselves.

Class consciousness intensified class conflicts in Europe in the 1890's and early 1900's. During the preceding centuries the middle class had developed a "common awareness and acceptance of similar attitudes and beliefs, linked to a common style of life."[4] But by placing a premium upon individual initiative, achievement, and responsibility its class awareness ordinarily denied the existence or reality of classes. In contrast, class consciousness in its most undeveloped form recognizes that similar attitudes and beliefs signify a particular class affiliation and that other classes do indeed exist. Its next level of development "involves a conception of class conflict: where perception of class unity is linked to a recognition of opposition of interest with another class or classes." Class consciousness as perception of conflict of interest tends to become revolutionary class consciousness only when people perceive the existing order as illegitimate and recognize the possibility of reorganizing it on a new basis through class action. Revolutionary class consciousness in our period was strongest among peasants and skilled workers whose traditional mode of production was being undermined by modern techniques. Middle- and upper-class leaders tried to deal with it by repressing it, defusing it with extensions of the franchise and welfare legislation, or diverting it into nationalist and imperialist channels.

But revolutionary class consciousness was the exception rather than the rule among most manual workers in our period. Even those who believed that the state supported the "capitalists" against them recognized the separation of the political and economic structures. (This separation is unique to capitalist society; it had not existed under feudalism and it has been eliminated under socialism.) On the one hand, they began to see that they could better their economic conditions through strikes and collective bargaining with their employers. On the other hand, they lost some of their earlier feeling of being outside the political process as the state incorporated them into a developed system of "citizenship rights."* They understood that the right to vote and join political parties had little to do with their mode of participation in the economic structure. But they became willing to express their class conflict with the owners and man-

---

*These rights, which were achieved at widely different times in different societies, are of three kinds: civil rights; the right to vote and to organize politically; rights of economic welfare and social security. See Thomas Humphrey Marshall, *Class, Citizenship, and Social Development* (Garden City, N.Y.: Doubleday, 1964), p. 84.

agers in the struggle for economic rewards. As the more advanced capitalist societies began to institutionalize this mode of class conflict in the form of collective bargaining, revolutionary consciousness failed to develop. It became widespread mainly in Russia, Italy, and Spain, where the capitalist-industrialist order was not yet dominant and where there was greater resistance to granting the workers citizenship rights.

The incorporation of the workers into a developed system of citizenship rights helped to stabilize class differentials in capitalist society and to maintain the distinction between the political and economic structures. Disraeli and Napoleon III had already seen that this could happen in the 1860's with regard to political rights. And in the 1880's Bismarck had initiated the modern welfare state in an effort to counter the revolutionary appeal of the socialists. During the next two decades the organization and control of the means of production did not change anywhere. In the modernizing liberal states of northwestern Europe the existing class system remained intact while allowing outstanding individuals to move upward. In Eastern Europe inefficient members of the landowning gentry were declassed, but the upper class remained more closed than in the West, and its hold on the political structure was not seriously threatened (except during the Russian Revolution of 1905). Even in northwestern Europe the political structure changed little, despite the increasing possibility for men from modest backgrounds to hold elected office. The extension of the franchise and the payment of parliamentary deputies actually consolidated the political structure.

There were marked variations in the social structures of different countries and in the kinds of class conflicts they engendered. The greatest contrast was between Great Britain, with its capitalist economic and social structures and liberal political order, and Russia, where the middle and working classes were still small and the authoritarian political regime preserved many of the assumptions of a society divided between dominant landowners and subordinate peasants. In Britain, France, and the other advanced countries of northwestern Europe the main antagonisms were between the urban middle and working classes; in Russia and the less advanced areas of Southern and Eastern Europe they were still between the big landowners and the peasants and agricultural laborers. The Russian social structure was least compatible with the requirements of modernization and the most ready to explode of any in Europe.

Social structures changed more in some modernizing countries than in others. The older conflict between the landowning aristocracy and the bourgeois capitalists and well-to-do professional men had been resolved in Britain and the smaller countries of northwestern Europe by their co-operation and partial fusion into a new upper class. In France this conflict had subsided with the retirement of the older aristocracy from most sectors of public life and the recruitment of the governing elites predominantly from the modern-minded upper-middle and middle classes. Germany's social structure had changed much more slowly than its economic structure and was able to survive only because of the power of the authoritarian state. As in Britain, the older aristocracy and big businessmen co-operated politically, but the social cleavage between them was much greater. (Until 1918 Prussian nobles put up a velvet rope between themselves and middle-class guests at gala balls.) As the urban lower and lower-middle classes became a majority of the population in Germany, its archaic social and political hierarchies could not remain intact for much longer.

Upper-class owners of the means of production still had strong ties with the conservative and liberal political parties, but they alone did not constitute a "ruling class" anywhere in Europe before 1914. The more advanced capitalist societies were ruled, rather, by a governing class or power elite in which capitalists were less active than other kinds of people recruited from the upper and upper-middle classes. These classes retained their monopoly over the highest nonelective positions in the state and the means of access to them: wealth, connections, and education. Not only did the universities and exclusive secondary schools reinforce their belief in their right to rule, but in some countries these institutions were also deliberately geared to careers in the higher ranks of the administrative structure. In fact some upper-middle-class people were able to use their wealth, connections, and education to become part of the new upper class.

EDUCATION AND THE CLASS SYSTEM

One day in 1895, Pascal Chaignon, the postman in the French village of Mazières-en-Gâtine, was thinking of how he could send his son to a nearby *collège* (classical secondary school) when Monsieur Proust, a self-confident wealthy bourgeois, came out of his château. Hoping that Monsieur Proust might help him financially, Pascal said:

"My son is doing well at school; he is 12 and I should like to send him on to the *collège*."

"To the *collège?* What do you want to make him? A misfit?"

"I don't know if I shall make him a misfit, but I very much hope I shall turn him into someone better than his father."[5]

This incident illustrates both the misgivings of the middle and upper classes about educating people beyond their station in life and the new aspirations of the lower and lower-middle classes. In Monsieur Proust's view Pascal's son would most likely end up in the growing ranks of unemployed secondary-school graduates and become a troublemaker. Pascal hoped to see his son become an employee in the higher grades of the Post Office—an improvement in status, though still far from the seats of power.

As education began to rival birth and even wealth in defining who one was, the people in power intensified their efforts to make it reinforce the existing class system and reproduce the elites that governed their nations. By 1914 they had instituted compulsory elementary education for the lower classes in all but the most backward countries. In Chapter 1 we noted that this was the first major effort by governments to "civilize" these classes by instilling in them the minimum standards of modern society: orderliness, discipline, patriotism, and the ability to read and write the national language. In addition, the "postgraduate" courses of the elementary track provided vocational training for jobs in industry, commerce, and teaching at the elementary level. But the elementary track was supposed to remain a dead end for the lower classes. Secondary and higher education were supposed to be reserved for the middle and upper classes. That was why Monsieur Proust and his counterparts in other countries resisted the efforts of people like Pascal to get their children onto these tracks. At most they were willing to allow some of these people to go to newly created dead-end "middle" schools offering practical training. But the classical high schools, the universities, the military and professional schools, and other institutions of higher learning retained their high entrance requirements, thus keeping out the masses.

The secondary school was regarded everywhere as a selective institution. According to the official report of the English Board of Education for 1908–09:

> The words "secondary" and "middle class" came to be thought of as meaning the same or nearly the same thing. The idea that elementary and secondary schools represent not successive stages of education but alternative kinds of education meant for different social classes is deeply rooted, and may be said to have dominated practice until recently.[6]

An elementary school classroom in France, c. 1900.

A few years earlier, when the Kaiser had suggested lowering the entrance requirements for high schools, the Chancellor, Prince Chlodwig zu Hohenlohe-Schillingsfürst, warned that this would help create an "educated proletariat."[7] Like many devoted teachers of Latin, the Italian Augusto Monti viewed the lower-middle-class students in his courses as a different race from the "intellectual bourgeoisie" to which the classical high schools had traditionally catered.

But in an age of rising aspirations the selective nature of the secondary schools and the career opportunities they opened made them appeal to people who had previously been excluded from them. Only a few lower-class people could afford the fees or provide the necessary cultural background for their children. But in the early 1900's, under pressure from the lower-middle classes, governments increased the number of secondary schools and, in some countries, provided tuition scholarships. As a result, some lower-class people sent their children to these new secondary schools, and the "postgraduate" courses of the elementary track lost much of their earlier attraction.

After 1900, England, Germany, and the Scandinavian countries led the way in creating public high schools that granted a terminal degree and "free places" for qualified children whose parents could not pay the fees. The German, Danish, and Swedish "middle" and "modern" schools corresponded to the English grammar schools. Most of their graduates did not go on to a university but they did receive a diploma that helped them to find modest careers in business, teaching, and the lower ranks of the civil service. By 1914 this high school diploma was also becoming a basic requirement by means of which the lower-middle classes distinguished themselves from the lower classes in many European countries. The middle classes, in turn, aimed for the bachelor's degree, which was granted by the more exclusive humanistic secondary schools and which was necessary for careers with more prestige. (In Sweden this degree was not granted until 1904 to graduates who failed their university entrance examinations; in Italy it was not granted until 1969.) By 1914 less than 3 per cent of the young people between 14 and 18 in the most advanced countries were enrolled in a secondary school of any kind. And about half of these were in technical, scientific, and commercial high schools from which it was almost impossible to go on to a university. In France as recently as 1950 only 19 per cent of the young people in this age group were in secondary schools, as compared with 70 per cent today.

Thus the ruling elites succeeded in reproducing themselves by controlling who went to the preparatory schools and what went on in them.

Friedrich Paulsen, a leading German educational philosopher, recalled how, in 1890, the Kaiser publicly criticized his own minister of education for supporting a more modern curriculum to supplement the classical one.[8] Nine years later former premier Alexandre Ribot complained about the way competition for government posts controlled the course of study in secondary schools in France, adding that the same thing was true in other countries.[9]

No one could gain a position of real power in the military, the bureaucracy, the judicial system, or even politics without an academic degree or without passing the state examinations for which certain institutions of secondary and higher education prepared them. Before 1914 almost all cabinet ministers had such a degree, particularly in the law. So did most members of Europe's parliaments. The era of semieducated dictators like Mussolini, Hitler, and Stalin and their unlearned party henchmen was to come during the interwar years and last only until 1945. After that a university or professional degree was once again to become the *sine qua non* for membership in the governing class.

Not only the degree but also the socialization process in the universities and professional schools reinforced the exclusiveness of the new upper class, from which the governing class was largely recruited. Just as lower-class young men completed their elementary-school socialization during their period of military service, so middle- and upper-class young men finished theirs as university students in the residential colleges at Oxford and Cambridge, at the *grandes écoles* (École Polytechnique, École Normale Supérieure, École Libre des Sciences Politiques) in France, and in the exclusive fraternities in Germany and Austria. By means of initiation rites, sports, dueling, pranks, songs, and special dress, institutions such as these gave their members an abiding group loyalty and confirmed their belief in their prerogatives as their nation's future leaders. University students were already privileged personages, entitled to reduced military service and welcome to compete for higher positions in the state service. Throughout the rest of their lives these men took the privileges of their social rank for granted. They also made special concessions to their former classmates, whatever field of endeavor they might be in. Their old-boy networks constituted a new aristocracy of professional men, entrepreneurs, and high civil servants.

In Germany a major recruiting ground for this new aristocracy was the exclusive clubs of university students in which dueling was a prominent activity. These clubs were of two main types: corporations, which were mainly middle-class, and corps, which were more aristocratic in

German student fencing (*Mensur*) at Heidelberg University, c. 1890.

tone. As in the officer corps of many European armies, the German student corps fostered aristocratic values and standards, even though the sons of titled nobles were a minority in them. Until the 1870's the corps, like the corporations, had had a large proportion of sons from middle-class families, but in our period they became more and more restricted to the sons of high officials, wealthy businessmen, and academic and professional men, with sons of landowning nobles in fourth place numerically.[10] These student corps remained exclusive not only in the types of recruits they accepted but also the numbers. Whereas the total number of German male university students doubled between 1890 and 1914, the numbers in the exclusive corps increased hardly at all. By the 1890's many of them were also specifically excluding Jews.

As in the more prestigious colleges at Oxford and Cambridge, the exclusive dueling fraternities in Germany imbued their members with an elitist mentality and oriented them toward careers in public service, but here the analogy ends. Student dueling—called *Mensur*—differed from dueling to satisfy wounded honor. It was rather like a feudal tournament in that its purpose was to give the participants self-mastery and imperturbability in disagreeable situations. Like the feudal barons of medieval times, the *Corpsstudenten* were trained to take care of themselves and their affairs without seeking legal redress or concerning themselves with the judgment of others. Their own honor would tell them what was right. It was ironical that so many of these students studied law and came to hold the highest posts in the civil service, which was based on the rule of law. Even more ironical was the fact that the *Corpsstudent* should have been an ideal image for the Wilhelmine era, with its rampant bureaucratization, industrialization, and urbanization. Dueling scars on the faces of industrial tycoons, high court judges, and professors of political science were supreme signs of snobbery—visible proof that one was something else from what one did.

In Germany more than in most countries there was a marked contrast between rapid industrialization and urbanization and the deliberate cultivation of certain antimodern aristocratic ideals among the nation's upper-middle and middle classes. In addition to the *Corpsstudenten* these ideals were embodied in the reserve officer corps. With his lieutenant's commission in it a well-to-do commoner could gain admission to circles ordinarily restricted to members of the aristocracy. The traditional military virtues were alien to his upbringing and to his business or professional activities, but he cultivated them gladly in order to enhance his image as a privileged subject of the Kaiser.

Aristocratic values and humanistic and legal education were not what modern society needed most in its governing class, but this class clung to them as marks of social exclusiveness. As the sociologist Max Weber observed:

> differences of education are one of the strongest . . . social barriers, especially in Germany, where almost all privileged positions inside and outside the civil service are tied to qualifications involving not only specialized knowledge but also "general cultivation," and where the whole school and university system has been put into the service of this [ideal of] general cultivation.[11]

But legal training and general cultivation did not produce the political skill essential for cabinet ministers, and Germany was particularly handicapped by the paucity of suitable candidates for ministerial posts.

In addition to the stiff entrance requirements for the higher ranks of the German and Austrian state service (other than the foreign office), the authorities used their right to favor qualified candidates whom they found acceptable politically or socially. In Prussia, Jews, Socialists, and radicals were automatically rejected; the landowning aristocrats did not compete for posts in the central bureaucracy but they dominated the provincial administration, where they resisted liberal government policies they opposed. In Austria a civil service examiner told a candidate of ancient lineage: "I know I won't prevent your being made governor of Upper Austria, Count, but at least I can delay it for a year."[12]

In Britain, France, and other liberal states of Western Europe qualified candidates were less subject to arbitrary discrimination in their competition for high civil service posts, but they still had to have gone to the "right" institutions of higher learning. These were Oxford and Cambridge in England and the École Libre des Sciences Politiques in France. In the period 1901–35, 113 out of 117 successful candidates in the competition for entry into the Conseil d'État were from "Sciences Po," 82 out of 92 for the Cour des Comptes, and 246 out of 280 for the ministry of foreign affairs.[13]

Whereas access to the "right" institutions of higher learning remained restricted to the upper-middle class, more and more middle- and lower-middle-class people were able to send their children to other universities. (Still, by 1914, in no country was more than 1 per cent of the total population of university age enrolled.) These middle- and lower-middle-class students tended to choose the fields of law and secondary-school teaching.

The universities of Germany and Russia were less exclusive than those of England and France. In Germany in the academic year 1902–03, 23.3 per cent of the university students were from the "noneconomic" upper-middle class (the professions and higher government service), but 22.6 per cent were the children of middle- and lower-level officials, non-commissioned officers, and teachers without university educations, and 26.3 per cent were the children of small independent merchants, shop-keepers, innkeepers, tradesmen, and craftsmen; only 6.3 per cent were the children of independent farmers and only 1 per cent of workers.[14] By 1914 children of workers and craftsmen accounted for 24.3 per cent of Russian university students and children of peasants 14.5 per cent. Thus, in Russia, the "trend toward broadening of opportunities to secure education and to develop one's talents was clearly evident as an accompaniment of the modernization process well before the revolution [of 1917]."[15] But it also reflected the small proportions of middle- and lower-middle-class people in Russia, compared with England, France, and Germany.

THE MIDDLE CLASSES

Within the upper, middle, and lower classes there were numerous divisions based on cultural differences. In Chapter 2 we noted the different "sets" within the aristocracy and the kinds of social hierarchy to be found in rural villages; we shall see presently that the urban working class had its own distinct strata as well. But it was within the broad spectrum of the middle classes that modernization encouraged the most changes and the greatest variety of values and standards of behavior. Each occupational group had its status, but, as the German novelist Theodor Fontane said: "A person outside his proper rank is miserable. Bankers' sons are treated with the utmost lack of esteem in officers' and professors' circles. Officers are regarded as needy wretches in bankers' circles."[16]

The strongest class antagonisms were at the bottom, not the top, of the middle class. There was far more hostility between the lower-middle class and the working class than between the upper-middle class and the aristocracy. In Germany many upper-middle- and even middle-class people abandoned their own traditional values for those of the aristocracy, which they sought to enter by way of the reserve officer corps or through marriage. The democratic writer Friedrich Spielhagen exemplified this new orientation. In his earlier novels—especially the ever popular *Hammer and Anvil*—he had expressed his hatred for the aristocracy, but in 1875 he depicted capable and honorable aristocrats in his novel *Sturmflut*. In Austria, Italy, and Spain many people tried to acquire noble titles in one way or another; in Britain and France, where titles were harder to come by, the life style of gentlemen and ladies was widely imitated among the upper-middle classes. These forms of snobbery were not new but they were spreading toward the end of the nineteenth century.

People at all levels of the middle class were more status conscious than those in the older sections of the upper class. Aristocrats took pride in who they were; they assumed that their class culture was something they were born with. Nontitled gentry in Britain and the older urban patrician families on the Continent also distinguished themselves by their ancestry and were relatively unself-conscious about their values and standards of behavior. In contrast, people in the middle class proper consciously tried to maintain or improve their status by means of their wealth, occupation, and culture. This class—middle-level entrepreneurs, administrators, and professional people—constituted no more than 10 or 15 per cent of the total population in the most modern countries and considerably less elsewhere. Its members tried to distinguish themselves from the classes below them by what they did and how they did it. And the lower-middle class, which was considerably larger and more amorphous, tried to emulate them.

Within the upper-middle and middle classes "cultivated" people tried to dissociate themselves from propertied people in their professional activities and their private values and standards of behavior. Long before our period bishops, army and navy officers, judges, high-level bureaucrats, university professors, and physicians had set themselves apart by their professional standards and codes of conduct, and other people had recognized their special status by addressing them by their professional titles. During the second half of the nineteenth century, lawyers, engineers, secondary-school teachers, and middle-level civil servants were trying to achieve a similar status by upgrading their occupations through professional associations and government charters and by making their life styles more cultured and refined. Their humanistic secondary education gave all of them a little Latin and a perfunctory interest in literature and the arts—the minimum requirements of a cultivated person. Professional status, which required government sanction, was more difficult to achieve. Consequently the groups that campaigned for it had to be as "pushy" as the businessmen they professed to despise.

Professional status was more closely identified with general cultivation on the Continent than in England. By the late nineteenth century the idea of social standing of many English professional men "was to get as close as they could to the pattern set by the landed gentry, or what they imagined the pattern to be."[17] This pattern involved a loftier code of ethics than that of tradesmen, to be sure, but an English gentleman was not expected to read "serious" books or go to the opera. The typical English professional man liked to think of himself as an esquire, whereas his Continental counterpart preferred to think of himself as an intellectual. In Central and Eastern Europe the middle classes in general regarded intellectual attainments more highly than the "superfluous" lives of the landed gentry. But in France too "the ideal of general culture remained the final crowning of life"[18] for doctors and other highly trained professional men because the prestige of specialized knowledge alone was not considered an adequate mark of success.

Because of the contempt for specialized training among the Victorian upper classes professional status was harder to achieve in England than on the Continent. Secondary and higher education in most Continental countries was more professionally oriented than in England. Thus, in the late nineteenth century, when surgeons, solicitors, and most branches of the civil service instituted qualifying examinations, applicants had to prepare for them by cramming with private tutors. The English public schools and older universities did not adapt themselves to the demands of the examining bodies to the same extent as their Continental counterparts. Besides, the English middle class wanted them to continue to turn their sons into gentlemen. Although new, professionally oriented public universities were created in England in the *belle époque*, the prosperous classes preferred Oxford or Cambridge, "not for any direct professional training but rather as a highly desirable finishing school, valued as much for social reasons as for any intellectual polish it might confer."[19] In law and medicine England lagged behind in the kind of training offered at the leading Continental universities. And it had nothing to compare with the Conservatoire des Arts et Métiers and the École Centrale des Arts et Manufactures in France or the higher technical schools in Germany, Italy, Switzerland, and Scotland until the founding of the Imperial College of Science and Technology in 1907. English civil engineers had a particularly difficult time gaining official recognition as a profession. They were unable to institute qualifying examinations until 1898, and apprenticeship still remained the main means of specialized training, as it did in most English professions.

The civil service offered the most opportunities for professional status in all advanced countries, but here too Britain lagged behind. Government employees constituted 9.3 per cent of the total labor force in 1895 in Germany and 5.8 per cent in 1901 in Britain; the figures increased to 10.6 per cent in Germany in 1907 and 6.9 per cent in Britain in 1911.[20] Of the 2,692,379 German government employees in 1907, over one million could claim the title of official (*Beamte*), including officers, teachers, and postal and railroad workers; 390,000 were civil servants in the narrower sense.[21] The three or four hundred top officials in the German and Austrian imperial governments and in Prussia had more power and prestige than their British counterparts.

Although the British Home Civil Service did not provide as many openings or as much prestige as the German, the imperial civil services offered unparalleled opportunities for advancement to young men from modest backgrounds. This was particularly true of the competitive examinations for the Indian Civil Service. Although the majority of the entrants were middle-class, "the rulers of late Victorian India—the sahibs of the British Empire in its glory—included an appreciable number of men whose fathers had been bakers, butchers, tailors, shoemakers, upholsterers, cheese factors, and undertakers."[22] They were better paid than their colleagues in the Home Civil Service and enjoyed many more perquisites. On retirement they were guaranteed a pension of £1,000 a year, which put them near the top of the middle-class income bracket. At home they would have been mere bureaucrats and excluded from Society; in the Empire they were part of the governing class and accepted into its narrow social world.

Parliamentary politics was also becoming professionalized in the liberal states of Western Europe. Most elected representatives were themselves professionally trained, particularly as lawyers. In France and Italy they were emerging as a distinct social group with its own code of conduct. Those deputies who could aspire to become cabinet ministers were especially careful to respect certain rules in dealing with their colleagues who held opposing views. Antoine Florent Guillain, president of the French iron and steel trade association, was minister for the colonies in the 1898 cabinet of Charles Alexandre Dupuy. And Joseph Chamberlain had left his screw-manufacturing business in the 1870's to become mayor of Birmingham and, in 1895, colonial secretary. But most big capitalists preferred to influence government policy behind the scenes and leave public politics to the professional politicians.

Ironically, secondary-school teachers, the people most directly involved in imparting general cultivation to the middle and upper bourgeoisie, had the most difficulty in improving their status. By the late nineteenth century more and more of these teachers were from the lower-middle class, particularly on the Continent. They had hoped that their learning and dedication would make the bourgeoisie accept them on a par with the other professions, despite their low salaries. Instead these *lycée* and *Gymnasium* professors found themselves socially isolated and regarded as less useful than other professions in modernizing societies. They formed their own professional associations to champion their cause. On March 12, 1901, in an article in the *Nationalzeitung*, Friedrich Paulsen said that the one thing the higher teaching profession could not tolerate "on grounds of principle" was the government's refusal to put it "on a formal equality with the legal profession, so as to make the upper teachers rank with the judges, since that was tantamount to belittling their professional honor, which it was the duty of all professions to uphold." In Italy the professors in the secondary schools had the special problem of distinguishing themselves from all sorts of people who called themselves "professor," including typing and swimming instructors.

In their private lives many upper-middle- and middle-class people felt that their status required them to engage in philanthropic and reforming activities. Industrialists like the Krupps in Essen, Stumm-Halberg in the Saar, and Schneider in Le Creusot sponsored canteens, medical services, picnics, and small bonuses for their workers. (French coal miners received twelve francs for each son's first communion.) And their wives joined the fund-raising drives of charities run by aristocratic ladies. These kinds of patronage were obvious imitations of *noblesse oblige*—the traditional sense of obligation of nobles toward their inferiors. In Edwardian England many middle-class liberals who felt guilty about "the condition of the poor" contented themselves with reading C. F. G. Masterman and John Galsworthy, "writers of the kind of social criticism that moves in the wake of the time, deploring faded injustices and admiring archaic virtues."[23] But the active Edwardian reformers were motivated by the desire to perform socially useful services. The Fabians, for example, reflected the rise of the salaried, professional, technical, and intellectual cadres of post laissez-faire capitalism.[24] They were self-conscious modernizers, the precursors of today's technocrats.

Doing good for the less fortunate gave the people involved a feeling of self-importance and served as a substitute for their lack of political influence in countries like Germany, Austria, and Russia; in the liberal states of the West doing good also allowed the bourgeoisie to impose its own class standards on its clients and sometimes on institutions and the law. We have already noted how the modern-minded middle and upper-middle classes used the state schools for this purpose. But they organized a host of other organizations as well for the prevention of or protection against activities they regarded as social evils. Almost every modern country had its societies for the prevention of alcoholism, prostitution, and white slavery, and offenses against public decency and for the protection of children and animals. In France the society for the protection of animals faced opposition from both the lowly farmers and the aristocratic hunters, but it managed to get some legislation on the matter by the turn of the century. In Britain the temperance leagues were able to force Parliament to limit the licensing hours for pubs. In Germany the organizations for the prevention of cruelty to children succeeded in making the institution of the *Engelmacherin* illegal.

Whereas the cultivated middle classes distinguished themselves in all these ways, businessmen and their wives became increasingly materialistic. The English novelist H. G. Wells described them as follows:

> With an immense . . . zest they begin *shopping,* begin a systematic adaptation to a new life crowded and brilliant with things shopped, with jewels, maids, butlers, coachmen, electric broughams, hired town and country houses. They plunge into it as one plunges into a career; as a class, they talk, think, and dream possessions. Their literature, their Press, turns all on that; immense illustrated weeklies of unsurpassed magnificence guide them in domestic architecture, in the art of owning a garden, in the achievement of the sumptuous in motor-cars, in an elaborate sporting equipment, in the purchase and control of their estates, in travel and stupendous hotels. Once they begin to move they go far and fast. Acquisition becomes the substance of their lives.[25]

In England some wives of less affluent businessmen tried to affect aristocratic manners, but on the Continent these middle-class people retained more of their older "philistine" outlook. They talked incessantly about the good, the true, and the beautiful while thinking only of their material comfort. The following description by Fontane could apply to the comfortable bourgeois almost anywhere:

> . . . with his pettiness and his endless desire to be admired for nothing. Father bourgeois has had his portrait painted, and asks that I declare this daub to be a Velasquez. Mother bourgeois has bought herself a lace stole and treats the purchase as An Event. Everything bought or "offered" is accompanied by a glance saying, "Happy person who is allowed to eat of *this* cake and to drink of this wine."

> . . . A dinner of roast goose and Zeltinger and meringues at which
> the hostess is all smiles and imagines that she has taken me out of the
> humdrum of my daily existence for two hours is cheap in itself and
> made doubly cheap by the attitude which accompanies it.[26]

Below the middle class proper was a larger, more motley stratum
known as the lower-middle class, *petite bourgeoisie, piccolo borghesia,* or
Mittelstand. Unlike "bourgeoisie" these terms were strictly modern.
They had come into use during the first half of the nineteenth century to
designate small capitalist entrepreneurs, occupational groups aspiring to
professional status (dentists, pharmacists, secondary-school teachers), and
lower-ranking "officials." During the second half of the century, as these
people tried to move up into the bourgeoisie, their places were sought by
older occupational groups that had previously been subsumed under the
labels "the people" or "the popular classes"—small shopkeepers, craftsmen, noncommissioned officers—plus a rapidly growing number of elementary-school teachers, shop assistants, and office clerks of "popular" origin.

These last three groups tried harder than any others to raise their status
through their attitudes and life style in our period. Objectively the main
differences between them and skilled workers were that they did not do
manual labor and that they were paid salaries for services rendered instead of wages for actual time worked. Many male clerks in insurance,
banking, and the civil service earned more than many skilled workers, but
the average salary of all clerks, shop assistants, and schoolteachers was
close to the average wage for all skilled workers. This situation was
caused mainly by a growing oversupply of aspiring white-collar employees and schoolteachers, particularly among women. Nevertheless
people in these "new" occupations tried to compensate for their "popular" origins and limited incomes by imitating middle-class speech patterns, styles of dress and grooming, and norms for "respectable" behavior. Meanwhile people in the "old" self-employed occupations considered
themselves middle-class in spite of their less than genteel manners and the
precariousness of their economic independence. When one is marginal,
small distinctions assume major importance.

Thus the lower-middle class was based primarily on perceptions of status rather than on the brute facts of economic organization in a capitalist
society. By the early 1900's this stratum constituted 20 to 30 per cent of
the total working population in the more advanced countries of Western
and Central Europe. But it included wide varieties of people, many of
whom felt little in common with one another and some of whom tried to
identify themselves with the bourgeoisie because of their income, train-

ing, or life style. An Italian secondary-school teacher would have been horrified to be classed as *piccolo borghese*, but that was how many other Italians still perceived him. The owner-chef of a Bordeaux restaurant, the proprietor of a Prague clothing store, the Liverpool pharmacist, and the master diamond cutter in Amsterdam were all lower-middle-class, even though they made more money than most clergymen and some doctors, lawyers, and engineers. At the central headquarters of the Siemens Electrical Corporation in Berlin the office managers and the clerks were both part of the *Mittelstand*, despite the authority of the former over the latter and the differences in their incomes. In governmental as well as corporate bureaucracies most administrators and technicians without a suitable education were lower-middle-class, regardless of their titles or cultural pretensions.

Modernization stimulated more changes in the status and outlook of these different kinds of lower-middle-class people than in any other social stratum. In the factories the search for increasing rationality in production and control not only blurred distinctions between craftsmen and semiskilled workers but also undercut the foremen's position as well. Before the 1890's the men at Siemens used to say "the foreman's will is God's will," but thereafter "not only the workers, but also the foremen performed work clearly controlled by another."[27] At the same time the gap between the factory and the office widened. Although the economic situation of white-collar employees increasingly resembled that of the better-paid workers, they were encouraged by their employers and the power elite as a whole to identify themselves with middle-class values and standards of behavior.[28] In Germany their organized agitation to keep their privileged status as salaried employees (*Angestellter*) prompted the government in 1911 to pass a special social security law giving them the same sort of protection as the workers but recognizing them as a distinct and separate group. Elsewhere white-collar employees found it more difficult to set themselves apart from wage earners on the one hand and all self-employed persons and employers on the other, but they tried to do so in their dress, manners, and cultural "interests."

The cultural philistinism of older lower-middle-class types was portrayed by many literary writers. Gustave Flaubert provided the classic examples in Bouvard and Pécuchet and the character Monsieur Homais in *Madame Bovary*. Other such types included Charles Dickens' Mr. Micawber, Peter Stockmann in Henrik Ibsen's *An Enemy of the People,* and the office manager in Maxim Gorky's *Enemies,* who prides himself on reading newspapers and knowing what is going on in the world.

Whereas all these characters are caricatures, the German writer Wilhelm Raabe treats the hero of his novel *Stopfkuchen* (1891) more sympathetically. Despite his sententious conversation and his idiosyncratic collection of ancient fossils Stopfkuchen emerges as a warm and humane individual—a latter-day Biedermeier* type who is morally superior to his former schoolmate, the merchant adventurer Eduard.

In *Stopfkuchen* and his other late novels Raabe presented the dilemmas of the "old" lower-middle classes in a materialistic age: "Should life be lived in conformity with changing patterns of society at the cost of spiritual and intellectual values, or in self-imposed seclusion? Are these in fact mutually exclusive? Can one be involved in the process of historical change without sacrificing one's humanity?"[29]

Stopfkuchen could still ask these questions in bourgeois comfort, but less affluent shopkeepers—the core of the petty bourgeoisie at the turn of the century—were fighting a seemingly losing battle against economic modernization. Just as the rationalization of manufacturing reduced the status of craftsmen and foremen, so the growth of department stores and consumer co-operatives threatened the very livelihood of some small shopkeepers. Yet opening a small business was still the main way to move up into the lower-middle class for individuals without marketable skills, and the number that did so kept increasing. In his novel *The History of Mr. Polly* (1910) H. G. Wells expressed the plight of this "vast mass of useless, uncomfortable, under-educated, under-trained, and altogether pitiable people" in modernizing societies. As long as they did not go bankrupt (as many did who spent less time than Mr. Polly reading about faraway places in books) they had a degree of economic independence. But many of them had to work more hours to earn less money than some skilled workers.

In some industrialized countries small tradesmen began to join political movements that emphasized their "reliability" against working-class "subversion," their importance for a "healthy" society, and their need for protection against big business.[30] In Germany some of them viewed the movement of white-collar employees for statutory social security benefits

---

* This term originally denoted the transitional style in art and home decoration between Neoclassicism and Romanticism as interpreted by the Central European petty bourgeoisie during the first third of the nineteenth century. It acquired a derogatory sense from the caricature "Papa Biedermeier," who symbolized middle-class comfort and conformity. The Biedermeier type was the "little man" who resigned himself to his humble lot in the political order and rejoiced in the little pleasures of family life and private hobbies.

A musical evening in a lower-middle-class English home, 1908.

(often at their employers' expense) as a threat almost as great as department stores and co-operatives. Thus economic realities kept the "old" and "new" *Mittelstand* apart and divided the "old" *Mittelstand* to some extent. The objective class position of neither group was the determining factor shaping their organization, political behavior, expectations, or life style.

> Both groups were organized primarily in order to present a front against those whose class position they shared: the small shopkeepers confronting and keeping apart from big capital and heavy industry, the white-collar workers confronting and keeping apart from manual workers. They constituted the most important phenomenon distinguishing Wilhelmine society from a clearly divided class society, forming, so to speak, a padding, which, tended by the state, dampened the growing class conflict. This padding fell apart in the world war.[31]

Economic realities also made it very difficult for most people with middle-class pretensions to maintain a middle-class standard of living. In 1901, out of 7 million households in England and Wales only 400,000 people had taxable incomes of more than £400 a year (the minimum for a middle-class standard) and fewer than a million had at least £160 a year (the minimum for a lower-middle-class standard). As the social historian Peter Laslett put it, "the famous middle class of literature and reminiscence turns out to be largely a matter of aspiration, imitation and snobbery. A third of the population was trying to live in a way that only a seventeenth of the population could live."[32] This proportion was almost as great in Germany, France, and other advanced countries. One could not keep a full-time maid on less than £160 a year, yet one could hardly claim lower-middle-class status without one; in one's "living room" one could afford to have lace curtains, antimacassars, and sham *objets d'art,* but not a piano. Easy credit was still a thing of the future. Besides, the buy-now-pay-later mentality was alien to lower-middle-class notions of propriety.

THE LOWER CLASSES

Everyone looked down on the lower classes. Social elites and their imitators have always perceived the traits of subordinate groups as somewhat barbaric and pathological. Monsieur Proust could be patronizing to Pascal the postman because he was a native of the village and had a responsible job. But during most of the nineteenth century French industrial workers were considered dangerous persons needing careful surveillance. The *livret* (a kind of internal passport) they were supposed to show to each new employer had fallen into disuse in the 1860's but was not legally abolished until 1890. English laws, reflecting the standards of the upper and middle classes, continued to conspire in explicit ways against wage earners and propertyless people in matters of debt, divorce, compensation, and jury selection.[33] In both urban and rural areas law enforcement agencies in most countries maintained a double standard in dealing with the lower classes and "respectable" people. Paternalistic industrialists and their wives showed sympathy for the poorer workers in their own locality as long as they were not drunk and did not come too close to smell. And liberal governments sometimes intervened on behalf of the unemployed in order to subvert or divert demands for greater state intervention.[34] But even the most sophisticated liberal intellectuals remained convinced that crimes are committed mainly by lower-class newcomers to the cities, particularly those of "inferior" ethnic stock.[35]

The middle-class myth that working-class people are intellectually and culturally inferior dies hard. In January 1914 a "serious" German magazine published an article called "The Culture Problem and the Worker Mentality."[36] It asserted that the gulf between the mentalities of bourgeois and workers is so great that these two groups confront one another like people who speak different languages. The article made the distinction—still current—between logical, abstract, bourgeois thinking and intuitive, analogical, working-class thinking. The worker sees everything in purely concrete terms, with himself as the center of any union or party he joins. (Hence middle-class people are wrong in perceiving him as a doctrinaire and wanting a new social system.) He consults his drinking companions on questions to which a bourgeois would seek answers from a specialist. Whereas bourgeois are individual islands, workers are at home only as part of the mass. And so on.

In Britain and elsewhere:

> . . . as a whole, the middle and upper classes, self-confident to arrogance, kept two modes of address for use among the poor: the first was a kindly, *de haut en bas* form in which each word, of usually one syllable, was clearly enunciated; the second had a loud, self-assured, hectoring note. Both seemed devised to ensure that though the hearer might be stupid he would know enough in general to defer at once to breeding and superiority. Hospital staff, doctors, judges, magistrates, officials and the clergy were experts at this kind of social intimidation; the trade unionist in his apron facing a well-dressed employer knew it only too well. It was a tactic, conscious or not, that confused and "overfaced" the simple and drove intelligent men and women in the working class to fury.[37]

The actual working class as it evolved around 1900 differed markedly from middle-class perceptions of it. These perceptions were largely a carry-over from the early stage of industrialization. At that time men, women, and children uprooted from traditional settings had had to be severely disciplined to convert them into effective instruments of industrial labor; their living standards had been extremely low, and their "uncivilized" behavior had made them seem as dangerous a class as criminals. But Britain, Belgium, France, and Germany were now entering a more mature stage of industrialization based on increased mechanization, a stepped-up pace of work, and larger organizational units with more impersonal employer-worker relationships. These changes created new tensions for both craftsmen and unskilled workers. They also reduced earlier distinctions between the kinds of work the two groups did and fostered their amalgamation into a single class. The unskilled—and the new stratum of semiskilled—workers still exhibited some of the traits that had helped form the middle-class stereotype of them. But they were becoming more settled and more family-oriented as their incomes became higher and more regular and as they became educated. Those craftsmen who managed to adapt themselves to the new stage of industrialization remained distinct from other workers in certain aspects of their life style, which in some ways was approaching that of the lower-middle class.

But for both craftsmen and ordinary workers

> a culture that had been painfully established or re-established after the first shock of industrialization was now challenged. What work was, what wives were for, what children were for all had to be rethought. Out of the variety of responses to these challenges came a recognizably modern, though highly differentiated, working-class life style.[38]

The working class in Britain, Belgium, France, and Germany differed from its emerging counterpart in Italy, Russia, and Spain. First of all it was a much larger proportion of the economically active population: by the immediate prewar years workers in manufacturing, transport, construction, and extractive industries constituted almost 50 per cent in Great Britain, over 40 per cent in Belgium, and almost 35 per cent in France and Germany. After 1900 children were increasingly withdrawn from industry, but a growing number of women entered it, provoking anxious reactions from male workers and the labor movement. As the over-all growth of the industrial labor force slowed, the average age of male workers increased. (In 1911 only 12.1 per cent were under twenty-four in France, compared with 19.1 per cent in 1896.) Moreover the majority of the men were second- and third-generation workers, whereas the majority in the less modernized countries were fresh off the farm. This difference made the workers in the advanced countries more conservative regarding changes in their work patterns. And their incorporation into a developed system of citizenship rights made them less politically rebellious than Italian, Russian, and Spanish workers.

Yet working-class consciousness was more highly developed in the maturing industrial societies. As the growth in the factory population slowed after 1900, workers saw fewer opportunities, "not in the middle-class sense of chances for advancement, but in the more genuinely work-

A Berlin shoemaker and his family working at home, c. 1900.

ing-class sense of being able to continue doing what one had started out doing."[39] The proportion of skilled jobs grew apace with unskilled ones, but technological displacement accounted for more reshuffling than new growth. The decline of the old craft hierarchies made it more difficult for ambitious young workers to use them as avenues into the lower-middle class, and many of them settled for the better-paying semi-skilled jobs rather than becoming apprentices. Only a minority of the more prosperous craftsmen managed to send their sons and daughters to secondary schools and on to white-collar careers.

The vast majority of workers—young and old, male and female, skilled and unskilled—felt locked into the working class. They found their jobs increasingly less satisfying but were only beginning to develop compensating satisfactions away from work. "Lacking basic control of the economic system, unwilling to fight the system directly, most workers made do with a mixture of disgruntlement and small pleasures—a mixture that confuses outside observers and serves the class still."[40]

The emerging working-class life style involved many ambivalent attitudes and contradictory goals. During the early stage of industrialization the workers and craftsmen had painfully constructed a culture that would protect them against change and give them a respectable status within their own circumscribed world. Now the economic system was subjecting them to novelties that made many of them close ranks in the face of seemingly declining opportunities to live as their parents and grandparents had lived. As they found less satisfaction in their jobs and as their real wages ceased to grow in the early 1900's, they also began to feel new economic grievances and a heightened class consciousness. The following observations about English workers during the immediate prewar years could apply to those in other maturing industrial societies:

> They were upset and not at all sure what to do. So they did many apparently contradictory things at once: they struck for wages and struck for status; they sent the TUC [Trades Union Congress] their money and bucked its leadership; they opposed national insurance while they collected their pensions; they voted Labour and agreed that Labour accomplished almost nothing.[41]

Most workers in the advanced countries of Western and Central Europe shared this outlook. A few engaged in radical protest; others began to find their major satisfactions in the new popular culture. The majority, however, remained preoccupied with the pressures involved in adapting to new work systems, without elaborate recreational outlets and without the organized capability for making these systems give them the kind of satisfaction in their work which they had traditionally felt.

The modern view of work is an instrumental one: a job is only a means for making money so that one can do the things one really wants to do. Lower-middle-class clerks were more modern than most workers in finding more satisfaction in their families and consumption patterns than in their work. Their jobs were also becoming routine, but they were less plagued by mechanization, physical fatigue, and disagreeable foremen. And, as we have seen, they felt a certain attachment to management and considered themselves superior to blue-collar workers. Even those white-collar employees whose meager earnings allowed them little in the way of costly recreation struck a sharply defined balance between work and private life which few workers could achieve. In contrast, most male workers still wanted to find dignity in and confirm their manhood through their jobs. Their drinking habits and their growing interest in sports were partly extensions of their concern with physical prowess as defined by their perception of man's work. They viewed most white-collar occupations, including teaching, as not only "soft" and "cushy" but also useless.

Aside from their frustrations on the job and their limited recreational outlets many married workers in the advanced countries continued to worry about being able to provide their families with enough food and other basic necessities. Real wages rose appreciably during the last three decades of the nineteenth century but leveled off thereafter. Although unemployment and underemployment affected mainly casual laborers, even semiskilled factory hands with steady jobs sometimes had trouble making ends meet. In 1892, when real wages were still rising, a German semiskilled machine-tool worker in Chemnitz earned twenty dollars a month, a semiskilled French steelworker in Le Creusot earned twenty-eight dollars, and a comparable English worker in Manchester earned forty dollars. But because food and housing were cheaper in Germany the Chemnitz worker with the same number of children had a standard of living not much lower than that of his English and French counterparts. The worker in Le Creusot had to pay over thirteen dollars a month for the mortgage and interest on a house provided by his company; when asked what he would do if he became ill he said that he would have to send his children out to beg.[42] When the Manchester worker's fifth child was born, an older brother told a neighbor: "We could have done without her. It's only another mouth to feed."[43] Only the better-paid married skilled workers and unmarried workers living with their parents could afford such luxuries as Sunday dress clothes, gambling, and a weekly visit to a cabaret or music hall.

Working-class people led segregated lives everywhere. Their neighborhoods were largely self-contained, and they rarely ventured out of them, except those who had to commute to their jobs. In school and the army they met other kinds of lower-class people who were strangers to them, but they had practically no personal contacts with the middle classes. In Saxony unmarried factory workers who dressed up to go to Sunday night dances frequented by "the higher classes" were still distinguishable "by their larger and coarser hands, and the absence of eyeglasses."[44] And in the Salford district of Manchester, "On Sundays the artisan in his best suit looked like the artisan in his best suit: no one could ever mistake him for a member of the middle classes."[45]

Workers who did not live in large cities were even more isolated from the rest of society than those who did. This was especially true in Belgium, where much heavy industry and mining were in rural areas and where compulsory elementary education was not instituted until 1914. But everywhere miners lived in segregated communities. In the Ruhr, where they had traditionally been recognized by the state as a specialized status group, they managed to preserve their intense community feelings even after they were treated as ordinary workers.[46] Some investigators see this sense of community among specific occupational groups as retarding the development of class consciousness by allowing these groups "to build up smaller sub-cultures with their own small-scale versions of success."[47] But in England and Wales the miners combined their sense of community and social isolation with a strong feeling of affinity with the rest of the working class.

Although the working class as a whole was not integrated into any national society in Europe before 1914, the mass organizations that claimed to represent it were able to accommodate themselves to the power structure in two distinct ways. In England and the Scandinavian countries the trade unions and socialist parties were accepted as legitimate interest groups, and the conflict between labor and management was institutionalized in the form of collective bargaining. In France, Italy, and Germany these organizations were permitted to exist legally but prevented from gaining access to the centers of power. The more radical elements in them stressed the need to build a revolutionary working-class society and culture in isolation from the rest of the nation, but they also developed vested interests in the legal status of their own organizations. Consequently, though their rhetoric stressed preparation for an ultimate seizure of power, their day-to-day behavior was primarily concerned with strengthening the structures of these organizations. This concern not only left the basic structure of the dominant system intact but also helped to integrate radical labor movements into it in a negative way.

The most important example of this kind of "negative integration" was the German Socialist Party.[48] During the 1880's, when its political activities had been legally restricted to running candidates for public office, it had developed a number of nonpolitical organizations to mobilize the working class. Chief among these was a network of trade unions, but there were also health insurance and other mutual-aid groups, athletic associations, and numerous educational and cultural organizations. After 1890 the party's political activities, now legal again, attracted a membership that reached 1 million on the eve of the war. By 1909 there were also seventy-nine Socialist daily newspapers with a circulation of 1 million, as well as many weekly and monthly periodicals. The Socialist press stressed indoctrination and intraparty information, thus contributing to the cohesion of the party's subculture and its relative isolation from the larger German society.

Adult male workers could satisfy almost all their off-the-job needs and aspirations in the party's subculture. The musical ones could sing in Socialist glee clubs or play in Socialist bands. Socialist hiking and gymnastic clubs attracted many younger workers. Those workers who wanted more education could take evening courses and read in party libraries. The party's trade unions looked after their members' economic interests and provided a feeling of social solidarity. Even Marxism was used less as a revolutionary ideology than as a means of enabling the workers to secure an independent class existence within the capitalist, middle-class order and to defend and improve their position as a class within that order.

Socialist women and young people were more radical than their male comrades in the German party, especially in its bureaucracy. This was so in part because most men in the labor movement were mainly interested in improving their living conditions and winning more freedom, and the Socialist trade unions made these reformist attitudes prevail in the party after 1906. But the party itself was also becoming more bureaucratic—more concerned with consolidating its own structure than with leading a revolution. Thus radical women like Clara Zetkin fought to expand the Socialist women's organizations and to isolate them from the male-dominated reformist bureaucracy. Zetkin also looked to the Socialist youth movement in her drive toward a more revolutionary course. The bureaucracy found it harder to control the youth movement, since it was outside the party and technically illegal in Prussia. It was the only German Socialist organization to operate underground. And its fight against militarism was embarrassing to the party leadership, whose commitment to negative integration involved a tacit agreement to let the army alone if the state let the party alone.

Negative integration failed to create a unified, self-contained working-class society and culture anywhere in Europe. Its proponents were hampered not only by divisions within their own ranks but also by the inescapable influences of the dominant culture in the press, the schools, and universal military training. Not even the German Socialist press could compete in quantity or quality with the mass-circulation dailies, which purveyed middle-class values and attitudes. At the time of the Boer War, English Marxists unsuccessfully opposed educational reforms aimed at bolstering Britain's imperialist role.[49] And during the years immediately preceding the First World War the French labor press expressed a certain distrust for the public elementary schools because of their attachment to the bourgeois state and their superpatriotism.[50] But most Socialist and labor leaders did not seriously try to counteract the nationalist orientation of the schools and the army. Nowhere were these leaders able to make working-class solidarity prevail over national loyalty. Nor could the majority of workers in the advanced countries ignore the efforts of the power elite to integrate them as individuals while opposing their interests as a class.

Even in their private lives the different strata of workers had their own values and standards of behavior. The more "respectable" families of craftsmen and skilled workers were the staunchest upholders of "discipline" regarding their children, but even the families of casual laborers were more closely knit than they had been during the early stage of industrialization. Evidence about working-class standards for child rearing is sketchy and conflicting for most countries, but the following observations by E. J. Urwick, an English investigator at the turn of the century, give some idea of the differences among strata.

Urwick, who lived in a working-class tenement for several years, divides the inhabitants into three types: casual laborers; regularly employed unskilled and semiskilled workers; skilled workers and craftsmen.[51] Of the first type he says: "Acts of wanton cruelty and violence are unquestionably condemned if the sufferer be a child or other weak person." "A theft committed on, or a lie told to, the parent meets with summary vengeance." But the chief moral training is "not to be found out." In the second type, "Truthfulness receives little attention; obedience the parents endeavour to obtain, but their efforts are rewarded with singularly little success." "Another lesson the mother strives to impress on the children is that of respect to elders and superiors, but this attempt meets with stubborn opposition from the children." "The chief characteristic of the class" is "a patient, plodding industry looking for nothing beyond its rights and receiving with a naive surprise any addition to its bare wage." (German workers were less patient, plodding, and appreciative than English workers.)

Of the third type Urwick says that "roughness and noisy brawling in the street are condemned as conduct unsuitable to the social position of the boys." Truthfulness—a middle-class value—was more stressed in theory in this stratum, but it was not always observed in practice. "The chief difference between this and the last type lies in the fact that the patient industry and endurance of the latter is replaced by a spirit of flourishing and self-assertive superiority, which manifests itself in a demand for some external and distinctive behaviour."

Urwick's reference to "noisy brawling in the street" confirms the middle-class perception of young male workers in general, but by the turn of the century this kind of behavior was restricted to the lowest stratum of the working class in the most advanced countries. This group was still closest to the *Lumpenproletariat*, and some of its young men did drift into petty crime. In Manchester street gangs of seventeen- to twenty-year-old youths called "scuttlers" fought one another as individuals and in groups. "Gangs 20–30 strong, armed sometimes with heavily buckled belts and mineral-water bottles, would from time to time engage in set combat, in which serious injuries were often inflicted."[52] These gangs were put down in the early 1900's by the police, but another type, the "ike," remained. "He is a loafer, an idler, at best a casual worker." His distinctive dress consisted of "a loose white scarf on the throat, hair well plastered down on the forehead, peaked cap tipped over one eye, bell-bottom fustian trousers." He was generally stupid and vicious, but not organized in gangs. Only rarely did these "ikes" join in muggings, like the London "hooligans" and the "peaky binders" of Birmingham.

The police, however, harassed even the peaceful street-corner gangs engaged in such innocent pastimes as card playing, as in the following incident involving a group of older teen-age boys in a Manchester slum:

> Suddenly one hears a shriek of warning. The gang bursts into a scatter of flying figures. From nowhere gallop a couple of "rozzers," cuffing, hacking, punching, sweeping youngsters into the wall with a swing of heavy folded capes. The street empties, doors bang. Breathing heavily the Law retires, bearing off perhaps a "hooligan" or two to be made an example of. The club is over for another night, leaving its young members with a fear and hatred of the police that in some perfectly law-abiding citizens lasted through life and helped colour the attitude of a whole working-class generation towards civil authority.[53]

The different strata of the rural lower classes also had their distinctive values and standards of behavior. As we have seen, the agricultural laborers were below the hierarchy of "proper" peasants, and their conduct reflected the precarious and sometimes brutal nature of their lives. This was particularly true regarding family relations.

"Proper" peasants everywhere treated the older members of their family with respect, not only because they were taught to do so but also because of pressure from the community, as is evident in the following letter published in July 1903 in the Polish *Gazeta Świąteczna:*

> In Makoszyn . . . Andrzej Lekarczyk, with the help of his son Antoni, beat with flails his father-in-law, a white-haired old man, Józef Majda. The wronged Majda brought a complaint against his son-in-law and his grandson and the court condemned Andrzej Lekarczyk to 3 months and Antoni to 3 weeks' imprisonment. But Majda begged the court to commute this punishment to a church-penance. And so . . . the Lekarczyks stood for three Sundays in the parish church . . . during the divine service with the flails with which they had beaten the old man, in such a place that everybody could see them. It was a great shame for them. Now people laugh at them, point to them with their fingers and will remind them for a long time about their disrespect for gray hair.

Many farm laborers and servants lacked these compunctions, particularly on the manorial estates of Hungary. On these *pusztas:*

> Up to a certain age parents beat their children, then there is a brief pause. When this is over, the situation is reversed and the children beat their parents. This is . . . an ancient tradition. There was a famous anecdote about Uncle Pálinkás. . . . His son used to drag him by the hair through the common room and kitchen, and when they reached the doorway of the servants' quarters, Uncle Pálinkás would shout, "Let me go here son, this is as far as I dragged my father!"[55]

Farm servants and laborers in Hungary beat one another and were beaten by their superiors more than in any other country, but they were the most mistreated social class everywhere. In many parts of Southern and Eastern Europe they could expect little redress for their grievances against their superiors even when they dared complain to the local magistrates or police. In Hungary many large estates were independent administrative bodies whose magistrates were normally the farm managers themselves; a law of 1907 confirmed the right of masters and their agents to assault any farm servant until he was eighteen. And in East Prussia the farm servants and laborers continued to be treated with abuse and contempt even after the village regulation of 1891 eliminated the remaining legal and administrative powers of the local landowners on their estates.

In Russia most peasants were also treated as second-class subjects. The emancipation had recognized them as free persons but limited their civil rights. Not only could they not own land as individuals, but, as we have seen, they had to get the approval of the head of their household and their commune before leaving their village for a lengthy absence. (This restriction was abolished by the Stolypin Reforms of 1906.) Special provisions of the criminal law applied only to peasants: corporal punishment by the authorities of peasant debtors was formally abolished in 1903, but other forms of discrimination lasted until the Revolution of 1917. In no other major country were the rural masses made as conscious of the rest of society's contempt for them as in Russia. Even when they were soldiers, peasants were still treated as peasants and excluded from public places frequented by the middle and upper classes. In his famous short story, *Peasants,* Chekhov expressed most cultivated Russians' perception of the muzhiks as follows: "They are coarse, dishonest, filthy, far from sober; they did not live in amity, were forever quarrelling; inasmuch as there was no mutual respect, they feared and suspected one another."

Rural life was much less brutal in Western Europe, yet, in societies supposedly dominated by genteel bourgeois standards, peasants and servants of peasant origin were still considered inherently inferior beings. Many French heads of household forced their young female servants to go to bed with them, though they left the village girls not in their employ alone. From Stockholm to Naples the middle classes viewed the country bumpkin as a retarded person whose feelings could not be hurt because he really did not have any. They called him a lad, or boy, even when he was an old man (just as they called an old female servant "the girl"). For a service rendered they dismissed him with a tip, assuming that he would use it to buy himself a drink and thus be content. Even well-meaning schoolteachers believed that corporal punishment was the only kind of discipline that rural children understood. Recalling his childhood in the English village of Akenfield, the farm worker Leonard Thompson said: "We were thrashed a lot at school. Fathers would be ordered to the school to hold their sons while the mistress thrashed them. Most of the teachers were big thrashers. But we were tough, very tough. Everybody said, don't-don't to boys then and after awhile we didn't listen."[56]

CULTURE AND CLASS: THE LIMITS OF IMITATION

Although class consciousness intensified class conflicts, people responded to this effect of modernization in diverse ways. Marxist ideologues told the workers that they should help History overthrow the class system along with the economic and political structures that sustained it. But the emerging class consciousness of most workers was directed mainly toward finding values and standards of behavior which would make their jobs and their daily lives more rewarding within the existing order. Their economic grievances were more related to this cultural goal than to a desire for political and social revolution. Before 1914 most workers did not perceive the possibility of rising out of their class as real, and they viewed the few who tried to do so by imitating bourgeois ways as traitors. Within the middle classes, however, many ambitious individuals did try to gain acceptance in the stratum or class above them by imitating its life style. This effort is another example of the importance of culture in defining one's status and identity under the impact of modernization. Capitalist societies have varied in the degree to which they have offered opportunities for this kind of upward mobility, but they have all done so as a means of *maintaining* the class system. The upward mobile individuals themselves acquire a vested interest in its maintenance. Otherwise how would they know that they had "arrived"?

At the beginning of this century few people in modern capitalist societies believed in the possibility of upgrading or "promoting" a whole class or social group. The more successful peasants became farmers and the more adaptable craftsmen skilled workers; the others disappeared as distinct social groups. Militant labor spokesmen demanded more openings for individual workers in the existing secondary schools rather than an alternative system for upgrading the educational qualifications of the working class as a whole. Surgeons, engineers, architects, and secondary-school teachers had managed to achieve professional status by enforcing standards similar to those of physicians and lawyers. Only in recent years, however, has the word "professional" used as a noun been appropriated by nonself-regulating occupations such as social work and TV repair service. In American advertising the adjective "professional" has been cheapened to mean merely skilled, while the barbarism "paraprofessional" has been introduced by schools and hospitals as a sop to the sensitivities of the semiskilled. But upgrading the names of occupations is simply another way of *not* changing the class system. Bank clerks remain on the lower fringes of the middle class, and the working class has yet to receive its "promotion," despite talk about the *embourgeoisement* of its more affluent members.

People's attitudes toward other classes and social groups were often ironic. A proletarian culture boastful of the alcohol consumed still prevailed in most places in the 1890's, but thereafter it began to give way to greater moderation. In Munich, for example, "working-class percentage expenditure on drink was matched by the much wealthier categories of university professors and upper bureaucrats."[57] The code of honor of the aristocracy was disgracefully belied during a fire at a charity bazaar in Paris in May 1897: of the 125 persons who died only five were male (three old men, one physician, and one twelve-year-old boy); the young male aristocrats present had kicked and trampled the women and children in their rush to get out. Yet those commoners who still wanted to believe that aristocrats were superior beings succeeded in rationalizing such incidents away. Newly rich millionaries who tried to gain recognition in English Society by displaying their material goods were condemned in 1913 by the *Times* (which spoke for that very Society) as "that modern class—the waste products of prosperity." The disdain with which cultivated bourgeois and businessmen viewed one another in most countries actually expressed a conflict between two ways of conforming to middle-class standards. And the efforts of white-collar employees to distinguish themselves from manual workers did not alter the fact that the economic position of the two groups was virtually the same.

The ideal of the reserve officer corps among German *Bürgers* was as incongruous as the ideal of the country house life style in Great Britain, the most highly urbanized country in the world. This ideal was reinforced in the exclusive secondary schools and colleges, which were like country houses, with their personal servants, meal rituals, outdoor recreational grounds, and gate porters. An eccentric bachelor like Sherlock Holmes could live in a modest flat and have his meals sent in, but most Londoners who could afford to preferred to live in a town house and, ideally, have a country house as well. Even the address of one's town house was made to resemble that of a free-standing country estate. One's house stood on a square with trees, and though it had a number, one avoided using it; instead one spoke of living in Eaton Place or Belgrave Square.

By the 1890's outward signs of class differences were becoming less obvious though not yet negligible. The middle-classes and "high-class" kept women had been "invading" the opera, expensive resorts, and other fashionable public places since the middle of the century and were almost indistinguishable from the aristocracy in their dress and grooming. Yet aristocrats still had a distinctive bearing and were usually slimmer than middle-class people. The average European worker was at least three inches shorter than the average bourgeois* and he (and especially his wife) got older-looking at an earlier age. Young female factory workers and shop assistants in passably fashionable dresses and hats often betrayed their plebeian background with their sloppy make-up and cheap perfume. And peasants in city clothes were always distinguishable by their facial features, the hue and texture of their skin, and the way they moved.

People trying to imitate the class above them were also limited by the residual values of their own class. Thus middle-class people who tried to imitate the nobility had difficulty shaking off the value of usefulness, which their class had developed and internalized in earlier times in its struggle against the nobility as a useless class. Most businessmen still left to their wives the cultivation of aristocratic norms for behavior such as patronizing the arts, observing the social niceties, and engaging in good works. (It was among their sons that the aristocratic values instilled by the elite secondary schools sometimes replaced their utilitarian, money-making ethos with an emphasis on public service.) When lower-class people tried to imitate middle-class ways, they were hampered by a resid-ual concern with good intentions and a sentimental attachment to justice in a milieu where it was "results that count." Just as a person to the man-ner born could spot a rich parvenu on horseback, so a hotel manager could identify a lower-class guest trying to "pass" by overtipping. In each case the behavior of the imitators showed that they had not in-ternalized the values and perceptions that gave it its true meaning.

Similar patterns of consumption do not necessarily put everyone in-volved in the same class. Even today people from different backgrounds often interpret and respond in quite different ways to the same products and themes of mass culture. "Far from being eradicated by the uniform content of the media, existing forms of differentiation in social structure may be actively reinforced by it, as a consequence of such selectivity of perception and response."[58] At the beginning of the century the patterns of consumption of different classes were much less homogenized. The middle classes were just beginning to acquire their image of "class" from

---

* In the early 1900's in England twelve-year-old children who went to pri-vate schools were, on average, five inches taller than those in state schools. This difference was largely due to the greater quantities of meat, milk, and other high-protein food consumed by well-to-do families.

newspapers, magazines, advertising, and department store window display. But then, as now, this image had more to do with fashion than social structure. As we shall see in Chapter 6, sports meant different things to aristocrats, bourgeois, and workers (and meant nothing to most peasants). Each class did have a distinctive mentality. And this mentality reflected not only opposing economic, social, and political interests but also different attitudes toward religion and morals.

CHAPTER 5

RELIGION AND MORALS

The wish to be free has become a commonplace of modern Western civilization. Few people want to have to do something because some authority says it has to be done or that it has always been done. That sort of thing went out with the bustle and the horse and buggy. Ask any advertising copywriter, politician, schoolteacher, parent, or even a modern-minded clergyman. Pamper yourself, think for yourself, find yourself, express yourself, you owe it to yourself, God helps him who helps himself. You have only one life to live, so live it as a Clairol blonde. Here are the facts; judge them for yourself. Only you know what is best for you. The choice is yours.

Another commonplace is everybody's insistence on being included as equals in all institutional structures. Everybody counts now: workers, women, children, ethnic minorities, servants, the mentally retarded, even criminals. Vote, join, speak up, participate. It's your government, your school, your neighborhood, your union, your company. You don't need education, money, or breeding; you've got rights.

These demands for autonomy and inclusion continue to provoke discontent and social action—as they did in the days of the horse and buggy —because modernization keeps raising the stakes. Then, as now, conflicts arose among groups that wanted to extend or limit the bases for full participation in society. Moreover, as society has become progressively differentiated its moral standards have forced individuals to take into account a variety of acceptable courses of action. "This need to make choices on the basis of personal morality, the pressures deriving from the desire to accept or reject different levels of autonomous activity, and the struggle for inclusion—these are in fact the general sources for persistent feelings of discontent."[1]

These feelings of discontent have been compounded by the declining importance of traditional religion in people's lives. Liberty and equality are rational, legalistic values; they are often perceived emotionally but they offer no solutions to the more basic emotional problems of human life. "The death of a loved one wrenches our emotions; the failure to achieve what we yearn for saddens and bewilders us; the hostility between ourselves and those around us infuses our social contacts with tension and prevents the achievement of mutual values."[2] Traditional religion expressed people's

> refusal to capitulate to death, to give up in the face of frustration, to allow hostility to tear apart their human associations. The quality of being religious, seen from the individual point of view, implies two things: first, a belief that evil, pain, bewilderment, and injustice are fundamental facts of existence; and, second, a set of practices and related sanctified beliefs that express a conviction that man can ultimately be saved from those facts.

As men and women lost this conviction, they became less willing to accept these "facts."

The decline of religion as a force for social integration also made many people less willing to accept their allotted places and roles in the prevailing secular order. Traditional religions were most successful in socializing their members to fit into a total system which their myths conceived as having been created "once and for all." Along with rituals and sacred laws, these myths defined and supported the social and cultural norms of a given society as part of its total religious "package." Religious beliefs and rites gave meaning to the life of the individual and that of his community in the face of the apparent senselessness of ordinary existence by putting him temporarily into close rapport with the mysterious generative powers of supernatural forces. But this kind of religion was unable to

Concert in the New Workers' Hall, Vienna, from an illustrated newspaper, 1902.

cope with a world that was being rapidly transformed by creative human efforts. Under these conditions religious indoctrination in traditional values and norms for behavior often led to "inadequate socialization," thus making the conflicts of interest between individual and group aspirations and the authorities more explicit.

These conflicts began at different times and took different forms in different social classes. In earlier centuries Western Europe's middle classes had renounced their dependency on the authority of many traditional institutions, but by the 1890's the authority they vested in the family and the secondary schools had become new barriers to the wish to be free for some middle-class adolescents and women. The new, more permissive morality these people longed for was not to prevail until long after the First World War, but it already had its champions and critics during the prewar decades. Those aristocrats who felt the wish to be free continued to express it in their private lives while publicly conforming to the traditional moral standards of their class. In contrast to the middle and upper classes, the lower classes, both rural and urban, had become increasingly liberated sexually during the course of the nineteenth century. Religion, the family, and the schools had little authority over them, but the urban workers developed new norms for personal behavior in their own environment. (Their conflict with the authorities over their desires for equality and justice for their class is a separate topic and will be discussed in Chapter 8.)

DECLINING RELIGIOUS BELIEF AND PRACTICE

Most observers simply assume that religious belief and practice decline in modernizing societies and give little further thought to the matter. In the 1950's the German sociologist Helmut Schelsky said:

> Religious life is submerged in an indifference which stems not from a conscious decision or changed disposition but from the overloading of life with other, more pressing, though also basic, material demands. In social classes continually hard-pressed by daily work religion had its roots in social customs and practices more than in inner experiences and crises. The uprooting of people by a ubiquitous social mobility and their leveling into a middle-class society has cut them off both from the freedom to respond to the spiritual stirrings of religious belief and from their ties with traditional religious needs. . . . These people still think of themselves as Christian in their creed and their self-assessment, but these suppositions have less and less motivating force in their conduct.[3]

Aside from the point about "leveling into a middle-class society" these observations already applied in Germany and much of Western Europe fifty or sixty years earlier. Even so they tell us only that in modernizing societies secular concerns override religious belief and practice.

First of all we must distinguish between the faithful and those people who had lost their religious belief but were reluctant to abandon their religious practices. For some people these practices represented the lingering effects of their former faith; for others they signified a loyalty to old customs. Before 1914 the overwhelming majority of Europeans still believed that birth, marriage, and death needed an outward sign of sanctification. Consequently they had their children baptized, were married in a church, and insisted on a religious funeral. Some people wanted the last rites of the church they had rejected only when their rationalism or agnosticism faltered at the moment of death. Others went through the motions of religious practice throughout their lives to avoid calling attention to themselves or isolating themselves in a society that formally observed the rules requiring it.

By the late nineteenth century most Europeans who went to church did so out of conformity or habit; so did most of those who stayed away. The proportion of churchgoers was usually highest among those groups with the strongest ties with their local community—landholding peasants and aristocrats, small-town and suburban middle-class people—and lowest among those with the weakest local ties—agricultural laborers and unskilled urban workers. For the first group going to church was mainly a matter of conformity; for the second group *not* going was a habit. This habit was a tradition dating back to premodern times, when agricultural workers, like their unskilled urban descendants, were the least integrated members of the social and religious communities in which they lived, especially those who moved from place to place. Many skilled and semi-skilled workers and their families not only lacked the habit of going to church but also felt that they would be defying and even dissociating themselves from their working-class surroundings by doing so. In all social classes many men stayed away from church because they associated religion with weakness and superstition, while their wives and daughters continued to attend out of habit. Barred from most clubs, bars, and other public meeting places frequented by men, many women also went to church to get out of the house.

The validity of these generalizations varied from place to place and according to the way religious practice is defined. Statistical studies usually define a practicing Lutheran or Anglican as someone who takes communion at least once a year; a practicing Catholic is supposed to do this at Easter. For those Protestant denominations in which communion is less important the definition involves attendance at Sunday services with some degree of regularity. (On the Jews see Chapter 9.)

By 1914 the proportion of practicing Catholics was highest (over 75 per cent) in Ireland and Poland, where the priests were closest to the daily lives of their parishioners, and which were under the control of foreign states with their own, non-Catholic, established churches. The proportion was lowest (less than 25 per cent) in France, Italy, and Spain, where anticlericalism was strongest. Nominal (baptized) Catholics constituted over one third of the total population of the German Empire, and 50 to 60 per cent of them still fulfilled their religious obligations at Easter.[4] This relatively high percentage, particularly in such heavily industrialized and urbanized regions as the Rhineland, Westphalia, and Upper Silesia, could be explained in part as the heritage of resistance to the Protestant Bismarck's efforts (*Kulturkampf*) to limit the public influence of the Catholic Church during the 1870's and in part by the continuing influence of local Catholic leaders, particularly in Bavaria.

Local comparisons are often more revealing than national ones. The proportion of practicing Catholics was generally higher in the country-side than in the cities, but there were also important differences between one rural community and another and within a particular city. In one of two apparently similar neighboring parishes in Brittany most of the men were fairly prosperous sailors and religious practice was widespread; in the other one the men were mostly agricultural laborers and agnosticism prevailed. In Paris over one third of the inhabitants of the fashionable western districts were practicing Catholics, whereas only one fifteenth were in the working-class eastern districts.[5]

Regional variations among Protestants were well illustrated in Germany.[6] Twenty-seven per cent took communion at least once a year in Brunswick in 1895 and 26 per cent in 1910, whereas in neighboring Lippe the figures were 53 and 50, and in Hanover, 57 and 49. In predominantly rural East Prussia the figures for these two years were 45 and 39—almost the same as in industrialized and urbanized Saxony, with 47 per cent in 1895 and 37 per cent fifteen years later. The proportions were lowest in the largest Protestant cities: 16 per cent of the inhabitants of Berlin were communicants in 1895 and 14 per cent in 1910; in Bremen the figures were 14 and 7 per cent; in Hamburg, 9 and 7 per cent. These low figures were not unique to Germany. In 1908 only 8 per cent of the adult Lutherans were communicants in the diocese of Uppsala,[7] thirty-five miles from Stockholm.

In London the proportion of churchgoers was higher than in the largest Continental Protestant cities, though it too fell during our period. According to a religious census reported in the Nonconformist *British Weekly*, on October 24, 1886, about 1 million out of a total of 4 million people attended a Protestant service on that particular Sunday. When the *Daily News* took a similar census 16 years later it showed that, while the total population of the city had increased by about 565,000, church attendance had fallen by 164,000. According to C. F. G. Masterman, in London and other large English cities:

> It is the middle class which is losing its religion; which is slowly or suddenly discovering that it no longer believes in the existence of the God of its fathers, or a life beyond the grave. . . . It is not becoming

> atheist. It is ceasing to believe, without being conscious of the proc-
> ess, until it suddenly wakes up to the fact that the process is com-
> plete.[8]

Since the habit of not going to church was already widespread among
most working-class people throughout Europe by the 1880's, the decline
in over-all church attendance thereafter is probably attributable to the
middle classes in other countries besides England.

Great Britain was unique in that its different churches were associated
with different social and ethnic groups. The Church of England included
most of the upper and upper-middle classes, though it still had members
among the rural poor. Middle- and lower-middle-class Englishmen predominated in the Noncomformist denominations, though some skilled
workers and craftsmen also attended their chapels, particularly Methodist
ones. Church attendance was higher in Welsh agricultural and mining
districts than in similar areas in England. In Wales Nonconformism had
long been an expression of national feeling, but after 1900, as working-
class grievances began to take precedence over this feeling, "the chapel
ceased to have the significance that it had so long maintained."[9] The Irish
Catholic workers in England and Scotland were even more loyal than the
Welsh to their religion as an expression of national feeling. But most
English workers did not feel the need to attend church or chapel for purposes of social identification. This also seems to have been true of
Scottish workers.[10]

In Russia the religious situation was also unusual, but for different
reasons. Unlike the established churches in other European countries, the
Russian Orthodox Church was completely dependent on the state, which
opposed all efforts to improve its administration or the quality and economic conditions of its priests. Yet the rural masses clung to their religion
more tenaciously in Russia than anywhere else. Contemporary foreign
observers and even later Soviet historians were struck by the pervasive religious outlook of the prewar Russian peasants.[11] Whereas village Orthodox priests were often inferior to their Western European counterparts
in moral and intellectual leadership, the leaders of the schismatic sects,
though intellectually even weaker, were morally inspiring. In Russia, as
elsewhere, a few individual members of the educated and upper classes
found new meaning in religion. Tolstoy is the best known example; other
notable converts included the economist Peter B. Struve and the philosopher Nikolai A. Berdyaev. But more than in most countries the intelligentsia in Russia had abandoned religious belief and practice precisely be-

cause the Orthodox Church was so dependent upon the autocracy they hated.

In his five-volume history of Christianity in the nineteenth and twentieth centuries Kenneth Scott Latourette sees the *belle époque* as one of growing "de-Christianization" among the majority of Europeans along with "revivals" of faith among certain minorities. During the nineteenth century Catholic popular piety, both among the clergy and the rank and file, had been mounting, especially in devotion to the Sacred Heart of Jesus and to the Virgin Mary.[12] According to Latourette, the fresh surge of life was even more striking in Protestantism, particularly in German biblical scholarship and in the efforts of English evangelical movements toward moral uplift. But these "revivals" failed to halt the decline in regular church attendance almost everywhere. For Roman Catholicism anticlericalism was less serious than "the apathy which betokened an indifference that dismissed the Church and its faith as irrelevant and looked upon baptism as a social convention to be observed but not to be taken too seriously."[13]

Yet many nonpracticing Christians continued to believe in the possibility of divine intervention in their daily lives. They saw little evidence that God or Providence punished evil and injustice, but this sort of retribution was implied in some of the popular fiction and melodrama to which they turned for escape. In the 1930's Marie Legrain, the wife of a militant French anarchist, recalled that three decades earlier, when she was nineteen, she had prayed to St. Expédit (patron of the dispossessed) for a job and got one. "Since that day, although I don't believe in religion, I don't go to Mass, and I don't say any prayers, as soon as I am in trouble I nevertheless call on Saint Expédit and, to tell the truth, I have always felt satisfied with his services."[14] An unbelieving English mother wishing to break the news of a sister's death to a child wrote a letter in the dead sister's name purporting to come from heaven, and describing her state of bliss in that place.

Regardless of the forms that religious belief and practice (or their rejection) took, Christian *moral* values were still important throughout Europe. Many people, perhaps the majority, no longer believed that their behavior would eventually put them in heaven or hell. Politics, business, and war were often conducted in an unchristian manner, but in private life hardly anyone could lie, steal, or kill without feeling guilty. Most people's attitudes regarding the family, male and female roles, and sexual deviations were also based on the authority of the Judeo-Christian tradition. Even most anticlericals and freethinkers followed a private moral code similar to that of religious people. Their very rejection of organized religion, like that of the socialists, was based on a strong moral sense. Christianity as they perceived it stood in the way of individual freedom and social justice and was therefore unredeemable. Yet their own version of these values was close to that of the Sermon on the Mount.

RELIGION AND SOCIAL CONTROL

During much of the nineteenth century religion had acquired an expanded role in the systems of social control in many countries. Reacting against the revolutionary upheavals of the period 1789–1815, the established and restored authorities were determined to revive the historic conjunction of religion and social power which had overlain substantial degrees of indifference, anticlericalism, and paganism for centuries. This change occurred not only in those Continental countries that had been directly affected by these upheavals but also in Great Britain. It was more important historically than the new personal religious commitment of rulers such as Alexander I of Russia and Charles X of France, literary figures such as François-René de Chateaubriand and Alessandro Manzoni, or the philosopher Sören Kierkegaard. After 1870 the authority and power of the established churches were undermined almost everywhere. In Britain, however, the evangelical Nonconformist churches retained a good deal of their political and social influence in certain localities until the beginning of the new century.*

We do not know why people at the top of the hierarchies of power and status began to rely less on religion as an instrument of social control, but when they did religious practice usually declined among the people under their influence. This point can be seen more readily in comparisons among regions than among whole nations. Religion had the most influence and the largest following in rural areas inhabited by peasants with land and dominated by local practicing Christians. It was weak in those rural areas in which most of the inhabitants were day laborers, the landlords were usually absent, and public officials were viewed as

---

* Thereafter one reason for the declining influence of laissez-faire, teetotaling Nonconformist Liberals in the power structure was their opposition to social imperialism (see Chapter 9), which other members of their party championed in the face of international competition and which won widespread popular support. See Hugh McCleod, *Class and Religion in the Late Victorian City* (London: Croom Helm, 1975).

exploiters, as in parts of southern Spain and southern Italy. On the other hand, religious influence was strong in the Spanish Basque provinces, which were dominated by pious businessmen and a vigorous church hierarchy. The same was true in the Italian province of Veneto, in contrast to Tuscany, where clerical influence was weak.

Although industrialization, urbanization, and social mobility undermined both religious practice and the social power of organized religion, this tendency was delayed in a number of places by the local power holders. The region stretching from northern France through Belgium and into the German Rhineland was one of the earliest to be industrialized and one of the most highly urbanized by the late nineteenth century. Yet Catholicism retained much of its influence and its following among the workers there well into the twentieth century. One reason was that the leading laymen and clergymen in this region were among the most active in Europe in organizing Christian trade unions and promoting the health, education, and welfare of the lower classes. Another reason was that the authority of the family remained strong in these classes. The fact that 50 to 75 per cent of the inhabitants of the predominantly Catholic regions throughout Germany voted for the Center (Catholic) Party in the late nineteenth century was a further indication of the continuing influence of the local clerical-oriented elites there.

In most places, however, working-class people rejected the churches and their lay organizations because they shared neither their outlook nor their frame of reference. Long before the 1890's they had become aware of the contradictions between their own visceral aspirations and traditional religious instruction, which stressed routine piety as the way toward personal salvation in the hereafter. People who spent most of their waking hours struggling to feed themselves and their families had few opportunities to commit most of the seven deadly sins. They might succumb to envy and covetousness, but pride, lust, gluttony, anger, and sloth seemed limited mainly to people with money and time on their hands. Peasants might accept Christian-inspired traditional culture because they knew no other. But most workers in cities, factories, and mines rejected its emphasis on obedience and acceptance of the existing order as ordained by God, and they developed their own working-class culture as a conscious reaction against it. The root of the divorce between the working-class world and the churches was a "divorce of mentalities."[15]

Nowhere was the "inadequate socialization" provided by traditional religious instruction more apparent than among urban factory workers in the Protestant sections of Germany. This was true of the unskilled laborers just off the farm, the city-bred semiskilled wage earners, and the skilled mechanics and foremen who had drifted to the city from small provincial towns. In the public schools they had all been forced to memorize the cátechism and taught to accept without question the authority of the Bible in secular as well as religious matters. This kind of instruction seemed completely irrelevant to the workers' adult experiences in the factory and in their daily lives. Consequently the workers forgot all about it and in many large industrial cities the majority of them came under the influence of the Socialist Party.[16]

In France, Belgium, Italy, and Spain most workers were hostile to the Catholic Church because of its contrasting behavior toward them and their employers. It always seemed to take the employers' side during strikes and it opposed all working-class organizations that escaped its control. Despite Pope Leo XIII's condemnation of capitalist exploitation in his encyclical *Rerum Novarum* (see Chapter 2) the workers saw little evidence of clerical efforts to combat it. They were mainly impressed by the Church's intransigent opposition to socialism because of its atheism and its emphasis on class conflict.

English workers were particularly conscious of the cleavage between their own pattern of life and the middle-class character of the churches and chapels. On February 3, 1897, a plumber wrote to the *Methodist Times* paraphrasing the call of Christians to the nonworshiping masses in the following way:

> We want you, the working "classes," to attend our church; but you must forget that you *are* the working "classes," and you must not on any account presume to be on an equal footing with ourselves, as you don't belong to our "set," and you should be grateful to us for our condescension in asking you to come at all.

In their public pronouncements on the relations between capital and labor both the Wesleyan Conference and the Congregational Union assumed that capitalism and social justice were incompatible. The Church of England seemed even more aloof and condescending toward working-class interests. In January 1898, its weekly, *The Guardian*, vigorously condemned a strike by the Amalgamated Society of Engineers, calling the union leaders radical troublemakers. As the liberal-minded Anglican clergyman T. C. Fry admitted later that year:

> The Church is mostly administered and officered by the classes; her influential laity belong almost wholly to the class; she is doing a great and growing work among the masses; but the deep sympathies of the

clergy with the poor are largely obscured to the eyes of the masses by the fact that social rank and social position secured by wealth and tradition still count for so much in her service, both amongst clergy and laity.[17]

Next to formal instruction, charity had been the churches' most important traditional means of social control over the poor. The English agricultural labor organizer Joseph Arch bitterly remembered how a local parson had demanded that the rural workers and their families who were given charity show deferential thanks and stay away from the Nonconformist chapel.[18] Like the Poor Law Commission and the Charity Organisation Society, the English churches and chapels distinguished between the "deserving" and "undeserving" poor and tried to foster the middle-class standard of self-help among their charity cases. In France the revolutionary syndicalist Pierre Monatte, one of the most perceptive observers of the pre-1914 working-class mentality, said:

> Among the mass of workers there is suspicion of everything that comes from the Church, the eternal accomplice of the Rich. Take the most indifferent worker, furthest removed from our struggles, take him, even when he is down on his luck and seeks charity from a religious source; he will always approach it with an instinctive mistrust that nothing will be able to modify.[19]

It was through their indoor, rather than outdoor, relief that the churches still managed to assert a considerable amount of social control over their dependents—in orphanages, asylums, and homes for the infirm and destitute—especially in the Latin countries.

As we saw in Chapter 2, the churches opposed all institutions and forms of entertainment that escaped their control, but they were slow in setting up competing agencies. The most successful of these were the English Sunday schools, which working-class children attended more than day schools during most of the nineteenth century. Although they lost much of their attractive power by the early 1900's, working-class parents still found some advantages in them, as is evident in the following observation by a resident of a Devon fishing community.

> The children go to Sunday School, of course; it is convenient to have them out of the way while Sunday's dinner is being cooked and the afternoon snooze being taken. Besides, though the Sunday School teaching is a fearful hotch-potch of heaven, hell and self-interest, the tea-fights, concerts and picnics connected with it are well worth going to.[20]

But most observers agreed that these working-class children gave up both Sunday school and church by their early teens and forgot whatever they had learned in them.

Another innovation of the English Nonconformists was the Pleasant Sunday Afternoon movement, which was most successful in the industrial Midlands. Nominally autonomous and nonsectarian, the local P.S.A. societies tried to lure workingmen to their meetings, sometimes in public halls, though in churches as well. Their motto, "Brief, Bright, Brotherly," set the tone of the afternoons' activities. Typically these began around two-thirty, after "welcomers" had shaken hands with each arrival and shown him to a seat; aside from a short prayer and a few hymns the "service" was secular and usually included a short talk by a prominent layman on some subject with a liberal and humanitarian slant. It would be difficult to estimate how many nonchurchgoers were lured to regular services by these Pleasant Sunday Afternoons, but this goal justified their very existence in the eyes of the more puritanical Nonconformist leaders.

Though only indirectly connected with the churches, the temperance movement also tried to operate as an agency of social control in Great Britain. Not only the clergy but the middle classes as a whole viewed working-class drunkenness as the country's greatest social blight. Even the "Christian Socialist" Baptist minister John Clifford argued that drunkenness was a major cause of poverty,[21] disputing the American WCTU leader Frances E. Willard, who said that it was the other way around. Particularly active was the Band of Hope, a temperance society for men, women, and children. At its weekly meetings people took the pledge, sang temperance hymns, listened to speakers, and then had their social hour. The Band of Hope attracted a certain number of workers to middle-class respectability, but, like the evangelical churches, it was concerned with moral uplift rather than poverty.

The one organization that tried to save the lower classes on their own ground was the Salvation Army. During the late 1850's, after a wide experience in several Methodist sects, William Booth and his wife Catherine concluded that the English class structure made it impossible for missionaries from the well-to-do classes to reach the masses for Christ. In Mrs. Booth's words, the poor could be made Christians only "by people of their own class, who would go after them in their own resorts, who would speak to them in a language they understood, and reach them by means suited to their own tastes."[22] In 1865 the Booths set up their first "Christian Mission to the Heathen of our Own Country" in London's Whitechapel. Their early collaborators were lower-class (a blacksmith, a ditchdigger, a policeman, a sailor, a chimney sweep, and a sometime professional boxer) in their manners and speech patterns and full of "the rapture of spiritual drunkards" in their battle against the devil. In 1878 their mission finally launched the Salvation Army, with "General" Booth at its head, to fight this battle. Their "military" uniforms were designed to be classless in a society where the poor viewed men in clerical garb as envoys of the rich. The brass band was first used to drown out the heckling of hostile crowds, but it also acquired the task of announcing and brightening the Army's revival meetings.

Spokesmen for respectable English society had mixed feelings about the activities of the Salvation Army. On April 26, 1882, the *Times* recognized the failure of existing religious organizations to instill Christian norms for behavior in the very poor and remarked that the noise made by sober converts was more tolerable than the noise they had previously made when drunk and unregenerate. But in June 1891 the mayor of Eastbourne publicly called the Army "an atrocious, infamous and degrading movement." As a result, on the twenty-eighth, several thousand citizens of that town attacked a large procession of Salvationists who had come there to welcome Captain Bob Bell and his four fellow prisoners on their release from the local jail.[23] By then, however, the Army's golden age was over, and William Booth had become anxious about his lack of success in making permanent headway among slum dwellers. In 1890, in his book *In Darkest England, and the Way Out*, he had proposed a plan to organize the unemployed into "self-helping and self-sustaining communities, each being a kind of co-operative society, or patriarchal family, governed and disciplined on the principles which have already proved so effective in the Salvation Army." Again the *Times*, and even the Queen, saw some merit in the Army's efforts. Like Booth, they perceived the submerged masses as not only workless and godless but also shiftless. But by the middle of 1891 the brief success of *In Darkest England* among the reading public was over. Thereafter Booth subordinated social work to making triumphal tours around the world, while the younger people who ran the Army forgot about his plan for alleviating poverty and concentrated on saving souls.

Unlike the Salvation Army, which directed its main efforts at the *Lumpenproletariat*, the English Christian Socialists wanted to help raise the status of the working class as a whole. The first Christian Socialists, such as Frederick Denison Maurice, Charles Kingsley, and Thomas Hughes, had been active in the co-operative movement in the mid-nineteenth century. By the 1890's a number of Nonconformist ministers had also declared themselves socialists, and their movement was acquiring a limited respectability. In a lecture given in early 1893 the Reverend John Clifford told his audience: "I do not say that Collectivism is the only thing needful . . . but within the area of Industrialism this is the advance we should seek."[24] The Reverend Reginald J. Campbell advocated a welfare state and declared: "The Socialism which is developing so generally in antagonism to conventional Christianity is far nearer to the original Christianity than the Christianity of the churches."[25] Even within the Church of England a few rare spokesmen such as the Reverend Henry Scott Holland of Oxford took a similar position. Christian Socialists may have helped to break down the prejudices of religious people toward socialism and to encourage social reform in the early 1900's. "Yet they failed in the end to break through the class barrier and to make sustained and successful communication with the urban masses."[26]

On the Continent, Christian socialism was more politically oriented than in England and more openly hostile to Marxism. The only Protestant Christian socialist party was that of Adolf Stöcker in Prussia, and this former chaplain of the German emperor based his appeal to working-class people more on anti-Semitism than on social welfare. Karl Lueger, the leader of the Austrian Christian Social party, did institute a kind of municipal socialism as mayor of Vienna during the early 1900's (see Chapter 9), but he did not challenge the Hapsburg power structure or the Catholic hierarchy. In 1899 Romolo Murri, a young priest from central Italy, published his Christian Democratic program calling for structural changes in the whole society in the interests of the workers. During the early 1900's he also helped to organize leagues of Catholic workers and, unlike most Catholics, he did not view Socialists with apocalyptic horror. But Pope Pius X denounced Murri both for his socialism and his "modernism" and excommunicated him. Whereas Pius X turned against Murri for wanting the Church to associate itself with socialist ideas he condemned the French layman Marc Sangnier and his Christian Democratic movement (the Sillon) for not being under ecclesiastical control. This too was a "modernist error."

Yet the Vatican recognized the usefulness of laymen's organizations as agencies for social control even before Pope Leo XIII's *Rerum Novarum*. One such organization was the Association Catholique de la Jeunesse Française, founded in 1886 by Albert de Mun and other clerical-minded Frenchmen who wanted to alleviate some of the social hardships brought by industrialization.[27] The ideology of the A.C.J.F. was Social Catholicism. Far from favoring independent action on the part of the workers, it wanted to unite them in Christian guilds with their employers and to place them under the guidance of directing committees recruited from the upper classes. It also sought to strengthen the faith of French Catholic youth and to reorganize French society on what it considered a Christian basis. The A.C.J.F. was much smaller and less influential than the Opera dei Congressi, established in 1874 in Italy.[28] By 1897 this movement had nearly four thousand parish committees and sponsored hundreds of mutual aid societies, associations of Catholic workers, rural banks, and youth groups. But it still taught that society's privileged had a responsibility to lead by example and discouraged workers from forming their own unions or engaging in political action that escaped their control.

By the immediate prewar years the Catholic hierarchy began to sanction new kinds of organizations to mobilize the faithful in their secular activities. It acknowledged the need to compete with the trade unions as well as the socialist parties in the struggle for the working class. As a result, Catholic unions under ecclesiastical control sprang up in Italy, Germany, France, and Belgium; these unions were to become more independent and militant after the war. Pope Pius X was also impressed by the increasing interest of young people in athletics. German Protestant pastors had sponsored gymnastic clubs for a long time, and the Church of England had made sports a part of the activities of the Church Lads Brigades. Now the Catholic clergy was encouraged to use athletics as a means of social control over Catholic youth.

Despite the efforts and good intentions of both clergymen and laymen, the Christian churches could not shake off their image as a conservative force until long after the war. They especially opposed the modernizing leaders of France and Italy, but even in England, where anticlericalism was not a major issue, the majority of the clergy and the churchgoers were less committed to social reform than the government itself, particularly under the Liberals after 1906. Throughout Europe organized religion remained on the defensive, still proclaiming traditional piety and morality as the best ways to deal with the discontents provoked by all the forces of modernization.

THE NEW MORALITY AND ITS CRITICS

Morality involves both standards of behavior and character, but these are not inseparable. In our period, as in others, there were well-mannered cowards and malicious prudes, teetotaling swindlers and prostitutes with hearts of gold. Traditionally, high character was assumed to be limited to people of noble birth, and the word noble has remained a synonym for it down to the present. But as money and culture superseded birth as the main criteria for identifying a person's social status, standards of behavior gained increasing importance. We have seen how nobility of character was taught as an ideal in military academies and in certain elite schools and student fraternities; in practice, however, the emphasis was on doing what was expected rather than being a good person. Many people of good character felt that organized religion itself was hypocritical in this respect. Thus our concern here is with standards of behavior, which are changeable, not character, which is usually fixed.

The wish to be free from the fetters of traditional authority in one's behavior has appeared in many forms and has been criticized from the time of the Old Testament prophets to today's American Legion.* Aristocratic licentiousness in England and France helped to spark the puritanical repression of the 1650's and the restraints of Robespierre's Republic of Virtue in the 1790's. By the early nineteenth century the established authorities in many parts of Europe were already complaining about a similar loosening of moral standards among the lower classes, particularly the youth and women. In 1833 the government of the Bavarian province of Oberpfalz said: "The truth of the matter is that people in general are becoming more sentimental and increasing in self-esteem, while the simple old customs in domestic family life are vanishing."[29] It depicted young people as having more "freedom of will," fearing their elders less, reveling in irresponsibility, wantonness, "tearing about," and mischief. The Bavarian government saw the root of the evil as an "emancipation from all control, an exaggerated feeling of independence."

As traditional moral standards loosened among both the middle and lower classes, they were replaced by new norms for behavior, not degeneration into normlessness. Between the sixteenth and late nineteenth centuries the middle classes in the West had renounced their dependent connections with the authority of traditional economic, political, and religious institutions. In their place they "tried to create the psychic and social structures that would bolster and sustain their wish for freedom"[30] and to make the family the decisive mediating agent between these struc-

---

* On August 16, 1974, Rear Admiral Jeremiah A. Denton received a standing ovation at the legionnaires' annual convention in Miami when he gave as examples of the moral decline in the United States "the Gay Liberation movement" and "an 800 per cent increase in premarital and extra-marital sexual relations" (*Miami Herald*, August 17, 1974).

tures. The middle-class family assumed the main responsibility for the socialization of its members. Ideally, the maximum goal of this process was "to foster in the individual a perception of self as a separate, independent actor without great guilt or anxiety, and to establish rewards for autonomous activities that are external to the family." This kind of socialization was designed to make the individual willing to perform in morally appropriate contexts and give him the ability to discriminate between the different aspects of authority. Middle-class parents tried to ration their affection not only to make their children sublimate their libidinal and aggressive energies but also to give them "the internalizations and identifications necessary both for independent activity outside the family and for tolerance of the diversity and complexity that is characteristic of pluralized societies."

While modernization transferred many of the economic and civil functions of the patriarchal family to the state, the factory, and the school, middle-class parents began to subject their children to a longer period of dependence than ever before.[31] In premodern times teen-agers in all classes had lived away from their parents—as servants in other households, as apprentices in their masters' homes, or as students in boarding schools. Although still semidependent, they had had their own traditions for social control and moral support in village youth groups and in student and craft brotherhoods in the towns. Industrialization and massive urbanization eroded or transformed most of these peer-group traditions and tied young people closer to their families. In the second half of the nineteenth century working-class youths, living in crowded quarters with numerous brothers and sisters, still organized a large part of their social life around peer groups outside the home, particularly in street gangs (see Chapter 4). By then, however, middle-class parents began to limit the number of their offspring as more of these survived and to extend the care and concern formerly reserved for very young children to adolescents.

As apprenticeship declined and secondary and higher education gained increasing importance for the future careers of their adolescent children, professional people and even businessmen assumed a much greater role in supervising their socialization and training. Secondary-school students had to submit to this supervision whether they lived at school, as in England, or at home, as in most Continental countries. Middle-class parents' concern for suitable careers for their sons and advantageous matches for their daughters also raised the average age of marriage. In England the proportion of all married males and females between the ages of fifteen and twenty-four declined from a peak of 17.4 per cent in 1871 to the nadir of 9.7 per cent in 1911, and in the middle classes the average age at marriage was five years above that in the working classes.[32] But whereas unmarried young men in all classes retained much of their earlier autonomy, middle-class adolescents became increasingly subject to the control of their parents and teachers.

The social controls exerted by both parents and secondary schools denied middle-class adolescents access to the economy and society of adults and made it difficult for them to develop their own autonomous subcultures. In England teachers and administrators in the elite public schools developed new peer-group networks and rituals to provide the internalizations and identifications they thought their boys needed for performing successfully as men (see Chapter 2). But their honor codes, sexual taboos, team sports, and debating societies were vapid imitations of Victorian ·adult ideals and merely postponed the adjustments required by the actual adult world. By 1900 most secondary-school students on the Continent were cloistered within the narrow confines of the home, leaving only when they went on to a university or began their adult careers. They were more burdened with homework and had fewer opportunities for sports than their English counterparts. And they had abandoned the political radicalism of their forebears, particularly in 1848 in France, Germany, and Austria.

Unlike the peer groups in English boarding schools, those on the Continent did not promote mutual trust but mainly helped to protect their members against their teachers in the enjoyment of their private interests. In France some peer groups in the *lycées* sought to destroy the authority of a teacher by discrediting him for his political views; in the German *Gymnasia* they could occasionally do this by exposing a teacher's moral lapses—as in Heinrich Mann's *Professor Unrat* (1905), later made into the movie *The Blue Angel*, with Emil Jannings and Marlene Dietrich. German fathers were particularly persistent in asserting their traditional patriarchal authority, and their teen-age sons, trapped between the tyranny of the home and the rigorous academic demands of the *Gymnasium*, looked back with nostalgia to premodern peer-group structures and the partial autonomy these had represented.

It was this feeling of being trapped and this nostalgia which attracted German teen-agers to the *Wandervogel* (birds of passage), the most influential youth movement in pre-1914 Europe. The original group was founded in 1901 in a Berlin suburb by Karl Fischer, a young stenography teacher with a flair for leadership. But Fischer seemed too dictatorial to some people, and beginning in 1904 new leaders split away from the *Wandervogel* and formed similar organizations. Between 1910 and 1913 the youth movement spread throughout Germany and took root in Austria and Switzerland. Although the *Wandervogel* and its offshoots had their regional and national leagues, their core groups—or "hordes"— usually consisted of less than twenty members, almost all between the ages of twelve and nineteen. Both the members and the leading personalities in the German youth movement were the sons and—after 1907— daughters of professional men in government, industry, and commerce.[33]

The main purpose of the *Wandervogel* was to go on hikes and excursions away from the city in order to escape the control of parents and teachers and to experience the kinds of autonomy and togetherness found in premodern youth groups. At first the movement took as its models the wandering scholars of the Middle Ages and the Romantic youth of the *Sturm und Drang* movement. But its members were younger than these models and much more integrated into the national society. They were also more self-conscious, deliberately trying to "rough it" by sleeping in barns and cooking their own food while making certain that their bare knees, flamboyant hats, and guitars distinguished them, as middle-class adolescents, from lower-class vagabonds.

These young Germans felt that they were protesting against a corrupt civilization lacking in warmth, vitality, emotion, and ideals. The *Wandervogel* gave them these things in walks at night and at sunrise, in the atmosphere of the campfire, in communal singing of folk songs, and in uninhibited friendships. But they disapproved of selfish and licentious behavior. They eventually chose as their ideal the hero of Hermann Popert's novel *Helmut Harringa*, which was published in 1910 and sold 320,000 copies in the next few years.[34] Helmut, a young Hamburg judge, carries on a relentless fight against premarital sexual intercourse, drunkenness, and the contamination of the Nordic race. The closing words of the novel are: "The world owes the idea of freedom to the Nordic peoples, the Germans."

The *Wandervogel's* idea of freedom was spiritual and peculiar to the German middle class. Its spokesmen made no demand for civil liberties. Unlike the attitudes of more recent movements of rebellious youth, the *Wandervogel's* vaunted sense of equality did not threaten the social order since it was confined to members of their own class. And their emphasis on brotherhood had sufficiently patriotic overtones to make it acceptable to the authorities. The public image of the *Wandervogel*—their bizarre dress, casual behavior, and alleged encouragement of homosexual relations

Wandervogel.

—made them seem like rebels against Wilhelmine social conventions. But their parents and the authorities tolerated their rusticated bohemianism as a harmless expression of that newly discovered phase of life—adolescence —and as a preferable alternative to real delinquency, or worse, socialism. Before 1914 only a few isolated radicals in the movement advocated free love. "Far from favouring any sweeping sexual reforms, the youth movement of those days might perhaps have been best characterized as an organization for sublimating the juvenile libido."[35] Thus it reinforced the socialization acquired in the middle-class family.

The lower-class family differed from its middle-class counterpart, though it too gained new importance in our period for a number of reasons. As the sprawling working-class districts of industrial cities developed into stable communities, romantic relationships became less transient and led increasingly to marriage and to the legitimation of children born out of wedlock. This happened not because the workers wanted to imitate the middle classes but because they were elaborating their own cohesive subculture with distinctive values and standards of behavior. Also, bourgeois society had begun to accept the idea of workers marrying at an early age. Previously, especially in Central Europe, it had legally restricted such marriages in order to prevent their offspring from swamping the local poor-relief funds.[36] But since the lower classes had already abandoned their premarital chastity, these laws had not served their purpose and they were repealed in the 1860's. From about 1875 until 1914 illegitimacy ratios declined almost everywhere, though the timing and rate of this decline varied considerably.* Nevertheless, the working-class family was much less effective than the middle-class family as an agency of social control.

This difference helps account for the different ways in which members of the middle and working classes asserted their wish to be free. Both

---

* According to a report of 1909—*International Congress of Women* (2 vols., Toronto: G. Parker & Sons, 1910, II, p. 221)—the percentage of illegitimate births each year between 1896 and 1900 was 4 to 5 per cent in the United Kingdom, Switzerland, and Spain, 6 to 7 per cent in Italy and Finland, 7 to 8 per cent in Norway, 8 to 9 per cent in Belgium, France, and Hungary, 9 to 10 per cent in Germany and Denmark, 11 to 12 per cent in Sweden, 12 to 13 per cent in Portugal, and 14 to 15 per cent in Austria. Numerous variables account for these differences, but the correlation between illegitimacy ratios and religion was the least significant. Both Catholic Spain and Italy and predominantly Protestant Britain and Switzerland had low illegitimacy ratios, whereas Catholic Portugal and Austria, along with Protestant Sweden and Denmark, had high ones.

classes had been influenced by the modern market-place economy, with its emphasis on rationally pursuing one's individual self-interest. And both had been exposed to formal schooling, which even at the elementary level helped to increase the individual's self-awareness by teaching him to think logically. According to the social historian Edward Shorter:

> It appears that liberal sexual attitudes probably flowed from heightened ego awareness and from weakened superego controls. Traditional European society internalized anti-sexual values which commanded repression. But, when new values began to replace old ones, the superego restrictions on gratification gave way to the demands of the ego for individual self-fulfillment as integral to this larger personality objective. I do not mean that people became "sexualized" human beings; instead they became pluralized, seeing sex as an intrinsic part of their humanity. This makes the sexual revolution an integrated movement of self-awareness, not a turbulent unleashing of carnality.[37]

Shorter goes on to point out the paradox that the middle classes who found their freedom in liberalism, laissez-faire capitalism, and universal suffrage were the most repressive people sexually, whereas the workers who favored economic collectivism and political community were the most liberated sexually, with a high degree of personal control and autonomy. The paradox can be explained by the difference in the roles of the middle- and working-class family.

Young urban workers of both sexes met freely in public places, especially dance halls, and felt little compunction about ending a Saturday night with sexual intercourse. In the early 1890's a perceptive firsthand observer said:

> I believe that in the whole labouring class of Chemnitz it would be hard to find a young man or a young woman, over seventeen, who is chaste. Sexual intercourse, largely the product of these dance-halls, has assumed enormous proportions among the youth of to-day. It is regarded quite simply as natural and customary; there is seldom a trace of consciousness that it can be looked upon as sin.[38]

Working-class girls in Manchester, Lille, and Turin might have worried a bit more than those in Chemnitz about losing their virtue in this way, but an enterprising lad could usually find one who did not. In any case it was regarded as only right that any boy over the age of fifteen should have one girl to whom he was supposed to be attached and should take a lively interest in any others he might happen to meet. These attitudes toward girls of one's own class distinguished urban workers from all other classes and social groups, whose courtship patterns remained more traditional and were regarded as necessarily leading to marriage.

The one approved outlet for young middle-class men responding to new aspirations for gratification was sleeping with lower-class women and prostitutes, a practice which they themselves also used to prove their manhood. Incredible as it may seem today, these young men took particular pride in asserting that they had had a venereal disease when it had been contracted from a whore. According to a contemporary study, no officer could be elected to a certain Swedish military club until he furnished proof of having once had syphilis.[39] This study adds that, in the early 1900's, most German men had had gonorrhea, and about one in five syphilis. The majority of these men were probably workers and peasants who had contracted these diseases from prostitutes before marrying, particularly while performing their military service. But young middle-class men in many Continental countries also imitated their upper-class counterparts by having premarital sexual relations with "girl friends" from the lower classes.

Unmarried middle-class women had no such outlets and once married they were often frustrated by their husbands' insensitivity to their need for sexual fulfillment. The prostitute and lower-class "girl friend" allowed the middle-class husband to preserve his belief that the pure woman he had married had no sexual needs. Freud summed up the Victorian husband's dilemma as follows:

> Full sexual satisfaction only comes when he can give himself up wholeheartedly to enjoyment, which with his well-brought-up wife . . . he does not venture to do. Hence comes his need for a less exalted sexual object, a woman ethically inferior, to whom he need ascribe no aesthetic misgivings, and who does not know the rest of his life and cannot criticize him.[40]

In 1905 an Oxford doctor, when asked if women enjoyed sexual intercourse, was quoted as saying that "nine out of ten woman are indifferent to or actively dislike it; the tenth, who enjoys it, will always be a harlot."

But in the early 1900's middle-class attitudes about the social role and sexual nature of women were beginning to change in the most advanced parts of Europe. Few young women dared go as far as the heroine of H. G. Wells's *Ann Veronica* (1909), who defiantly left home, seduced an attractive older man, ran off with him to Switzerland, and lived happily ever after. But thanks in part to books like Havelock Ellis's *Man and Woman* (1894; 5th edition, 1914), sexual relations could be accepted, at least in print, as a subject for discussion and as a potentially enriching experience for women as well as men. In addition to being the first scientifically trained Englishman to write objectively about the psychology of sex for the general reader, Ellis was a leading champion of what he called the New Spirit, which for him also included socialism and the emancipation of women. As we shall see in Chapter 8, these two movements made considerable advances in the *belle époque*. Meanwhile, in Protestant countries educated middle-class people began to take a less rigid position on contraception, marriage, and divorce. And in Catholic countries respectable young women were less strictly chaperoned and could indulge openly in minor vices like smoking.

One of the earliest and most influential literary advocates of the liberation of middle-class women (the feminist movement itself will be discussed in Chapter 8) was the Norwegian playwright Henrik Ibsen (1828–1906), especially in *A Doll's House* (1879). Until the last scene of this play Nora Helmer tries to cling to her Doll's House standards and values, which define her role as a loving, cheerful, cajoling wife and mother. Earlier in her marriage she had borrowed money from the unscrupulous Krogstad and forged her dying father's signature on the I.O.U.s in order to restore her husband Torvald's health by sending him to Capri. Now Krogstad's blackmail threatens to expose her unless Torvald takes him on as a business associate. Nora, expecting Torvald to insist on shouldering her burden, lets him read Krogstad's fatal letter and plans to drown herself to prevent this sacrifice. Instead, Torvald abuses her for ruining his new position as manager of the local bank. Then another letter from Krogstad arrives returning her I.O.U.s (thanks to the intervention of an old female friend of Nora). But Torvald, again thinking only of himself, cries: "I am saved! Nora, I am saved." Numbly realizing that her life has been an elaborate make-believe, Nora becomes transformed by a new self-awareness and tells Torvald that she is leaving him. The fortuitous return of her forged I.O.U.s no longer means anything to her; she sees that the real crime is the male conspiracy to debase the female. Both her father and her husband, she declares, had treated her as a doll-child. As she walks out the door she assumes the stance of a liberated woman, releasing her husband from his obligations to her and renouncing her duties as a mother, since these mean bringing up her own children as if they too were dolls. She knows that the outside world will be hostile to her, but she is determined to educate herself and find some dignity as an independent person.

Today these notions seem like something out of an unliberated woman's magazine, but in the late nineteenth century they were truly radical. *A Doll's House* and Ibsen's other plays were performed in avantgarde theaters in the major cities of Europe as open attacks on bourgeois hypocrisy and sexual repression. It would be difficult to demonstrate a direct connection between these plays and the changed behavior of some middle-class Europeans in the twentieth century, but they certainly expressed the new attitudes that prompted this change.

The German playwright Frank Wedekind (1864–1918) was far more daring and pungent than Ibsen in his assaults on the hypocritical bourgeois conventions that repressed the sexual instincts of teen-agers. He glorified physical vitality and advocated full sexual freedom for all members of society. His play *The Awakening of Spring*, published in 1891 and first performed in 1906, examines the sexual problems of puberty with unprecedented candor. Melchior and Wendla fall in love and consummate their passion in a hayloft. When Wendla becomes pregnant her parents force an abortion on her and she dies from it. In the concluding scene Melchior is standing at her grave when the ghost of a school friend who has killed himself after failing an examination appears and tempts him to commit suicide too. But Melchior is saved by a Masked Gentleman in top hat and tails who persuades him that life is a better alternative.

In this play Wedekind uses Expressionist techniques (see Chapter 10) to heighten his attack on the German school system and the society that produced it. While the innocence of the young people is emphasized by the lyrical quality of their language, the language and behavior of the schoolteachers are imbecilic. At a crucial meeting in which they are to decide Melchior's fate they spend most of their time arguing about whether the window should be open or shut. Wedekind shows how the school system is rooted in the tyrannical authority of the father and how its hypocritical puritanism and moral cowardice are grotesque distortions of that authority. The very names of the teachers—Flydeath (Fliegentod), Tonguelash (Zungenschlag), Hungerbelt (Hungergurt)—make them travesties, soulless automata in a world deliberately portrayed out of focus.

Homosexuals had far greater difficulty in freeing themselves from traditional moral standards than heterosexual women and adolescents. André Gide first insinuated homosexual longings in his novel *The Immoralist* in 1902. But only twenty-seven years later did he publish his autobiographical *If It Die*, which acknowledged the experiences of his first novel's hero in Algeria as his own—including a couple in the company of

Oscar Wilde. Edward Carpenter, like Ellis, wanted to liberate sexual behavior from social definitions. ("There is no rule except that of Love.") An avowed homosexual himself, Carpenter openly defended the right of his kind to follow their sexual orientation without fear of social and legal repression. In 1896 the Manchester Labour Press published his book *Love's Coming-of-Age,* and by 1914 other editions were to sell 50,000 copies and be translated into several languages. But the Oscar Wilde scandal in 1895 set back Carpenter's efforts for at least a decade, outside of a small socialist circle.

The reactions to this scandal illustrate the hypocrisy of the upper class and the conservatism of middle- and lower-class attitudes toward nonconformist behavior. In 1895 Wilde was tried and imprisoned because of the public exposure of his relationship with Lord Alfred Douglas by the latter's father, the Marquess of Queensbury. Until then this gifted playwright and darling of London Society had been forgiven his eccentricities of dress and his flamboyant aestheticism and praised for his wit, which could dismiss traditional moral standards with remarks like "There is no sin except stupidity." However, once Wilde was publicly identified as a homosexual, Society abandoned him. In its eyes, his unpardonable "sin" was not so much his sexual inclinations as his "stupidity" in getting caught. In England, as in other parts of Europe, many upper-class people tolerated deviant behavior in private as long as the rest of society, which was intolerant, could not point to examples of it among their own. It was, after all, the tradesmen, clerks, and cabdrivers who were the most scornful of Wilde's behavior when it was publicized in the press and the law courts.

The most active movement for homosexual liberation was in Germany, though it too received a major setback because of a scandal in high places. Led by Magnus Hirschfeld, a university professor of sexology, the Scientific-Humanitarian Committee campaigned vigorously for the removal of legal penalties against homosexuals. Hirschfeld also published a *Yearbook for Intersexual Variants* for a small number of doctors and jurists and a *Journal of Sexology,* in which both Sigmund Freud and Alfred Adler published articles in 1908. But by that time Hirschfeld's cause was gravely compromised by the publicity given to a trial in which Count Kuno von Moltke was suing Maximilian Harden, editor of the left-wing liberal review *Die Zukunft* (The Future), for libel. Harden had unmasked Moltke, Prince Philip zu Eulenburg, and several other members of the Kaiser's inner circle as homosexuals as an indirect way of attacking the autocratic regime itself. (Needless to say, the regime survived the scandal by relegating the exposed victims to obscurity.) Hirschfeld himself testified in court that, in his expert opinion, Moltke was homosexual, thus allowing his integrity as a scientist to override his commitment to homosexual civil rights. More significant, however, was the willingness of highly educated middle-class "liberals" like Harden to use the homosexuality of people they disliked as a means of ruining them.

In Germany, as in England, a number of socialist leaders defended the movement for homosexual liberation against the hypocrisy of these liberals. On January 13, 1898, in a speech in the Reichstag, August Bebel, the head of the German Socialist Party, supported the petition of the Scientific-Humanitarian Committee for reform of the section of the penal code that made homosexual acts a crime. Bebel argued that the law was hypocritical in assuming that homosexuality was restricted to a small number of antisocial monsters. He insisted that there were thousands of otherwise law-abiding homosexuals in all social classes. When challenged on this point by other deputies, Bebel asserted that if the state prosecuted all known violators "it would have to build two new penitentiaries . . . in Berlin alone."[41] The authorities themselves were well aware of the situation, and the Berlin police tolerated the existence of almost forty taverns and cabarets catering exclusively to homosexuals.

"Revelations" concerning both male and female homosexuality enjoyed a certain vogue among self-righteous people in all classes during our period. Until then such people had considered the subject taboo, but they now made homosexuals the scapegoats—along with criminals and prostitutes—of their indignation against their perception of the New Morality. In his book *La Corruption fin de siècle* (1891) the sensation-mongering journalist Léo Taxil fascinated his readers with his exposés of Lesbianism among Paris society ladies. He named their meeting places and told how a devotee of Sapphic love could be recognized by "the magnificent, curled, bedecked, prettified and sometimes even beribboned poodle which accompanies her on her outings" on the Champs-Élysées or on a certain path in the Bois de Boulogne. In May 1913 the Viennese public was shocked to read in its newspapers that Alfred Redl, a high official in Army Intelligence, had been selling information to Russia in order to pay for his expensive life style and that of his current male lover. Even more threatening than Redl's treason and homosexual activities was the realization that such a man had been able to succeed in both endeavors by assuming the mask of the ideal officer and by keeping up the proper appearances in his public behavior.

Degeneration! That was the title and judgment of Max Nordau's widely read book on the New Morality. Originally published in German in 1893, *Degeneration* was quickly translated into many languages and went through several editions during the next two decades. In it Nordau, a skillful journalist and one of the founders of the Zionist movement, abandoned the traditional belief that people who behaved immorally were evil and adopted the modern "liberal" diagnosis that they were sick.

The thesis of Nordau's book is that the moral and mental degeneration it catalogues in over 550 pages was the direct result of physical degeneration. Nordau documents his arguments with footnote references to medical doctors and psychiatrists and dedicates his work to Cesare Lombroso, Professor of Psychiatry and Forensic Medicine at the University of Turin. He begins by defining the New Morality of the *fin-de-siècle* as "a practical emancipation from traditional discipline, which is theoretically still in force."[42] Although he notes that the pace and pressures of modern urban life were causing physical degeneration among all classes, he insists that the malady he is concerned with was most rampant among rich educated people. Then he devotes the bulk of his book to exposing the intellectuals and artists whom these degenerates lionized as the champions of the New Morality: the French Decadents and Symbolists, Richard Wagner, Leo Tolstoy beginning with his *Kreutzer Sonata* (1889), Joris-Karl Huysmans, Oscar Wilde, Henrik Ibsen, Friedrich Nietzsche, etc. According to Nordau, these "antisocial beings" were as physically and morally degenerate as Lombroso's "born criminals." The only difference was that "the former content themselves with dreaming and writing, while the latter have the resolution and strength to act."[43]

Nordau directs some of his sharpest barbs at Ibsen and Nietzsche and their admirers. He chastizes Ibsen for advocating sexual freedom for married women in a society in which marriage was still the main institution that protected them from philandering husbands who might otherwise desert them and their children. Only hysterical women and masculine masochists could find any sense in Ibsen's New Morality, but unfortunately their numbers were increasing among the upper classes in the 1890's. Just as their "ego-mania" found its poet in Ibsen, so it found its philosopher in Nietzsche, the most monstrous enemy of traditional morality in all its dimensions. And while Ibsen, according to Nordau, was clinically a masochist, Nietzsche was a sadist and mad in every sense of the word.

> From the first to the last page of Nietzsche's writings the careful reader seems to hear a madman, with flashing eyes, wild gestures, and foaming mouth, spouting forth deafening bombast. . . . So far as any

meaning at all can be extracted from the endless stream of phrases, it shows, as its fundamental elements, a series of constantly reiterated delirious ideas, having their source in illusions of sense and diseased organic processes.[44]

Nordau accuses Nietzsche of sanctioning the most barbarous crimes in the name of fostering individual self-expression and flouting allegedly false values. In the popular mind this was what Nietzsche continued to stand for until the middle of this century. (See Chapter 7 on the "real" Nietzsche.)

Traditional religious beliefs and norms lost much of their influence on behavior in the modernizing societies of Europe. The majority of Europeans still considered themselves Christians out of conformity or habit, but most urban workers rejected the authority of the churches. Individuals in all social classes expressed their wish to be free in challenges to traditional moral constraints and in a heightened sexual awareness. Some moralists viewed these responses as signs of alienation from all values and norms; others saw them as fulfillments of the liberating promise of modernization. Before 1914 only a few critical thinkers (see Chapter 7) saw the ultimate paradox of modernization, which encourages us to think for ourselves and be ourselves while at the same time forcing us into new kinds of regimentation and conformity. But there were already signs of this paradox in the popular culture of the prewar decades.

CHAPTER 6

POPULAR CULTURE

The new media of popular culture combined lip-service to the conventional morality of the time with an outlook that was secular, materialistic, and naïvely empirical. We have seen how this modern-minded middle-class mentality was fostered in the state schools, including those that gave perfunctory instruction in traditional religion and morals. Widely read novels such as Mrs. Henry Wood's *East Lynne* still alluded to divine Providence, but most popular fiction written after 1890 ignored it. So did mass-circulation newspapers, magazines, and motion pictures—except for an occasional epic such as *Quo vadis?* Advertising campaigns and department store window displays stressed products that could be seen, touched, and consumed right now, with the clear implication that tomorrow they might be out of date. Although the middle classes still deferred some kinds of gratification and saved for a rainy day, they became increasingly willing to spend money on recreation, amusement, and newly fashionable goods and services. The mass media encouraged this "consumerism" in the lower classes as well.

These media also fostered the naïve notion that "I read it in the newspaper" (or, later on, "I saw it on television") gives one a perception based on a firsthand experience. Traditional arts and crafts had provided a limited number of stylized perceptions of things beyond daily experience, but in modern society the mass media bombard people with secondhand images and ideas of everything under the sun. Unlike artistic imagery—which evokes inner feelings—or critical thought—which looks for underlying functions and processes—the perceptions derived from the mass media are literally superficial. Newspaper coverage of the travels of royalty and government leaders does not explain international relations. And photographs of train wrecks, natural disasters, and military battles are just that; they tell us something about what these events "look like" without involving us in them in any way.

As popular culture became increasingly mass produced and designed to appeal to a mass public, the perceptions it purveyed were not only secondhand but ready-made as well. The mass culture of the pre-1914 period was still a long way from foisting nonplaces like Marlboro Country, nonpersons like The Bloomingdale Man, and nonevents like the contract negotiations of sports stars. But it was already producing "programmed" novels of adventure and romance, hit songs with prepackaged sentimentality, and the formula comedy and glamour of the variety theater—all of which are still with us in today's electronic media. Spectator sports were becoming a major item of mass consumption, though they still meant different things to different social classes. Early phonograph records of Enrico Caruso singing operatic arias brought into the home a version of "culture" that had none of the impact of a live performance of the opera itself. Early motion pictures emphasized photographic glimpses of outer reality in a way never before possible, giving the viewer canned images of that reality and its marvels. "Programmed" learning and visual aids came to children in the form of picture postcards and the card series that became part of the packaging of cigarettes before 1914 and breakfast cereals and bubble gum later in the century.

GOING OUT FOR A GOOD TIME

In the big cities more and more people sought recreation and entertainment in a growing number and variety of public places. The formerly thrifty and prudish middle classes no longer considered it frivolous or wicked to spend money in this way; the younger generation of workers also found more places to go than their parents had. People from all classes frequented bars, gambling places, theaters, sporting events, parks, and brothels. But each class had its "suitable" grades and varieties of such facilities, or at least separate sections in the same one.

Before 1914 the middle classes still considered the movies too plebeian for their taste, but the growing number of these people who now went to the "legitimate" theater and the opera wanted lighter entertainment than these genres had traditionally provided. Cultivated bourgeois considered Richard Strauss the most important new opera composer (see Chapter 10), but Giacomo Puccini was more popular not only because his music was more accessible but also because the structure of feeling in his operas was closer to that of the less cultivated middle and lower-middle classes. (Unlike Elektra and Salome—haughty princesses who willfully brought about their own downfalls—Tosca, Mimi, and Cio-Cio-San could be perceived as poor dears who became the unwilling victims of injustice, prejudice, or their own sentimentality.) In the theater, tragedy—except when performed by superstars such as Sarah Bernhardt or Eleonora Duse—was far less popular than drawing-room comedy or farce. In the guise of spoofs Georges Feydeau's plays allowed middle-class audiences to be titillated by the forbidden delights of adultery without feeling guilty. Franz Lehár's *The Merry Widow* (1905) and other new operettas also used the spoof increasingly to meet the demand for this kind of gratification.

In the early 1900's middle-class people also frequented hotels and resort areas more than their parents had, thus spurring a great expansion in the number of these facilities. Dining and dancing at London's luxurious new Piccadilly Hotel, the Ritz in Paris, or the Adlon in Berlin became the height of fashion for newly rich commoners. And some ordinary middle-class families in big cities were beginning to celebrate Christmas and other holidays in tourist hotels. Seaside resorts and "fun cities" like Paris and Venice also attracted increasing numbers of middle-class visitors from abroad.

Although a few English seaside resorts were beginning to attract a working-class clientele, for many workers the shortest way out of Manchester (or Essen, St. Étienne, and Genoa) was getting drunk. Drunks on the streets were still a major problem in working-class districts, but the number of arrests for drunkenness continued to decline: from 98,482 in 1875 to 52,025 in 1906 in France and from 207,000 in 1905 to 162,000 in 1910 in England and Wales.[1] The proportion of workers who drank remained the same, but in the maturing industrial countries

Scarborough, England, with the Grand Hotel in the background.

their per capita consumption of alcohol declined. Unlike their predecessors during the early stage of industrialization the majority of these
workers drank to be sociable rather than to drown their sorrows.

Social drinking in taverns was the principal form of recreation for
married working-class men well into the twentieth century.[2] Before the
advent of radio and television there was little to keep them at home, and
before 1914 few of them thought of going anywhere else for an evening's
relaxation. Unmarried workingmen sometimes took their sweethearts to
music halls, variety theaters, and the movies. But married workingmen
rarely took their wives anywhere, except on an occasional Sunday outing.
In Britain they began to attend soccer and cricket matches with their
cronies on Saturday afternoons, and Sunday afternoon sporting events
were beginning to attract the better-paid Continental workers in the
early 1900's. Nevertheless the tavern remained the habitual recreational
and social center for male workers from day to day. "Tables for ladies"
notwithstanding, it was a refuge from their families—a place where they
could speak freely about whatever they pleased, flirt with the barmaids,
engage in good-natured kidding and horseplay, and leave with a warm
glow inside them.

Like the hotel for the middle classes, the tavern for the working class
was a place where one could do things one would not do at home in a
setting close enough to one's familiar surroundings so that one did not
have to worry about unpredictable consequences resulting from unfamiliar behavior patterns. But some people liked to venture into more novel
settings for greater excitement. They could go to the dance halls and
cafés-concerts of Montmartre or to amusement parks like the Prater in
Vienna, which had the largest Ferris wheel and roller coaster in Europe.
On the rides, in the fun house, and at the shooting galleries one was still a
participant, but in an obviously artificial world. The circus provided
purely vicarious thrills in an even more exotic setting.

In Germany the Busch circus featured a water extravaganza starring
Wasserminna (Water Minnie). Mounted on horseback, she jumped from
a great height down a waterfall into a pool.[3] This uncomplicated, exciting spectacle continued to attract a heterogeneous audience into the early
1890's. Thereafter, however, variety theaters became more popular in
Germany, not only because circuses ran out of sensational new acts but
also because people could smoke in variety theaters and music halls.*

* After 1900 cigarette smoking increased dramatically among all classes everywhere and was fast becoming one of the commonest small pleasures in
modern society. For women and boys it was a more acceptable symbol of liberation than drinking; even working-class men cut down their consumption of

The "8 Germania Girls" in their first appearance at the Wintergarten Theatre (Berlin) in early 1914.

Variety became the key word in show business at the turn of the century. The most famous variety theater in Berlin, the Wintergarten, had music, acrobats, clowns, and magicians, as well as cabaret and operetta artistes and Parisian chorus girls. Its dancing stars included La Belle Otero, Mata Hari, and the Australian Saharet. The "uncultivated" middle classes sat at tables for six marks a seat, while the shop assistants and office clerks filled the one-mark seats in the auditorium, where evening dress was optional.

People went to the variety theater (including the music hall, the revue, and vaudeville) to laugh and to forget their daily cares. At the Wintergarten the singer-comic Otto Reutters had his audience rolling under the tables with laughter when he did a skit in which he comes home late at night and sings in a drunken voice:

---

alcohol in order to pay for cigarettes. The role of the cigarette in modern life —the attitudes, rituals, and promotional campaigns connected with it—awaits its social historian.

A man stands by my dresser—
He says: You! Give me a hand!
This thing is too heavy for me alone . . .
I won't be surprised by anything anymore.[4]

One of Reutters' most popular songs was a series of couplets about life's little cares and woes—a lost lover, a trip to the dentist, etc.—each followed by the refrain: "in 50 years everything is over and done with" (*"in fünfzig Jahren ist alles vorbei"*). This "look for the silver lining" theme was the universal message of the world of entertainment.

The medium of the variety theater was itself a message: Variety is the spice of life. English music-hall audiences laughed and cheered as Charles Coborn sang about the man who broke the bank at Monte Carlo and expressed mock sympathy as Vesta Victoria sang of the bride left waiting at the church. The turn of the century was the heyday of the English music hall; there were fifty-seven in London alone. Unlike the fashionable variety theaters, most music halls catered to "the masses"; the seats were cheaper, dress was more informal, and the performers encouraged the audience to respond more demonstratively to their antics and to sing the choruses of their songs with them. A large part of the comic effect of certain songs was conveyed by the gesticulations and deportment of the performers. The stage policeman was a stock butt of hostile jokes in lower-class music halls. For working-class youths the main attraction was often

> the "get up" and general whimsicality of the artist, and still more the conjurer, gymnast, or some extraordinary genius who is both an acrobat and a musician combined. Sandow, for instance will crowd a hall, and the lads come away filled with a desire to strengthen their own bodies and muscles.[5]

More than any other medium popular songs "packaged" the feelings of the modern urban masses. Unlike folk songs these "hits" were not rooted in the experience of a particular social group. Instead they deliberately catered to purely personal sentiments, thus encouraging the most pervasive of all responses to modernization: *privatization.* Every country had its sentimental love songs whose main theme was: As long as you and I are true to one another the rest of the world does not matter. But the French "blues" described more realistically the plight of the lower-class woman: Life is hard, so be grateful for any kind of love, no matter how bad the man is. And the following stanzas from two typical songs expressed the irony and insolence of which Berliners were so proud:

Think, think
Berliner lad
Think that I love you
When I am dancing with you.

Mom, the coal man is here!
Kid, shut up, I see him already.
I have no money, you have no money,
Who sent for the coal man?

The Viennese, on the other hand, preferred nostalgic songs that made their city the setting of their dreams—as in *"Wien, Du Stadt meiner Träume."* Just as mawkish, but of a different order, was the nostalgia expressed in the English hit "If Those Lips Could Only Speak":

If those lips could only speak,
If those eyes could only see,
If those beautiful golden tresses
Were there in reality.

Could I only take your hand
As I did when you took my name,
But it's only a beautiful picture
In a beautiful golden frame.

The appearance of two modern types—the celebrity and the fan—indicated the growing importance of popular entertainment in ordinary people's lives. Before the 1890's a few outstanding performers in the theater, the opera, and the circus had gained fame and adulation within limited circles of *cognoscenti*, and Jenny Lind, the Swedish Nightingale, had admirers on both sides of the Atlantic. But these performers were esteemed for their talents, not their images. It was the music hall and the cabaret that attracted the first fans of stars such as Marie Lloyd in London, Yvette Guilbert in Paris, and Cläre Waldoff in Berlin. Their appeal was not the quality of their singing voices but rather their stage personalities and the points of view they expressed. When, for example, Marie Lloyd sang "A Little of What You Fancy Does You Good," her whole manner invited her audience to adopt this permissive attitude. Her fans became interested in her behavior offstage, her views on current events, and her taste in clothes and men.

An early example of the performer as public personality was the comedian Alexander Girardi, who, from about 1870 to 1910, "paraded the image of the typical Viennese through the town, on and off the stage."[6] People of all classes delighted in his song, delivered in dialect, about the

Marie Lloyd.

Fiaker (horse-drawn taxi driver) who boasted that he did his job better than cabdrivers in other great cities because he was a true-born Viennese. Girardi also gave his personal stamp to the character parts he played, such as the pig breeder Zsupan in Johann Strauss's operetta *The Gypsy Baron*, one of his most copied triumphs. A whole generation of celebrity-conscious young Viennese walked in a certain way, struck certain poses, and repeated certain phrases because Girardi had done it that way. He was especially popular among the lower-middle classes because he seemed to personify their ideal image of themselves as witty, good-natured, easygoing citizens of the most *gemütlich* city in the world.

Whereas the fan delighted in seeing his attitudes glorified in a familiar setting, another modern type, the tourist, confirmed his belief in the superiority of his own culture while amusing himself among "foreigners." In the early 1900's a wealthy Englishman could

> proceed abroad to foreign quarters, without knowledge of their religion, language or customs, bearing coined wealth upon his person, and would consider himself greatly aggrieved and much surprised at the least interference. But, most important of all, he regarded this state of affairs as normal, certain, and permanent, except in the direction of further improvement, and any deviation from it as aberrant, scandalous, and avoidable.[7]

The Cook's tour made this kind of travel possible for people who did not have their own servants to smooth the way. Wherever the tour went there were guides who spoke one's language, explained the "quaint" native customs, and showed the men where to dally and the ladies where to shop. One also had oneself photographed with the Eiffel Tower, the Coliseum, and the Parthenon as backdrops for one's own presence. Unlike the true traveler, who tried to understand the local people on their own terms, the tourist treated them as "foreigners" whose only function was to cater to his wishes.

The tourist mentality was not restricted to the small number of people who traveled abroad. In the *belle époque* Paris Society discovered the joys of slumming among the cabarets and dance halls of Montmartre; at the Moulin Rouge they could watch La Goulue do her notorious version of the *chahut*, a frenzied dance whose high kicks and "splits" freely displayed the performer's animal spirits and underclothes. One could respond to anything that was foreign to one's own culture or subculture with the tourist mentality—like the Victorian lady-in-waiting who commented to her companion after a performance of Shakespeare's *Antony*

Alexander Girardi in the role of Valentin in Raimund's *Der Verschwender* (*The Big Spender*).

and Cleopatra: "How very different from the home life of our own dear Queen!" By our period this mentality expressed itself in another way among the middle and lower-middle classes when they visited museums or used artifacts from other times and cultures to decorate their homes. When one does this sort of thing one is always oneself while consciously consuming something alien on one's own terms. In other words, one domesticates something that is foreign to one's day-to-day experience by perceiving it and using it as something whose very foreignness is at one's disposal.

The *chahut*, in a Montmartre night club in the 1890's.

SPECTATOR SPORTS

By the early 1900's spectator sports were becoming another form of commercialized entertainment that provided vicarious thrills and excitement. The concepts of sport and sportsmanship originated in England and spread to the modernizing Continental countries in the late nineteenth century. Continental aristocrats had developed horsemanship and hunting on their own, but they borrowed athletic sports from the English aristocracy. Our main concern, however, is the development of sporting events for mass audiences as an example of modern popular culture. This development also began in England and spread from there, but sports continued to mean different things to different social groups in Western and Central Europe right up to the war.

The most obvious example of a sport that meant different things to different social groups was horse racing. It had originated in England in the eighteenth century among aristocrats and it was the "sport of kings" as well under Edward VII and his successors, who regularly attended the

The segregation of the upper and lower classes at the Ascot Race Track, England, 1907.

great races to see their own horses run. Whereas aristocrats and kings were primarily interested in thoroughbred racing as a sport, the lower classes were almost exclusively interested in it as an opportunity for gambling. Some English workers would back only King Edward's, Lord Derby's, or Lord Rosebery's horses—"winning, they felt for a brief moment a glow of unity with the greatest in the land."[8] But most lower-class racing fans thought of betting on horses as the only way, other than stealing, to get money without earning it. By the 1890's they flocked to the race tracks in England and France, but even more of them placed their bets with bookmakers in their own neighborhoods. These lower-class gamblers also became a mass market for a press specializing in information about past performances, tips, and racing results. Much to the disgust of socialist and union leaders, some workers spent most of their free time reading their racing forms and handicap books.

Outside of France the majority of Continental horse-racing fans was middle-class. Harness racing was popular with all classes in Austria by the turn of the century, but horse racing, like most English sports, came to Germany later. Although in 1913 many new tracks opened in Germany, the grandstands were still small, and there was no open standing area for lower-class spectators, as there was in France and Italy.

In the early 1900's the most popular lower-class spectator sport on the Continent was bicycle racing. The biggest long-distance races in France and Italy were becoming national events and attracting the sponsorship of certain newspapers and commercial advertisers. In Paris, Berlin, and Milan there were also huge indoor arenas where thousands of spectators watched six-day bicycle races. Not only was the bicycle more plebeian than the thoroughbred horse but the riders were also more clearly working-class than the jockeys. Consequently the spectators felt a special affinity for the heroes of six-day bicycle races as they watched them compete. Another reason for the popularity of this sport among lower-class spectators was the fact that they themselves rode bikes. To be sure, the bicycle was primarily a means of transportation, but bicycle-riding was also the only active sport for tens of millions of Europeans, especially in Italy, the Netherlands, Belgium, Denmark, and northern France.

Except in the United Kingdom, active participation in most sports was still largely limited to aristocrats and middle-class boys and young men. By the time the middle- or working-class man had the beginnings of a family he had neither the time nor the energy left for participation in sports. And, although highland games in Scotland and hurling in Ireland were popular among simple country people, most European peasants

Program for the opening of the first bicycle-racing arena in Turin, Italy, 1894.

and farmers showed no interest in any kind of sports. Thus, aside from upper-class hunters and fishermen, participation in sports was an urban phenomenon, and only in England did it attract working-class lads. In most northern English cities they began playing soccer at the age of eight or ten. And as teen-agers they raced through the streets on Saturdays in their running pants and thin vests, to the consternation of many pedestrians and of lovers in the quieter byways.[9]

Different classes of people perceived the meaning of sport and sportsmanship differently. On their neighborhood soccer teams working-class Manchester lads played rougher than public-school boys and without their *esprit de corps;* they felt no loyalty to their teams and often deserted them during losing streaks.[10] To upper-class adults sport still meant primarily horsemanship, hunting, shooting, and fishing, and these were the only kinds covered in a book called *Sport in Europe,* published in 1901. By the immediate prewar years the expensive German illustrated weekly magazine, *Sport im Bild,* also stressed these traditional sports, along with newer ones like tennis and skiing; the only spectator sports it covered were horse racing and soccer, which had no working-class fans in Germany before 1914. In France most athletic sports remained the preserve of upper-class teen-agers until after the war.[11] Although Pierre de Coubertin, the "father" of the modern Olympic Games, wanted to bring sports to French workers, in the 1890's "the very idea of sporting activities for the common people evoked laughter when raised in a municipal council."[12] What could they know of sportsmanship? The Duchesse de Clermont-Tonnerre, commenting on some noisy working-class rowers on a lake outside Paris on the eve of the war, declared: "True sport is noiseless."[13]

But the development of spectator sports into commercialized entertainment altered the traditional meanings of sport and sportsmanship. Today the mass-media image of the athlete is someone from a poor family who earns a lot of money playing on a big-league team, reaches his peak around age thirty, and then earns even more money endorsing deodorants, beverages, and colognes. (He also tends to have a big head and a loud mouth.) He is entirely different from the well-born teen-age amateurs who first played football (soccer)* while their schoolmates, teachers, relatives, and friends watched. This game originated in mid-

---

* To most Europeans football meant what North Americans call soccer (derived from Assoc.—the abbreviation of Association Football in England), but in the English Midlands, Ireland, and especially Wales it could also mean rugby. To avoid confusion, the word soccer will be used in the text hereafter.

Victorian England as an activity for socializing young gentlemen and as a safety valve for their youthful high spirits and repressed sexual drives; by the 1890's it was spreading to the exclusive secondary schools and colleges in France. But in England it had already "gone public" in 1867 with the founding of the Football Association, and in 1888 the professional clubs broke away and formed the Football League. The working-class supported professional soccer teams in the Midlands, and the north quickly outclassed the amateur, middle-class supported clubs of the south; until the end of the century no southern team reached the cup final. So popular had the game become by then that 110,820 spectators, including many workers from the north, attended the Crystal Palace final in London in 1901.

By the turn of the century professional soccer games were providing millions of British workers with an exciting form of Saturday afternoon entertainment that allowed them to release emotions pent up by their drab urban lives.

> The Edwardian football follower regarded booing of players or referee as his right. . . . Yet the players of the time recall crowds as generous and essentially good mannered: certainly their reactions included nothing so studiedly cruel as the slow handclap of later years. Perhaps the fairest and clearest definition of these very masculine hordes is that they were supporters rather than spectators. Many of them had watched their local clubs grow up from waste-land play to the heights of success and they felt themselves passionately involved in the fortunes of their team.[14]

To heighten their emotional involvement, they often made bets on the outcome of a game.

Since soccer was still a sport, both the spectators and the players accepted the upper- and middle-class values of athletic prowess, teamwork, and fair play, but they interpreted them in their own way. Though less brutal than rugby or American football, a professional soccer match was also perceived as a kind of simulated battle. Thus, contrary to the public-school ideal, winning was felt to be more important than sportsmanship. Just as the spectators recognized the necessity of moral inhibitions in their interpersonal relations they also accepted the need for a referee to keep the competition in the game from getting out of hand. But subconsciously some working-class fans began to perceive him as a partisan, fallible, and possibly corrupt representative of bourgeois law and order. (This perception was to become more widespread on the Continent later in the twentieth century.) The players had a more conscious grievance against the established order after their union, founded in 1908, was denied official approval when it affiliated with the Federation of Trades Unions. Their work was far more fulfilling than that of most people in their class, but even the biggest stars earned modest incomes and faced uncertain futures once they could no longer play.

By 1914 professional soccer was becoming popular in several Continental countries. In Italy a number of today's major teams—Genoa, Turin, Milan, Juventus, Pro Vercelli—were established between 1898 and 1913. At first many of the players on these teams were from England, Switzerland, and Austria-Hungary, but after 1908 they were mostly Italians. Belgium, France, and Sweden also had professional teams, and the first international competition was held on May 15, 1910, in Milan. Before the war only in Italy were the crowds anywhere near as large as in England, but after 1919 Sunday afternoon soccer matches were to become the number one spectator sport in most of Western Europe.

The Germans showed little interest in team sports; both in and out of school they remained faithful to their own form of athletics, called *Turn*. This term has no English equivalent but includes what we call gymnastics and group calisthenics. Like English public-school sports, *Turn* was used to socialize young people, though it was not restricted to the upper and middle classes. *Turn* was also used as a public spectacle. Today we associate mass calisthenics performed in front of an audience with "totalitarian" regimes, but this kind of spectacle originated in Germany in 1860. The twelfth German *Turnfest*, held in the Leipzig stadium in July 1913, involved 17,000 participants and a crowd three times as large. An outsider finds it difficult to think of this sort of thing as entertainment, but it certainly was a form of popular culture.

Spain's national spectator sport, bullfighting (*corrida*), was older and more ritualized than most others, but it served similar functions. It provided vicarious thrills and excitement for tens of thousands of fans on Sunday afternoons in every major city. By stressing the bravery of the performers it also reinforced the process of socialization in which all Spaniards were taught that a coward is not a man. There had been famous matadors in the past, but by 1913 the twenty-one-year-old Juan Belmonte was gaining unprecedented popularity with his new approach to the role. He shifted the emphasis from killing the bull to mastering it and dominating it through the skillful use of the red cloth (*muleta*) and cape. "Playing" with the bull in this way made the matador more of an athlete than a gladiator. Although his performance still ended with the

The 1913 *Turnfest* at Leipzig, Germany, from *Sport in Bild*.

death of the bull, the crowds became more interested in cheering his various passes and identifying themselves with this aspect of his prowess. It should also be noted that bullfighting was more truly a *national* spectator sport than any other one in any other country. This was a remarkable phenomenon in view of the intensity of class and regional antagonisms in Spain.

POPULAR FICTION

Each class, each age group, and each sex had its own genres of popular fiction. Grown men read less escapist fiction than women and children, though the mystery-thriller was beginning to attract them. Middle-class women had been reading sentimental novels about "true romance" among the well-born since the middle of the nineteenth century (Emma Bovary had been an avid reader of novels such as *Amélie de Mansfield* and *Les Aventures d'une grande dame*), and by the 1890's this kind of women's fiction gained a mass audience among teen-age girls and working-class women. Middle-class boys devoured adventure stories, such as those of the German Karl May about the North American West featuring "The Redskin Gentleman" (an Apache Indian with the unlikely name of Winnetou), the Italian Emilio Salgari's tales of sixteenth-century pirates and freebooting soldiers, and the Frenchman Michel Zévaco's "*romans héroïques*." English working-class boys preferred comic books and the tales of reckless and impossible daring, bloodshed, successful thieving, and ridiculous adventure in the "penny bloods," but by the immediate prewar years some of them also became addicted to Frank Richards's magazine stories about the adventures of five well-born youths at a fictional public school called Greyfriars.

In his study *The Classic Slum*, Robert Roberts says that working-class boys in Manchester's Salford district tried, not very successfully, to emulate "the Famous Five" at Greyfriars.

> Greyfriars gave us one moral code, life another, and a fine muddle we made of it all. . . . It came as a curious shock to one who revered the Old School when it dawned upon him that he himself was a typical sample of the "low cads" so despised by all at Greyfriars. Class consciousness had broken through at last. Over the years these simple tales conditioned the thought of a whole generation of boys. The public school ethos, distorted into myth and sold among us weekly in penny numbers, for good or ill, set ideals and standards.[15.]

The "realistic" literary works of Spielhagen in Germany, Meredith in England, Zola in France, and Balzac and Tolstoy throughout Europe remained staple articles of consumption among middle-class adults. Although many of their readers were only interested in the stories and the emotions of the characters, these novels also reassured them that Literature still supported their familiar structure of feeling. In a world in which the ritual language of religion had lost most of its meaning Literature was still conceived as a code which signified something other than its content and its individual form. The signs and categories expressed in this code made Literature an institution capable of reinforcing the bourgeois mentality, which perceived individual heroes and heroines making responsible choices in an ordered world of "real life." In other words, the medium itself was this "message," regardless of any other messages the author meant to convey.

In Chapter 10 we shall see how this function of Literature disintegrated under the impact of modernization; here we are concerned with forms of popular fiction whose main purpose was to entertain the reader and offer him an escape from his mundane existence. Their authors receded into the background, often using pseudonyms, and replaced the ritual language of Literature with prefabricated clichés. Literary critics dismiss this kind of writing as "trash," and so it is from their point of view. But from our point of view escapist popular fiction is important because it fed the fantasies of its readers and helped to shape their perceptions.

Popular fiction for women certainly influenced their perceptions of the pitfalls of illicit love affairs and the virtues of marriage; a famous example was *East Lynne*. Written by Mrs. Henry Wood in 1861, this novel was originally published as a serial in the *New Monthly Magazine*. In book form it had sold over half a million copies in England by the end of the century and remained a best seller throughout the Edwardian period. As a play, it was still popular into the 1920's in both England and America. Mrs. Wood addressed her "tearjerker" specifically to "young ladies," but by the turn of the century it found special favor among women of all ages in the lower-middle and working classes. (Indeed this type of melodrama was to appeal to this audience in "true romance" magazines, movies, and radio and television "soap operas" until the more permissive attitudes of the middle of this century found their way into these media.)

The main plot of *East Lynne* concerns the sin, shame, and retribution of Lady Isabel, the only child of the Earl of Mount Severn, a peer of the realm. Reared for a life of luxury and leisure, she discovers at the age of eighteen that her father's death has left her penniless and homeless. Not only has he dissipated his income of sixty thousand pounds a year but he has also been forced to sell East Lynne, his palatial home, to a young local lawyer, Archibald Carlyle. Archibald saves Lady Isabel from her plight by marrying her and establishing her as the mistress of East Lynne. She does not love him but she respects him and bears him three children. Then she falls in love with a handsome but ignoble young acquaintance named Francis Levison. He plays on her unfounded suspicion that the reason Archibald is less attentive than he had been at first is that he loves another woman. But it is really her illicit passion that prompts Lady Isabel to run off with Francis to Grenoble, France. After less than a year Francis deserts her when he inherits a barony of his own, just a few weeks before she is to bear his child. Meanwhile Archibald divorces her and marries the woman whose business relations with him (actually concerned with the second plot of the novel) Lady Isabel had mistaken for amorous encounters.

So now Lady Isabel is twice fallen. Not only has she deserted her husband and children but she has also lost all possibility of being made an "honest woman" by her lover. A train wreck kills her new child and she

herself is reported as dead, though she is only disfigured. In order to earn
a living she becomes a governess on the Continent under the French name
of Madame Vine. Ten years later she hears that Archibald and his new
wife need a new governess and, disguising herself as best she can, she returns to East Lynne in that capacity. No one recognizes her except her
former maid, and she feels a certain contentment in being near her own
children and her former husband. But her oldest son dies of tuberculosis
(called "consumption" in the nineteenth century), and she contracts the
disease herself. Knowing that she too will die, she resolves to leave East
Lynne, but she delays too long. She cannot resist revealing her true identity to Archibald and asking for his forgiveness, and the tearful deathbed
scene between them ends the story.

East Lynne can be easily criticized on literary grounds, but the very
weaknesses of the novel helped account for its enormous success. Its melodrama, pathos, and lack of development in most of the characters were
just what its sentimental readers wanted. Lady Isabel's improbable behavior—particularly her desertion of Archibald for inadequate reasons
and her return incognito to East Lynne—allowed the reader to empathize
with her while at the same time condemning her. Although Mrs. Wood
keeps her story moving breathlessly along, her occasional asides directly
stimulate this response.

> Young lady, when he, who is soon to be your lord and master, pro-
> tests to you that he shall always be as ardent a lover as he is now, be-
> lieve him if you like, but don't reproach him when disappointment
> comes. He does not wilfully deceive you; he only forgets that it is in
> the constitution of man to change, the very essence of his nature.
> The time will arrive when his manner must settle down into a
> calmness, which to you, if you are of an exacting temperament, may
> look like indifference or coldness; but you will do well to put up
> with it, for it will never be otherwise.

Commenting on the early awakening of Lady Isabel's remorse—which is
to be expected "when a high-principled gentlewoman falls from her
pedestal"—Mrs. Wood says:

> O reader, believe me! Lady—wife—mother! should you ever be
> tempted to abandon your home, so will you awaken! Whatever trials
> may be the lot of your married life, though they may magnify them-
> selves to our crushed spirit as beyond the endurance of woman to
> bear, *resolve* to bear them; fall down upon your knees and pray to be
> enabled to bear them; pray for patience; pray for strength to resist

the demon that would urge you so to escape; bear unto death, rather than forfeit your fair name and your good conscience; for be assured that the alternative, if you rush on to it, will be found far worse than death!

The author's final "dialogue" with the reader hammers home the expected response toward Lady Isabel's "tragic" end.

She brought it upon herself! She ought not to have come back to East Lynne! groans our moralist again. Do I not say so? Of course she ought not. Neither ought she to have suffered her thoughts to stray in the manner they did towards Mr. Carlyle. She ought not to have done so; but she did. If we all did just as we "ought," this lower world would be worth living in. You must just sit down and abuse her, to calm your anger. I agree with you that she ought never to have returned; that it was an act little short of madness; but are you quite sure that you would have not done the same, under the facility and the temptation?

Here the moralizing is clearly an excuse for the secret titillation of the reader who puts herself in the fallen heroine's place while at the same time rejecting the idea that she could behave in a similar way. This kind of vicarious thrill was exactly what the new mass of compulsorily educated readers of both sexes wanted from popular fiction about victims and criminals as well as swashbuckling heroes and clever avengers. The fascination of this kind of fiction was heightened when there was an element of mystery in one of the principal protagonists.

Even more popular than *East Lynne*—and a good deal more "realistic" —was Mary Elizabeth Braddon's mystery-thriller *Lady Audley's Secret*. Published first in 1862 as a serial in the *Six-penny Magazine*, in book form it had sold one million copies by 1914. (As in the case of *East Lynne* the numerous dramatic versions were pale shadows of this book.) The title character is also a beautiful young lady, but unlike Lady Isabel, she was born a commoner and reared in poverty. She first appears under the name of Lucy Graham, a governess, and moves up in the world by marrying Sir Michael Audley, a rich country widower with a daughter almost her own age. Early in the story the reader begins to suspect Lady Audley of having murdered George Talboys, a friend of Sir Michael's nephew Robert Audley. But this is not her secret, which only comes out toward the end as a result of Robert's efforts to solve the mystery of his friend's unaccountable disappearance. Since the plot and motivations can still appeal to today's reader it would spoil his or her pleasure to divulge Lady

Audley's real secret here. But her behavior is both more wicked and more plausible than Lady Isabel's. And Robert Audley's role as amateur detective set a standard for the modern mystery story.

In addition to the continuing large sales of their books Mrs. Wood and Miss Braddon were the "queens of the circulating libraries." A 1907 survey of twenty-one of the largest public libraries in England showed that they had an aggregate of 2,296 copies of Miss Braddon's eighty novels with an average per library of 109; the figures for Mrs. Wood's forty novels were 1,903 and 91.[16]

The most popular women's fiction written before the war was more manipulative and more frankly escapist than *East Lynne* or *Lady Audley's Secret*. In France it was mass produced for the series popularly called the Bibliothèque Rose and in England by writers like Elinor Glyn and Rita (Eliza Humphreys). Even in "backward" Russia Anastasiya Verbitskaya contributed to this genre in her six-volume *The Keys of Happiness* (1910–13). But the most successful of all was the German writer Hedwig Courths-Mahler, who published her first story in 1905.

During the next thirty-five years Courths-Mahler wrote two hundred novels, which sold 30 million copies in Germany alone and which were translated into a dozen languages.[17] In 1912 her *Wild Ursula* became an immediate best seller, and her next book that year, *I Won't Let You Go*, was quickly made into a play and a film. Other typical titles are *Be Still My Heart* and *I'll Love You Always*. Courths-Mahler did not think of herself as a literary writer but as a purveyor of a particular product for a specific type of consumer. Like other mass-production writers of her time she "turned out" her stories very quickly according to a "programmed" formula.

Courths-Mahler's novels are all love stories. Sometimes the lovers are both from the aristocracy; sometimes the man is an aristocrat and the woman a peasant or servant; occasionally the woman is an aristocrat and the man an overseer on her father's estate. The second case was of course the Cinderella theme in its folk version, but the more familiar Charles Perrault version of this theme also occurred in the first case when Courths-Mahler's heroine was the illegitimate or impoverished daughter of an aristocrat, whose antecedents become known toward the end of the story—as in *The Beggar Princess* (1914). In the third case the heroine's family raises objections to a match with the overseer, but, though a commoner, he is presented as morally good and his virtues and those of his family are contrasted with the wickedness and ignoble qualities of some of the noblewoman's relatives. In one story a wealthy doctor has difficulty convincing the poor girl he has married that she does not have to skimp on the family budget; he always takes coffee and cake with his mother in town rather than suggest that his wife provide him with such "luxuries." This petty bourgeois conception of delicacy of feeling among the rich and well-born is naïve (Courths-Mahler had never moved in such circles) but it fed the fantasies of the reader.

These "harmless fairy tales" about the present—as Courths-Mahler herself called them—had special appeal to teen-age schoolgirls, as well as women of all classes. Like teen-age schoolboys with their adventure stories, these girls read the novels of Courths-Mahler in defiance of their teachers, who considered them unworthy. Whatever the variations in plot, the stories all have a happy ending: Love conquers all. And living happily ever after also meant sharing in the conventional life style of the aristocracy, which is presented as exalted and undisturbed by the sordid and boring details of daily life. Courths-Mahler's stories set forth this fantasy in an uncomplicated style that excited the reader's interest and provided an escape from the worries of this world. Only the intimate feelings of the characters matter. Social barriers and economic concerns, if mentioned at all, fade into insignificance in the face of triumphant romance.

Sociologists of literature overemphasize the "reactionary" influence of the aristocratic-authoritarian settings in Courths-Mahler's novels and in much turn-of-the-century popular fiction. In escapist fiction aristocratic settings served the same function as they did in operetta: they evoked a world of set conventions inhabited by carefree characters with nothing else to do but cultivate romance, glamour, excitement, and adventure. These settings certainly did suggest that in the fantasy world of the good old days things were better than they are in real life, and far more predictable. But when one is reading for relaxation or to pass the time, one usually blots out everything that gets in the way of instantaneous gratification. The reader accepts the social settings and clichés as purely formal conventions that smooth the way toward this gratification.

The serial story is another typical cultural product for mass consumption. It originated in the mid-nineteenth century in the form of the serialized novel in daily and weekly newspapers. At that time it still had a beginning, a middle, and an end and was often published in book form as well. Those novels of Charles Dickens and Eugène Sue which dealt with social injustice in an emerging industrial society touched the liberal conscience of educated middle-class men and women. In Germany the novels of Gustav Freytag and Friedrich Spielhagen dwelt more specifically on the contrast between the moral goodness of the middle class and the arrogance and decadence of the aristocracy and showed less sympathy than Dickens and Sue for the lower classes, though they appealed to a similar audience. Their outlook was taken over by E. Marlitt (Eugenie John) and W. Heimburg (Berta Behrens), whose novels were first serialized in the *Gartenlaube*, Germany's most popular family magazine, which had a less educated and predominantly female audience. The novels of these two women still stressed the petty bourgeois values of sentimentality, perseverance, and respectability, but plot and character development were less important than the evocation of emotional reactions to purely personal and family affairs. By the 1890's writers like Natalie von Echstruth in Germany and the serial novelists in the mass-circulation daily newspapers in Britain and France turned this kind of novel into the formula that has survived in the soap opera down to the present. They made no reference to the problems of the larger society or to the public events of the time; their characters simply moved through an endless series of "programmed" emotional states.

Like much of mass culture the serial story trivialized earlier forms whose purpose was moral or aesthetic enlightenment into products to be consumed and forgotten. In doing so these stories reinforced their readers' views of life as an ongoing series of loosely related episodes and *faits divers*. To be sure, some working-class and lower-middle-class readers who knew better consciously turned to serial stories for escape; they also did this with adventure and detective stories, sports, the music hall, and newspaper accounts of the comings and goings of public personalities. Nevertheless, these media all carried the "message" that modern life is a day-to-day affair with no ultimate purpose, such as individual development or salvation or social justice.

During the immediate prewar years a more up-to-date type of series dealing with "cops and robbers" became immensely popular in France; the most famous one dealt with the adventures of the clever and elusive criminal Fantômas. Each month, beginning in 1911, Marcel Allain and Pierre Souvestre "turned out" a new novel in the series—a total of 580 in less than fifty years. (The first three alone were to sell over 11 million copies during that time.)[18] When Allain was interviewed in 1965 he summarized the mass-production technique that he and his co-author had used as follows:

> We made the *plan* together, very carefully, in detail. Then we drew
> lots to see who would write the odd and even numbered chap-

ters. . . . In order to keep track we arranged that I would begin the first page with an "all the same" and Souvestre with a "nevertheless." Thus, if a chapter had to be reworked later on, we knew which one was responsible for it.[19]

Unlike Jean Valjean or Edmond Dantes, Fantômas is not a victim of injustice, but the forces of law and order which he eludes are far from blameless. (Two early titles in the series are *The Burglar Judge* and *The Hooligan Policeman*.) His perennial pursuers, the detective Juve and the young reporter Fandor, are upright and courageous—even intelligent. Yet their unending struggle with Fantômas is a dialectical one in which the reader constantly switches sides, depending upon which one has the upper hand at the moment. Thus there is no personal involvement in the emotional states of the characters, as in the serial stories for women. Fantômas appealed to women because he was athletic and sexy; he appealed to men because he was daring and fearless. And he appealed to all classes and age groups because he was a man of mystery and intrigue. With his many disguises and disappearances he was more mythical than real (his very name is derived from the French word for phantom) and therefore a kind of Superman of crime.

For the modern mass audience this type of persona offered a comforting sense of continuity in a discontinuous world. Each adventure in the Fantômas series, in films as well as books, was episodic in itself and usually left the audience hanging at the end. Yet one knew that Fantômas, Juve, Fandor, and Lady Beltham would reappear in another adventure in a month in novel form or in a week in the movie serial. Life on that level at least was "to be continued."

A typical example was the installment called "The Simplon Express Disaster" in Louis Feuillade's 1913 movie serial *Juve versus Fantômas*. Preceded by shots of Fantômas and Juve in various disguises, the episode begins with Juve and Fandor working on an unsolved crime: Is the body really that of Lady Beltham? They watch the house of the mysterious Dr. Chalchek (Fantômas). Then Juve follows him after a young woman, Josephine, hands him a message which the audience learns involves a plot to rob some wine merchants of 150,000 francs. Juve's taxi runs out of gas, but Fandor has better luck in shadowing Josephine in the Métro. Josephine meets one of the unsuspecting wine merchants at the railroad station and they board a train, with Fandor lurking behind them. Two bandits are also lurking about and one of them, Loupart (Fantômas), recognizes Fandor. The other bandit uncouples the coach while the train is moving very fast. Then at Josephine's signal ten masked men rob the wine merchant and Fandor. Both men untie themselves and leap off the coach, which is rolling backwards, just before the Simplon express crashes into it. The bandits meanwhile discover that the 150,000 francs in banknotes are torn in half, the other half to be handed over when a certain agreement is signed. Chalchek-Loupart plans to get the other halves and do away with Juve. He sends Juve a telegram signed "Fandor" in order to trap him at the warehouse of the wine merchants. Fandor and the wine merchant from the train are also there and are shot at by the bandits. Juve and Fandor become trapped by flaming wine barrels ignited by the shots, but they roll into the sea in a barrel and swim away. In the next scene Juve and Fandor encounter Josephine in a fancy Montmartre restaurant and order her to tell them where Chalchek is. Actually he is sitting at another table with two lady friends. When he realizes that Juve sees him he runs out the door. He is apprehended but he escapes on the street and flees in a taxi, returning to the restaurant after Juve and Fandor have gone. The scene shifts to the deserted villa of Lady Beltham, now living in a convent outside Paris. She has come to her old room to meet Gurn (Fantômas). Disguised as Chalchek, he merely tells her that he has grown a beard. Though she knows he is a criminal she cannot resist him and agrees to return once a week at midnight. Juve and Fandor follow Lady Beltham on her next visit to the villa and spy on her and Chalchek through an air vent near the floor of her bedroom. They hear Chalchek tell Lady Beltham that he will take her away and that Juve will be killed by his "Silent Executioner." In the next scene the "Silent Executioner," a boa constrictor, slithers into Juve's bedroom through a window but fails to kill him and leaves. Then, back at the villa, Fantômas, masked and sheathed completely in black, feels himself surrounded by invisible enemies (Juve and Fandor). He binds a stick of dynamite to the wiring in the servants' quarters. Juve and Fandor lead the police in and pursue Fantômas, who submerges himself in a rain-water cistern in the cellar and breathes through a broken bottle. Juve hears the breathing and has the furnace lit, expecting the smoke in the air vents to force Fantômas out of the villa. Fantômas escapes through the cellar window and blows up the villa. But are Juve and Fandor really dead? To be continued next week.

This summary description may seem to exaggerate the episodic quality of this ancient silent film, but it is not meant to be a parody. Even today the film holds the viewer's interest. Given the genre, the acting is somewhat stilted, but no more so than in the average television soap opera or

Fantômas.

"private eye" series. Feuillade was a director of great talent, and his cutting is smoother than this summary indicates. In fact, for 1913, *Juve versus Fantômas* was ultramodern. Its episodic character is important in the context just discussed, but it also offered moving picture images of technological innovations which had been rarities less than fifteen years earlier: automobiles, electric trams, subways, electric lights, the telephone.

EARLY MOVIES

By the time of the Fantômas serials, motion pictures had captured an international audience, yet they had been invented less than twenty years earlier. In France the Lumière brothers created the first short factual film: *Excursion of the French Photographic Society to Neuville* (1895). Other early films of this type included *Gold Rush Scenes in the Klondike* (1898), *The Funeral of Queen Victoria* (1901), *McGovern-Corbett Fight* (1903), *San Francisco Earthquake* (1906), and *First Wright Flight in France* (1908). By 1910 scenes and incidents such as these were to be incorporated into newsreels and were to give mass audiences ever since their fleeting images of life in the modern world. The first short fictional films included the American Alfred Clark's *The Execution of Mary Queen of Scots* (1895), the fantasies of the Frenchman Georges Méliès such as *The Conjurer* (1899), *A Trip to the Moon* (1902), and *The Palace of the Arabian Nights* (1905), and the American Edwin S. Porter's *The Great Train Robbery* (1903). Slapstick comedy was introduced to film by the French comedian Max Linder in 1905 and the American actor-director Mack Sennett in 1911. During the immediate prewar years feature-length fictional films were being produced mainly in France, the United States, and Italy and distributed in most modern countries. On the eve of the war England alone had 3,500 movie houses, just six years after the first one had opened there.

Much of the content of early silent feature films was borrowed from the medium of the popular theater: farce and vaudeville in France; adventure and melodrama about simple folk in the United States; historical spectacles and melodramas about modern high life in which statuesque women overreact to grand passions in Italy. But since the new medium was purely visual—with a minimum of printed dialogue and exposition*—new effects had to be improvised to hold the audience's attention and interest. It was these effects, rather than the traditional content and mannered acting, that gave the filmgoer new perceptions of modern civilization. These perceptions were bound to be superficial since, more than any other medium, movies concentrated on the surface reality of things.

Motion pictures made it possible for the first time to reproduce the effect of speeding trains and automobiles. The earliest internationally popular example was *The Great Train Robbery*. In this 1903 one-reeler a group of bandits rob the mail car and take over the locomotive of a fast-moving train. Then the content becomes more traditional. Like highwaymen attacking a stagecoach the bandits force the passengers outside and, after robbing them too, they ride away on their horses but are captured by a local posse after a gun battle. Since most of the people who saw this film were uneducated city dwellers who never rode on trains, the impact must have been startling. They knew that the scenes they were watching were plausible, yet to them they were fantasy. Even more

---

* Some attempts were made to use phonographs with the film projector (see illustration) to bring in music and other kinds of sound, but it was impossible to synchronize the voices with the actors' lips in this way. Also, amplification and speaker systems were inadequate for large movie palaces.

New mass media: A "Chronophone," in the Gaumont Palace movie theater in Paris in 1910. The first fairly successful experiment with phonograph records playing background music and sound effects with a silent film.

startling were the chase scenes in the immediate prewar films involving the Keystone Kops. They gave European audiences an exceedingly superficial and distorted notion of what life was like in America, the symbol of modern civilization at that time.

These audiences were predominantly youthful and working-class. In most countries the middle and upper classes looked down on the movies and the phonograph before 1914 as they were to disdain radio and television later on. Children were barred from movie houses in some countries, but in England working-class children begged, worked, and even stole to obtain the price of admission. (In 1912 the governor of Durham prison was appalled by the number of boys there for having stolen in order to get money to go to the movies.)[20] Although cultivated adults would not go even to the most luxurious movie palaces, middle- and working-class courting couples were attracted by the prospect of sitting together in semidarkness in the back seats.

The closest the early silent films came to depicting the discontents of

Max Linder.

their viewers toward modernization and the injustices of capitalist society was through the antics of a sympathetic underdog or "loser." D. W. Griffith's *A Corner on Wheat* (1909), based on Frank Norris's muckraking novel *The Pit*, was an isolated exception and not nearly as popular as his *Comrades* (1911). In this film Mack Sennett and Dell Henderson are tramps trying to crash high society. One of them steals some fancy clothes, pretends to be Marmaduke Bracegirdle, a "wealthy British MP," and gains entry into a burlesque version of an upper-class American home in this disguise. While he is courting the daughter of the owner (all rich people are fat and pompous in these slapstick films), his pal keeps following the couple around. But the real Marmaduke finally arrives and the impostor is thrown out into the cold. The clumsy but lovable tramps in *Comrades* were precursors of the type made world famous a few years later by Charlie Chaplin. Another prototype whom Chaplin himself acknowledged was the Frenchman Max Linder.

Max Linder was the most popular and most imitated movie comedian in Europe. Between 1905 and 1915 he made hundreds of one-reelers in which he played a dapper but inept victim. In the opening scene of *Troubles of a Grass Widower* (1908) Max is reading a newspaper at the table at lunch. His wife objects and goes home to Mother. Max puts on white gloves to do the dishes but after washing a few glasses in a pan he takes the pile outside and hoses it. Then he goes shopping for food but hides the bundles from a female acquaintance and her small son for fear that they will make fun of him. Back in the kitchen Max plucks a chicken, puts wine and vegetables inside it, and tries to cook it over a small burner. The next morning he cannot find his necktie and empties all the drawers in the house looking for it. In *Max and His Dog* (1912) Max and another young gentleman vie for a young lady's favor by serenading her. Then they draw lots. Max wins the girl and marries her. A few weeks later, while Max is at his office, his former rival appears in the house. Max's dog telephones him to warn him, and he comes home to confront the couple. The dog brings in the wife's hatbox, and Max sends the lovers off. In the last scene Max and his dog (wearing a large bib) share a meal at the table. Max Linder combined the slapstick antics of a vaudeville comic with whimsicality and trick photography. Although individuals in all classes loved him, his one-reelers were shown mainly in the cheaper movie houses.

Queen Elizabeth, a 1912 filmed French stage play starring Sarah Bernhardt, was designed to entice a more "respectable," better-paying audience into the movie theaters. But only the most devoted fans of "the divine Sarah," one of the greatest box-office attractions of her time, could find it worthy either as a play or a movie. The plot is a hodgepodge of intrigue, adultery, and betrayals involving Elizabeth and Essex. Through it all Bernhardt is always Bernhardt playing a QUEEN (though hardly an English one). The film is full of incongruities that strain the most willing suspension of disbelief: the hair styles are 1912, the gestures 1880, the costumes 1588; after Essex's head is chopped off, Elizabeth visits the body—with the head back on. At the end of the film, after the character she has played dies, Bernhardt "emerges" from the corpse on the bed and takes curtain calls!

The 1912 Italian film *Quo vadis?* did succeed in attracting a new audience by abandoning the techniques of the theater for those of the cinema. Set in Rome after the death of Christ, this first version of the much-filmed Henryk Sienkiewicz novel was both "elevating" and spectacular. It seems stilted today, but in 1912 the wild animals, the masses of extras, and the three-dimensional sets made it an international success. With *Quo vadis?* the feature-length historical melodrama came into its own. A year later the Italians produced *Cabiria,* another epic set in ancient Rome. D. W. Griffith gave the genre new dimensions in *The Birth of a Nation* (1915) and *Intolerance* (1916).

Although the content of most feature films remained traditional, the new medium transformed it into a canned fantasy world for millions of people. Silent movies could be inspiring aesthetically—as in Robert Wiene's *The Cabinet of Dr. Caligari* (1920)—or politically—as in Sergei Eisenstein's *Potemkin* (1925)—but for most viewers they were simply entertainment on a scale and at a price never before available to the masses. They also provided a worldwide audience of fans with celebrities as seemingly real yet remote as the stars in the heavens—from Max Linder, Mary Pickford, and Charlie Chaplin in the immediate prewar and war years to Pola Negri, Douglas Fairbanks, Rudolph Valentino, and Greta Garbo in the 1920's.

Before the war Garbo's prototype was Lyda Borelli, the embodiment of noble, if deceived, womanhood, in the 1913 Italian film *Love Everlasting* (*Ma l'amore mio non muore*). The Italian star had a fuller figure than her Swedish successor, and her acting was more flamboyant, but they played similar roles. Indeed in the closing scene of *Love Everlasting,* Borelli dies singing the same role in *La Traviata* that Garbo was to play twenty-five years later in *Camille.* But in the film itself Borelli is no lady of the camellias; she is Elsa Holbein, the daughter of an aristocratic colonel in the army of a contemporary German grand duchy. Elsa is forced to take up a career as an opera singer only because of an intrigue in which she was an innocent dupe.

The opening scene of *Love Everlasting* is the drawing room in the home of Colonel Holbein. An adventurer named Moise Sthar is charming Elsa at the piano while her father and the war minister are looking over plans for the fortifications for the grand duchy. Then, while Elsa and her father are escorting the war minister to the door, Moise steals the plans. After he leaves the house Moise returns to his hotel and checks out. The next morning the colonel discovers that the plans are missing. "A terrible suspicion enters Elsa's mind." She goes to the hotel and is told by the doorman that Moise has left town. Her father is disgraced and is executed.

Elsa flees to Paris to earn her living as a singer under an assumed name. When she gets her first contract the title on the screen says: "So begins Elsa's new life." She is a big success and has many male admirers. One

Lyda Borelli in *Love Everlasting*.

day she sees Moise in an outdoor restaurant in Nice and is reminded of her family tragedy. She languishes in her dressing room, looks at her father's picture and puts flowers around it. (The overdecorated dressing room, like the other interior scenes, gives a foretaste of Hollywood in its heyday.) When Elsa tries to find Moise at his hotel, he has disappeared again. In the next scene she is out riding and stops at a church. She plays the organ and sings. Outside Prince Maximilian, son of the grand duke, is sitting reading a newspaper. He hears Elsa singing, he goes into the church, and they fall in love.

For the moment Elsa seems to have everything a modern woman could want. Her singing career goes on triumphally and a handsome prince is in love with her. Then Moise reappears and exposes her true identity to the newspapers. Back in Germany the grand duke reads about Elsa and sends his son a message ordering him to renounce "that singer," whose father had been shot as a traitor. Prince Maximilian leaves, and Elsa has a big "abandoned" scene. Later she writes to him saying that, though they must be parted, her love is everlasting. Now the prince has a big lamentation scene. Elsa mopes around for a while and then goes back to the opera. Then her prince risks his own future by returning to her. But when he leaves her dressing room, Elsa takes poison before going on stage. She collapses as she begins to sing and just before *she* dies she says: "But my love does not die."

Love Everlasting was a pioneer product of twentieth-century popular culture. It was a cinematic rendition of a late nineteenth-century operatic version of an early nineteenth-century poetic conception of a late medieval romance about early medieval love *à la* Tristan and Isolde or Lancelot and Guinevere. Not only was it thus a fourth-hand derivation but it was also "cleaned up" for a period in which the conventional morality was still that of *East Lynne*. (Unlike Elsa, Isolde and Guinevere were adulteresses.) The manipulative techniques of the silent film made *Love Everlasting* a more effective tearjerker than the same theme in earlier media. For all their wet handkerchiefs most of its female viewers knew that love was not a disembodied emotion, capable of lasting forever. They also knew that what they saw on the screen was only an illusion. Yet *Love Everlasting* showed them that at the movies they could temporarily escape from their daily frustrations and enjoy a good cry while watching a glamorous celebrity triumph and suffer in luxurious modern settings. Once the mass market for such films was established, mass production kept it supplied.

THE PRESS

Daily newspapers were the most pervasive medium of the emerging mass culture.* By 1914 *Le Petit Parisien, Le Petit Journal, Le Journal,* and *Le Matin* alone printed a total of 4.5 million copies a day, which

* This section deals exclusively with mass-circulation newspapers and magazines aimed at a general audience. There were of course many newspapers and periodicals specializing in political, literary, financial, and religious affairs. We have already noted the emergence of a sports press and a children's press. French newsstands also sold sensational magazines featuring crime, adventure, and sex; even little boys could buy them. (See illustration.)

amounted to 75 per cent of all Parisian dailies and 40 per cent of all French dailies.[21] These four morning dailies were truly national newspapers, distributed throughout France by a smoothly co-ordinated network of trains, trucks, and news dealers. In Great Britain the London *Daily Mail* was the largest national newspaper, bringing the standards and images of the metropolis to the rest of the nation in the same way. The fact that many readers abandoned the provincial press for the *Daily Mail* and other national British dailies helps account for the doubling of their readership between 1896 and 1906 and again by 1914. In Germany, where even the biggest Berlin dailies did not have a comparable national circulation in the prewar decades, the readership of the local dailies almost doubled in provincial cities such as Bremen.[22]

Like other forms of popular entertainment and enlightenment the press had different levels for different social groups. In Paris the morning daily *Le Gaulois* was aimed at the aristocracy, *Le Figaro* at the upper-middle and middle classes, *Le Journal* at the lower-middle class, and *L'Humanité* at the workers. In Great Britain the London *Times* and *Telegraph*, the *Manchester Guardian, Glasgow Herald*, and *Birmingham Post* "were written for men already established, or on the way to being established, in their business or professions: top-hatted, frock-coated men with serious minds. Neither women nor the lower classes came within their view."[23] The same was true of the *Neue Freie Presse* and *Wiener Tageblatt* in Vienna, the *Vossische Zeitung* and *Berliner Tageblatt* in Berlin, the *Corriere Della Sera* in Milan, and the *Neue Zürcher Zeitung* in Zurich. In England workingmen preferred the Sunday *News of the World*, which concentrated on violent and salacious crimes, to the *Daily Mail*, which carefully avoided "indecent" material. French workers read the daily picture newspaper *Excelsior* rather than the weekly *L'Ilustration*, which —like the *London Illustrated News, Illustrazione Italiana*, and the *Gartenlaube* in Germany—provided the nonintellectual middle and lower-middle classes with predigested information about modern developments.

Not only did daily newspapers reach more people than any other medium but they were also more influential. The fact that people read them every day made their impact more continuous. They also gave more "product" for less money; by the 1890's all the big dailies had reduced their price to about two cents, and in the early 1900's they increased their size from four to eight or ten pages. Newspaper readership increased partly because of growing literacy and technological changes that made it possible to print several editions a day. But the most important reason for the great influence of newspapers was the basic functions that all

QUESTION D'ART

— Dans lequel qu'on aura l'plus d'femmes nues pour deux ronds?

New mass media: Three French boys at a newsstand debating which magazine will offer them the most naked women for two sous.

news media perform, namely giving a feeling of continuity in modern mass society and making sense out of what happens in it. These functions were especially important to millions of people who lacked other cultural means for coping with the forces of modernization. (On the press and nationalism see Chapter 9.)

Newspapers and other news media domesticate the modern world by making it comprehensible to masses of people who would otherwise feel bewildered by it. (The fact that it *is* bewildering is unacceptable to most people.) By communicating with the average reader at his own level of understanding newspapers make knowledge universally understandable. Thus in mass society universal comprehensibility becomes the criterion of knowledge. Newspapers make knowledge public: "All the news that's fit to print." Thus in mass society publicity becomes the criterion of truth.[24] In other words, when I understand what I see or read, seeing or reading is believing. All the news media foster this naïve empiricism, and most readers automatically perceive whatever they *report* as *information* about things that actually happened.

Modern newspapers also give their readers a common universe of discourse. In traditional society one's universe of discourse was limited to what could be expressed in the dialect of one's native region. But urbanization, social mobility, and the growing use of national languages made people aware of a wider world while at the same time making it necessary for them to communicate more and more with strangers. It was therefore reassuring to know that the information and attitudes one got from one's newspaper were shared by millions of other people. Newspapers also provided mutually familiar topics for casual conversation with strangers: What do you think of that scandal, fire, murder, ball game, etc.? Many of the perceptions people got from newspapers of events, pseudoevents, and celebrities had little if any relevance to their daily lives. Yet they felt the need to respond to them somehow: with indignation over the Armenian massacres, pride concerning the activities of royalty, curiosity about scandals and crimes.

Founded in 1876, *Le Petit Parisien* had the largest circulation of all the dailies in our period—1 million in 1902 and 1.4 million on the eve of the war.[25] It also reached a more heterogeneous audience: many middle- and lower-middle-class men and women read it, and it was supposedly *the* newspaper of the concierges, but the majority of its readers seem to have been working-class. Although Jean Dupuy, its publisher from 1888 to 1919, supported the policies of the liberal republican regime, his paper did not cater to the interests of any particular social group and was not openly hostile to the aspirations of labor, as many big dailies were. As its title indicates, *Le Petit Parisien* was aimed at the "little man," the ordinary citizen (called John Q. Public in the United States). This was the mass audience that all the news media have tried to reach. And what it wanted in its newspapers was information, excitement, novelty, and variety, all packaged as appealingly as possible. *Le Petit Parisien* was so successful because it met these demands so well.

Like other major dailies *Le Petit Parisien* constantly increased the scope of its coverage to satisfy the new interests of its readers. The main new topics after the turn of the century were sports and human interest stories. There were also regular sections on fashion and finance, serial novels, and contests. The front page of the October 18, 1903, issue of *Le Petit Parisien* contained the following items: two columns announcing its first contest, one column on technological progress in agriculture, a half column on the visit of the King and Queen of Italy (with the first photographs in a French daily), one column on a double murder in Aix-les-Bains, a boxed list of one-sentence headlines about the day's events, and, on the bottom third of the page, a serial novel. *The Fiancé of Lorraine,* by Jules Marie. Within a few years, the serial novel was moved to a later page and replaced by more photographs and more crime stories. *Le Petit Parisien* had fewer big exposés than its English and American counterparts but it did offer articles on public issues based on series of interviews with well-known personalities.

Le Petit Parisien's first contest set a trend in the new popular culture. Its objective was to guess how many grains of wheat there were in a bottle which was shown in an illustration and whose dimensions were given in detail. Each entry had to be accompanied by ten mastheads of the newspaper. There were 250,000 francs (600,000 1975 dollars) in prizes, including a first prize of 25,000 francs in cash, a suburban house, a seaside cottage, two automobiles, and 12,000 other items of merchandise. This contest required mathematical rather than verbal aptitude (as in crossword puzzles) or miscellaneous information (as in later contests on radio and television). It not only titillated its current readers but also served as a promotional device for attracting new ones. Still, it was a real challenge, unlike the *Daily Mail*'s March 3, 1908, contest supplement—a jigsaw puzzle of seven pieces to be arranged to form a complete elephant.

Founded in 1896 by Alfred Harmsworth (later Lord Northcliffe), the London *Daily Mail*[26] was consciously aimed at the interests and aspirations of the modern-minded, upward-striving members of the lower-middle class. Its circulation jumped to almost 1 million during the excitement of the Boer War and averaged three quarters of a million during the Edwardian years. The *Daily Mail* called itself "The Busy Man's Daily Journal"—a "bright" newspaper for lower-middle-class commuters. Harmsworth told his staff to think of their readers as men aspiring to a life style of "£1,000 a year people." None of the white-collar employees who actually read the *Daily Mail* had such an exceptional income but, as we saw in Chapter 4, many such people identified themselves with the class that did. The *Daily Mail* was also one of the first British dailies to appeal to female readers. When it inaugurated its women's page it declared: "Movements in women's world—that is to say, changes in dress, toilet matters, cookery and home matters generally—are as much entitled to receive attention as nine out of ten of the matters which are treated of in the ordinary daily paper." Harmsworth accurately discerned what his readers wanted. Emphasizing the attractively trivial over the solidly serious he gave them two categories of "news": "actualities" and "talking points." The first, he told an employee, "is news in its narrowest and best sense—reports of *happenings*, political resignations, strikes, crimes, deaths of famous people, wrecks and railway smashes, weather storms, sporting results, and so on. The second is getting the topics people are discussing and developing them, or stimulating a topic oneself." One way the *Daily Mail* stimulated a topic was to run stunts such as the £10,000 London-Manchester air race in 1910.

The *Daily Mail* appealed to "those who had no complaint against society but simply wished to improve their own position in it, satisfied to feel themselves a cut above the labouring poor and happy to be governed by their betters."[27] Thus it opposed labor reforms and gave favorable coverage to the doings of royalty and London Society. On April 21, 1908, it published a three-column letter from a brewer named Henry Boddington who, though currently unemployed, was for laissez-faire and the Empire and against creeping socialism. The *Daily Mail's* serial stories all concerned the lives of the well-to-do—as in *The Ways of Men*, by Herbert Flowerdew, "author of *The Third Kiss, Maynard's Wives*, etc., etc." Even rich London Jews were treated favorably in Pierre Costello's *A Sinner in Israel. A Drama of Modern Jewish Life.*

A typical pre-1914 issue of the *Daily Mail* contained at least four columns of stories about crimes and sensational accidents, one full page on sports, one full financial page, and a women's page. There were book and theater reviews, a column for farmers, and feature articles on medical science, history, and great men. In additon to advertisements for the usual consumer goods—particularly beauty aids and nerve pills—there were ads for "how to" books, *The Children's Encyclopaedia*, and *The Historian's History of the World*, which was sold by the *Times* Book Club. (Harmsworth had bought the *Times* in 1907 and the *Evening News* several years earlier. He had also launched the *Daily Mirror* and several weeklies.)

Newspaper publishing became big business earlier than any other mass medium. Soon after they were founded both the *Daily Mail* and *Le Petit Parisien* became public companies, inviting investors to buy shares not because they were interested in politics or newspapers as such but simply to earn profits from a successful commercial enterprise. Whereas the profits of *Le Petit Parisien* came mainly from its large circulation, the biggest English and German papers—like their American counterparts—derived theirs increasingly from advertising revenue. In place of the traditional classified ads the *Daily Mail* ran large illustrated displays for brand-name products such as Pear's Soap, Players Cigarettes, and Beecham's Pills ("for all bilious and nervous disorders"). When Selfridges department store opened in 1909 it took six whole pages and three quarter pages in the *Daily Mail* within nine days. Not only did

Advertisement in the *London Illustrated News*
for Beecham's Pills.

newspapers thus become linked with the business of mass marketing but
they themselves were a market for another business, the major wire services: Reuters in the United Kingdom, Havas in France, and Continental
Telegraphen in Germany.

Aside from daily newspapers there were mass-circulation weeklies that
provided the average reader with unsophisticated entertainment and enlightenment and helped him make sense out of the modern world. The
English prototype was *Tit-Bits* "from all the most interesting books, periodicals and contributors in the world." Founded in the 1880's, it quickly
achieved a circulation of 700,000. *Tit-Bits* specialized in the type of information found in almanacs: "What is the greatest height from which a
person has fallen without receiving an injury?" "Which football field
allows the largest number of spectators an uninterrupted view of the
game?" It also included patriotic little stories and traveling salesmen's
humor such as:

Cleverton: "Do you think it possible to love two girls at the same time?"

Dashaway: "Not if they know it."

Always alert to new markets, Alfred Harmsworth launched a rival to *Tit-Bits*, called *Answers*. The formula was the same: potted information conveyed in short brisk paragraphs of two or three lines. But Harmsworth actually wrote the questions himself. ("He had an appetite for unrelated facts as insatiable as a competitor in a television quiz show.")[28] The readers of the first issue of *Answers* (June 2, 1888) were able to learn about "What the Queen Eats," "How to Cure Freckles," "Why Jews Don't Ride Bicycles," and "Narrow Escapes from Burial Alive." They were also told: "Anyone who reads our paper for a year will be able to converse on many subjects on which he was entirely ignorant. He will have a good stock of anecdotes and jokes and will indeed be a pleasant companion."

Some of the big Continental dailies published inexpensive illustrated weekly supplements that were widely read by the half-educated lower and lower-middle classes, but one of the most successful and enduring family weeklies, the *Gartenlaube*,[29] was a medium-price magazine aimed directly at the middle class proper. Although peculiarly German in many ways, the *Gartenlaube* was a forerunner of the American *Saturday Evening Post* and *Ladies' Home Journal*. Its circulation was considerably smaller—around 250,000 around 1900—but its influence was more profound because it had less competition from other media. The *Gartenlaube* was viewed as an institution by both its readers and its critics because it embodied the mentality of the middle-brow German bourgeoisie.

The *Gartenlaube* domesticated everything. Its very title, which means an arbor, symbolized the domestication of nature. The serial novels it published, especially those of E. Marlitt, domesticated human relations through an effective mixture of idealism and sentimentality which few of its readers could resist. Unlike the "harmless fairy tales" of Courths-Mahler, they were presented as stories of real life in a prettied-up but not distorted world. Indeed Marlitt's forthrightly hostile portraits of evil aristocrats have been interpreted as a form of social protest.[30] But in the world depicted in news stories in the *Gartenlaube* evil and excess were avoided as unsuitable for the innocent schoolgirls and sensible housewives who were its ideal readers.

By the turn of the century, however, the *Gartenlaube* had decided to enlighten its readers about various aspects of modernization, though still in a domesticated version. In 1899 it gave considerable coverage to the International Women's Congress in London, including pictures of some of the militant feminists there. Although the *Gartenlaube* still believed that women's place was in the home, it played up and illustrated new activities like bicycle-riding and amateur photography. On the scientific-technological "front" it reported Marconi's invention of the radio and Blériot's flight across the English Channel, as well as advances in "feminine hygiene," a topic heretofore taboo in family publications. In 1906 it ventured into the realm of social problems with a major illustrated article on the plight of poor women forced to do sweated labor in their homes. Its news of the world increasingly paralleled that presented in the other mass media: the doings of royalty, Germany's new overseas colonies, the world's fairs in Paris in 1900 and St. Louis in 1904. In 1912 the *Gartenlaube* showed its readers "How a Paris Art Exhibition Is Organized" but neglected to tell them about the avant-garde artists who shunned such official exhibitions.

Neither as enlightenment nor as entertainment did the emerging mass culture show the real effects of modernization on people's lives. The mass-circulation press was already treating its readers as self-centered consumers to whom the events and developments it reported were "about" other kinds of people than themselves. The very format of newspapers and magazines reinforced the perception that whatever they presented was a discrete unit, unrelated to structured, interconnected processes. Melodramatic fiction and popular songs like "Heaven Will Protect the Working Girl" reduced the problems of women in the labor market to the fending off of amorous employers. Popular fiction in general—along with the variety theater, the movies, and spectator sports —reassured people that emotions and interpersonal relations are always the same, no matter how superficially modern the setting.

The new mass media encouraged a consumer mentality that began to regard all cultural products in terms of "I like it" and "what it means to me." An individual with this mentality personalized, domesticated, and sentimentalized great works of art ("We Fell in Love at the Parthenon") while completely missing their meaning as symbolic forms created to help people experience something beyond themselves. The same individual responded in the same ways to popular songs, serial novels, and Schlock art—attaching his own personal meaning ("They're playing our song") to something mass-produced and with no meaning beyond *itself*. But this way of using cultural products leads to the opposite of enlightenment, empathy, and understanding.

Thus the emerging mass culture presented a superficial view of reality which offered no way of understanding how modern structures and systems worked. Some forms of popular fiction and theatrical entertainment provided predigested morsels of a sentimentalized past for momentary escape from the unappetizing aspects of real life in the present. And the naïve empiricism fostered by the news media was a mystification rather than an explanation. Instead of showing objects as the constituents of which events and relations are built mass culture presented them as self-contained miscellaneous items to be consumed or disregarded. From their personal experiences people did become aware of the class structure, the political system, and the market economy. But mass culture gave them no guidance in understanding how these functioned or how they were interrelated. Unlike traditional popular culture it was not supported by explanatory myths. Its main message was: All that counts is here and now, so consume whatever you can.

CHAPTER 7

NEW CONCEPTS AND PERCEPTIONS

While most Europeans became more materialistic and secular in their outlook, some philosophers and social theorists sought new ways to understand the complexities and contradictions of modern life. In their efforts to do this they rejected traditional rationalism and the positivism and scientism of their immediate predecessors. They particularly stressed the importance of the irrational and the unconscious in human affairs. Friedrich Nietzsche and Henri Bergson concerned themselves with the role of the individual will and the possibility of free spirits creating new values. Sigmund Freud, Émile Durkheim, and Max Weber sought new concepts of the individual's place in the society of their own time. These social scientists began to assume the relativity of all cultural values and norms and to view alien cultures as valid on their own terms. Indeed psychoanalysis itself is, in part, a theory about the ways in which the culture of a particular society is assimilated and handed on.

During the prewar years philosophers and social scientists followed a separate path from that of physicists like Albert Einstein and Max Planck toward the relativistic outlook that came to dominate the twentieth century. Weber recognized that competing value systems and diverse national cultures were inescapable facts of modern life. Durkheim specifically acknowledged the similarity of the assumptions of his sociology with those of pragmatism. "Man is a product of history and hence of becoming; there is nothing in him that is either given or defined in advance. . . . Everything in man has been created by mankind in the course of time. Consequently, if truth is human, it is also a human product."[1] Bergson's idea of creative evolution also rejected the fixed, "objective," quality ascribed to truth by rationalism. And Ludwig Wittgenstein said that the terms used in a proposition derive their meaning from their relationship within the proposition.

But neither the intellectual establishment nor the educated bourgeoisie was prepared to cope with these new concepts and perceptions. Most academic philosophers paid no attention to Nietzsche or Bergson and continued to elucidate traditional ideas. And though these two thinkers became fashionable with some pseudointellectuals who considered themselves forward-looking, the most popular "philosophy" among the "enlightened" public was Ernst Haeckel's monism. In the late nineteenth century Haeckel had been Germany's leading champion of Darwinism, and in 1900 he published *The Riddle of the Universe*, which announced that man was completely merged with nature and denounced all distinctions between mind and matter, body and soul, spirit and substance. This book sold 300,000 copies by 1914, including numerous translations. Its solution to the problem of modernization and its discontents was a substitute religion derived from mid-nineteenth-century scientism.

During the early 1900's Europe also experienced its version of the American "great awakening"—a call for a moral regeneration. Like monism, voluntarism, and antirationalism this call dismissed modernization as a bad thing, rather than confront the complex, interrelated structures and systems it had brought into existence. Besides, talk about moral virtues covered the absence of a realistic analysis of prevailing social conditions which would have threatened the vested interests of the readers of the *Revue des Deux Mondes*, the *Preussische Jahrbücher*, the *Nuova Antologia*, and the *Quarterly Review*. These "serious" media of public enlightenment gave as distorted a version of the ideas they professed to explain as Max Nordau's book *Degeneration* (see Chapter 5).

REORIENTATIONS IN PHILOSOPHY

The real Friedrich Nietzsche (1844–1900) was far different from the distorted image of him popularized by Nordau and others. He was certainly the most notorious nineteenth-century philosopher of the wish to be free from passive submission to the authorities of the past. But he directed his nihilism at traditional moral values in order to clear the way for the creation of new ones, not to encourage degeneration into normlessness. Nietzsche preached the need to tame our all-too-human drives, which he subsumed under our will to power. After his death his sister Elizabeth edited his unfinished notes on "The Will to Power" in a book that seemed to make him a proto-Nazi.[2] Nietzsche himself would have been horrified by this distortion. Recognizing the chaos that would result from the unbridled expression of man's will to power, he argued that we must sublimate this basic drive by redirecting it toward constructive objectives controlled by our reason. He also admitted that this was a superhuman task in a world in which God was dead as the symbol of all universal certainties.

Nietzsche struck a responsive chord with his admonition: "Become who you are!" Although he wrote all his finished works in the 1870's and 1880's, their full impact on European thought came only after 1900. By then modernization was prompting innovative thinkers in all advanced countries to question traditional certainties. The American pragmatist philosopher and psychologist William James asserted each individual's right to choose the beliefs that were best for him from the existing moral heritage. Nietzsche did not share James's democratic optimism. He believed that only a few outstanding individuals could fulfill their will to power through self-perfection. And only this kind of effort could save the human race from its current decadence.

Like Socrates, Nietzsche saw himself as the gadfly of his society and the vivisectionist of contemporary conceits and hypocrisy. Although he loved Wagner's music he despised the cultural philistinism of the German middle classes who "appreciated" it at the Bayreuth festivals and tried to see in it an expression of their anti-Semitic nationalism.[3] Nietzsche's response to modernization was not Wagner's romantic mixture of Christianity and "blond beasts." It was a reasoned search for new values. In his *Untimely Meditations* and *The Birth of Tragedy*, Nietzsche argued that culture, by which he meant the spontaneous creation of original values and norms, was the only end that could give meaning to life. In *Thus Spake Zarathustra* and *Beyond Good and Evil* he exposed the inconsistencies involved in attempts to harmonize the ancient moral code of Christianity with modern civilization and the compromises that were constantly being made between moral theory and social practice. Nietzsche also opposed liberalism, socialism, nationalism, and democracy as inimical to culture. According to him, "the goal of humanity" could not lie in ends such as these; it could only be born "in humanity's highest specimens." This assertion from the *Untimely Meditations* gives the clue to Nietzsche's conception of values and to his aristocratic ethic.

Nietzsche is justly famous for his concept of the superman, though what he meant by it has often been misunderstood. He believed that "free spirits"—poets and philosophers like himself—should show superior individuals how to surpass themselves in order to make a better world for the future. But he did not intend these supermen to exercise political power. They were antipolitical individuals seeking self-perfection far from the modern world. Their will to power was directed more toward overcoming their own limitations than toward transforming society. And society was to be censured insofar as it insisted on their conformity and impeded their development.

The shrill and provocative quality of Nietzsche's rhetoric often obscured his main intentions. He insisted that "war and courage have done more great things than brotherly love," figuratively using "war" to mean strife, "courage" to mean exertion, and "brotherly love" to mean the ineffectual sentiment of sterile souls who fled their task of self-perfection. In an age when science and technology made bourgeois life complacent, and when the state began to take the masses in tow, Nietzsche urged, in *The Gay Science*, "that a human being attain his satisfaction within himself. . . . Only then is a human being at all tolerable to behold. Whoever is dissatisfied with himself is always ready to revenge himself therefore; we others will be his victims."

Nietzsche's perception of the "resentment" of such people, along with his idea of sublimation, highlights the psychological dimension of his thinking. Like Freud, Nietzsche thought in ways that transcend the rules by which knowledge can be tested. For him, true wisdom was much more than a body of established fact and self-conscious theory. The central confusion in his writings arises from his having treated knowledge as if it were a form of art, and art as if it were a form of knowledge. At the heart of this confusion lies his belief—which repelled Nordau and so many others—that destruction itself is joy, and inseparable from creation. According to the accepted rules of reasoning, this idea is illogical. But Nietzsche wanted reason to abandon the conventional logic of causal explanation and to use psychological insights as the means for interpreting the origins of concepts. Instead of describing and defining, philosophy must interpret. In a note (dated 1888) for "The Will to Power" he gives an example of this kind of thinking regarding the origin of religion:

> . . . In the psychological concept of God, a condition, in order to ap-
> pear as effect, is personified as cause. The psychological logic is this:
> When a man is suddenly and overwhelmingly suffused with the *feel-
> ing of power*—and this is what happens with all great affects—it
> raises in him a doubt about his own person: he does not dare to think
> himself the cause of this astonishing feeling and so he points to a
> stronger person, a divinity, to account for it.[4]

Nietzsche's idea that superior individuals could surpass themselves had widespread appeal in Europe in the early 1900's.[5] It attracted the humanitarian-socialist Irish playwright George Bernard Shaw and the elitist German poet Stefan George (see Chapter 10). In different ways each of these influential writers was reacting against the complacency and smugness of his own society. To them, nineteenth-century civilization had come to a dead end, and they wanted to move forward. They accepted Nietzsche's credo that the artist must be a creator of new values "away from the market place." The Frenchman Henri Bergson (1859–1941) expressed the desire for personal liberation and creative change in ways that made him the most popular and most widely translated philosopher of the prewar decade.

Like many of his contemporaries Bergson rejected scientism and positivism, the extreme forms that faith in the progressive role of science in human affairs had taken in the 1870's and 1880's. Scientism was the belief that science could solve all man's problems through its knowledge of natural and social processes. Positivism went a step further by asserting that science would wrest all cosmological theory from the province of religion. Auguste Comte and Herbert Spencer based their sociological theories on positivism, and this outlook reached a wide audience in a watered-down form. In 1872 the popular English writer Winwood Reade said in his book *The Martyrdom of Man:*

> When we have ascertained, by means of Science, the methods of Na-
> ture's operation, we shall be able to take her place and to perform
> them for ourselves. . . . Men will master the forces of Nature; they
> will become themselves architects of systems, manufacturers of
> worlds. Man will then be perfect; he will be a creator; he will there-
> fore be what the vulgar worship as a God.

But in February 1889 Thomas Henry Huxley, one of the most influential prophets of this kind of evolutionary optimism, already sounded a note of pessimism in an article in the review *Nineteenth Century* on "Agnosticism," a term he himself had invented. According to Huxley, we are not only ignorant of any divine plan for man's salvation but there is also no assurance that the process of natural selection will make men and society better. The German physiologist Emil Dubois-Reymond was also torn between his positivism and his agnosticism. On the one hand he proclaimed: "There is no other form of knowledge than the mechanical one and no other form of scientific thinking but the mathematical physical."[6] On the other hand he expressed his pessimism about the limits of human knowledge in a speech entitled: "*Ignoramus, Ignorabimus.*"

Bergson replaced faith in science with a new kind of optimism in his book *Creative Evolution* (1907). He urged his contemporaries to shake off their complacency and sterile theorizing and to seek direct contact with life instead. Only in this way could they achieve a higher stage of evolution. According to Bergson, living was a far more basic process than knowing. The knowledge revealed by science and mathematics is abstract. It is a practical device to facilitate action. (The pragmatist James praised Bergson for making this point.) But it does not penetrate to the instinctual stream of consciousness that surges beneath it. Bergson argued that only at this level of experience do we become aware of the life force (*élan vital*), which is the true reality. Men raise themselves to a higher plane through an increasingly precise, complex, and supple adaptation of their consciousness to the conditions under which they live.

"You must take things by storm; you must thrust intelligence outside itself by an act of will." In saying this Bergson was emphasizing the primacy of intuition and instinct over intellect. He was reacting against the mechanistic-materialistic-deterministic view of life with which the scientists and positivists had tried to strait-jacket human freedom. Bergson insisted that there was room for real freedom and real change once men threw off the strait-jacket "by an act of will." The life force, rather than mind or matter, is the fundamental reality. Intuition alone brings us into immediate contact with real life. The intellect misses what is unique and original, unforeseeable and irreversible. And it is from these sources that true human progress stems. This exciting and liberating point of view appealed to artists and writers, to religious thinkers, and to the fashionable ladies who came to Bergson's crowded lectures at the Collège de France.

Bergson's voluntarism, his antirationalism, and his glorification of the life force were the culmination of the romantic effort to cope with the loss of faith in traditional certainties. This effort had begun a century earlier in response to the French and Industrial Revolutions. These upheavals had cleared the way for modernization by creating new political, social, and economic structures, but they had also disillusioned sensitive thinkers and artists concerning intellectual and cultural traditions dating back to classical Greece. Just as classicism had assumed that art could impose order and beauty on life, so the rationalism and intellectualism of Plato and Descartes had assumed that philosophy could discover true ideas about man and his world. The romantics could no longer accept the certainty of these assumptions. Georg Wilhelm Friedrich Hegel tried to create a new certainty that explained ordinary facts, human actions, historical changes, and institutions as the progressive realization of the World Spirit. He also invented a new, dialectical logic to account for change and development in ways unexplainable by means of traditional logic—with its insistence that a thing must either have or not have an attribute at a given time. But during the first half of the nineteenth century the two philosophers who stressed the unqualified absurdity and cruelty of life most completely—Sören Kierkegaard and Arthur Schopenhauer— were also the most pessimistic. Nietzsche held out some hope for the gifted few, but Bergson was optimistic about the possibility of redemption for the many. He was also moving toward a mystical faith (fully formulated in his last work, *The Two Sources of Morality and Religion*) in each individual's capacity to make his energy and will transcend the bounds of nature and self and reinsert them into the creative movement of spirit.

During the early 1900's other European philosophers also tried to invent new philosophies of life in place of the traditional certainties that modernization—beginning with the scientific revolution—had destroyed. In Italy, Benedetto Croce (1866–1952) championed the idea of the free spirit rejecting conventional notions, creating new values, and, through his intuition, apprehending the pure throb of life in its actuality. But Croce also tried to restore the importance of the intellect:

> Those intellectuals who see salvation in the withdrawal of the artist or thinker from the world around him, in his deliberate non-participation in vulgar practical contests . . . do without knowing it compass the death of the intellect.[7]

The true philosopher seeks concrete knowledge about life through the study of history. Indeed Croce argued that philosophy and history are identical. This is so because all concrete knowledge comes from the understanding and judgments the philosopher derives from studying the lives and actions of the past which he finds relevant to his own time. And the knowledge he gains in this way should be translatable into action.

Vienna, the Ringstrasse in front of the Parliament building.

In Spain, Miguel de Unamuno (1864–1936) rejected Croce's demand for action based on reason and advocated an activist irrationalism. In his essay "*La Cruzada,*" in the review *España Moderna* in February 1906, Unamuno demanded a "crusade" to rescue Don Quixote from the fearful and cowardly prudent spokesmen for reason, who considered him the knight of folly for having fought without asking the "why" of everything. According to Unamuno, the purpose of life is to believe in what there is hope for and to fight not for victory but "for love of the combat itself." In *The Tragic Sense of Life*, first published in 1913, Unamuno argues that the only possible position from which to face existence is one of uncertainty.

Rejecting all forms of traditional speculation, another group of philosophers redefined their task as the critique of language. The German Gottlob Frege and the Englishman Bertrand Russell concentrated on deriving mathematical languages from a purified logic. The Austrian Ludwig Wittgenstein (1889–1951) believed that the only way to disengage ourselves from the traps of traditional philosophies was by a careful, scrupulous description of language as most people actually use it. Wittgenstein's philosophy is more difficult to summarize than that of any of his contemporaries because of the unconventional way in which he expressed his insights. Yet the effort must be made, not only because his reorientation of philosophy was so radical in itself but also because Wittgenstein was closely tied to the cultural setting of pre-1914 Vienna and the reactions of other modern-minded writers and artists against it.

Nowhere else was the contrast between traditional and modern culture as extreme as in Vienna in the years 1900–14. As we shall see in Chapter 10, Paris was the main center in which avant-garde painters tried to strip away traditional values and perceptions and invent new pictorial languages, but the Viennese Oskar Kokoschka also participated in this effort. We shall also see how Adolf Loos banished ornament from art and architecture and how Arnold Schoenberg rejected the trappings and theatrical effects of late romantic music and sought new ways of developing the purely logical character of musical ideas. Each of these men, along with Wittgenstein himself, acknowledged the inspiration of Karl Kraus, the maverick critic of language and society and editor of the satirical review *Die Fackel* (The Torch). Kraus was the most incisive and uncompromising polemicist against the corruptions, distortions, and falsifications of traditional Viennese culture in all its aspects.[8]

Kraus also attacked the journalism and psychoanalysis of his day for what he considered their distortions. According to him, the prestigious Viennese daily *Neue Freie Presse* not only distorted the news generally because of its upper-middle-class bias but it also distorted specific news events by freely mingling fact and opinion, subjective and objective reactions. Kraus charged that the worst distortions appeared in that paper's short, "serious" essays (*feuilletons*), which Carl Schorske, the leading historian of the prewar Viennese cultural scene, describes as follows:

> The subjective response of the reporter or critic to an experience, his feeling-tone, acquired clear primacy over the matter of his discourse. To render a state of feeling became the mode of formulating a judgment. Accordingly, in the feuilleton writer's style, the adjectives engulfed the nouns, the personal tint virtually obliterated the contours of the object of discourse.[9]

In one of his most often quoted aphorisms—"Psychoanalysis is that spiritual disease of which it considers itself to be the cure"—Kraus was referring to Freud's "myth" explaining aesthetic and moral values as the products of the frustrations of irrational, egocentric, antisocial impulses in the unconscious. According to Kraus, psychoanalysis thus made creative fantasy a manifestation of the illness it sought to cure, whereas Kraus saw it as the source of everything that was healthy in the individual and society.[10]

Although Wittgenstein did not publish his *Tractatus Logico-Philosophicus* until 1921, this work reflected the modernist reaction in prewar Vienna against intellectual self-indulgence and aesthetic sloppiness in all fields. Kraus preached the need for a "creative separation" of factual discourse from artistic and moral discourse. Only in this way could his contemporaries eliminate the falsification of the factual and the debasement and distortion of the aesthetic and moral, which permeated their culture. What Kraus tried to do in the fields of letters and journalism Wittgenstein attempted in philosophy. His method was also Krausian, with its ironical and paradoxical aphorisms designed to shock the reader into rearranging his mental patterns.

Above all Wittgenstein sought to bar philosophical speculation from interfering with the way we live and to prevent rationalizations from stifling our spontaneous feelings.[11] Like Nietzsche, Bergson, Croce, and Unamuno, Wittgenstein condemned rationalism and positivism for assuming that all human concerns could be meaningfully discussed in logical language. He insisted that only the artist can show us the higher truths and that there should be a clear separation of creative fantasy from reason. Wittgenstein tried to prove that logical language can deal only with facts, whereas feelings can only be *evoked* and values can only be *shown*, not *said*. This is the meaning of the last proposition of the *Tractatus:* "Whereof one cannot speak, thereof one must be silent."

Few twentieth-century philosophers were ready to "be silent" about ethics, politics, aesthetics, and even logic itself, which Wittgenstein maintained is a model we impose on facts, not a fact in itself. Propositions "model" situations by relating objects in configurations. The logical relation that a proposition expresses between the symbols gives it its sense. A proposition is true when the objects named or symbolized in it form the configuration that the logical relation "models." Otherwise it is false. "Only propositions have sense; and only in the nexus of a proposition does a name have a reference."[12] By themselves names are without sense; they become intelligible only in the context of the logical relations between them. With his model theory of propositions as the basis of his new critique of language Wittgenstein was also able to solve a critical problem that plagued other theorists of logic. A classic example is whether the proposition "The pot of gold at the end of the rainbow is full" is true or false. Wittgenstein's model theory resolved the dilemma by pointing out that this proposition itself has no sense and therefore cannot give the "pot of gold at the end of the rainbow" a reference it lacks in fact.[13]

The logical basis of Wittgenstein's model theory *showed* how the structure of propositions determined the limits of rational and scientific discourse. Wittgenstein insisted that his critique of language solved the philosophical problem of how knowledge of the world was possible. Such knowledge could only be *said* in the mathematical representations of scientists or in straightforward descriptive language. But the "meaning of life" could not be *said;* it could only be *shown* by the metaphors of the poet and other forms of "indirect communication." The next to last aphorism in the *Tractatus* seems to admit Wittgenstein's failure in his own effort to go beyond the sayable:

> My propositions serve as elucidations in the following way: anyone who understands me eventually recognizes them as nonsensical, when he has used them—as steps—to climb up beyond them. (He must, so to speak, throw away the ladder after he has climbed up it.) He must transcend these propositions and then he will see the world aright.[14]

But, like Kraus, Wittgenstein is using a paradox to make his point that the "meaning of life" can only be "seen" outside the realm of rational discourse—through fantasy and in the way one lives. Traditional philosophy should therefore go out of business altogether.

SOCIAL SCIENCES

At the end of the nineteenth century the scientific study of behavior became separated from traditional philosophy as natural science had done in the eighteenth century. During the Age of Enlightenment philosophy dealt mainly with the mind of man, the nature of his thought, and the ends of his action, whereas science, disregarding the idea of purpose, sought causal laws that would explain the world of matter. Thought about man and society remained largely philosophical during most of the nineteenth century. For all their claims to being scientific, Comte, Spencer, and even Marx did not succeed in supporting their theories with adequate empirical data. The founders of scientific sociology were Émile Durkheim, Max Weber, and Vilfredo Pareto. Psychology as the science of mental life evolved out of physiology and neurology in the early work of Wilhelm Wundt and out of the treatment of mental illness, most notably in the work of Pierre Janet and Sigmund Freud. Except for Ivan Petrovich Pavlov, the theories of these early scientific sociologists and psychologists still had a significant philosophical dimension. Meanwhile, Edward B. Tylor, Sir James Frazer, Lucien Lévy-Bruhl, and other precursors of modern anthropology were armchair ethnologists imbued with the philosophical assumption that people in "primitive" cultures lacked the capacity to think "logically." Bronislaw Malinowski and A. R. Radcliffe-Brown began their scientific field work in social anthropology before 1914, though their major impact came after the war.

DEPTH PSYCHOLOGY

One of the most momentous discoveries of the prewar generation was that mind and consciousness are not one and the same. Wundt and James pointed out that consciousness is selective and that what it chooses to notice or suppress at a given moment is governed by a collection of symbols and feelings in what Freud called the preconscious mind. This nonconscious mental storehouse of momentarily rejected but potentially conscious ideas allows us to make those intuitive leaps that help us understand and cope with the oceans of information and stimuli in which we are constantly swimming. If we could not draw on it to select what is important in a given situation, we would drown. But our ability to understand and cope with a given situation is also influenced by what goes on in the darker recesses of the mind—the *unconscious*—which is ordinarily inaccessible to consciousness. The unconscious and its workings became a major concern of psychologists in our period. Janet, Alfred Adler, and Carl Gustav Jung conceived of it in different ways and devised different methods of dealing with it.[15] Earlier, Freud also drew on the research and theories of others, but his contributions to the understanding of the unconscious as a dynamic system with its own rules were the most influential, both before and after the war.

Sigmund Freud (1856–1939) founded psychoanalysis as a theory, a therapeutic method, and an organized movement. The power of his writings and the breadth and audacity of his speculations

> revolutionized the thought, the lives, and the imagination of an age. He contradicted, and in some cases he reversed, the prevailing opinions, of the learned as well as of common people, on many of the issues of human existence and culture. He led people to think about their appetites and their intellectual powers, about self-knowledge and self-deceit, about the ends of life and about man's profoundest

passions and about his most intimate or trivial failings, in ways that
would have seemed to earlier generations at once scandalous and
silly.[16]

Even more original than his theory was his new method of dealing with
the unconscious. Freud maintained a medical practice in Vienna from
1886 until his exile in 1938. As a means of treating the emotional disturbances of his patients he invented the psychoanalytic method, based on
free association and the analysis of resistances and transference. And almost from the beginning he made psychoanalysis into a "school," with its
own organization, publications, and the training analysis of the would-be
member, which also served as an initiation rite.

The original stimulus that set Freud on the path toward psychoanalysis
was his association with Josef Breuer, who had first stumbled on the talk-
ing-out cure. An important additional influence was his searching self-
analysis, which was literally the first psychoanalysis. Freud soon came to
assume that ideas helped to form hysterical symptoms and that the words
used in hypnotic suggestion were effective against them. At first Freud
believed that these symptoms occurred because the patient had repressed
some horrible memory into his unconscious and resisted all efforts to
bring it into consciousness. On May 2, 1897, however, in a letter to his
friend Wilhelm Fliess, he wrote: "The psychical structures which in hysteria are subjected to repression are not properly speaking memories . . .
but impulses deriving from the primal scenes."[17] A few months later he
told Fliess that the patients' recollections of seduction or rape in these
primal scenes were fantasies, not real events. By then Freud had also
abandoned hypnosis for the technique of free association as the means of
overcoming his patient's resistance to consciously recognizing and coping
with these crippling fantasies.

Although Freud is famous for his theory of hysteria (*Studies in Hysteria*, 1895) and other forms of mental illness, this theory constitutes only
one of his major contributions to depth psychology. Other early ones are
his theory of dreams (*The Interpretation of Dreams*, 1900), his theory of
the errors we make in everyday life (*The Psychopathology of Everyday
Life*, 1901), and his theory of jokes (*Jokes and Their Relation to the Unconscious*, 1905). Unlike the theory of hysteria, these three theories are
primarily concerned with exploring the unconscious mind in its normal
workings.

"The interpretation of dreams is the royal road to a knowledge of the
unconscious activities of the mind."[18] This is so, according to Freud, because the great majority of dreams are disguised fulfillments of repressed

wishes. In 1909, anticipating his postwar theory of the roles of the ego, superego, and id, Freud said in his *Introductory Lectures on Psychoanalysis*, that "a dreamer's relation to his wishes is a quite peculiar one. He repudiates them and censors them—he has no liking for them, in short."[19] Freud goes on to say that two separate people are somehow united in the dreamer: one who rejects the wish and another who has it and is satisfied by its fulfillment in his dream. The one who rejects the wish does so because it is incompatible with his other wishes; for example, he rejects the wish to kill his father and sleep with his mother partly because he also wishes to gain the love of his father and partly because he wishes to avoid castration as punishment for his incestuous impulse. But even in dreams the profoundly disturbing wishes that would give satisfaction are only latent. If the wish did not express itself in the disguise of a dream, the wisher would have a nightmare and be awakened. The "manifest content" of the dream, which is what we remember, disguises the "latent content" so thoroughly with symbols through the mechanisms of displacement and condensation that only the analyst can decipher its true sense with the method of free association.

Freud's theory of dreams derived from his general conception of the mind and its unconscious workings.

> It was discovered one day that the pathological symptoms of certain neurotic patients have a sense. On this discovery the psycho-analytic method of treatment was founded. It happened in the course of this treatment that patients, instead of bringing forward their symptoms, brought forward dreams. A suspicion thus arose that the dreams too had a sense.[20]

Freud further developed his conception of the unconscious as a dynamic system with its own rules in his studies of the "slips" and jokes we make in everyday life. Even an apparently innocent forgetting of a name, according to him, is the outcome of a conflict between the conscious and the unconscious; there is an unconscious *reason* for the conscious forgetting. Slips of the tongue often express the "counter-intention" or "counter-will"[21] of what is actually said, as in the case of the President of the Lower House of the Austrian Parliament who opened a session by declaring it closed. In cases like this one the "counter-intention" reveals itself in an obvious way. But "counter-intentions" that express more deeply repressed wishes require more elaborate disguises. Freud gives the following example:

> A young man of twenty introduced himself during my consulting

hours in these words: "I am the father of So-and-so who came to you for treatment. I beg your pardon, I meant to say I am his brother: he is four years older than I am." I inferred that he intended this slip to express the view that, like his brother, he had fallen ill through the fault of his father; that, like his brother, he wished to be cured; but that his father was the one who most needed to be cured.[22]

Many jokes are even more oblique expressions of unconscious impulses than Freudian slips. Freud distinguished "innocent" jokes, whose only purpose is to evoke a smile with a playful use of language, from tendentious jokes, which have the ulterior purpose of giving vent to repressed wishes in a socially acceptable way. Tendentious jokes give more pleasure because they serve this purpose. The hostile gibe allows a person to "get away with" expressing an aggressive impulse by claiming that he is "only kidding." The obscene joke allows the teller and his companion(s) to strip or seduce a third party mentally through the fantasy it evokes.

Freud's preoccupation with sexuality was neither original nor unique in our period. In 1886, the year Freud began his medical practice, Richard von Krafft-Ebing published his *Psychopathia Sexualis* in Vienna. Thereafter the number of titles on this subject grew so large that in 1905 Magnus Hirschfeld's yearbook, part of which tried to cover the current bibliography, had 1,084 pages. Thus, when Freud published his *Three Essays in the Theory of Sexuality* in that same year, he was synthesizing a vast body of scattered and partially organized ideas. But the synthesis itself was both original and unique.

Several themes dominate Freud's sexual theories. First there is the concept of the sexual drive itself (which in his 1915 revision of the *Three Essays* Freud calls the libido), its manifestations in infancy, its successive phases of evolution, and its metamorphoses. Second, Freud emphasizes the vicissitudes of choice regarding a love object, giving particular attention to the Oedipus complex. Third, based on the preceding, he interprets certain types of neuroses and sexual deviations as the result of fixations at the oral and anal phases of sexual development. Fourth, he posits a system of sexual symbolism. Fifth, he inquires into the early events of sexual life, childhood sexual fantasies, and their functions in the emotional life of adults.

In recent years Freud's sexual theories have been attacked because they seem to downgrade the sexuality of women, but throughout his life he was attacked for defaming the innocence of childhood with his radical ideas on infant sexuality. For Freud sex included all forms of sensual gratification, not just genital ones. "Sucking at the mother's breast is the starting-point of the whole of sexual life, the unmatched prototype of every later sexual satisfaction, to which phantasy often enough recurs in times of need."[23] Freud thought sexuality fundamental not only because it began so early but also because its aims do not readily tolerate frustration and because it can influence the ways we think and see things. ("A man's attitude in sexual things has the force of a model to which the rest of his reactions tend to conform.")[24] Finally, Freud insisted on the proneness of sexuality to maldevelopment. The conflicts about sexual impulses and fantasies and the resulting anxieties that led to their repression were for him the number one cause of most neuroses and other psychopathologies of everyday life.

Depth psychology was not without competing theories. Behaviorism so-named also originated in the immediate prewar years and, in one form or another, has come to dominate the psychological establishment in recent decades. In its most extreme form it reduces all behavior to conditioned and unconditioned reflexes. In 1903 Pavlov gave his first definitions of these reflexes in his paper "Experimental Psychology and Psychopathology of Animals" at the International Congress on Medicine in Madrid; he was awarded a Nobel Prize a year later. Most behaviorist psychologists have taken "softer" positions than Pavlov (who never considered himself a psychologist anyway). Some have tested performance and skills; others have adapted their hypotheses to their patients' symptoms. Freud's theory about childhood rests on interpretations of adult memories, fantasies, and neuroses, whereas the theories of Alfred Binet and Jean Piaget reflect their empirical observations of the actual behavior of children. In contrast to Freud and other early advocates of depth psychology, many behaviorists have insisted on meeting what they considered the standards of science as objective inquiry and operationally definable concepts. And by these standards they take the mind, both conscious and unconscious, to be a mere ghost in the machine.

CLASSICAL SOCIOLOGY

It has often been argued that Freud's psychological theories reflected the bourgeois culture and society of pre-1914 Vienna and are therefore inapplicable in a world that has moved into a later stage of modernization. Whether or not the second part of this argument is true, the first part certainly is. Similar charges have been leveled at the "Classical Sociology" of Émile Durkheim, Max Weber, and Vilfredo Pareto, which the sociologist Alvin W. Gouldner recently said:

> was the great achievement of the middle class of Western Europe, in the late nineteenth century, when the individual, competitive entrepreneur was being supplanted by increasingly large-scale and bureaucratized industrial organization, and when in general, the middle class was increasingly threatened by the rise of Marxist socialism.[25]

Durkheim, Weber, and Pareto dissociated themselves from the Marxist charge that capitalist society and its values functioned only for the benefit of the ruling class. Just as Freud accepted as fixed the dynamics of the nineteenth-century bourgeois family, so Pareto and Durkheim (though not Weber) seemed to preserve the nineteenth-century middle-class view that existing social arrangements served a useful function for the whole society.

Durkheim, Weber, and Pareto also rejected all explanations of human behavior which disregarded what takes place in consciousness. All three strove "to comprehend the newly recognized disparity between external reality and the internal appreciation of that reality."[26] They stressed the importance of consciousness both as a mediating factor between behavior and rationalizations of behavior and as the means for understanding these two phenomena. In an age when traditional religion was all but exhausted and individuals began to feel entrapped by increasingly autonomous and bureaucratized forces, they placed special emphasis on the kinds of beliefs that held groups and societies together. These shared beliefs, or consensus, could not be understood "from without," as a mere adjunct of material conditions, institutions, or the policies of powerful leaders. They were something internal, in the thoughts and feelings of the average member of a given society; sometimes they went against his self-interest. The classical sociologists believed that this social bond, however nonrational its components might be, helped explain much social behavior.[27]

The Italian Vilfredo Pareto (1848–1923) was primarily concerned with the impact of mental processes on society. His sociology reflects his early training in civil engineering, particularly mathematics, and his professional interest in laissez-faire economic theory. (He held the chair in political economy at the University of Lausanne, Switzerland, from 1893 to 1907.) Indeed his graduation thesis on mechanical equilibrium became the model for his conception of both economy and society. In 1897 he hit upon the second main assumption for his sociology: the idea that most human activity is due to feelings rather than logical thinking. Pareto began writing *The Mind and Society: A Treatise on General Sociology* in 1907 and completed it in 1912, though this four-volume work was not published until 1916.

Pareto believed that the true objects of sociological inquiry are the basic impulses and attitudes in individual minds. He called the various forms of these emotions *residues*. These residues differ among the social strata of a society and between one society and another, but they change little in any given society as a whole. Pareto distinguishes six classes of residues of which the first two are the most important socially. Class I, the "instinct for combining," is essentially innovative; Class II, "the persistence of aggregates," is the propensity to conserve elements already combined. Actions based on interests, particularly the pursuit of wealth and power, are usually logical. In contrast, most actions based on residues are nonlogical.

But human beings take great pains to convince themselves and others that such actions are logical by means of "verbal manifestations" which Pareto calls *derivations*. These derivations—or, more loosely speaking, rationalizations—serve as a "logical veneer," as "emotional veils" for nonlogical actions that "are mere manifestations of instincts, inclinations, etc."[28] Hence Pareto's sociology seeks to strip the realities behind these rationalizations, since the nonlogical actions based on them are crucial elements in any social system.

Derivations in their various forms are important because, once accepted, they lend "strength and aggressiveness to the corresponding sentiments, which now have found a way to express themselves."[29] Nationalist and socialist ideologies make people more conscious of their residues of group solidarity and thus help them act more effectively. Pareto applied his theory of propaganda specifically to newspapers, whose power was growing in his time.

> But that [power] does not come of any special facilities which they possess for forcing their points of view upon the public, nor of the logico-experimental validity of their reasonings—these are often childish enough. It is all due to the art they have developed for working at residues through derivations.[30]

According to Pareto, society is held together only by residues. There is no scientific standard for judging whether or not these residues are true, but their "truth" is irrelevant. What matters is their functional effectiveness, their social utility. Feelings expressed in manners, family organization, and religious beliefs constitute the foundation of society. They resist transformation even after a revolution has changed the identity and ideology of those who govern and, eventually, the organization of public power.

Pareto conceives of society as a dynamic system of interdependent forces. He recognizes external forces such as climate, geography, and race, but assumes that their effect came early in history. The crucial interactions occur between four variables: interests, residues, derivations, and the ways in which these maintain the equilibrium between elites and masses in a given society. When this equilibrium is upset, the society moves into a new cycle. Shifts in the mutual dependence of the masses and the governing and nongoverning elites are determined by fluctuations in their motivations and psychological states. But Pareto concerns himself especially with the role of governing elites.

"History is the graveyard of aristocracies." By this statement Pareto means that the history of societies is the history of a succession of privileged minorities—or governing elites. Normally there is a *circulation of elites*—that is, able and vigorous members of the lower strata of society move up into the governing elite while its more ineffective and degenerate members are eliminated. But "if one of these movements comes to an end, or worse still, if they both come to an end, the governing class crashes to ruin and often sweeps the whole of a nation along with it"[31]; then a new governing elite takes over and the normal circulation is resumed. This was what had happened to the various aristocracies of the past and it would inevitably happen again. For example, Pareto foresaw that the men who made the Bolshevik Revolution in Russia in the name of the masses would become a new governing elite themselves.

Pareto's theory of the mind and society is pessimistic. It recognizes the progress of reason and innovation in modern science and technology but sees little hope for similar progress in social and political conduct. Pareto is cynical regarding the humanitarianism, parliamentary democracy, and socialism of his time.

> Almost all great newspapers, not excepting a goodly number that are professedly Socialist, have connexions, direct or indirect, with the plutocracy that is the ruling power in civilized countries today, and with the governments in which it plays a part.[32]

He uses the term "pluto-democracy" to describe the tacit alliance he perceived between the trade-union bosses and the employers in modern industrial society. His theory of the "political process" as the interaction of mutually dependent variables in a given society has been taken over by twentieth-century political scientists, though without his cynicism. And his replacement of reason and morality with function as the dominant factor in human affairs was a typical response of most social scientists to the effects of modernization before the war. But his elaborate classification of residues and derivations has been dismissed by almost everyone as arbitrary and unverifiable.

The Frenchman Émile Durkheim (1858–1917) rejected Pareto's and Freud's assumption that the source of human behavior is individual states of mind or feelings; for him social constraints determined behavior. These social constraints emanate from *collective representations*—the customs, traditions, ideas, and values that a given society has institutionalized to educate and socialize individuals so that they will become functionally useful members of that society. Collective representations are part of a cultural symbolic system. According to Durkheim, they have a reality of their own and are beyond the control of the individuals who have incorporated them into their basic outlook. And, like the collective representations and moral code it creates, society itself is autonomous. It is *sui generis*—real but not physical.

For Durkheim the most important function of any institution or practice is to maintain social stability. Social constraints function in this way through education and also through punishment. The identification and punishment of deviants reinforce both the moral code and the society that produced it. Whatever other uses to which it might be put, such as deterring crime or rehabilitating individual criminals, punishment has as its object not the offender himself but the violation done to the *conscience collective* (translatable as collective conscience or collective consciousness) of the society. This collective conscience expresses itself in the shared moral code, which is made sacred by religion. Religion too is a creation of society and it functions, through its rites, symbols, and moral constraints, as the principal force for maintaining social stability and order.

Only religion or its functional equivalent can provide the sacred bond that holds society together. In archaic and traditional societies religion sanctified the collective representations and moral code accepted by all their members. But it no longer served this function in modern society, which was especially threatened with disintegration because of the "forced division of labor." Durkheim distinguished between the forced division of economic activities among people who are born rich or poor and the "organic" division of social roles; he perceived the latter as good because it encouraged individual liberty. Thus, in all his major books— *The Division of Labor* (1893), *The Rules of Sociological Method* (1895), *Suicide* (1897), and *The Elementary Forms of Religious Life* (1912)—Durkheim tried not only to make sociology a science but also to find in a society in the throes of modernization the source of a new secular morality that would restore order and stability to it.

For Durkheim the worst effect of modernization was what he called *anomie* (normlessness). In the highly differentiated and pluralistic French society of his time the highest value seemed to be respect for individual autonomy and judgment. But how could the individual find his true personality and make personal judgments in a meaningful way in a society in which traditionally accepted norms were losing their force and no new ones were taking their place? In this situation of *anomie* the individual became disoriented. He had difficulty performing, and even finding, a useful social function. Nor did his improved material well-being alleviate his moral distress.

> With increased prosperity desires increase. At the very moment when traditional rules have lost their authority, the richer prize offered these appetites stimulates them and makes them more exigent and impatient of control. The state of de-regulation or anomy is thus further heightened by passions being less disciplined, precisely when they need more disciplining.[33]

In extreme cases *anomie* led to suicide. Individual suicides occurred in all societies, but, according to Durkheim, the increasing *rate* of suicides was an index of "the general unrest of contemporary societies."[34]

Durkheim made a major contribution to modern sociology with his perception of *anomie;* his idea of function influenced social anthropology as well. He criticized the so-called comparative method of Comte and Spencer and the ethnologists Tylor and Frazer, who catalogued instances of a given trait in many different societies but disregarded the utterly different functions it might have served in each of these societies.

> In the first place, for the sociologist as for the historian, social facts vary with the social system of which they form a part; they cannot be understood when detached from it. This is why two facts which come from two different societies cannot be profitably compared merely because they seem to resemble each other; it is necessary that these societies themselves resemble each other.[35]

For instance, the monogamy that is frequent among the Australian aborigines serves a quite different function from monogamy in modern

Western societies. Another mistake is to assume that practices considered "pathological" in modern society could have no "normal" function in archaic societies. Like Durkheim, the anthropologist Radcliffe-Brown believed that magic solemnized the activities with which it was associated among primitive peoples, thus promoting social solidarity. Although Malinowski disagreed, his contention that magic reduced anxieties so that these peoples could go about their business and get their work done was also a "normal" function, albeit a different one.

Like Pareto, Durkheim accepted modern capitalism as functionally useful, though he recognized the ways in which its "forced division of labor" undermined social solidarity. Durkheim renounced criticizing the capitalist system because that would have meant adopting a socialist point of view. And as a scholar-professor he believed that championing an ideology was incompatible with preserving academic sociology as an objective science. In contrast to those theorists who predicted the eventual triumph of socialism, Durkheim argued that social scientists could not predict the future. Their task was to examine social facts and their functions in the existing system.

Despite his preoccupation with social stability Durkheim was a liberal in his desire to see modern society enhance moral individualism. In order to complete the liberating effects of the Revolution of 1789 he advocated the abolition of the hereditary transmission of private property as the way to end the "forced division of labor" of his own day. "Spontaneous division of labor" would reconstitute society "in such a way that social inequalities exactly express natural inequalities."[36] At one point Durkheim suggested a modified kind of guild socialism, in which occupational organizations and other intermediate institutions between the individual and the state might supply the moral values needed to give anomic individuals a sense of purpose. But he did not approve of forced or revolutionary change of any kind and he never demanded basic changes in the capitalist structure of modern industrial society itself.

Functionalism allowed Durkheim and most of the succeeding generation of social scientists to avoid questioning the justice of the capitalist economic and political order. Instead they searched for ways to bolster social solidarity *within* it. But accepting the existing order involves an implicit value judgment just as surely as claims to complete objectivity in human affairs are a form of self-delusion. We are all limited by the "social construction of reality" that we have internalized from our own culture.[37]

Durkheim the would-be empiricist comes close to philosophical idealism when he describes the collective consciousness as having a real existence of its own. "Being placed outside of and above individual and local contingencies, it sees things in their permanent and essential aspects, which it crystallizes into communicable ideas."[38] The collective consciousness, according to Durkheim, was developed by rooting out the subjective elements in collective representations. Thus "the way was opened to a stable, impersonal and organized thought which then had nothing to do except to develop its nature."[39] Durkheim asserts that "Despite its metaphysical appearance, this word [collective representations] designates nothing more than a body of natural facts which are explained by natural causes."[40]

The trouble comes from Durkheim's use of "social" as a synonym for "natural." Social behavior may be motivated by collective representations, but these are not empirically verifiable in the same way as the behavior itself. They are analytical concepts which the sociologist imposes on the behavior in order to make sense out of it, not "natural facts" in themselves. Collective representations are thus intellectual, not "social," explanations of social facts (behavior). These may be as "real" as physical facts, as Durkheim insists, but it is more likely that the concepts used to explain both kinds of facts emanate from individual minds than from the facts themselves.

The German sociologist Max Weber (1864–1920) acknowledged the distinction between social facts and the concepts we use to explain them. Trained as a jurist and economist, he also acquired professional competence as a historian and philosopher. Unlike Durkheim, Weber was not significantly influenced by the positivist tradition, according to which the "laws" of nature and social behavior exist "out there" waiting to be discovered. His struggle was rather against the Hegelian idealist tradition, which reified ideas. Although Marx himself tried to avoid this fallacy, Weber criticized the young Marxist metaphysicians of his own time for defining the proletariat as an entity that was infallible in pursuing its interests. Weber insisted that such an idea could not be derived from empirical data. He did not discuss Durkheim's collective representations but he insisted that all such concepts were abstractions invented by social scientists in order to understand action that is social—that is, whose "subjective meaning takes account of the behavior of others and is thereby oriented in its course."[41]

Weber distinguishes two types of understanding of the subjective meaning of social action. Observational understanding derives the meaning of an act or symbolic expression from immediate observation. Interpretive or explanatory understanding requires that the particular act "be placed in a broader context of meaning involving facts which cannot be derived from immediate observation of a particular act or expression."[42] We can understand by direct observation both the rational action of somebody who reaches for the knob to shut a door and the irrational exclamations or movements of someone becoming angry. When the motive of the action is not directly observable, the social scientist must try to interpret it within the complex of meaning in which it belongs. Thus he must scrupulously avoid applying his own values and ideas to it and try to understand those of the actors he is studying. In order to do this he must consciously adopt the mentality of these actors, no matter how different they are from him culturally.

The following quotation summarizes Weber's argument that sociological and historical studies can be made scientific by delimiting their subjective dimension and by using empirically derived concepts, especially "pure" or *ideal types*.

> A correct causal interpretation of a concrete course of action is arrived at when the overt action and the motives have both been correctly apprehended and at the same time their relation has become meaningfully comprehensible. A correct causal interpretation of typical action means that the process which is claimed to be typical is shown to be both adequately grasped on the level of meaning and at the same time the interpretation is to some degree causally adequate. If adequacy in respect to meaning is lacking, then no matter how high the degree of uniformity and how precisely its probability can be numerically determined, it is still an incomprehensible statistical probability, whether we deal with overt or subjective processes. On the other hand, even the most perfect adequacy on the level of meaning has causal significance from a sociological point of view only insofar as there is some kind of proof for the existence of a probability that action in fact normally takes the course which has been held to be meaningful. For this there must be some degree of determinable frequency of approximation to an average or a pure type.[43]

A familiar example of an ideal-type is that of modern laissez-faire capitalism. "It offers us an ideal picture of events on the commodity-market under conditions of a society organized on the principles of an exchange economy, free competition and rigorously rational conduct. . . . [But] this construct in itself is like a *utopia* which has been arrived at by the analytical accentuation of certain elements of reality."[44] It helps us to understand the characteristic features of the market-conditioned relationships it refers to; it also offers us guidance in the construction of hypotheses about the processes of economic behavior.

Weber first formulated his own ideal-types on the basis of comparative historical evidence and then tried to analyze a particular subject to see how far it approximated or deviated from them. Some of his familiar ideal-types are bureaucracy, charismatic authority, patrimonialism (as distinct from feudalism), the Occidental city, and the Protestant ethic. Unlike Pareto, Durkheim, and many other sociologists, Weber did not believe that such abstract concepts could make explicit the class or average character of social and cultural phenomena. This goal was scientifically unattainable because the concepts themselves do not describe any existing or historical reality. Weber's purpose in constructing his ideal-types—both in his sociological and his comparative historical studies—was to understand the unique individual character of meaningful social action.

> How then, can we attain objectivity in the behavioral sciences? The *objective* validity of all empirical knowledge rests exclusively upon the ordering of the given reality according to categories which are *subjective* in a specific sense, namely, in that they present the *presuppositions* of our knowledge and are based on the presupposition of the *value* of those *truths* which empirical knowledge alone is able to give us. . . . In the empirical social sciences . . . the possibility of meaningful knowledge of what is essential for us in the infinite richness of events is bound up with the unremitting application of viewpoints of a specifically particularized character, which, in the last analysis, are oriented on the basis of evaluative ideas. These evaluative ideas are for their part empirically discoverable and analyzable as elements of meaningful human conduct, but their validity can *not* be deduced from the empirical data as such. The "objectivity" of the social sciences depends rather on the fact that the empirical data are always related to those evaluative ideas which alone make them worth knowing and the significance of the empirical data is derived from these evaluative ideas. . . . The *cultural significance* of *concrete historical events and patterns* is exclusively and solely the final end which, among other means, concept-construction and the criticism of constructs also seek to serve.[45]

This position poses difficulties that Weber never resolved. The "*presuppositions* of our knowledge" can never be completely separated from the social construction of reality we have internalized. It is one thing to claim that we can discover what is worth knowing to us with evaluative ideas; it is quite another thing to presuppose that we already know what is worth knowing in another culture.* Perhaps Weber's effort to move from evidence to the formulation of concepts, and from concepts back to evidence is as close as we can get to a scientific understanding of anything. But the "objectivity" of this kind of understanding is still relative not only to the presuppositions of the social scientist or historian but also to the ways in which the data available to him—such as statistics on income, unemployment, crime, and literacy—have been ordered and classified. Nevertheless, Weber made a lasting contribution to the methodology of the social sciences with his emphasis on a precise, specialized terminology.

Weber applied his new methodology in a number of fields, including economic action, the sociology of law, and the sociology of religion. In addition to his books about the religions of China and India and ancient Judaism he postulated a novel connection between religion and modern capitalism in his *The Protestant Ethic and the Spirit of Capitalism* (1905). His theory of the types of domination forms the core of his most important work, *Economy and Society*, and has influenced many subsequent studies on this subject.

Like Pareto, Weber was preoccupied with the ways in which power is exercised in modern society. But whereas Pareto treated this question in terms of the composition and techniques of ruling elites, Weber concentrated on the more impersonal aspects of bureaucracies. For Weber, bureaucratization—making collective activities functionally rational—was the most important aspect of modernization. It was brought about to a large extent by the inordinate concentration of all organizations, particularly the units of production. Within large organizations there developed a system of impersonal rules. These rules served as much for the definition of functions and the division of responsibilities as for the ordering of careers. Weber recognized the superior efficiency of bureaucratic organization and also its democratizing effect. "This results from its characteristic principle: the abstract regularity of the exercise of authority, which is the result of the demand for 'equality before the law' in the personal and functional sense—hence, of the horror of 'privilege,' and the principled rejection of doing business 'from case to case.' "[46]

Yet Weber worried about the dangerous amount of standardization that modern bureaucracies imposed on their members.[47] According to him, "the march of bureaucracy . . . destroyed structures of domination

---

* Anthropologists have recently discovered that they can miss certain aspects of another culture even when using their supposedly objective cameras. Consequently they are now letting the natives take photographs of what *they* think is important.

which were not rational," that is, "with rules, means-ends calculus, and matter-of-factness predominating."[48] Weber contrasted modern bureaucracy and the rule of law with patriarchal and patrimonial domination—in which tradition prescribed social action—and with charismatic domination—in which individual authority was based neither on rational rules nor tradition. Like these earlier types of domination, bureaucracy must have some kind of legitimacy and thus rely ultimately on consensus. Weber insisted that the basis of legitimation has distinct consequences for the way that power can be organized and applied, particularly on a routine or day-to-day basis. What bothered him most was the predictability requirements of bureaucratic organization and the standardization of behavior which alone can meet these requirements.

In explaining the functioning of his ideal-type of bureaucracy as a combination of impersonality, expertness, and hierarchy, Weber concluded that these tend to stifle the feelings and sentiments of its members. He foresaw "charismatic" revolts against it through youthful antiscientism and was himself a critic of the "iron cage" of bureaucracy. But many sociologists during the interwar years refused to see that bureaucratization could not entirely stifle human feelings any more than scientific work-organization (Taylorism) could. Indeed those who accepted the ideal-type of Weber without his own qualifications asserted that "the routine and oppressive aspects of bureaucracy are so many elements of what may be described as a 'vicious circle' that develops from the resistance of the human factor to the mechanistic rationalist theory of behavior which is being imposed on it."[49]

Bureaucratization for Weber produced a malady similar to that of Durkheim's "forced division of labor": alienation. And, like Durkheim, Weber did not believe that socialism was the cure. Since it was the central feature of modernization, bureaucratization would continue even if capitalism were replaced by socialism. More than any other thinker of our period Weber perceived the pathos of the effects of modernization on the human longing for faith and freedom.

Sociology was the social science most directly concerned with the transition from traditional to modern society. This concern had first been expressed by Comte, Tocqueville, and Marx and was approached in a more empirical way beginning in the 1890's. The dichotomy between traditional and modern society became a commonplace in the sociological literature. Herbert Spencer saw the fundamental contrast as one between social relations based on status in traditional society and on contractual arrangements in modern society. Ferdinand Tönnies saw it as communal ties versus voluntary associations in his *Gemeinschaft und Gesellschaft* (first published in 1887). Durkheim and Weber stressed the new functions that traditional institutions and values—particularly religion and authority—were forced to perform and their frequent failures in the face of forced division of labor and bureaucratization. They also dealt with the pathetic situation of individuals whom modernization made aspire increasingly toward personal autonomy in the face of growing efforts of modern organizations to mobilize them.

Perhaps the most important new perception of the classical sociologists was that modernization did not necessarily bring social and political progress. Until the 1890's the dominant bourgeois-liberal assumption in Britain and France, culminating in Spencer, was that the disintegration of traditional communal institutions was a good thing because it allowed the individual to develop his personality and satisfy his wants without the fetters of the past.[50] Marx too had been hostile to localism, community, and co-operation, but his view of industrial capitalism as merely a stage in the evolution toward an ideal society was unacceptable to both Spencer and the classical sociologists. Spencer stressed the progressive evolution from ties rooted in tradition and community to ties based on restitutive sanctions and division of labor. He believed that the society of his time could find rational and useful alternatives to the remaining irrational drives in men which still impeded progress. For example, man's natural aggressive instincts could be tamed by replacing their destructive expression in wars and revolutions with vicarious, hence harmless, experiences of violence in boxing matches, football games, and other forms of physical competition. But the classical sociologists showed that the forms in which most irrational drives expressed themselves were not individual but social. Without internalized cultural values, which were mostly nonrational, individuals became alienated, thus making social and political progress impossible.

Pareto, Durkheim, and Weber were all preoccupied with the impact of culture on social behavior. This impact became increasingly obvious in a period when traditional social status and social roles were losing their function of helping people find their identities. But the classical sociologists still reflected the outlook of the modern-minded middle-class culture of their own time. Pareto acknowledged the cultural influence of nationalist and socialist ideologies on group behavior but assumed that these could be manipulated by the governing elites. Weber doubted that the new working-class subculture that was developing in response to modernization in German society could provide an alternative to the dominant national culture. And Durkheim was unable to conceive of cultural pluralism as a workable concomitant of the social diversification he took such pains to analyze. Thus the theories of the social scientists of the turn of the century (including Freud) are interesting for us not only as "science" but also as data for understanding the subjective and objective realities from which they emerged.*

Nevertheless, the classical sociologists introduced a new conception of social reality which is still with us. Society, according to them, is built up by activity that expresses subjective meaning. But, once constructed, society has an objective reality of its own and it shapes each new generation through its institutions, norms, and values. "It is precisely the dual character of society in terms of objective facticity *and* subjective meaning that makes its 'reality' *sui generis*."[51] In other words, people construct their social reality. The construction is based on subjective meanings, but the reality is objective in the sense that it cannot be wished away. This is true of institutions like the state and the family and of the values and ideologies that legitimate such institutions. Weber and the sociologists who came after him saw more clearly than Pareto and Durkheim the dialectical character of social reality: "Society is a human product. Society is an objective reality. Man is a social product."[52] This dialectic appears in its totality as each new generation internalizes the values and perceptions of its society through the process of socialization.

The contrast between the spread of the wish to be free and the pessimism of philosophers and social thinkers concerning modernization was to dominate the Western world long after the First World War. Champions of progressive education remained optimistic about the possibility of developing individual potentialities for self-expression, but they no longer shared Spencer's faith in education as the means for eliminating moral disorganization, social alienation, and the growing power of the state. Although Durkheim also believed that education could help, he never found

* Some of today's European sociological theorists, recognizing the impact of computer languages and programmed behavior, have perceived that capitalistic technological society weakens the autonomy of the individual not through domination by the apparatus but through the supplanting of undistorted rational communication by technological rationality. "What is inexorable in the modern world is the rationalisation of culture." See Jürgen Habermas, *Legitimation Crisis* (Boston: Beacon Press, 1975), pp. 130–143, and Anthony Giddens, *The Class Structure of the Advanced Societies* (London: Hutchinson, 1973), p. 278.

a satisfactory way to socialize people for both individual liberty and order and stability in society. Even Freud, who tried to liberate individuals from their own psychological blocks, was almost as pessimistic as Nietzsche about the possibility of making modern society and culture more responsive to the wish to be free. (See especially his *Civilization and Its Discontents*, 1930).[53] One perception shared by both the champions of the New Morality and the philosophers and social scientists was that reason itself was often used to provide rationalizations for the status quo. This perception and the new value placed on equality and social justice were vigorously exploited by new radical protest movements.

CHAPTER 8

RADICAL PROTEST

Capitalism can't last forever.
The working class must emancipate itself through direct action.
Women are as good as men.
The land belongs to those who work it.
My nationality must be freed from foreign rule.

These were the moral orientations of the leading movements of radical protest in countries at all levels of modernization during the *belle époque*. They were adopted by minorities of workers, women, and peasants (see Chapter 9 on subject nationalities) as battle cries against a society that provided no solution for their discontents. These minorities wanted positive alternatives to the alienation and *anomie* felt by other people whose internalized standards no longer helped them cope with the effects of rapid social change. But they rejected bourgeois society's institutionalized solution to the discontents of modernization: the separation of private from public life. Conforming in the public sphere in order to be free in the private sphere "worked" only for people who did not consider themselves repressed by the established order. As the minorities we are concerned with became conscious of their own repression, they refused to internalize *it*. Instead they rejected the dominant mentality in their society and the perception of reality that was used to rationalize it. They based their collective actions on their own, "correct," perceptions of reality.

The conflicts provoked by this kind of radical protest expressed the incompatible outlooks of the opposing sides. Consequently they could not be resolved by appeals to reason or interest. The conformist middle classes could not comprehend the "irrational" answers they received when they asked: "What do those people want?" And when "those people" "went too far" in asserting their demands, even the most conscience-stricken liberals called out the police and the troops. In the summer of 1892 Jules Huret, a reporter for the Parisian daily *Le Figaro*, concluded his interview with the Italian anarchist labor agitator Errico Malatesta in London with the following question: "As a matter of principle, do you approve of thefts and killings perpetrated against capitalists, for example, as legitimate reprisals by the poor against the rich?" Malatesta replied:

> My goodness, principles have nothing to do with it! The poor are so oppressed by the rich that, if they rebel and take vengeance, and try to better their lot by the most ferocious means, that's the most understandable thing in the world. It's up to the rich to give up their privileges. As for us anarchists, we are doing our best to bring about, as soon as possible, a society in which there will be no more sufferers, no more oppressors, and where love will reign among men.[1]

Members of the intelligentsia were more concerned with principles than were agitators like Malatesta. Because of the importance of the intelligentsia in leading radical protest and criticizing certain aspects of modernization, this social group must be distinguished from intellectuals in general. Its members do this themselves when they condemn "ivory tower" intellectuals and "mandarins" who work for the established order. An intelligentsia consists of those people whose exposure to new ideas, especially in the universities, makes them intensely conscious of the confrontation between modernizing trends and traditional society and whose cultural contacts with both pose certain problems, issues, and dilemmas. Their education tends to alienate them from their own society and to make it difficult to find an acceptable place in it. This can happen not only to literary writers and free-lance journalists but also to educators, lawyers, doctors, engineers, and even army officers in countries at an early stage of modernization—as in Russia during the Decembrist Revolt of 1825. Indeed, during the next two decades many members of the Russian intelligentsia were nobles. Later in the nineteenth century, in Russia and the rest of Europe, some sections of the intelligentsia tried to "ignite" the "pent-up revolutionary energy" of the peasants or workers. Only in this way, they felt, could they give meaning to their own lives and lead the way to an ideal society in which no one would be discontented any more.

The intelligentsias we are concerned with tried to resolve their discontents in a variety of ways. Only a handful of their members rejected the traditional order completely and became enthusiastic modernizers. The traditionalists rejected modernization completely and often became nostalgic aesthetes or populists. A third group sought to reform and renovate certain features of the traditional order to make these compatible with modernization. Thus the intelligentsia in each country was a heterogeneous social group. It was disunited in its responses to modernization and in the moral orientations its members chose in order to overcome their feelings of repression.

WORKING-CLASS PROTEST: ANARCHISM, REVOLUTIONARY
SYNDICALISM, SOCIALISM

Several caveats are necessary in any discussion of working-class protest.[2] First of all, national differences in political, economic, and social structures—particularly in the most and least advanced countries—influenced the predominant orientation to action. Second, different kinds of workers in the same country often behaved differently and had incompatible goals: artisans and factory workers (and different occupational groups within these two categories), the organized and the unorganized, urban and rural workers, Catholic and Protestant workers, native and foreign workers. (Although foreign workers were already attracting attention in certain occupations in England, France, and Germany before the war, they were not a major factor in the development of the labor movement in Europe, as the mass of foreign-born workers was in the United States.) Third, the rank-and-file members of organizations claiming to represent the workers did not always accept the doctrines and tactics of their leaders. Our purpose, however, is not to construct a theory[3] that takes care of these caveats but rather to examine major examples of radical protest.

Anarchism was the most extreme orientation to action against the existing order and all it stood for.[4] It combined a belief in the possibility of a violent and sudden transformation of society with a confidence in the reasonableness of man and the possibility of human improvement and perfection. Not only capitalism but also government in all its forms had to be eliminated before the anarchist dream could come true.

The principal adviser and philosopher of the anarchist movement was Prince Peter Kropotkin (1842–1921). Like its founder, Michael Bakunin (1814–76), Kropotkin was a fugitive Russian noblemen, but their contributions to the movement were quite different. Bakunin had been primarily a conspirator and agitator. When he was not battling Marx in the First International* he was trying to win converts to the anarchist revolutionary mentality among the Western European masses, particularly in Italy. In contrast, throughout the *belle époque.* Kropotkin led a quiet, respectable, and scholarly existence in England. During the 1890's, when many anarchists turned to the "propaganda of the deed," Kropotkin denounced some of the individual bombings and assassinations this entailed but not the belief that in certain situations terrorism might well be the only means of making the Revolution.

Kropotkin was a utopian but he did not oppose all aspects of modernization. In his view it was capitalism, not scientific and technical progress, that had brought about man's moral regression. He believed that man was originally innocent and sociable and that throughout history his instincts to co-operate had asserted themselves until they were crushed by the evils of capitalist society. In the good society private property and the right to inherit it would be destroyed, thereby eliminating greed and exploitation. Then morality would be based on man's own good instincts and would need no outside sanction to enforce it. The Revolution was necessary to bring about the total reorganization of society into a form that Kropotkin called "anarchist communism." Only through mutual co-operation and free association, rather than direction from a centralized state, could the purpose of this ideal society be achieved: "From each according to his ability, to each according to his needs."

By the very nature of their principles all anarchists spurned large-scale organization to achieve their goal of a completely libertarian society. Some of them founded short-lived magazines and secret societies, but anarchism was never a coherent political or philosophical movement. Dedicated to the emancipation of the working class, its creed attracted people from all walks of life. In the United States the Russian-Jewish im-

* The First International Workingmen's Association had been founded in 1864 and had collapsed twelve years later. The Second International, founded in 1889, was predominantly socialist and soon became completely so by expelling the anarchists.

migrant Emma Goldman ("Red Emma") worked in a sweatshop for $2.50 a week in the late 1880's before turning to agitation for all the libertarian causes of our period. Errico Malatesta, the renegade son of a well-to-do Italian bourgeois family, worked as an electrician and led numerous unsuccessful working-class insurrections in Europe and the Americas. Anarchism also attracted the artist Camille Pissarro, the journalists Émile Pouget and Vigo Almereyda, bohemian intellectuals, and tough working-class labor bosses, as well as the lonely misfits who perpetrated spectacular acts of violence and terrorism. Many of these terrorists lacked the ideal of a better society to come, yet it was they who created the image of the anarchist among "respectable" people.

Anarchist violence and terrorism reached their peak in the 1890's. In March 1892, François-Claudius Ravachol, a part-time worker, thief, and murderer, bombed the Parisian homes of the judge and prosecuting attorney responsible for jailing two anarchist demonstrators. No one was killed in these bombings, but Ravachol was condemned to death for his earlier murders. On hearing this verdict he cried: "Long live anarchy!" and thus became a martyr of the movement. In February 1894, Émile Henry bombed a cafe in a suburban railroad station in Paris during the rush hour. When the judge asked him how he felt about killing innocent citizens, Henry replied: "There are no innocent people." By this he meant that the white-collar commuters in the cafe represented bourgeois society and supported all its evils. Four months after Henry's bombing an Italian anarchist assassinated President Sadi Carnot of France; three years later another Italian anarchist assassinated Prime Minister Antonio Cánovas del Castillo of Spain. Other self-styled anarchists assassinated Empress Elizabeth of Austria in 1898, King Humbert of Italy in 1900, and President McKinley of the United States in 1901.

During the early 1900's the anarchist leaders in France, Italy, and Spain renounced individual acts of protest. They decided that the Revolution could be achieved only through more positive efforts. And such efforts needed planning and co-operation. The Spanish anarchists who planned to assassinate King Alfonso XIII on his visit to Paris in May 1905 assumed that their republican allies in Barcelona would also launch a coup and seize power in Madrid: "With the death of the King, there'll be Revolution in Spain." But this kind of organized conspiracy also failed. Meanwhile, as in France and Italy, many anarchist leaders in Spain had already concluded that terrorism and the repression it provoked had lost them the sympathy of the workers. Thus, when individual terrorists resumed their bombings in Barcelona during the years 1904 to 1907, these leaders disavowed them. They founded the Federation of Trade Unions (Solidaridad Obrera) and began moving toward their own brand of revolutionary syndicalism. Since they could not hope to mobilize the workers in an atmosphere of government repression, some of them actually informed on the terrorists in their zeal to wipe them out.[5]

Revolutionary syndicalism was far more influential in working-class circles than anarchism had ever been. It became the official ideology of the largest confederation of trade unions in France and of important federations in Italy and Spain.* In the United States the International Workers of the World adopted revolutionary syndicalism, though by 1914 this organization had only one hundred thousand members, compared with the 2 million in the American Federation of Labor. On the eve of the war some of the biggest strikes in Great Britain also reflected the influence of syndicalist ideas. These ideas are perhaps best known through the writings of the French publicist Georges Sorel, but in the context of this chapter they are best understood through the outlook of the people who tried to put them into actual practice.

The development of revolutionary syndicalism[6] reflected the differences between Fernand Pelloutier (1867–1901), secretary-general of the Fédération des Bourses du Travail from 1895 to 1901, and Victor Griffuelhes (1874–1923), head of the CGT until 1909. Pelloutier had grown up in a bourgeois family and attended the *collège* of St. Nazaire until he failed his baccalaureate examination in 1885. During the next seven years he edited a local newspaper and turned to anarchism. Between 1892 and 1895 he tried to propagate the idea of the general strike at trade-union and socialist congresses. Thereafter he subordinated the final goal of revolution to the means of achieving it: the organization and education of both artisans and industrial workers in the Bourses du Travail.

In Pelloutier's time the Bourses "constituted a provisional synthesis between old crafts and new industries, between occupational solidarity and class consciousness, between revolutionary millenarianism and trade-unionism."[7] In each town the Bourse tried to unite workers in different unions through its function as a labor exchange and its educational

* Founded in 1895, the Confédération Génèale du Travail had six hundred thousand affiliated members by 1912. The Unione Sindacale Italiana claimed one hundred thousand members at the time of its founding in 1912 and seems to have doubled its following by the outbreak of the war. Founded in 1911, the national organization of the Spanish anarcho-syndicalists, the Confederación Nacional del Trabajo, had only fifteen thousand members by 1915 but grew to six hundred thousand by 1919. (Spain was neutral during the war.)

efforts. Its goal was to prepare all these workers to emancipate themselves through direct action. Far from being a simple panacea, the "myth" of the Revolution—or General Strike—was used by the Bourse as a moral orientation to remind the workers of the need for discipline and co-operation as well as the evils they had to combat. According to Pelloutier:

> The Bourse du Travail is at the same time a center of resistance against capitalist oppression and the kernel of that just society whose establishment we are all striving to achieve. The Bourse, by bringing together diverse unions, by accustoming them to discuss questions of common interest together, shows them that all the evils they suffer are the same in all aspects of social life—in the workshop and in the home—and that the same means are necessary to gain a better life. In this way the feeling of solidarity develops to which the proletariat will owe its emancipation.[8]

In 1902, a year after Pelloutier's death, the Federation of the Bourses entered a formal alliance with the CGT, but, though the two organizations continued to exist side by side until the war, the CGT represented the dominant trend of revolutionary syndicalism as reflected in the newer, industry-wide trade unions. Whereas Pelloutier had opposed individual strikes because they fostered the dangerous illusion that the capitalist system could be ameliorated, Griffuelhes viewed them as better training for revolutionary action than the kind of discussions that went on in the Bourses. Griffuelhes took this position not only because of his own background as a shoemaker and official in the leatherworkers' federation but also because in the early 1900's the CGT seemed capable of organizing effective national campaigns directed against both the government and employers for concrete, though limited, concessions for the working class as a whole. And he undoubtedly caught the mood of the majority of the workers affiliated with the CGT when he attributed their preoccupation with everyday struggles to the expansion of trade-union activities.[9]

Griffuelhes' successor, Léon Jouhaux, was especially concerned with modernizing and expanding these activities in the newer and larger industrial combinations in order to cope more effectively with their organized efforts to resist unionization. The CGT could not ignore the growing effectiveness of these efforts, particularly on the part of the Federation of Industrialists. According to Jouhaux, "We must therefore adapt our movement's methods to the development and evolution of industry; if not, we will act in a vacuum."[10]

Yet, despite this modernizing, reformist trend in the CGT, the moral orientation of revolutionary syndicalism, in France and elsewhere, continued to reflect its anarchist origins. Its view of reality was that the working class would remain exploited as long as there was a distinction between wage earners and employers. Thus the working class must reject the positions of those groups that held a different view of reality. Obviously the workers must reject the outlook of their capitalist employers, who see them as perpetual wage earners and try to mollify them with better wages, working conditions, and fringe benefits. They must also reject the outlook of the liberal state, which sees them as individual citizens, like any others, who can be integrated into the larger society by means of legislative reforms. "Statism" is an illusion under any economic system; even under state socialism the workers would still be exploited— by government bureaucrats instead of private employers. Finally, the working class must reject the leadership of the Socialist Party, whose revolutionary wing sees it as a historical agent—a means rather than an end in itself—and whose reformist wing accepts the reality of parliamentary government and the possibility of emancipating the working class through electoral politics and progressive legislation.

Right up to the war the CGT maintained the position it had adopted in 1906 in the famous Charter of Amiens, which renounced all ties with Socialist political action. The only exceptions were in 1913, when it agreed with the Socialist Party on the use of the general strike to oppose the threat of war and on opposition to a law extending compulsory military service from two to three years. Even then Jouhaux feared that too much emphasis on the general strike and antimilitarism might alienate many workers at a time when the CGT was seeking new recruits. The increased strength of the Socialists after the 1914 elections made them difficult to ignore. Yet Jouhaux and his closest colleagues hesitated to abandon the revolutionary syndicalist orientation.

Socialists viewed reality differently from anarchists and revolutionary syndicalists. Despite Marx's theory, no socialist in our period believed that the state would ever "wither away." Both the centralized state and the concentration of the means of production were here to stay. Thus the goal of socialism must be to capture the state in order to take the means of production away from the capitalists and run them for the masses. Whereas anarchists and revolutionary syndicalists viewed this kind of collectivism as a deterrent to individualism, socialists considered it the only true means for liberating the individual *in modern society*.

Although all people who called themselves socialists shared this view of reality, they differed considerably in their orientations to action. The British Fabians and the Russian Bolsheviks represented the two extremes and were outside the mainstream of the pre-1914 European socialist movement. But even within the mainstream differences between revolutionaries and reformists periodically threatened the fragile unity of the movement—in the Second International and within the individual Socialist parties that tried to work together in it. The history of this movement cannot be covered here.[11] For our purpose its periodic shifts between reformism and orthodox Marxism are less important than the basic appeal of socialism as The Answer to the discontents of millions of Europeans.

On October 20, 1891, at the Erfurt Congress of the German Socialist Party, August Bebel assured the assembled delegates that the last crisis of capitalism was at hand: "I am convinced that the fulfillment of our aims is so close that there are few in this hall who will not live to see the day." Here was a revolutionary myth comparable to that of the general strike but reinforced by Marx's "scientific" theory of historical determinism. The laws of History made the downfall of Capitalism and the triumph of the Revolution inevitable. When Bebel died in 1913, the Revolution seemed much less imminent than it had twenty-two years earlier. Yet he was mourned by millions (and not just in Germany) for the hope he had given them for a better future.

The individual socialist parties sustained this hope in different ways, depending in part on the political structure and level of modernization in the country in which they operated. We have already noted how the labor parties in Britain and Scandinavia became increasingly committed to legislative reforms and trade unionism as they gained access to the centers of political power. Since they felt little need for theoretical reinforcement, they were relatively immune from the doctrinal splits that afflicted the avowedly Marxist parties. In Russia, on the other hand, the autocratic political structure and low level of modernization severely limited the options of the socialists. Most of the time they had to operate underground or in exile. Hence they had little possibility of organizing mass parties and trade unions. The Social Revolutionaries were populists rather than Marxists. As we shall see, they tried to mobilize the peasants during the Russian Revolution of 1905, but otherwise their hope was based on the peasants' collectivist and revolutionary potential. Led by V. I. Lenin, the Bolsheviks maintained that the masses did not know what they wanted until the revolutionary vanguard told them. Unlike the Mensheviks, who clung to the orthodox Marxist blueprint of a class-conscious proletariat overthrowing capitalism at a certain stage in history, Lenin insisted that the Revolution could be achieved only by a "con-

scious minority" of full-time conspirators. Also unorthodox was his pre-
scription for an alliance with the peasantry as a means of isolating the
bourgeoisie.

Another pattern emerged in Central Europe, which was more modernized than Russia but where parliamentary institutions offered little hope
for the achievement of the Revolution by peaceful means. Like Bebel in
Germany, Viktor Adler in Austria devoted himself to developing a mass
party as the only instrument capable of sustaining a working-class consciousness (see Chapter 4 on the German Socialist Party's subculture) and
of directing society along the difficult path to Socialist power. And, like
Bebel, Adler placed the highest priority on party unity as the best bulwark against external and internal divisive forces. In Austria the main
divisive force was pressure from the non-German Socialists for greater
representation. This issue was partially resolved in 1899 by giving the six
chief national groups—Germans, Czechs, Poles, Ruthenians, Italians, and
Slovenes—autonomy under the "umbrella" of a common party executive.
The main divisive force in the German Socialist Party was an ideological
one, and it highlighted the conflicting orientations within European socialism.

In his book *Evolutionary Socialism: A Criticism and Affirmation*
(1899) Eduard Bernstein argued that Marx's theories needed revision because they conflicted with the reality in the maturing industrial societies.
Contrary to Marx's predictions, working-class living standards were rising instead of falling, and the middle classes, far from being proletarized,
were thriving and their ranks were being bolstered by a new class of
technicians. These and similar observations about the effects of modernization made Bernstein challenge some of the underlying assumptions of
Marx's thought, such as historical determinism, dialectical materialism,
and the inevitability of class struggle. Like the Fabians, whom he had
come to admire during his stay in England, Bernstein advocated a gradual
evolution toward socialism through an alliance between the working
classes and the progressive bourgeoisie.

No one in the German Socialist Party denounced Bernstein's revisionism more devastatingly than Rosa Luxemburg, the most brilliant
theorist of radical protest since Marx himself.* According to her,

---

* In recent years Luxemburg has replaced Trotsky as the model of the ideal
revolutionary among young Western neo-Marxists who reject democratic socialism but who find Lenin, Stalin, and Mao uncongenial because of the elitist
role they ascribed to the party. During the early 1900's, Luxemburg was already challenging Lenin on this point. According to her, the Revolution could
not be merely the passive reward of benefits from the hands of a conquering

revisionism would lead to bourgeois conformism rather than to socialism. She did not oppose Socialists sitting in parliament and voting for certain reforms as long as these helped prepare the way for the final triumph of the working class. But she insisted on the primacy of the theory on which this triumph would be based. According to Luxemburg, Bernstein's "empiricism" (such as his statistics on rising working-class living standards) confused appearances with reality. The true reality is the evils inherent in capitalist society, which Marx's theory alone had correctly perceived. But Marxism was not a body of received beliefs, immutable in its purity. As a theory of the historical process it was subject to the feedback generated by this process. It postulated a continuing class struggle in which socialist revolutionary activities necessarily reinforced "not merely the fulfillment of the laws of dialectical materialism but the liberation and progress of humanity."[12] Thus Luxemburg condemned reformist tactics and Bebel's concentration on preserving the legal status of the Socialist Party structure as contrary to Marxist theory.

The German Socialist Party repudiated revisionism at the turn of the century, but not because of Luxemburg's arguments. Bebel and the ma-

---

elite. It could only come about as a result of the direct *participation* of the masses in false tries and premature seizures of power. Only this kind of participation could generate the friction that would lead to the revolutionary energy necessary to the maturity of class consciousness, which alone would assure the inevitable success of the Revolution. The best study of this remarkable woman is J. Peter Nettl, *Rosa Luxemburg* (New York: Oxford University Press, 1966). John Murray Cuddihy treats Luxemburg as an example of the European Jewish intelligentsia's search for a "radical *social* fulfillment" of their "wholeness-hunger" on page 106 of his book *The Ordeal of Civility: Freud, Marx, Lévi-Strauss, and the Jewish Struggle with Modernity* (New York: Basic Books, 1974). According to Cuddihy, these people rejected the vulgarity and materialism of their bourgeois parents but transferred their hostility to modern society itself. This they opposed because its differentiations between public and private behavior and between manners and morals required emancipated Jews to "be nice" by bourgeois Gentile standards as "the price of admission" (p. 13). Members of the Jewish intelligentsia were unwilling to pay this price, partly because they unconsciously longed for a replacement for the traditional Jewish community, where such differentiations did not exist, and partly because they consciously felt their alienation from modern European society, which treated them as troublemakers. Many turned to Marx, whose ideology was one of "dedifferentiation, at once nostalgic and utopian" (p. 235). This interpretation does not account for non-Jewish Marxists like Lenin and Bebel, but in any case our main concern is the appeal of revolutionary leaders to their followers rather than why they became what they were.

jority of his colleagues used these arguments to bolster their public image as orthodox Marxists and to help them resist "contamination" from non-Socialist forces in Wilhelmine society. At the same time they became increasingly reformist in their day-to-day policies. They saw no dilemma in being revolutionary in theory and reformist in practice.

In France and Italy the Socialist parties faced greater "contamination" from the more liberal political environment in those countries. The reformist leaders Jean Jaurès and Filippo Turati felt less need than Bebel to parade their impeccable revolutionary credentials in order to preserve party unity. Their revolutionary rivals would not have been deceived anyway. Jaurès and Turati still believed in a thoroughgoing transformation of their society, but they also believed that this could be achieved through electoral politics and progressive reforms. In both countries the Socialists entered coalitions with parliamentary liberals but opposed their governments' militaristic and imperialistic policies.

By 1914 the Socialist parties of Western and Central Europe had far more support than any other protest movement. In that year the Swedish party won one third of the seats in the lower house of parliament. The German party had won 30 per cent of the votes in the most recent Reichstag elections, and in several other countries the Socialists had received more votes than any other single party. Many people who were neither Marxists nor workers voted for Socialist candidates as the most forthright spokesmen for various progressive causes: universal suffrage, civil liberties, agrarian reform, welfare legislation.

But these electoral successes diverted the Socialist parties from what their more orthodox party executives considered their true function. In their view the function of a Socialist party was to mobilize the working class while abstaining from all co-operation with bourgeois governments until the forces of History allowed it to "inherit" power from them. Instead the nominally Marxist parties, along with the British and Scandinavian labor parties, were becoming pressure groups trying to right specific wrongs and competing for immediate rewards for their discontented constituents. Their parliamentary delegates behaved increasingly like other politicians. And in August 1914 the majority of socialists quickly abandoned their moral condemnation of militarism, nationalism, and imperialism and supported the war efforts of their own bourgeois governments.

The reformist trend of the immediate prewar years in both socialism and the labor movement was neither universal nor lasting. In Italy, for example, the revolutionary wing of the Socialist Party won out over the reformists in 1912 and the revolutionary syndicalist unions grew while the reformist ones lost members. Even in Great Britain the 1911–13 wave of industry-wide strikes (see pp. 281–83) expressed a radical form of protest that was out of keeping with the usual reformist orientation of that country's labor movement. The outbreak of the war brought the collapse of the reformist position almost everywhere, and the war itself

> led to the radicalization of the working-class movement. Communist movements, after all, were the product of the disintegration of the prewar working-class organizations. They arose in the immediate aftermath of the war. The period between the wars, moreover, was characterized by savage combat between reformists and revolutionaries.[13]

WORKING-CLASS PROTEST: STRIKES AND DEMONSTRATIONS

During the 1890's and early 1900's the rising level of strike activity in most European countries reflected the initial mobilization of the workers for collective action as a means of competing for political power with other organized groups.[14] In Great Britain, where the trade-union movement was older and larger than anywhere else, the level of conflict reached its peak in the years 1911 through 1913. Although the majority of strikes everywhere seemed to be over grievances against a particular employer—wages, working conditions, the arbitrary firing of colleagues —they all implicitly asserted the workers' *political* right to engage in collective action.

Before 1914 this right was far from being accepted in most countries, either by the government or the employers. Only after the repeal of the Taff Vale decision in 1906 (see p. 36) was it unencumbered by financial liability to the employers in Great Britain. Elsewhere only in the Scandinavian countries was collective bargaining, with or without strikes, institutionalized as a legitimate means of resolving industrial conflicts. Except during the Revolution of 1905 and its immediate aftermath, most kinds of strikes remained illegal in Russia. In France, the Netherlands, Belgium, Germany, Austria, Italy, and Spain many employers fought the unionization of their workers, and the governments of these countries, as well as Britain, regularly intervened against strikes that inconvenienced the general public. Some of the most massive strikes in Belgium (1893 and 1913), Austria (1905), and Germany (1910) were protest demonstrations aimed at forcing the governments of those countries to broaden the suffrage. And in 1911 and 1912 British railroad workers and miners used nationwide strikes to achieve gains directly from parliament. Strikes that momentarily united the entire working class against the existing order occurred in Milan in May 1898, in most major Russian cities in October 1905, and in Barcelona in July 1909.

In general, however, the active minorities of workers that engaged in collective action did so to affirm the interests of their own stratum or occupational group.[15] Most craftsmen joined the labor movement to avoid sinking into the proletariat and losing their independence, special skills, and relatively privileged social status. Miners formed the largest unions, launched the largest strikes, and put the most political pressure on governments. (Only among German miners did the use of immigrant and Catholic workers delay this tendency somewhat.) But they remained isolated from the other most active occupational groups in the labor movement: textile and leather workers, metal workers, and unskilled male workers, particularly longshoremen.

Industry-wide strikes were most effective in mobilizing unskilled and semiskilled workers; in 1889 this movement began with the great London dock strike and a strike by the Ruhr coal miners.[16] Both were launched against the employers by informal leadership groups, both involved large-scale violence and the massive use of police and army troops, and both led to the formation of national unions. But there the resemblance ends. The Ruhr miners were protesting the loss of their earlier protection by the state and striking to regulate their own status and conditions of work without outside help. In 1905 they struck again for the same reasons against the wishes of their union leaders and the Socialist Party. Not until 1912 was the German miners' union able to mobilize its members in a joint effort with other national unions in a strike for higher wages. The British dock workers, on the other hand, struck for higher wages and shorter hours in 1889, co-operated with other categories of unskilled workers who imitated them, and idolized the leader of their union, Tom Mann. They were beaten in 1893, but when they went on strike again in the summer of 1911 for the recognition of their union they were joined in many cities by the carters, seamen, and railroad workers. In Liverpool the situation was close to a general strike, and troops attacked workers wherever they gathered.[17] Tom Mann (now a revolutionary syndicalist) helped the Liverpool workers win their demands as chairman of their Strike Committee. But in another strike a year later the dock workers' union failed to achieve its goal of a closed shop.

Although the history and organization of trade unions cannot be covered here, the trade-unionist orientation to action must be noted as an alternative to revolutionary syndicalism and socialism. It was, after all, the one most directly involved with the day-to-day concerns of the workers themselves. As in the United States, trade unionism in Europe combined collective bargaining with employers with efforts to influence the government and public opinion. But whereas American trade unionism never had its own political party, this was not the case in Europe. The British Labour Party was actually created by the Trades Union Congress just after the turn of the century, and the Scandinavian Socialist parties were also largely controlled by the trade-union federations. In Germany the Socialist trade unions had at first been subordinate to the party but, beginning in 1906, they gained effective control over it.[18] Thus, despite its overriding concern with the workers' economic interests, European trade unionism was strongly oriented toward political action. Unlike the socialists and revolutionary syndicalists, however, the trade unionists tried to thwart overt attacks on the existing order.

Revolutionary syndicalist ideas were as pronounced in British trade-union circles from 1911 to 1914 as they had been in France during that country's great wave of protest strikes in the spring of 1906. The active syndicalists were a tiny minority in the otherwise reformist British trade unions. But the role of Tom Mann in the 1911 transport and dockers' strikes radicalized many workers impatient with parliamentary politics and convinced that their employers would never accept the union shop. These strikes had led to the creation of the Transport Workers Federation. In his 1912 pamphlet, *The Miners' Next Step*, Mann urged the creation of a national miners union as well. These industry-wide unions would then work together for the emancipation of the working class through direct action. Once the full syndicalist goal was achieved, the state would disappear, except for a Central Production Board, which,

> with a statistical department to ascertain the needs of the people, will issue its demands on the different departments of industry, leaving to the men themselves to determine under what conditions, and how, the work should be done. This would mean real democracy in real life, making for real manhood and womanhood. Any other form of democracy is a delusion and a snare.[19]

The closest that British trade unionism came to Mann's blueprint was the so-called "Triple Alliance," whereby the federations of miners, transport workers, and railroad men agreed to terminate their contracts at the same time in order to fight more effectively for new concessions from the employers. This alliance was to come into effect in 1914 but was postponed because of the war. In any case, most British trade unionists viewed it as a new technique of mass mobilization rather than a means to a social revolution.[20] (See pp. 329–30 on the politicization of the 1913 strike of Dublin transport workers.)

In contrast to industrial workers, craftsmen used collective action mainly to protest technical and organizational changes that threatened to reduce their power and status in their place of work. During the early 1890's British shipbuilders considered certain kinds of skilled work as "theirs by custom"; in the Dundee shipyards, for example, the joiners struck to protest the employment of semiskilled workers to operate a machine they considered their own. In that instance neither the executive committee of their own union nor sympathetic workers in other unions supported the strike, and the joiners had to give in. But in the summer of 1895 the union of the glassworkers of Carmaux, France, launched a strike against the local factory owner which climaxed five years of struggle for control of the factory itself.[21] The union had been founded to prevent the transformation of the craft through mechanization and the employment of semiskilled operatives. By 1895, however, it "no longer represented skill alone but a force with a power of numbers, with an internal organization which gave it control over punishing apprentices for not paying dues and which gave it a personality that could be insulted and could seek revenge." But, "though consciousness of the need for solidarity had enabled the glassworkers to resist Rességuier for several months, the impossibility of the goal of saving their positions as craftsmen meant they would inevitably lose the strike of 1895."

A more momentous example of collective action among threatened crafts workers was the Berlin beer boycott in the summer and fall of 1894.[22] Although unique in German labor history, this event illustrates a number of aspects of workers' protest. As in other crafts, concentration and mechanization had transformed journeymen brewers into lifelong wage-workers, with no prospect of future independence as brewmasters. These same forces also threatened the status of the masters themselves, who decried the employment of unskilled labor in their craft. But it was the unskilled and semiskilled workers whose informal leadership groups led the protest against their twelve- to fourteen-hour workday, the paternalistic policies of their employers, and the master-apprentice power relationship, which they felt was no longer justified in view of their permanent status as wage earners. The strike they launched on May 1, 1894, forced support from the brewmasters' craft union. It eventually gained the backing of both the Socialist and non-Socialist unions in the city, all of which agreed not to buy beer made in the struck breweries. The brewery owners retaliated with a lockout of 20 per cent of their employees and a boycott of the Berlin unions' labor exchange. They also gained the backing of many tavern owners, whose business dropped because of the decline in beer production and because Berlin workers refused to patronize taverns that sold beer from the struck breweries.

The Berlin boycott dragged on until Christmas before it was finally resolved. At first the strikers refused to listen to those party leaders, including Bebel himself, who urged them to negotiate a compromise with the employers; they even called them traitors. To the strikers and their supporters the boycott was a test of strength between two social classes. They could not hold out indefinitely, however, because their union and state unemployment benefits ran out and both the apprentices' and helpers' organizations lost half their members. In the final settlement the employers agreed not to fire workers who joined unions or the Socialist Party and to hire its workers through the unions' labor exchanges. But these small political victories were less important than the raising of the class consciousness of tens of thousands of Berlin workers and the growth in union membership that this prompted.

Much more was at stake in the rebellion in Milan in May 1898 (*Fatti di Maggio*). Behind it "lay a tradition of street protest with wide participation by various occupational groups, as well as a period of intense organizational activity centering on the more modern industrial workers but reaching into most occupational categories."[23] To the workers involved in this rebellion the issues were the right to demonstrate, to organize, and to participate in the political process. The authorities in turn treated the workers' demands as revolutionary and sent in troops with blanket orders to shoot.

On May 6 a group of demonstrators gathered outside a Milan police station to demand the release of several men who had been arrested for distributing Socialist propaganda at a nearby factory. The police opened fire on the demonstrators, killing several workers. On the next morning a strike spread in the industrial neighborhoods, and the workers threw up makeshift barricades to defend themselves against attacks by the troops. By the afternoon of May 7 violence had spread throughout the city, and the authorities declared a state of siege. Although Turati and other Socialist leaders opposed the workers' violence and tried to mediate the dispute, they were arrested along with almost seventeen hundred real and imagined troublemakers. Meanwhile, using heavy artillery and several thousand armed troops, the military quelled the rebellion by May 10, leaving hundreds of killed and wounded in their wake. Not since the Paris Commune of 1871 had a major European city experienced popular agitation and government repression on such a scale.

Unlike the *Fatti di Maggio*, the "Tragic Week" in Barcelona (July 26–31, 1909) began as a well-planned general strike and degenerated into mob violence against the established order.[24] The strike was originally conceived as a protest against Spain's unpopular war in Morocco and the government responsible for it. It was launched by metal workers under the leadership of the Radical Party, which expected similar strikes to occur in other parts of the country. Many factory owners and shopkeepers in the Barcelona area closed down their operations, thus seeming to support the general strike at first. The strikers paralyzed most transportation and communication facilities and were therefore unaware of the lack of support elsewhere in Spain. By the afternoon of July 26 their attacks on police stations showed that the striking workers were going beyond an antiwar protest demonstration. Those who belonged to the Catalan anarcho-syndicalist labor federation, Solidaridad Obrera, wanted to transform the strike into a revolution. Just after midnight they burned their first Catholic school. They viewed the philanthropic organizations of the Church, especially their wealth, as symbols of the established order they were determined to overthrow. But the Radical politicians were unwilling to lead a revolution, and the movement expended itself in the next few days in the destruction of twelve churches and forty convents and other religious institutions.

Shooting, burning, and looting by the Barcelona insurgents confirmed respectable people's nightmare of the "dangerous class" running wild. While the approximately thirty thousand activists camped freely in the streets, the city's 526,000 residents remained locked in their homes. In addition, a contingent from the *Lumpenproletariat*—prostitutes, procurers, and petty criminals—set up barricades in their own district to protest police harassment of their activities. But the unco-ordinated mob violence prevented the popular uprising from developing into a revolution and alienated potential middle-class allies. By July 29 military reinforcements from other parts of Spain drove the anarchist snipers into the suburbs and crushed the rebellion within the next two days. As in Italy eleven years earlier, the central government took severe repressive measures against both the Radical politicians and the labor unions. Even after parliamentary rule was formally restored in 1912, their reaction against the "Tragic Week" made Spain's political leaders fearful of the revolutionary potential of the working class. More than ever they believed that any reforms would only lead to further violence.

The "Great October Strike" in Russia in 1905 was the most important example of workers' protest in pre-1914 Europe. It was also the most successful, since it forced Tsar Nicholas II to issue the October Manifesto (October 17),* which granted all Russians civil liberties and representative, responsible government. No other strike or demonstration had political consequences of this magnitude. (The only other political revolution in our period was the overthrow of the monarchy in Portugal in October 1910, but it took place without significant mass participation.) And despite the strong traditional ties of many Russian workers they behaved more like the modern proletariat of Marxist theory than the workers in the most advanced countries.

How was all this possible? The Revolution of 1905 was a complex affair, and other aspects of it will be discussed presently.[25] Urban strike activities were most directly influenced by the unpopular and unsuccessful war with Japan and the growing consciousness of the workers of their repression by the tsarist regime. Russia was the only major country whose laws still prohibited trade unions, strikes, and any other kind of collective action by workers. Thus they had no legal way of seeking redress for their grievances against their employers. Some of them struck anyway in 1903 and 1904, and it was partly to sidetrack such domestic unrest that the government went to war against Japan. But by the beginning of 1905 Russia's disastrous military defeats had weakened the prestige of the government and emboldened illegal opposition groups of many kinds. A strike in the Putilov Ironworks in St. Petersburg escalated within a few days into a major demonstration at the Winter Palace. On January 9 ("Bloody Sunday") thousands of unarmed men and women, led by a popular priest, pressed into the palace square with a petition to the tsar for political change as a prelude to economic change. When they refused to disperse, the guards fired directly into the crowd. More than anything else this bloody act of repression dramatized to the Russian people the brutal injustice under which they lived.

After Bloody Sunday workers' strikes became larger and more numerous, adding demands for cessation of the war and the calling of a constituent assembly to those for increased wages and better working conditions. In May the strike committee in St. Petersburg began calling itself a *soviet* (council) of deputies; it soon assumed administrative re-

* All dates in this section are those of the calendar used in Russia until 1918 and are thirteen days earlier than those of the Western calendar.

Soviet painting: Dispersing of striking workers at the Putilov metal and machine works (St. Petersburg), January 3, 1905.

sponsibilities such as organizing a workers' militia and prohibiting shop-keepers from raising prices. Although it arose spontaneously, the soviet corresponded to the orthodox Marxist conception of a revolutionary body that would ultimately seize power from the central government. By June there was also growing unrest in the countryside and a major mutiny in the navy. Finally, in early October, the Moscow railroad workers went on strike and were joined by the administrative and technical personnel. Since Moscow was the railroad hub of the empire, the tie-up of its lines affected the rest of the country as no previous strike had.

On October 9 the Moscow railroad strike became a general strike that quickly spread throughout the empire. In most cities it followed a similar pattern. First the railroad workers struck and were joined by other workers. Then the various liberal and socialist political organizations issued formal calls for a general strike. Unlike other general strikes in Europe, the one in Russia was joined by the middle classes, thus emphasizing its goal of political change. Students and members of the intelligentsia were the most active agitators, but the strikers included store and office employees, teachers, doctors, lawyers, pharmacists, and even civil servants. Opera singers and ballet dancers refused to perform. Printers prevented newspapers from being published. Hospitals accepted only emergency cases. All public transportation and communication facilities came to a standstill. Within a week the general strike involved one million factory workers, seven hundred thousand railroad employees, fifty thousand government employees, and tens of thousands of professional people, students, and clerks. In every major city socialists, anarchists, and liberals harangued large audiences with their proposals for "liquidating the old regime." Meanwhile dozens of urban strike committees transformed themselves into soviets. Most of them accepted leadership by the socialists less because of their ideology than the vigor of their tactics.

Although the general strike ended with the granting of the October Manifesto, the most serious revolutionary disturbances were yet to come. The peasant uprisings will be discussed presently. In the cities the trade unions and the socialists mobilized many new members and demanded a full-scale political revolution. By the beginning of December the Moscow soviet called for another general strike with the slogans:

> We demand a constituent assembly!
> Long live the democratic republic!
> Long live the struggle of the proletariat under the banner of the Russian Social Democratic Labor Party!

The strike began on December 7 in Moscow and a day later in St. Petersburg; the other cities in the empire soon became involved as well. But despite its greater levels of bitterness and violence the December general strike was less effective than the one in October. It had less support from the middle classes, and the disruption of transportation and communication was less complete.

The government saw that the various centers of strikes and uprisings could not bring about an actual seizure of power and finally launched its counteroffensive. On December 15 it dispatched elite troops from St. Petersburg to Moscow. The strikers there resisted against artillery and rifle fire for two days in the Presnya district until it had been reduced to a smoking waste. By December 19 all resistance in Moscow ceased; one thousand civilians had been killed in the fighting and many thousands had been arrested. Soon thereafter government forces ended the strikes and uprisings in the other cities. Although constitutional government was granted from above, the Revolution was delayed for another twelve years.

PEASANT UPRISINGS

Peasants as well as workers rebelled when they perceived the existing order as illegitimate. Large-scale peasant revolts occurred only in those parts of Europe where there had been no earlier commercial revolution in agriculture led by the landed upper classes and where the peasants' surviving traditional expectations and forms of organization were subjected to new stresses and strains from the world outside the villages.[26] As we have seen, by the 1890's landholding peasants in northwestern Europe were already becoming modern, independent farmers. They were no longer bound in an exploitative relationship with the upper classes, they had learned to raise the products that the market demanded, and some of them were adopting new co-operative methods for getting these products to the market. During the early 1900's the winegrowers of southern France engaged in militant collective action to gain financial assistance from the government, and Italian agricultural workers in the Po Valley began to join unions, but neither group sought to overthrow the established order. In much of Central Europe agriculture had also become commercialized and traditional peasant institutions were disappearing; there were no peasant rebellions there either. The main peasant uprisings in our period took place in Sicily, Russia, and Romania.

These three uprisings were all protests against modernizing forces that defied traditional peasant attitudes toward justice, land use, and class relations. In earlier centuries the kinds of peasants involved in these three revolts had seemed insensitive to the disdain of outsiders. Outwardly they had kowtowed to landlords, tax collectors, priests, and other established authorities and found more equitable human relations in their supposedly immutable village cultures. They had known how much exploitation to expect and had felt fairly secure in their tenure of the land available for their use even when they did not own it. Hence they perceived the new demands of capitalist entrepreneurs and government officials as undermining their whole way of life. For this reason their indignation was more diffuse and elemental than that of workers and middle-class women. And because they were less articulate and less easily organized they expressed their protest with greater violence. Once their rebellions were under way some peasants became convinced that if the new order outside their villages would not let them alone it would have to be overthrown.

All of these emotional ingredients were present in the Sicilian, Russian, and Romanian uprisings. In Sicily and Romania the overwhelming majority of peasants were forced to lease small plots of land with unstable tenure and rising rents. Even in Russia, where much of the land was owned in common by the villagers, population pressure forced many peasants to lease additional land from the managers of large private estates at what they considered exorbitant rents. In all three areas capitalism came to the countryside not through aristocratic landowners but through these estate managers and the large tenants who subleased the land they rented in Romania. The peasants had no traditional class relations with these people or with the middlemen who marketed their produce. Their resentment against the arrogance and exploitation they suffered from these upstarts had been building up for several decades and had sometimes erupted into local acts of violence. In Sicily and Romania the peasants also resented the appropriation of formerly common land by people they believed were not entitled to it. In Romania and Russia they thought they had received less land than the government reforms of the early 1860's had promised to them, and they often could not meet their redemption payments to the state for this land. Finally, all these peasants felt overtaxed by their governments.

The Sicilian peasants rebelled in 1893, the Russians in 1905, the Romanians in 1907. What distinguished these from earlier forms of peasant protest was large-scale mobilization for the purpose of changing the economic and social order through political means. In all three cases many of the instigators were village men whose horizons had been widened during their period of military service. And in Sicily and Russia socialist organizers from outside the villages tried to turn the uprisings into a real revolution.

In 1893 the Sicilian peasant rebellions were part of a larger movement led by new organizations called *fasci* (leagues of people bound together —like the sticks of a Roman lictor). This movement began on December 4, 1892, when one thousand members of the workers' *fascio* in Palermo demonstrated in the streets of the city with banners carrying slogans such as "Where there is no equality liberty is a fraud." The urban *fasci* were modeled on the French labor exchanges, which included all occupational groups in a particular locality. Their organizers then went into the countryside to enlist peasants and agricultural workers in the movement. On January 20, 1893, in the nearby village of Caltavuturo eleven peasants were killed and forty were wounded when they tried to occupy six hundred acres of formerly common land illegally expropriated by village officials. The Palermo *fascio* took up the cause of the victims, but, under pressure from the large landowners, the police intervened in May and arrested its representatives who were agitating in the countryside. By then there were ninety *fasci* throughout the island. Many of these were nominally members of the Italian Socialist Party, but they were autonomous organizations. They had their own insignia (a red cocarde with a white button), security services, musical bands, and meeting halls; many also had their own co-operatives.

Rosario Garibaldi Bosco, the Socialist leader of the Palermo *fascio*, was unable to unite all the Sicilian *fasci* under the leadership of his party and had to settle for a loose federation. His principal rivals were the radical Napoleone Colajanni and the anarchistic Giuseppe De Felice, both parliamentary deputies. There was also a certain religious tone in some of the *fasci*. Some women took their newborn babies to be baptized at the local *fascio* headquarters instead of the church; other *fascio* headquarters displayed the crucifix. But these gestures expressed defiance of the priests and the established church. According to a police report in June 1893 from Piana dei Greci, both male and female peasants said: "Jesus was a true socialist and wanted exactly what the *fasci* demand; it's the priests who don't represent Him well, especially when they engage in usury."[27] The Socialist leaders of the federation of *fasci* accepted this kind of feeling and tried to use it to give their members a humanitarian conception of social justice along with a class consciousness. Atheism could come later.

The significance of the revolt of the Sicilian *fasci* was that even those of its members who were not socialists or anarchists were no longer willing to accept their traditional place in Sicilian society. Not only the urban workers but also the miners and agricultural laborers were acquiring the modern notion that all persons have rights. In addition, small peasant proprietors, hard-pressed by the agricultural depression, often had to farm additional land as sharecroppers to make ends meet, and they hated the landowners and overseers, who treated them like animals. Indeed they believed that all the authorities, often including priests, denied them justice.

Thus the Socialist leaders of the *fasci* concentrated on the nonideological demands of the Sicilian masses. They championed the demands of the peasants for better contracts with their employers and landlords, rather than the ultimate socialization of the land. In the cities the *fasci* also supported the workers' economic demands, such as higher wages and an eight-hour day. The number of strikes and demonstrations mounted throughout the island in the summer and fall of 1893. Led by the *fasci*, many of Sicily's fifty thousand sulphur miners—the island's

A group of Sicilian *fasci* sacking the headquarters of the prefect at Mazara del
Vallo in December 1893, from *Illustrazione Italiana*.

largest single group of workers—struck against the lowering of their
wages. Agricultural workers in the interior of the island also struck
against their employers and sometimes succeeded in forcing them to
agree to higher wages. But the employers soon reneged and refused to
deal with the *fasci* leaders. Then there were more disturbances, and
police and soldiers were called in. Not only were these organized strikes
new but the agricultural workers and some sharecroppers were also demanding an end to the remaining "feudal" relations between them and
their employers in an economic structure that was already capitalist.

Encouraged by the militancy of the workers and peasants, craftsmen,
small landowners and shopkeepers, and other lower-middle-class people
in rural centers began agitating against the burdensome taxes on consumer goods. Unlike organized strikes this kind of protest was not new.
But local hirelings of the Mafia, especially in the rural constabulary, encouraged acts of violence against local government offices and tax registers

so that they could use repressive force against them. The *fasci* had difficulty controlling this antitax movement, and violent demonstrations against town governments increased in the last months of 1893. The most important demonstration was on December 24, in Corleone, where four thousand people listened to the head of the local *fascio* tell them to stop paying all local taxes until the central government investigated graft and injustice in their collection. The crowd in Corleone dispersed without incident, but other demonstrations were violent. On October 10 the one in Syracuse ended with the sacking of the town hall. Elsewhere the mayors' policemen fired on the crowds and, after seeing their fallen comrades, some of the demonstrators assaulted the hated village authorities. In one instance they killed both the mayor and his wife, who had poured water on them from her window during a demonstration.

The antitax riots of late 1893 were the culmination of the revolt of the Sicilian *fasci*. In many demonstrations people carried portraits of the king and queen and shouted "Long live the king" and "Down with taxes." This loyalty to the monarchy may seem "primitive" (it was also widespread in Russia), but the rebels themselves were modern in the way they were mobilized and in their political goals. Their main targets were the local mayor, his constabulary, and his other henchmen, whom the citizens accused of intimidating them and of favoring themselves in levying taxes. All these demonstrations and riots—whether organized by the *fasci* or spontaneous—sought to put pressure on the local authorities to redress grievances. They were not the revolution that leaders like De Felice wanted and the possessing classes feared, but they sparked a major counteroffensive by the national government in Rome.

This counteroffensive began in the summer of 1893. At that time Giolitti, the minister of the interior, instructed his prefects to investigate those *fasci* that included people convicted of illegal acts, along with lower-level Mafiosi. When reports on this matter showed too few of these people to justify dissolving the *fasci*, representatives of the central government turned to intimidation, firing local officials who were secretly members of a *fascio* and refused to withdraw from it. In October they also looked for possible subversive contacts between the *fasci* and France and began moving army troops to some parts of the island to maintain order. By then there were over one hundred and sixty *fasci* in Sicily, with eleven thousand members in Palermo, ten thousand in Catania, and five thousand in Messina; even the village of Corleone had twelve hundred according to the prefect and six thousand according to other sources. At the end of the year ninety-two demonstrators throughout the island had already been killed, mainly by the local police but also by soldiers. In the rest of Italy the main counteroffensive against the *fasci* involved the mobilization of public opinion among the middle and upper classes around the fear of revolution.

The more ideologically oriented leaders of the Sicilian *fasci* undoubtedly considered a mass insurrection as the best way not only to defend themselves against government intimidation but also to bring about a revolution. But Bosco himself was hesitant, and even De Felice wanted to postpone the revolution until the *fasci* movement had spread sufficiently in the rest of Italy. By the beginning of January 1894, De Felice seemed ready to launch a revolution but the Socialists were not. Instead, on January 3, the leaders of the central committee of the Sicilian *fasci* met secretly in Palermo and sent to Rome a petition including all their demands. This petition denounced the existing order and insisted that the bourgeoisie stop its brutal repression and meet the needs of the poor. It also demanded structural changes in land tenure.

Prime Minister Crispi's response was martial law and mass arrests. On January 3 forty thousand additional army troops were sent to Sicily to enforce the martial law decree. A decree of January 11 authorized the arrest of all people who had been given warnings by the police, as well as "people of ill-repute." Almost two thousand people were arrested in these two categories alone. The martial law decree was also used to prohibit all public meetings, to declare all the *fasci* dissolved, and to bring to trial the members of the central committee for conspiracy and incitement to civil war. All were convicted and sentenced to long prison terms.

Although the *fasci* were successfully repressed in these ways, they had succeeded, for the first time, in mobilizing the downtrodden Sicilian masses, especially the peasants in the backward interior areas of the island. The Socialist press in other European countries hailed their activities as the first mass movement of the Italian proletariat. But the Sicilian *fasci* were not as revolutionary as the agrarian socialists and anarchists who tried to mobilize Russia's peasants in 1905.

By the summer of 1905 radical protest in Russia's cities stimulated rural violence in the Baltic provinces, and the political groups involved made their first effort to mobilize the peasants in the Russian heartland with the founding of the Peasants Union. The growth in the number of its branches, as with the Sicilian *fasci*, indicated the willingness of some peasants to abandon their traditional conservatism and to act as an organized political force. Unlike the *fasci*, however, the union's central leadership was dominated by liberals, who were more concerned with political reforms than with changing the economic and social structures. Italy's constitution already provided the representative government and civil rights that Russia still lacked, and the union's leaders in Moscow soon succeeded in persuading peasant meetings in the provinces to adopt petitions calling for these reforms. They also supported the nationalization of large private estates, with partial compensation to the landlords, leaving the details to be worked out by a constituent assembly. But the peasants' petitions often added more immediate demands for additional land and the elimination of onerous taxes.

Although the central leadership did not view the Peasants Union as a revolutionary agency, some of the local leaders did. As in Sicily and Romania, some of these local leaders were young men whose outlook had been broadened during their period of military service. In Russia, however, this experience was especially vivid among those peasant soldiers and sailors who were just returning from the Russo-Japanese War. Some of them brought revolutionary propaganda they had picked up in the service; others brought tales of the military fiasco, thus adding to the existing discontent. Another source for the local leadership—both formal and informal—was returning peasant-workers. We noted in Chapter 3 that a large proportion of Russia's urban workers spent part of each year in their native villages. They had been difficult to integrate into the urban working class before 1905, but the strikes and upheavals in the cities in that year raised their social consciousness. Thus they helped to channel urban ideas and attitudes to the countryside in the summer and fall.[28]

"Professional" agitators in the countryside wanted to transform the Peasants Union into a revolutionary agency. This was particularly so in the Don Cossack region and in Saratov Province, where the Social Revolutionaries had already gained positions of prominence in the formal leadership during the summer. By the fall, 50 per cent of the districts in the south-central part of European Russia were experiencing waves of agrarian revolt, including the burning of manor houses and the murder of landlords. In their passion for retribution the peasants relayed their cry "The red cock is crowing!" from estate to estate, while the provincial governors clamored for more troops to deal with the rebellion. Anarchists were sometimes able to persuade the peasants to demand independence from all superior organized authority. In the Olkhovskaya district, in Saratov Province, a group of peasants did this under the leadership of Avrahm Yushko, a local veterinarian. Their program called for the conversion of the churches into schools and hospitals, an elected clergy, and the replacement of the army with units of voluntary local militia.[29] In their draft program the Social Revolutionaries also demanded broad autonomy for urban and rural areas and village communes as well as the socialization of all privately held land.[30] But they cautioned the working class against "state socialism," which would make it dependent on a ruling bureaucracy.

The strikes in the cities, the granting of the October Manifesto, and the inability of the government to stop their outbursts made the Russian peasants a more aggressive political force than those in the Sicilian *fasci.* By November the Peasants Union had over two hundred thousand members in twenty-six provinces and the peasants' radicalism forced its Second Congress to demand the immediate transfer of land without compensation. Meanwhile rumors that the possibility of achieving this goal was near increased the number of violent acts by the peasants themselves. In the Nizhne-Lomonovsky district of Penza Province they demanded grain and timber from the managers of the Naryshkin estate. When they were refused they beat off the local police with clubs and looted and destroyed much of the landlord's property. In Saratov Province Social Revolutionary peasant fighting detachments went so far as to sabotage the operations of local officials.

But the rural revolt was not co-ordinated with the general strike in the cities in December, and once that strike was crushed the government was able to use all its repressive forces in the "pacification" of the countryside. Typically troops would descend on a village, order a public meeting, and demand that known troublemakers be turned over to them. If the villagers refused, Cossacks would drag the suspects to the village square and beat them. Then the village meeting would be forced to request that the alleged culprits be sent into exile in Siberia. If the peasants resisted, their punishment was particularly brutal and humiliating. The authorities burned many of their homes and ordered them to fall on their knees and beg for mercy. With these methods the government gained the upper hand by the beginning of 1906 in the six provinces where they were tried. "Pacification" in the rest of the empire took many more months, but it did not remove the causes of peasant discontent.

Socially and economically Romania resembled Russia. Though it had a liberal constitution, it was dominated to a much greater extent by the noble landlords (boyars) than the tsarist regime. The emancipation of the Romanian peasants in 1864 had been carried out in a manner similar to the emancipation in Russia three years earlier. In both cases the peasants were allowed to buy a portion of their former masters' land through long-term redemption payments, but they had to rent additional plots in order to feed their families. And in Romania common land, forests, and pasture were appropriated by the new capitalist landlords, who also brought new land under cultivation as Western European markets for their wheat grew. Whereas the Russian peasants' freedom of movement was limited by their obligations to their village households, the Romanian peasants refused to become migrant wage laborers and there was no work for them in Romania's preindustrial cities. They doggedly clung to their tiny plots of land.

In neither country did the emancipation reform foster small modern farms on the Western European model or large-scale farming based on wage labor, as in England and Prussia. Instead it created a chronically land-hungry peasantry, too poor and ignorant to adopt modern farming techniques and resentful toward the large landowners and their proxies, who exploited and humiliated them. Even more than in Russia the capitalist grain market made the Romanian landlords and large tenants raise the rents on the land that produced cereals for export, thus aggravating the peasants' feeling that land was being unjustly withheld from them. (By the outbreak of the First World War little Romania was the world's fourth largest cereal exporter.)

This contrast between a new, market-oriented agriculture supported by a landlord government and traditional peasant forms of organization and expectations regarding land use accounts for the fierce and bloody peasant rebellion of March 1907. It began in northern Moldavia against certain Jewish estate managers, but it quickly spread to other parts of the country and was directed against all large tenants and absentee landowners. The most violent episodes occurred in south-central Wallachia, where anti-Semitism was not an issue and where the clash between capitalist agriculture and peasant traditions was most severe.

Unlike the uprisings in Sicily and Russia the one in Romania was opposed by the Socialists. In 1907 the weak Romanian Socialist Party told the peasants: "Urprisings benefit only the boyars. The peasants afterward become even weaker and more depressed. . . . Peasants, you will not be delivered by uprisings, you will achieve profitable and lasting results not through violence and plundering but through seeking to destroy the political power of the boyars, landowners, and tenants."[31] Insofar as the peasants had any help in mobilizing themselves it came from village leaders: ex-army sergeants, clerks, and schoolteachers. Nevertheless, within a few weeks they succeeded in organizing revolutionary bands and seizing a large amount of land.

The Romanian peasant revolt was put down much more quickly than the one in Russia. There were no urban strikes or political revolution to deal with and no problem of moving demoralized troops over long distances after a lost war. In less than a month the Romanian army restored order in the countryside. Its reprisals were far more severe than in Russia: over eleven thousand peasants were killed during the brief but thorough "pacification." And, unlike Russia, Romania was on the winning side at the end of the First World War, and its government partially relieved the peasants' demand for land—though not their poverty and backwardness—in the agrarian reforms of 1918–21.

FEMINISM

Unlike peasant and working-class unrest, radical protest by feminists was concentrated in the most modern countries. The exceptional militancy of the English suffragettes* during the early 1900's was partly a reflection of the personalities of their leaders, but there was more to it than that. England was the most highly industrialized and urbanized country in Europe; it also had the highest standard of living and the most deeply rooted commitment to civil and political liberties. The contrast between these fulfillments of the promise of modernization and the continuing repression of women as women was felt to be especially intolerable by all English feminists. But feminists everywhere based their protest on the perception of this kind of contrast. They felt neither the hostility of the peasants nor the ambivalence of the workers toward modernization. Their main complaint was that changes in their status and roles were not occurring fast enough.

Yet even in the most modern countries feminism attracted only a small minority of women. With a few outstanding exceptions aristocratic women did not take part in movements for social reform or women's rights; their philanthropic activities were an expression of *noblesse oblige* and had little to do with feminist demands. Many young rural women left home to find work and a freer life in the cities, but those who remained on the farm were oblivious to their relative deprivation. Most urban lower-class women worked until they got married and many continued to do so thereafter, mainly to supplement their husbands' incomes

* The word "suffragettes" refers only to the members of the Women's Social and Political Union, to be described presently. Other champions of womens' suffrage are called "suffragists."

but sometimes to get out of the house. In general female workers did not try to compete for men's jobs or to demand equal pay for equal work, but a growing minority became willing to join trade unions and go on strike for economic gains. Although a few working-class women were prominent in the feminist movement, it was primarily an expression of the discontents of self-conscious middle-class women. Indeed the middle-class tone of the movement made the more revolutionary female Socialist leaders reject it. Rosa Luxemburg, Clara Zetkin, and Angelica Balabanoff argued that working-class women could only advance their social, political, and economic status through the Revolution, not through reforms wrested from middle-class men.

In her book on feminism in Germany and Scandinavia before 1914 Katharine Susan Anthony expressed the moral orientation of the movement everywhere: "The basic idea of feminism . . . is the emancipation of woman as a personality. The struggle for self-consciousness is the essence of the feminist movement."[32] Its goal is the restoration of woman's self-respect, and the main value of its political victories is to

> teach women not to depreciate their own sex. When the whole tale of objective achievements has been completed, when the schools have been opened to women, the dress fetich [*sic*] banished, state maternity insurance introduced, the legal protection of motherhood and childhood within marriage and outside of it guaranteed, the economic independence of women assured, and their political enfranchisement accomplished,—the sum of all these cultural victories will be more than needed to wipe out the psychological residue of subjection in the individual woman soul.

Feminists preached that only by achieving equality for their entire sex could individual women fulfill their wish to be free. They demanded the same rights that men had concerning life, liberty, and property. Unlike the radical spokesmen for the working class or the peasants, the feminists did not advocate the overthrow of the existing order but rather the "promotion" of all women as women through legal reforms and changed attitudes. Yet what they wanted amounted to a cultural revolution, given the internalized standards of the majority of Europeans—male and female—regarding the status and role of women. And their challenge to these standards provoked a more emotional reaction than the demands of most socialists.

Many feminists were more concerned with emancipation from traditional social and cultural restraints than the right to vote. A major impetus for this concern was the growing number of "surplus women." By the early 1900's there were over one million more women than men in England and Wales; the surplus was eight hundred thousand in Germany, six hundred thousand in Austria-Hungary, and three hundred thousand in the four Scandinavian countries. Although perhaps one third of the "surplus women" were below the customary age for marrying, the majority were spinsters and widows. There was always productive work for unmarried women to do in traditional peasant households, and working-class women could usually find employment in factories, sweatshops, or domestic service. It was the unmarried middle-class women who most needed outlets for their energies which would also be remunerative. Yet it was they who were most restricted in the kinds of careers available to them. Hence their first struggle was to gain admission to schools and professions traditionally reserved for men.

This struggle met with stiff resistance. Middle-class parents argued that study would make a girl bald and spoil her figure. Conservative clergymen charged that exposure to books and ideas would corrupt a girl's innocence. Distinguished publicists asserted that the feminine mind was incapable of logical thinking. To respectable society everywhere the very notion of lady doctors, lawyers, and administrators was scandalous. A lady was supposed to be passive and beautiful; even if she were neither she would be treated as a sex object in a man's world. At most an unmarried lady who had to support herself should be allowed to care for young children, as a governess or teacher. But the idea of a lady teacher in a secondary school—let alone a university—was considered preposterous.

In the face of these kinds of resistance male and female feminists achieved notable but limited gains in opening certain schools and careers to women.[33] During the last third of the nineteenth century secondary schools for girls were established in most countries, but many of these did not prepare women to meet the entrance requirements of the universities. In France the graduates of these "finishing" schools were given only a certificate, rather than the state *baccalauréat*. Only in 1908 did the Prussian government pass a law reorganizing and upgrading girls' high schools on a separate-but-equal basis. This law also admitted women to universities on the same conditions as men—three decades later than in England and Switzerland. Denmark's classical high schools were opened to girls in 1903, but ten years later the number admitted was still small and coeducation remained the exception in Copenhagen and the larger provincial towns. The Netherlands had the highest proportion of females in coeducational secondary schools and universities. Women's right to become physicians was first recognized in England* and Russia in the 1880's, in Germany, France, and Switzerland in the 1890's, and in Sweden during the first decade of the twentieth century. But the legal profession remained closed to women in most countries. (Denmark and the Netherlands were notable exceptions.) As late as 1911 the census for England and Wales recorded no women lawyers or engineers and only nineteen accountants. Nursing, elementary-school teaching, and clerical work were the main careers open to unmarried middle- and lower-middle-class women without restriction. In 1911 there were 117,000 women clerks in England and Wales but only 477 women doctors.

Once alternatives to marriage as a career existed, the feminist struggle against traditional social and cultural restraints focused on the institution of marriage itself. The Married Women's Property Acts of 1882 and 1893 improved the economic circumstances of English women, and married women gained some property rights in Germany and Scandinavia. But there was no such protection for women in France, Belgium, Italy, and Spain, which operated under the Napoleonic Code. Divorce was a more emotional issue than property rights, especially when feminists tried to justify it on the basis of the New Morality. Ellen Key, the leading Swedish advocate of libertarian causes, asserted that the monogamous union was still the highest ideal of marriage but that it was immoral when either partner found it oppressive.[34] During the prewar decade this radical notion was put into practice only in Sweden and Norway, where divorce was made possible by mutual consent. In most other Protestant countries, including England, only the husband could sue for divorce and only by proving his wife to be an adulteress. Thus, as in Catholic countries, the double standard of morality continued to prevail.

The most radical feminist campaign against traditional social and cultural restraints concerned the protection of unwed mothers—particularly by the German Union for the Protection of Motherhood (Bund für Mutterschutz). Here too the inspiration came from Ellen Key, whose book *Love and Marriage* appeared in German in 1904. According to her version of the New Morality, an unwed mother and her child should not be penalized by forced separation and the stigma of illegitimacy. In late October 1904, Ruth Bré, herself an illegitimate child, took up this idea and issued a call in the German press to "Unmarried mothers who are seeking a place in the world where they can keep their children with

---

* A few pioneer women had obtained their licences to practice earlier because the rules spoke of "persons," without distinction of sex.

them and rear them themselves can find a home and occupation immediately in the country."[35] She received so many replies that she decided to found the Union for the Protection of Motherhood on November 12. Its goals, for both married and unmarried women, included state maternity insurance, the right to use birth control, and a reform of sexual ethics.

An offshoot of the Union's activities was a campaign for the unity-title (like Ms. today) for all women. Originally conceived as a protection for unmarried mothers, the unity-title quickly came to symbolize the broader feminist demand for the same rights as men. As one of its advocates, the Swiss social psychologist August Forel, said: "We have no 'Herrlein' and 'Herren' and we should not have 'Fräulein' and 'Frauen.'"

The German feminist movement was one of the most varied and active in Europe.[36] Under the "umbrella" of the Union of Women's Clubs (Bund Deutscher Frauenvereine) there were organizations of Christian feminists, anticlerical feminists, Socialist feminists, suffrage-feminists, and feminist-feminists. In 1905 the largest group, the General Women's Union (Allgemeiner Deutscher Frauenverein), issued its minimum demands: 1) equal education, 2) equal pay for equal work; 3) equal responsibility in a marriage; 4) equal participation in all aspects of public life—including politics. (Until 1908 women, like youths, were prohibited from belonging to political organizations in most states of the German Empire.) Three years later Alice Salomon founded the first school for women social workers and devoted her life to raising the status of disadvantaged German women. The German feminists also pioneered the revolt against conventional female dress, particularly the corset. Like the bra sixty years later, the corset became the physical symbol of the traditional constraints from which women should be liberated.

Although middle-class feminists in a number of countries[37] concerned themselves with the rights of unwed mothers, they were divided on the issue of prostitution. A minority of them viewed female prostitutes as victims of masculine depravity and tried to protect them from gross infringements on their civil rights by procurers and the police. A larger group of feminists opposed registration and medical inspection of prostitutes as giving legal sanction to the double standard of morality. Most middle-class feminists viewed prostitution as an evil in itself and fought to make it illegal. Those with a socialist orientation contended that a more just and equitable economic order would make it unnecessary for women to sell their bodies. Capitalist-oriented feminists were too steeped in conventional moral standards to defend the prostitute as an independent entrepreneur who might even enjoy her work.

Working-class feminists understood the exploitation of women workers better than their middle-class sisters did. In 1892, at a Votes-for-Women meeting in Vienna, the Austrian Socialist Adelheid Dwořak-Popp[38] represented the Working Women's Educational Association. She startled the educated middle-class ladies present with her account, based on her personal knowledge, of the reasons some factory girls took to the streets: low wages, long hours, unhealthy working conditions, and lecherous foremen. The French feminist Marguérite Martin, in her book *The Rights of Woman*, stressed the double exploitation of working women as workers and women and, like Adelheid Dwořak-Popp, she urged that they be given the vote in order to better their lot.[39] Annie Kenney, a suffragette who had begun working part time in a Lancashire mill at the age of ten, was particularly resentful of the double duty that working women had to perform as factory hands and housewives.

> When work was over I noticed that it was the mothers who hurried home, who fetched the children that had been put out to nurse, prepared the tea for the husband, did the cleaning, baking, washing, sewing, and nursing. I noticed that when the husband came home, his day's work was over; he took his tea and then went to join his friends in the club or in the public house, or on the cricket or football field.[40]

This double duty also prevented most working-class women from becoming active in public or union affairs. By 1914 the four hundred thousand women in English trade unions constituted 10 per cent of the total membership, and the two hundred and fifty thousand women in the German trade unions 8.5 per cent of the total. Though small, these percentages were double what they had been two decades earlier. But the proportion of women in executive positions in the unions remained much smaller. Most working-class women had neither the time nor the energy to hold such positions or to participate in demonstrations and public debates.

No other movement of radical protest prompted as much public debate as feminism—in the press, in books and pamphlets, in the halls of parliament, and in open meetings. Few consciousnesses were raised by this debate. Instead it typified the modern middle-class notion that one should express one's opinions on current issues. The main issue was not the "unladylike" tactics of the English suffragettes, which will be dealt with presently. It was the whole question of what women are for and what rights they should have. Unlike the worker, peasant, Irish, Polish, and

Jewish "questions," the "woman question" involved people from the same social and cultural backgrounds. Thus they were arguing with one another not only about politics and economics but also about their own norms for behavior and their very identities.

Antifeminist men used every conceivable argument. French literary mandarins like Émile Faguet and Théodore Joran[41] charged that feminism was a menace to the family and that marriage was its born enemy. The English writer E. Belfort Bax, an admirer of Jean-Paul Marat, accused the feminists of wanting not equality but "female ascendancy"[42]; Bax specifically condemned the White Slave Traffic Act of 1912—which added flogging to the imprisonment of pimps—as discriminatory against male procurers. Charles G. Harper rehearsed the familiar argument about women's innate inferiority:

> Woman is the irresponsible creature who cannot reason nor follow an argument to its just conclusion—who cannot control her own emotions, nor rid herself of superstition. What question more pertinent, then, to ask than this: If mankind is to be led by the New Women, is she, first of all, sure of the path?[43]

The eminent Oxford professor of English Law Albert Venn Dicey argued against women's suffrage for reasons of state, particularly in view of the female majority in the total population:

> We are asked to weaken English democracy by far more than doubling the number of English electors; we are asked to place the government of England, nominally at least, in the hands of women. Of these the best are ignorant of statesmanship; the least trustworthy are fanatics who, in their passionate desire to obtain a share in the sovereignty which determines the policy of the British Empire (including the fate of millions of inhabitants of dependent countries), have conclusively shown that they have not yet mastered the most elementary principles of self-government or of loyal obedience to the laws of the country.[44]

On May 5, 1911, in a speech in the House of Commons, H. J. Mackinder echoed Dicey's arguments and added:

> I believe that if you do grant this vote it will do very great harm to men in their relations to women. I believe that the whole history of society has lain in this, that woman has succeeded in placing the burdens upon the shoulders of man, and I think she ought to keep them there. [Hon. Members: "Oh, oh."[45]]

Some female antifeminists used similar antimodernizing arguments. A self-styled English working woman, M. E. Simkins, asserted: "If we succeed in setting up the old ideals again in the minds of our young women, something of far greater might and power than the building of Dreadnoughts will have been done for the future of our nation."[46] Marie Corelli, author of numerous best-selling sentimental novels, entered the debate as a career woman: "I earn every pound I possess; I am a householder, paying rates and taxes."[47] Yet she rejected the "right" to vote because

> the very desire for a vote on the part of a woman is an open confession of weakness,—and proof that she has lost ground, and is not sure of herself. For if she is real Woman,—if she has the natural heritage of her sex, which is the mystic power to persuade, enthral and subjugate man, she has no need to come down from her throne and mingle in any of his political frays, inasmuch as she is already the very head and front of Government.

The debate between female suffragists and antisuffragists was based more on philosophical and political arguments than on the nature of women as such. Mrs. Humphry Ward, a leading sponsor of the Women's Anti-Suffrage League, appealed to women's "patriotism" and "common sense" in opposing parliamentary suffrage, which would be bad for the Empire and would pose the needless threat to men of a female majority.[48] To the suffragist argument that working women needed the vote to better their economic conditions the antisuffragists answered that "men are sweated as well as women, which would not be the case if the vote was the way out."[49] To the antisuffragist argument that only a small minority of women wanted the vote Dr. Ethel Smyth replied:

> If Miss Sinclair thinks me deficient in political instinct . . . I wonder what she would say of Wilberforce, who declared that if only one slave looked upon chains as a degradation it was reason enough for the abolition of slavery; or of Lord Beaconsfield, who cried that if his opponents were right in saying not one agricultural labourer wanted the vote, that was the strongest argument he had heard for their enfranchisement![50]

There were also basic disagreements among the feminists themselves. The more militant ones insisted that the majority of women were capable of being raised from a state of dependence to an independent existence as soon as the pressure of outside circumstances ceased simultaneously with the pressure of prevailing standards. They refused to acknowledge any inherent inequalities between women and men. Ellen Key and the Austrian Rosa Mayreder disagreed. They accepted the average woman's role as mother and homemaker but insisted on the right of any woman to reject this role to pursue a career of her own choosing.

> In the woman's movement the female minority is fighting for a normal social status; and why should not a highly developed state of society, furnished with all the means to a heightened perception, grant, even to a minority, the position to which it is entitled?[51]

Many Continental feminists felt that social and cultural emancipation was more important than political enfranchisement. But in England after the turn of the century most feminists "supported the rigid code of Victorian morality rather than claiming for women emotional and sexual freedom as well as civil rights. In demanding, as Christabel [Pankhurst] did, 'Votes for women and chastity for men,' women's chastity was taken for granted."[52]

Mrs. Emmeline Pankhurst (1859–1928) and her daughter Christabel (1880–1958) dominated the Women's Social and Political Union from its founding in October 1903 until the end of its militant campaign in August 1914.[53] In October 1906 these well-educated middle-class rebels renounced their earlier ties with the Labour party, though Sylvia, another daughter, continued her efforts to organize working women within the WSPU until she was formally ousted in January 1914. Between early 1906 and July 1908 the movement tried to impress the government with large public meetings for women's suffrage. The largest of these rallies, attended by over a quarter of a million people, occurred in London's Hyde Park on June 21, 1908. As early as October 1905, however, Christabel had decided to use violence and shocking behavior to gain publicity for the feminist cause. At that time she had spat at a policeman in order to be sent to jail and hence gain sympathy from prominent people who might put pressure on the government to give women the vote. But as public rallies and abusing policemen failed to get the government to change its policies, the WSPU raised the level of its violence and shocking behavior—culminating in the arson campaign of 1913 and 1914.

Christabel and her loyal followers were the most militant feminists of their time. Though the *Daily Mail* dubbed them "suffragettes" on January 10, 1906, their war was against men rather than the electoral system. In a letter written on August 1, 1913, Christabel said: "Another mistake that people make is to suppose that we want the vote only or chiefly because of its political value. We want [it] far more because of its symbolic value—the recognition of our human equality that it will involve."[54] Christabel insisted that women should have nothing to do with men either politically or sexually. According to her, men not only dominated women through male laws but they also inflicted venereal diseases on them. As she wrote in the September 12, 1913, issue of *The Suffragette*, young women had to be "warned of the fact that marriage is intensely dangerous, until such time as men's moral standards are completely changed and they become as chaste and clean-living as women." In the March 28 issue she had asserted: "In fighting against evil, the few are stronger than the many, women stronger than men."

The suffragettes' tactics antagonized even most women who wanted the vote. In October 1906 the National Union of Women's Suffrage Societies, led by Mrs. Millicent Fawcett, expressed its sympathy for ten suffragettes who were jailed for disrupting a session of the House of Commons but rejected militancy for its own members, who called themselves suffragists. By August 1909 imprisoned suffragettes regularly went on hunger strikes, and medical officers began to use force to feed them. As the militant feminists of the WSPU became more aggressive in their efforts to rush the House of Commons to demand the vote, the police became more brutal. On November 18, 1910—"Black Friday"— "women were kicked, their arms were twisted, their noses were punched, their breasts were gripped, knees were thrust between their legs."[55] Rather than submit to further mistreatment of this kind the suffragettes adopted the new tactic of anonymous attacks on property: window-smashing, setting mailboxes on fire, and widespread arson. In January 1913, Mrs. Pankhurst called the suffragettes "guerillists" who would "do as much damage to property as they could" to gain the vote. They also adopted an increasingly military stance, with bodyguards, marching bands, and "generals" on horseback.

Instead of seeking popular support for its cause the WSPU now used terrorism to *coerce* the public and the government to give women the vote. The government in turn abandoned the forced feeding of hunger-striking prisoners because this made them seem like martyrs. In April 1913 it instituted the so-called "Cat and Mouse Act," which released these prisoners so that they could recuperate before being reincarcerated. Meanwhile the militant suffragettes burned down more and more railroad stations, castles, churches, and cricket pavilions. In 1913 and 1914 they sometimes caused £50,000 fire damage a month. By the outbreak of the war this kind of violence and Christabel's intolerance of anyone who

The arrest of a suffragette following an "attack" on Buckingham Palace.

challenged her autocratic decisions had alienated many supporters and made the WSPU "a harried rump of the large and superbly organized movement it had once been."[56]

Like labor strikes and unrest in Ulster (see p. 331), the suffragettes' militant campaign ended with Britain's entry into the First World War. Mrs. Pankhurst and Christabel ceased calling their country "decadent" and urged men to join the army to fight the "Huns." After the war Christabel changed her ideas again and became an ardent believer in the Second Coming of Christ. The active contribution of hundreds of thousands of British working women to the war effort was largely responsible for persuading the government to grant female suffrage. Nevertheless, in the 1930's Mrs. Pankhurst was honored with a statue and Christabel was made a Dame Commander of the British Empire for their prewar leadership of the movement for women's rights.

The discontents of the English suffragettes were far different from those of Sicilian peasants and Russian workers. In fact most of these women, with notable exceptions such as Annie Kenney and Sylvia Pankhurst, felt little sympathy for the discontents of workers in their own country. European feminists accepted most aspects of modernization and demanded that women share in its benefits as men's equals as soon as possible. Most movements of radical protest by workers also aimed at accelerating the "promotion" of their class in modern society. In contrast, rural revolts expressed the reaction of a traditional peasant mentality against modern economic and social structures.

Yet despite their different goals and tactics all these movements had certain common features. They all reflected a new consciousness of the mistreatment of the social groups they claimed to represent. And they all tried to mobilize their followers for collective action in the political arena. When the authorities used force to repress their collective violence, many of their members became more convinced than ever of the rightness of their moral orientation and the perception of reality on which it was based. The First World War temporarily made most of these people shelve their discontents and defend their national societies. But their contributions to the war effort were to give them an even more compelling justification for the renewal of their demands.

CHAPTER 9

NATIONALISM

Nationalism was the main rival of all the protest movements discussed in the preceding chapter and of internationalism and pacifism as well. Growing international tensions helped to make it more and more influential throughout Europe, but that familiar story will be largely ignored here. Our concern will be with the relationships between nationalism and modernization and the social and cultural responses to these relationships.

The term nationalism has two distinct meanings.[1] It is most often defined as a consciousness, mentality, or

> state of mind, permeating the large majority of a people, and claiming to permeate all its members; it recognises the nation-state as the ideal form of political organization and the nationality as the source of all creative cultural energy and economic well being. The supreme loyalty of man is therefore due to his nationality, as his own life is supposedly rooted in and made possible by its welfare.[2]

National consciousness is more specific and more demanding than patriotism, an attitude common to all ages, which holds that one's own society is good because it *is* one's own. Typically patriotism has been centered on a "country" (*pays, paese, Land*) that is smaller than the great modern nations and ethnically more homogeneous: Quebec, Bavaria, Wales, Brittany, Catalonia, Tuscany (or even individual towns within it). Only when this kind of patriotism adds the demands for political independence

Emperor Francis Joseph reviewing a parade on the centenary of the "Battle of the Nations" in the Schwartzenbergplatz, Vienna, 1913.

and a sovereign state does it become a form of nationalism. And these demands are the basis of nationalism as an ideological movement.

According to its second meaning, nationalism is an ideological movement "for the attainment and maintenance of self-government and independence on behalf of a group, some of whose members conceive it to constitute an actual or potential 'nation' like others."[3] Its core doctrine is constructed from the following propositions: 1) Humanity is naturally divided into nations; 2) each nation has its peculiar character; 3) the source of all political power is the nation, the whole collectivity; 4) for freedom and self-realization, men and women must identify with a nation; 5) nations can only be fulfilled in their own states; 6) loyalty to the nation-state overrides other loyalties (unlike patriotism, which was often overriden by religious loyalties); 7) the primary condition of global freedom and harmony is the strengthening of the nation-state. Logical corollaries of these propositions include the stressing of cultural individuality by accentuating "national" or ethnic differences, a drive for economic autarchy and self-sustaining growth, attempts to expand the nation-state to maintain international power and status, renewing the nation's cultural and social fabric through sweeping institutional changes in order to compete successfully with other nations.

In the generation before the war both modernizers and antimodernizers adopted nationalism as an ideology—a program of action for achieving national goals variously defined. They did this partly because it seemed to resolve their subjective dilemmas in coping with modernization. But they also saw that, objectively, national consciousness had become the most pervasive and most readily mobilizable force of their time.

National consciousness develops

> as individuals among a people become involved in common enterprises, are able to and do communicate with others of like mind, and do act or interact with these others, their fellow citizens, "within a context of shared understandings, mutual expectations, and accepted norms."[4]

"A people" here means an ethnic group that comes to think of itself as a nation after modernization has uprooted many of its members from the traditional social structure and roles that had once given them their sense of identity and status. In Chapter 1 we noted the increasing importance of culture in serving this purpose for masses of individuals who moved into cities and new occupations and who were mobilized by large, impersonal organizations. And we saw in Chapters 1 and 4 how national governments tried to assimilate them politically and culturally through the extension of citizenship rights and public educational systems. All these forces helped the development of national consciousness, which looks on a nation as a "home" from which the individual derives his identity and self-respect. Nationalist movements politicized the importance of a particular nation as a "home" by insisting that the people who shared its culture should rule themselves and be independent economically and militarily.

The divisive and destructive consequences of nationalism, particularly during the two world wars, should not blind us to the constructive function it has played in aiding modernization. When traditional religious images lost their hold, it gave people a new faith and goals which were satisfying, credible, and meaningful. Nationalism has also fulfilled people's yearning for dignity and solidarity

> within an anthropocentric image of the world, which does not involve a leap of faith beyond the scientific-technological premises of modernizing societies. One can indeed claim that nationalism is one of the most convincing collective realizations of the principles of the Enlightenment.[5]

The ideologies of many antimodernizing nationalist movements belie this claim, but they were only part of the story.

There were nations without nationalisms and nationalisms without nations. Many of the nationalisms without nations involved only small minorities of intellectuals and conspirators. And some of the nations without nationalisms had a more developed national consciousness than other nations with active nationalist movements. But everywhere it appeared, nationalism had to cope with the effects of modernization.

NATIONAL CONSCIOUSNESS AS AN INTEGRATING FORCE

Although a common language has usually been a strong force for assimilating individuals politically and culturally into a nation, a shared structure of feeling is more basic, as is evident in the case of Switzerland. In his reminiscences the editor of a prominent German-Swiss newspaper recalls conversations in which his German was more closely akin to the French of a French-Swiss friend than to the German of a foreigner. "The French-Swiss and I were using different words for the same concepts, but we understood one another. The man from Vienna and I were using the same words for different concepts, and thus we did not understand one another in the least."[6] The Swiss spoke four different languages and still could act as one people because they had a common outlook based on shared personal associations, memories, learned habits, preferences, symbols, patterns of landholding and social organization, and events in history.

The Swiss had a strong national consciousness but no nationalist movement in our period, whereas the Italians, most of whom could speak the same language, had a less developed national consciousness but, as we shall see, an extremely articulate nationalist movement. One reason for these differences was historical: Switzerland had been politically united and independent for a much longer time than Italy, and participatory democracy in the Swiss cantons antedated modernization. Another reason was that the Swiss government was more responsive than the Italian in extending citizenship rights and in coping with the transformations brought by economic and social modernization. The small proportion of Swiss who emigrated overseas, in comparison with Italians, was an important reflection of the differences in national consciousness as an integrating force in the two countries.

National consciousness was nurtured beginning in each citizen's childhood by almost all institutions and forms of expression. Every public elementary-school pupil in France read *Le Tour de la France par deux enfants: devoir et patrie.* The purpose of this illustrated story, according to the preface of its author, G. Bruno, was "to make the fatherland alive and visible" through the travels of André Volden, age fourteen, and his seven-year-old brother Julien. These two boys begin their odyssey in 1871, soon after the Franco-Prussian War, as homeless orphans who leave their native town in that part of Lorraine annexed by Germany to find their true home in another part of France. In three hundred pages and as many illustrations they cover a lot of territory—from Lorraine to Brittany, from Dunkirk to Marseilles—savoring the local foods, observing the local geography, and learning about the artistic and scientific achievements of France's great men. In the words of the author:

> Each invention made by these illustrious men, each contribution they have made toward progress, becomes an example for the child who reads about it . . . and takes on more interest by being mixed with descriptions of the localities where these great men were born. . . . We want to show the children the *patrie* in its noblest aspects.

The metaphor of the homeless orphans (with a German-sounding name) was cleverly chosen as a means of instilling national consciousness. And the fact that André and Julien are homeless because of a humiliating defeat in a war with Germany made the metaphor all the more poignant. They are orphans because they have already lost their mother, and their father, a hard-working carpenter and war veteran, has just died in an accident. Thus they also need a new "father," which they finally find in their uncle Frantz on a farm in good old Gascony. ("Home" was automatically assumed to be "in the country" rather than a city.) But their travels also give them a father*land* and a set of perceptions, attitudes, and values designed to make them conscious of its unique virtues. At the end of the story Julien becomes ecstatic when Uncle Frantz proposes to put the national flag on the roof of the restored farmhouse: "Yes, yes, let's do it. When I think of the trouble we have endured to be French and that we have finally made it! . . . With all my heart I love France."

German educators tried to stress national consciousness in all elementary-school subjects. The homeland (*Heimat*) was to be presented as everything that gave the child his identity: birthplace, mother tongue, family and friends, religion, customs, history. Because Germany was only recently united politically and industrialization and urbanization were uprooting more people at a faster pace than in France, German textbooks took special pains to idealize the far from integrated character of the homeland's changing society.

> The Empire is unified, powerful, and respected in the world. The divisions between classes no longer exist. All paths are open to personal industriousness and talent. The people take part in the government. In all areas there breathes the spirit of tolerance. The condition of the lower classes has improved.[7]

German school children also learned to express their national consciousness in patriotic songs like "My Fatherland":

> Undying loyalty to you unto death
> I swear with heart and hand,
> For what I am and what I have
> I thank you, my fatherland!

Although instilling national consciousness in children helped achieve the integrative goal of modernization, like other kinds of social mobilization it tended to conflict with the goal of personal liberation and autonomy. We have noted this conflict in a number of contexts, and the struggle between the proponents of conformity and liberty has continued to the present. During the early 1900's a libertarian socialist like Ellen

Key foresaw the emancipation of the child from adult social constraints through "progressive education" not only as a desirable end in itself but also as a means toward reducing national rivalries and promoting world peace. But the schools and the major youth movements in most modern countries were adopting an increasingly nationalist and militarist tone during the prewar years. This tone permeated the Jungdeutschlandbund, which had 750,000 members in 1914, but it influenced even the Boy Scouts.

The Boy Scouts were organized in 1908 in England by Sir Robert Baden-Powell, a retired general and hero of the Boer War.[8] Baden-Powell borrowed ideas from the American Woodcraft movement and the Scottish Boys Brigade in the hope of mobilizing lower-class boys through a combination of camping and premilitary training. Within two years his organization attracted over a hundred thousand members, but from the beginning the British Boy Scouts came mainly from the middle and lower-middle classes. The working classes were less attracted to it not only because they could not afford to pay for the uniform but also because they resented military training in general and the movement's pressure to attend religious services. The scouting slogan "Be Prepared" meant not only knowing how to make a fire without matches and helping old ladies across the street but also cultivating physical fitness and discipline for future service to the nation. According to a 1966 survey, 34 per cent of British men born between 1901 and 1920 claimed to have been Boy Scouts. Thus the movement may well have conditioned a large number of middle-class boys to become patriotic soldiers during the First World War. Certainly a large percentage of its adult leaders were ex-soldiers, and both the War Office and the National Service League put pressure on it to help militarize the young in the absence of universal military training.

In most Continental countries universal military training programs continued the efforts of the schools in developing young men's national consciousness.[9] They prepared their recruits for good citizenship as well as combat. Those recruits who had not learned to read and write in elementary school were given special courses in the army. They were also taught modern notions of discipline, hygiene, and self-sacrifice for the fatherland. In France and some of the smaller countries of Western Europe the citizen army was conceived as a "melting pot" in which young men could develop close personal ties with their compatriots from all parts of the nation. This was undoubtedly the army's most successful function as an integrating force.

For adults mass-circulation newspapers were the most important medium promoting cultural assimilation and propagating standardized "national" attitudes, perceptions, and expectations. This was especially true of morning dailies like *Le Petit Parisien*, the proportion of whose sales in the provinces increased from 40.5 per cent in 1890 to 66.6 per cent by 1914.[10] In the issue of October 13, 1893, an editorial writer asserted: "Thus in a great country like France the same thought, at the same hour, excites the whole population. It is the newspaper that establishes this sublime communion of minds across space." Despite its rhetoric this assertion was justified in many ways.

Partly because the political consensus was more fragile in France than in England *Le Petit Parisien* tried more consciously than the *Daily Mail* to champion the existing regime. (Another reason was that its publisher, Jean Dupuy, was more interested—and more influential—in national politics than Alfred Harmsworth.) In addition to its consistent and open defense of the institutions and policies of the Third Republic it stimulated the national consciousness more subtly in its many special features: sports, fashion, serial novels, contests (see Chapter 6). These features were packaged in appealing ways that neither the schools nor the army could hope to match. Also, the fact that Frenchmen bought *Le Petit Parisien* because they wanted to give it an edge over these two institutions as an integrating force.

All forms of popular culture appealed to the national consciousness of their respective countries both directly and indirectly. Not only in England, France, and Germany but also in Italy and Austria-Hungary vaudeville entertainers, particularly fetching young women in tights and military headdress, included a patriotic song as one of their "numbers"; often the audience sang the chorus along with the performer. People supported their national teams in all sports competitions with foreigners; not even the modern Olympic Games, founded in 1896 to promote international understanding, could escape these national biases. In popular adventure stories for both children and adults the heroes and heroines personified the virtues of their own nation and perceived all situations in terms of its particular mentality. They knew who they were and what was right, whereas their enemies were rootless, antisocial, evil, and often foreign. Marxist critics have argued persuasively that the national consciousness disseminated in these ways was a "false consciousness" for the workers. But its very pervasiveness was difficult to counteract, particularly during the diplomatic crises of the immediate prewar years.

People saw images of the nation everywhere. The national flag was displayed in all public buildings, schools, theaters, and sporting arenas. In France the words Liberté, Égalité, Fraternité and the letters R.F. on public buildings were symbols of the activities and presence of the French national state in the smallest villages. Each capital city had its national monument commemorating some real or legendary hero: the mammoth Victor Emmanuel II monument in Rome glorified Italy's recent past, whereas in Budapest the block-long panoramic sculpture of ancient Magyar conquerors evoked events one thousand years earlier. Coins and postage stamps were also illustrated with national themes.

But national images and symbols meant less to some individuals than to others. Those who were already mobilized by economic and social modernization were more open to their messages than those who were not. If the content or form of the message was too unrelated to the expectations of the receiver it passed over his head. Because of their upbringing and travels the concept of the nation meant much more to Julien and André Volden than to an illiterate Russian peasant woman who stayed in the same village all her life. Even among city dwellers the white-collar employees were more receptive than the casual laborers to the media that reinforced national consciousness. If an individual had no roots anywhere, his range of expectations usually did not extend beyond himself and his immediate family. But if he was conscious of the recent loss of the communal or religious ties that had given him his identity and self-respect, he was more susceptible to the appeals of national sentiment. This was especially so if he already had some degree of familiarity with the language, culture, and major institutions of the national society.

It was the extension of citizenship rights and their use by people in countries undergoing economic and social modernization that helped the most in promoting national consciousness in all states. This was as true in imperial Germany as it was in the democratic nation-states of northwestern Europe. In Germany the average citizen had less influence on his government's policies than his counterpart in England, France, or Switzerland, yet his national consciousness was just as strong because he could vote, expect fair treatment from the bureaucracy and legal system, and avail himself of the numerous welfare services sponsored by the state.

The promotion of a national consciousness by the extension of citizenship rights also helped to increase the demand for political independence in countries where it did not yet exist, as in Norway. Until the 1860's only about 10 per cent of the adult male Norwegians voted regularly.[11] Thereafter the percentage increased rapidly among men who already had the right to vote and, with further extensions of the franchise, reached

40 per cent by 1900. At the same time Norwegian politics was transformed by the rise to power of the radical peasant Venstre Party and a growing demand for ending the existing Swedish-Norwegian Union. In 1905 the Norwegian parliament finally declared the union dissolved. Within a few months the Norwegian voters ratified this action in a plebiscite, and the Swedish government accepted the decision.

National consciousness was much less of an integrating force in Eastern than in Western Europe. Its function as a *dis*integrating force in Austria-Hungary and the Balkans and among the subject peoples of the Russian Empire is well known. The tsarist policy of forced Russification was resented and resisted by the national minorities in Poland, the Baltic provinces, Transcaucasia, and the Ukraine. Most Russian Jews felt particularly alienated (see pp. 340–43) because of the forced segregation, poor living conditions, and periodic persecutions that plagued them, and over 1.5 million of them emigrated abroad, almost three fourths of them to America, during the so-called *belle époque*.

But even among the Great Russians national consciousness was largely restricted to sections of the intelligentsia and the middle and lower-middle classes in the cities. As we have seen, at the turn of the century most Russian workers did not feel integrated into their own class, let alone the nation. The peasants—over three fourths of the total population—were still legally second-class subjects, the majority of them illiterate. Despite their ethnic and linguistic homogeneity they felt no national bond among themselves and only a vague loyalty to the tsar. Universal military training helped to lower illiteracy, but it did not promote national solidarity in Russia as it did in Western Europe. And the schools, where they existed, could do little to counteract the cultural deprivation and economic backwardness of most of Russia's peasants.

The Revolution of 1905 dramatized the inability of the tsarist regime to hold the Russian people together.[12] It was an outstanding example of what can happen when political modernization does not keep up with economic and social modernization. Since 1890 industrialization, urbanization, and structural differentiation had been developing at an accelerated pace, and liberal, socialist, and populist movements had been trying to mobilize sections of the middle classes, workers, and peasants. But the activities of the socialists and populists were illegal, and even the liberals had no national parliament in which to exercise their citizenship rights. Indeed the Russian people were not citizens but subjects of the tsar, who ruled them as an autocrat. Consequently, when the Russian army suffered disastrous losses in its war with Japan in 1904 and early 1905, the majority of the people became alienated from the regime, and large numbers of them joined the revolution against it.

We are concerned here only with the relationship of the Revolution of 1905 with modernization and national consciousness. Not only the national minorities but different classes of Russians also made their own separate revolts. The middle-class liberals demanded a national parliament (Duma) and went on strike until Tsar Nicholas II issued his October Manifesto promising to meet their demands. As we have seen, urban workers, led by socialist agitators returning from exile, tried to continue their own general strike in Moscow until an army regiment from St. Petersburg crushed it. Meanwhile peasant disorders continued into December, when the government began its forceful pacification of the affected areas.

Thus in 1905 the Russian people acted not as a nation but as separate and often conflicting social groups in their own interests. The promulgation of a constitution and the setting up of a Duma seemed like steps toward political modernization, but after 1907 the Duma was less representative than it had been at first. In 1906 the Stolypin Reforms aimed at transforming the traditional Russian peasants into the kind of individualistic property-owning farmers who seemed so loyal to the national states of Western Europe. But these reforms, like the institution of compulsory elementary education two years later, would have needed at least a generation to assimilate the majority of the Russian people politically and culturally. As the tsarist government was to discover in 1917, not even mass mobilization in a modern war against a foreign invader could sustain a national consciousness as underdeveloped as the Russian.

National consciousness developed best when political modernization kept up with economic and social modernization, but this development was handicapped in a recently unified nation such as Italy, where the northern and southern halves of the country were at different stages of modernization in all respects. Despite regional differences and a paucity of political maturity, the general conditions in the north at the time of unification "pointed to a reasonably swift and successful integration of the state with the civil society."[13] The ruling elites there placed a high value on parliamentary government, economic progress, and social responsibility. The south, on the other hand, was hampered in adapting to a modern industrial society based on working representative institutions and civil equality because of its economic backwardness, its tradition of political clientism, and a social frame of reference often restricted to family interests.

Well into the twentieth century many northern Italians looked down on their southern compatriots as an inferior "race," and many southerners continued to resent the central government as an alien force working against their interests. (Their saying, *E piove, governo ladro,* meant that even when there was a destructive rainstorm, the government caused it as a way of stealing their crops.) We have seen how the former radical Francesco Crispi crushed the revolt by his fellow Sicilians who were demanding social justice, just as his northern predecessors had done with earlier unrest in the south. During the early 1900's the liberal Piedmontese prime minister Giovanni Giolitti, heeding pressure from the working classes, introduced a number of labor reforms and widened the franchise. But these extensions of citizenship rights did little to integrate the south into the nation. The economic and social gap between the two halves of the country actually increased as the north continued to modernize while the south became poorer because of overpopulation and clung to its traditional reliance on local bosses and "amoral familism."

In all countries even those people who had a national consciousness spent most of their time thinking about family and personal matters. People who joined nationalist movements were more dedicated and active in promoting their cause. This was so in unified states like France, Germany, and Italy and in emerging nations still seeking unity and independence.

NATIONALISM AS A PROTEST AGAINST FOREIGN RULE

Since the early nineteenth century nationalism as a protest against alien rulers had served as an integrating force among oppressed peoples. In most cases—Greece, Belgium, Italy, Romania, Hungary, Serbia, Bulgaria —it had required diplomatic and military maneuvers by the major powers to achieve the goal of independence. In regions under foreign rule cultural and political nationalist movements took a wide variety of forms, and it would be impossible to cover them all here. Some, like the Irish and the Czechs, tried to win home rule from the "foreign" parliaments in which their representatives sat (when they were not shouting, filibustering, or otherwise trying to obstruct the normal proceedings). Others, like the Poles, tried to preserve their language and religion against their rulers' efforts to denationalize them. Still others, like the Serbs, abetted their compatriots under foreign rule in acts of terrorism such as the assassination of the Archduke Francis Ferdinand, which sparked the outbreak of the First World War. Whatever form they took, these nationalist movements tried to awaken and politicize the ethnic consciousness of the people they wanted to liberate from alien rule.

Ethnic consciousness is one of the principal ingredients of nationalism, but many of Europe's emerging nations included diverse ethnic groups within the same territory. When Metternich called Italy "a geographical expression" in 1815, he was right. Almost fifty years later, after the political unification of most of the peninsula, the patriot Massimo d'Azeglio acknowledged: "We have made Italy; now we must make Italians." Ireland was another example of ethnic disunity in a clearly defined geographical area. Legally a part of the United Kingdom through the First World War, this island had an Irish Catholic majority dominated by an English and English-oriented Protestant minority in the Dublin region and a "Scottish" and English-oriented Protestant majority in Ulster (where the conflict between Catholics and Protestants still rages). Bohemia also had a native majority (Czechs) that felt oppressed by a sizable "foreign" minority (Germans) in its midst. In Eastern Europe, from the Baltic to the Black Sea, mixtures of Germans, Magyars, Romanians, and various kinds of Slavs made it almost impossible to give each people with an ethnic consciousness a national territory of its own.

One of the most ethnically diverse Balkan regions with a militant nationalist movement was Macedonia. This province was the central core of Turkey's remaining possessions in Europe, which included Thrace to the east, Thessaly and Epirus to the south, Albania to the west, and the Sanjak of Novi-Bazar to the north. In 1878 the Treaty of San Stefano had given Macedonia to Bulgaria, but a few months later, at the Congress of Berlin, the great powers had returned it to Ottoman rule with the proviso that the Turks institute reforms favorable to its Christian peoples. Macedonia's population, which reached 2.3 million in 1912, was 50 per cent Slavic, 20 per cent Turkish, 11 per cent Greek, 8 per cent Albanian; the remaining 11 per cent included Vlachs (who spoke a language akin to Romanian), gypsies, Jews, and others. Although most Macedonian Slavs who thought about the matter at all considered themselves ethnically Bulgarian,* Serbia called them Old Serbians, and Greece called them Bulgarian-speaking Greeks. In any case, by the 1890's a growing number of Macedonians were becoming conscious of themselves as an oppressed

---

* Linguistically, however, Macedonian was as distinct from Bulgarian as Norwegian from Swedish or Slovak from Czech.

Guerrilla fighters of the Internal Macedonian Revolutionary Organization, 1903.

people under the Turks, who failed to carry out the reforms urged by the powers.

In 1893 a part of the Slavic Macedonian intelligentsia, including men with military training, founded the Internal Macedonian Revolutionary Organization—IMRO—for the ultimate purpose of liberating their "country" from Turkish rule by means of an armed insurrection. First they recruited teachers, students, priests, and professional men in the towns to help make the peasants conscious of their oppression and to enlist them in the cause. The IMRO then tried to set up an underground government with representatives throughout the province as a means of mobilizing the political consciousness of the Macedonian Slavs. It also operated a clandestine press and its own courts of justice. But in 1897 the Turkish authorities discovered the IMRO's secret activities and took reprisals against the movement and its followers.

After that the IMRO began to build a guerrilla force and to counter Turkish reprisals with its own acts of terrorism. All of its armed partisan fighters (*chetniks*) took the following oath on the Bible, dagger, and revolver:

> I swear on my faith, conscience and honor, that I will work for the liberty of Macedonia and the Adrianople Vilayet with all my strength and means, and that I will never betray the secret of the revolutionary work of the IMRO. Should I do such a thing, may I be killed by this revolver or by this dagger which I kiss. Amen.

The IMRO also collected a "revolutionary tax" from the Macedonian peasants wherever it could, but it was always short of money and arms. By 1902 several of its top leaders were in Turkish prisons and the remaining local leadership felt threatened by a rival partisan group subsidized by Bulgaria. In order to outflank this "External Organization" and gain money for arms the IMRO band in northeastern Macedonia kidnaped the American missionary Ellen M. Stone and held her captive for six months until the Turkish government paid them a ransom of sixty thousand dollars. Meanwhile other bands of *chetniks* engaged in skirmishes with Turkish troops and tried to enlist more village youths in their ranks. The IMRO resembled the Palestine Liberation Organization of the 1970's in many of its tactics, including appeals to foreign powers. But, except for little Bulgaria, the powers gave no effective help to this people that had always lived under foreign rule, despite William Gladstone's slogan: "Macedonia for the Macedonians!"

In August 1903 the IMRO launched its first and only armed insurrection. Some of its leaders may have hoped that the powers would intervene on their behalf, as they had for other emerging nations in the nineteenth century. But the IMRO was politically and militarily ill-prepared for a full-scale guerrilla war in such an ethnically mixed province. Even its most enthusiastic chronicler admits that the Turks, Albanians, Greeks, and "Grecianized Bulgarians"—over 40 per cent of the total population of Macedonia—fought *against* the insurrectionists.[14] Only in the mountainous district of Monastir, in the northwest, were the Slavic village militias called upon to fight alongside the *chetniks*. In the rest of the province the IMRO had too little time to develop the cover of a nationalist mentality among the masses, which every guerrilla army must have if it wishes to survive. Thus, within three months, a Turkish army ten times as large as the IMRO forces crushed the insurrection and destroyed the movement's fighting capacity on Ottoman soil. The powers once again imposed reforms on the sultan, but, as in the past, these were not effectively enforced.

Macedonia's fate was decided by the Balkan Wars of 1912-13. The armies of Greece, Serbia, and Bulgaria (including a contingent of IMRO partisans) succeeded in driving the Turks out of Europe, but instead of creating an independent Macedonia the Balkan allies partitioned it, with the lion's share going to Greece and Serbia. Consequently over six hundred thousand Macedonian Slavs found themselves under Serbian rule and almost three hundred thousand under Greek rule, with only one hundred and sixty-five thousand under Bulgarian rule. From then on most of those in Greece were forcibly Hellenized and those in Serbia (later Yugoslavia) were urged to think of themselves as Serbs. The IMRO was to resume its propaganda and terrorist activities after the First World War, particularly against Yugoslavia, but Macedonia as the IMRO's leaders conceived it was never to become an independent nation. One reason was that they urged Bulgaria to enter the war against the Entente powers and thus found themselves on the "wrong" side at the Paris Peace Conference. Another was that, once the Turks were out of the Balkans, most other Europeans ceased to care about oppressed nationalities in that area. To them Macedonia was merely a name for a mixed fruit salad.

The oppressed people most familiar to Western Europeans and Americans was the Irish. Throughout the Middle Ages the Irish bards (*filí*) had preserved a Gaelic national consciousness in the face of Danish, Norman, and English colonization. Although the Irish language had gradually given way to English after the sixteenth century, a large majority of the island's inhabitants had clung to their Catholicism as a cultural bond in defiance of their Anglican overlords. Another grievance of Irish Catholics was the fact that most of their land had been confiscated in the seventeenth century.* Modern Irish nationalism first expressed itself in the rebellion of 1798, led by Theobald Wolfe Tone. Two years later, in retaliation, the English government closed the Irish parliament in Dublin and incorporated Ireland into the United Kingdom.

From 1800 right up to the First World War, Irish nationalism took two main political forms[15]: revolutionary movements aiming at an independent republic and a movement among the hundred or so Irish representatives in the House of Commons for Home Rule. The most active revolutionary movement was the Fenians (also known as the Irish Republican Brotherhood), organized in the 1850's with Irish-American help. These Fenians led another abortive rebellion in 1867. Reconstituted in

* Whereas in 1641 59 per cent of the land in Ireland was owned by Catholics, 14 per cent of it was Catholic-owned by 1703. Unlike the settlement of Ulster by Presbyterian and Anglican immigrants from the border areas between England and Scotland, this confiscation did not displace the local peasantry. But it did reduce them to the status of tenants on plots of land too small to sustain a burgeoning population in the late eighteenth and early nineteenth centuries.

1905 by Arthur Griffith as Sinn Fein (Ourselves Alone), this organization tried unsuccessfully to unite all the other separatist movements in the face of the Home Rulers. The Home Rule movement reached its first zenith under the leadership of Charles Stewart Parnell in the 1880's, both in the House of Commons and in Ireland itself. Parnell's disgrace (as the exposed lover of a married woman) and death in 1891 left the movement leaderless and divided for the next nineteen years, but it came closer than ever before to achieving its goals during the five years preceding the First World War.

Because of the loss of the Irish language, cultural nationalism was more difficult to organize than political nationalism. By the middle of the nineteenth century only 30 per cent of the population was able to speak Irish whereas over 90 per cent could speak English; by 1891 85 per cent could no longer speak Irish. Paradoxically, passive mass support for political nationalism had begun with Daniel O'Connell and the Young Ireland movement of the 1840's

> at the very point when the Irish language was in full retreat. An obvious result is that popular nationalist sentiment consisted of yearnings of the type . . . seen in our folksongs, while the fulfilment was restricted to what various leaders could build up, almost all of them having to start from scratch with a people still thinking themselves into English usages.[16]

The movement to revive the Irish language was restricted to scholars and antiquarians and had little influence before 1914. But the Gaelic Athletic Association, founded in 1884, spread rapidly through the country at the end of the century, reviving local and national patriotism and promoting enthusiasm for Irish football and hurling. There was also a spectacular literary renaissance at that time. Led by William Butler Yeats, it included such luminaries as Lady Gregory, George Russell, Douglas Hyde, George Moore, and the playwright John Millington Synge. (The Anglo-Irish writers Oscar Wilde and George Bernard Shaw did not participate in this movement for cultural nationalism.)

One of the best-known literary efforts to glorify the unmodernized, though already English-speaking, rural Irish was Synge's *The Playboy of the Western World* (1907). In this play Christopher Mahon, a shy young peasant who thinks he has killed his bullying father, stumbles into an inn on the wild coast of Mayo, in Ireland's "western world." This world is still relatively untainted by the modernizing "eastern world" of Dublin and Belfast. The local women look on Christopher as a hero and try to catch him for a husband. Even the men are impressed when he wins a series of sporting events. Actually it turns out that his father is still alive, but Christopher himself is transformed by the adulation of the local people. When he finally leaves them he says: "Ten thousand blessings upon all that's here, for you've turned me a likely gaffer in the end of all, the way I'll go romancing through a romping lifetime from this hour to the dawning of judgment day."

But the reaction against this play signaled the decline of the Anglo-Irish literary movement. When it was performed at the Abbey theater riots broke out. Both the middle-class Dubliners in the audience and the Anglo-Irish literati strongly objected to the base and squalid life style it portrayed and to what they considered the degenerate attitudes of its protagonists. Yeats began that withdrawal into aristocratic contempt which was to become central to his later attitudes. Synge himself died in 1909, and George Moore left Dublin for England two years later. The intensive effort to create a modern Irish literature in English proved to be an impossible substitute for political nationalism. It had been based on the erroneous assumption that collaboration between classes, religions, and races in art, as in society, would fill the political vacuum that the fall of Parnell had produced.

Only occasionally did the Irish masses participate actively in the political struggle. The first time they had come onto the stage as leading players rather than extras had been in the Land Wars of 1879–82. Under the leadership of the Fenian-inspired Irish National Land League they refused to pay what they considered exorbitant rents and they heeded Parnell's admonition "not to bid for farms from which others have been evicted, and to use the strong force of public opinion to deter any unjust men amongst yourselves . . . from bidding for such farms." They also applied this kind of moral pressure to one large landowner's agent, Captain Boycott, "the breaking of whose nerve after a long struggle not only gave a new word to the language but also provided an object-lesson to a closely observant peasantry."[17] But the mass of peasants did not condone most acts of violence, especially the murder of two high British officials in Dublin's Phoenix Park in May 1882 by members of a secret society, the Invincibles. Thereafter land reforms initiated by the British government, plus large-scale emigration, allowed a growing number of tenants to become small proprietors and made them less active in the nationalist cause (see p. 17).

The other major episodes in which large numbers of Irishmen took an active part occurred in the cities of Dublin and Belfast during the imme-

Trade union rally during the Dublin transport workers' strike, 1913. (Note the movie palace on the left.)

diate prewar years. In the Dublin transport workers' strike in August 1913, as in the Land Wars, the initial grievance of the insurgents was economic oppression. Unlike Belfast, which had begun to industrialize in the 1850's, Dublin had a decaying commercial and distributive economy that could not absorb its growing number of rural immigrants. Thirty per cent of the population of the city lived in slums and earned less than a pound a week; the majority of the men were general laborers who could only hope for casual work. Thus the brilliant labor organizer James Larkin was able to attract ten thousand members to his Irish Transport and General Workers Union by the time of the 1913 strike. Initially called to force the United Tramways Company to recognize the union, the strike quickly gained the passionate support of a large section of the population when the British police arrested Larkin and killed two demonstrators and wounded four hundred others on O'Connell Street in September. Now cries of "freedom" and "independence" were intermingled with abuse against the employers for trying to starve the workers into submission. The strike was finally broken in January 1914. But "Larkin had broken the bond of deference and had created a conscious sense of identity among the unskilled workers, the most degraded single sector of Irish society."[18] Many of these same workers were to take to the streets again during the Easter Rebellion in 1916 and the full-scale struggle for independence in 1920–22.

Meanwhile the Protestant workers in Belfast were stepping up their own traditional violent efforts to keep the Catholics at bay. In the 1840's their rural forefathers had brought their guns as well as their prejudices to the newly industrializing city, and in 1857 they had fought a pitched battle there with Catholic workers.

> Religion became the opium of the working classes in their struggle for status and jobs. Industrialisation and urbanisation, providing the only hope that the rural roots of prejudice might wither away, became instead powerful agencies for the perpetuation and accentuation of sectarian animosity.[19]

Both Catholic and Protestant workers reinforced their ethnic consciousness by attending separate schools, supporting separate lodges (Green and Orange), and living in separate neighborhoods whose boundaries they periodically disputed. Every riot resulted in voluntary evacuation or intimidation which redrew the territorial borders and reinforced neighborhood identity. Urban guerrilla warfare grew more dangeous and less contollable as the territory and the numbers of the belligerents increased.[20] By 1913, facing the imminent prospect of the passage of a

Home Rule bill, both sides were arming themselves for a civil war. The police reported that there were ten thousand rifles and thirty thousand revolvers hidden in Belfast.

In addition to the amassing of these private arms the organization of one hundred thousand Ulster volunteers in 1913 prompted the nationalists to recruit their own volunteer army among the Catholic masses throughout the island. By May 1914 this "army," the Irish Volunteers, had seventy-five thousand members, mostly urban workers. The support of the leading Home Rulers for Britain's entry into the First World War on August 4 temporarily weakened the Irish Volunteers. But a week earlier their own leaders had successfully landed one thousand German rifles under the very eyes of British soldiers at Dublin harbor. This exploit so fired the imagination of Irish Catholics that by September one hundred eighty thousand had joined the Irish Volunteers.

The fact that the civil war in Ulster and the rest of Ireland was postponed until 1920 did not alter the paradoxes of the island's ethnic complexity. The English-speaking Irish were separated from the English by the same language and united with their remaining Irish-speaking compatriots. There were Anglo-Irish Protestants who felt closer to their Catholic compatriots than to the English or the Ulster Protestant extremists. And in Ulster itself the most intractable animosities were based on religion.

NATIONALISM AS A REACTION AGAINST MODERNIZATION UNDER "LIBERAL" LEADERSHIP

Unlike the situation in Ireland, nationalist movements in politically independent states were unable to mobilize large masses of people, particularly in the working class. Among the numerous patriotic societies only the British Primrose League had a membership of over a million, consisting mainly of old gentlemen and ladies and middle-class conformists. The more militant and nonconformist nationalist movements—such as the Pan-German League, the Action Française, and the Italian Nationalist Association—each had fewer than forty thousand members before 1914.

These organizations were often dominated by an antimodernizing intelligentsia. They rejected the ways in which many of the most influential modernizing government leaders used nationalism to rally popular support for their policies: Sergei Y. Witte and Peter A. Stolypin in Russia, Joseph Chamberlain and David Lloyd George in Britain, Giovanni Giolitti in Italy, Raymond Poincaré and Louis Barthou in France (and Theodore Roosevelt in the United States). The nationalists we are concerned with were outside the ruling circles and felt that their governments were betraying their nation's true interests. Many of them postulated an unbridgable gulf between the official, or legal, country and the real country—that is, those people who retained their traditional values.

The Action Française[21] based its whole ideology on this distinction. Founded in 1899 at the climax of the Dreyfus Affair, it constantly attacked the Third Republic, the *pays légal*, whose president pardoned the Jew Dreyfus in that year and whose highest court of appeals completely vindicated him seven years later. The Action Française tried to use nationalism as a means of restoring France's cultural purity and traditional institutions, particularly the monarchy and the church. It contended that the *pays légal* was ruled by a clique of Protestants, Freemasons, resident aliens, and Jews. These people were "un-French" because they opposed these institutions and corrupted the real nation's culture with "German" scholarship, "English" parliamentary government, the "Jewish" credit economy, and an egalitarianism that was part of the "Judeo-Masonic conspiracy" known as the Revolution of 1789. Charles Maurras, Léon Daudet, and the other members of the antimodernizing Parisian intelligentsia who led the Action Française also condemned the impersonal and cosmopolitan aspects of the modern city. They insisted that only people with native roots in the countryside were truly French. But though they praised the simple virtues of rural life, Saint-Germain-des-Prés was as close to the country as they themselves cared to live.

Clearly the nationalism of the Action Française expressed a reaction against all aspects of modernization. It championed monarchism and clericalism as the only alternatives to the liberalism of France's modernizing political leadership. In addition, it opposed social mobility and the legal elimination of class distinctions: if everybody were as good as everybody else, nobody would be anybody. With few exceptions the Action Française intelligentsia was also hostile to the scientific-technological premises of modernizing societies. Although Maurras considered himself a "positivist," Daudet and others condemned everything from the theories of evolution- and psychoanalysis to medical serums and canned foods.

The Action Française was a well-organized and active movement with thirty to forty thousand members in the immediate prewar period. It published a daily newspaper and a number of periodicals, pamphlets, and books. The social composition of the League of the Action Française reflected the antimodernizing bias of its ideology: 20 per cent petty nobility and clergy, 50 per cent upper-middle and middle class (especially in the older professions such as law, medicine, and the military), 30 per cent lower-middle class (especially white-collar employees, teachers, and noncommissioned officers). The Students of the Action Française came from similar backgrounds, but the Camelots du Roi, the young men who sold the movement's newspaper and fought its campaigns in the streets, were predominantly lower-middle class, particularly commercial employees. The Students and Camelots gave the movement far more publicity than its ideology by heckling republican politicians, disrupting the classes of "liberal" professors, beating up pacifists and socialists, and getting themselves arrested during their illegal demonstrations for Joan of Arc.

Despite its traditionalist ideology and the rowdyism of its younger members the Action Française gained a good deal of sympathy outside its ranks as a result of the nationalist revival of the prewar years.[22] This revival was a response to increasing international tensions. But it was men like Raymond Poincaré, premier in 1912 and president of the republic thereafter, who led the campaign to strengthen the nation's defenses and to encourage patriotic sentiments among the people. Maurras and his colleagues had no direct influence on the government's policies and they continued to pit their own brand of nationalism against the Third Republic. Only on August 4, 1914, did the movement's daily newspaper announce that it was abandoning its anti-Semitism and its attacks against the regime for the duration of the war.

There were also antimodernizing nationalists in Germany and Austria, where the political leadership was hardly "liberal." Unlike Maurras, the German writers Paul de Lagarde (1827–91) and his disciple Julius Langbehn (1851–1907)[23] were mystical and romantic, but they shared his hostility to the centralized modern state, democracy, industrialization, urbanization, and materialism. Lagarde and Langbehn also shared Nietzsche's cultural pessimism in the face of these trends but, unlike him, they identified true culture with the soul of the whole German people (*Volk*) rather than with an elite of philosophical supermen of all nations. Lagarde excluded the Jews from this *Volk* because they were bound together by a non-Christian and non-Germanic religion, but Langbehn's anti-Semitism became increasingly racial. For Langbehn the soulless Jews embodied modernity and materialism and were thus automatically opposed to the spiritual character of the German nation. Although they founded no movements, Lagarde and Langbehn articulated the resentment of many members of the German intelligentsia against the shallowness of their prosperous modernizing society. And their Volkish ideology appealed to the more militant nationalist movements in the German-speaking areas of Europe, including the Christian Social parties of Adolf Stöcker in Prussia in the 1890's and of Karl Lueger in Austria in the early 1900's.

The career of the unsuccessful Austrian politician Georg von Schönerer illustrates the ways in which antimodernizing nationalism could spread under the guise of "Christian" or "national" socialism.[24] His father was a railroad engineer ennobled for his services, and Georg began his own career as an "improving landlord," concerning himself with the welfare of the peasants in the vicinity of the family estate at Rosenau, near the Bohemian frontier. While a member of parliament, from 1873 to 1891, Schönerer organized several German nationalist clubs, stressing German racial superiority, a union of Austria with Germany, and anti-Semitism. He also tried to combine his nationalism with a pseudosocialism, attacking mobile "Jewish" capital while extolling landed property. Schönerer never commanded a mass movement and never achieved a political base outside of his home constituency. But this failure did not disturb him unduly, for he was more concerned with spreading an idea than leading a party.

In the late 1890's, if Schönerer and his dwindling band appeared pathetic and ludicrous, the feelings they tried to exploit were gaining ground. By the turn of the century several Austrian and German political parties had dissociated themselves from Jews. Whereas Schönerer was too doctrinaire and unbending in his hatreds to be a success in politics, Lueger used anti-Semitism, Christian socialism, and German-Austrian nationalism pragmatically to make himself one of the most popular men in the country and lord mayor of Vienna until his death in 1910. His popularity also rested on his modernizing reforms, which included a municipal gas works, an electrified tramway system, an expanded water supply, new hospitals and schools, and a municipal employment bureau and savings bank. But Lueger continued to condemn modern liberalism by identifying it with Jews: "I know only one destructive element in Austria, and that is the Jewish liberal party."

The ambivalence of "reforming" nationalists like Schönerer and

Lueger toward modernization and their tendency to blame its undesirable aspects on the Jews dominated the most important nationalist movement in Germany: the Pan-German League. Founded in 1890, this movement consistently championed an expansionist foreign policy. It also adopted the Volkish idea that blood and soil, rather than the state and citizenship rights, formed the basis of the true German nation. From the beginning the league concerned itself with agrarian interests. But since imperialism required industrial power it gradually abandoned the Volkish ideology's opposition to industry and modernization. It noted that a number of industrial enterprises contained "healthy German elements" within them. In his book *If I Were Emperor* (1912) Heinrich Class, the league's head beginning in 1908, singled out the Krupp works for special praise. But Class still followed the Volkish line in denouncing banks and department stores as parts of the Jewish conspiracy to exploit the German people. He accused the Jews of being the agents of modern materialism, which was undermining the Germanic *Volk* spirit.

Because it was not openly hostile to the existing regime, the Pan-German League had a more influential following than the Action Française. In 1901, of its 18,184 members,[25] 5,339 were university professors and lecturers, 4,905 small businessmen, 3,760 officials, artists, and teachers, and 2,673 artisans, mostly self-employed. The high proportion from the academic intelligentsia included "liberals" like the sociologist Max Weber and the historian Karl Lamprecht. "Liberal" politicians like Gustav Stresemann and Friedrich Naumann also joined the league, though Weber and Stresemann soon left it because of its proagrarian and antilabor biases. During the two decades before the war sixty Reichstag deputies belonged to the Pan-German League, along with a larger number of high officials. Other high officials and military leaders welcomed the league's support for an aggressive foreign policy, while its conformist lower-middle-class members were partly attracted by the respectability it conferred on Volkish nationalism.

The Italian nationalist movement resembled the Action Française more than it did the Pan-German League, but it lacked the traditionalist following of its French counterpart. Indeed it was the archetype of a political movement designed to express the reaction of a particular section of the disgruntled intelligentsia against modernization under liberal leadership. And because this was its purpose, its spokesmen were in constant disagreement over what its ideology should be. Until 1914 only two ideas united these literary journalists: that they represented the real Italy against official Italy and that only the violence of an imperialist war could close the gap between the state and the people.

Enrico Corradini typified the hostility of these men to the baseness of Italian life under liberal leaders like Giolitti.[26] In the late 1890's Corradini had begun writing novels filled with cultural pessimism regarding the positivism, materialism, and humanitarianism which seemed to dominate the ruling bourgeoisie. But he soon abandoned this passive response for a more "revolutionary" stance. Between 1903 and 1906 he edited the review the *Regno* (Kingdom), which called for a violent upheaval of "the people" against official Italy. At first Corradini advocated a war for colonies in North Africa to give poor Italian emigrants an alternative to settlement in the New World. He also flirted with revolutionary syndicalism, but he was too authoritarian to accept real popular participation in his revolution and too uninterested in economic issues to understand the concerns of real workers. By 1910 he argued that the nationalist elite should lead Italy, which was a proletarian nation just as the workers had been a proletarian class when the socialists had first tried to mobilize them.

> Just as socialism teaches the proletariat the value of class struggle, so we must teach Italy the value of international struggle. But international struggle is war? Well, then, let there be war! And nationalism will arouse in Italy the will for a victorious war . . . the only way to national redemption.[27]

Corradini made this declaration at the founding congress of the Nationalist Association, in October 1910 in Florence. Within a year this organization had branches in over sixty towns and cities. Total membership figures are not available, but the youth group in Rome alone had four hundred and fifty members.[28] In early 1914 a dozen cities also had small newspapers inspired by the Nationalist Association, whose semiofficial weekly, the *Idea Nazionale*, was sold throughout the country. By then, however, the movement had been upstaged by the Libyan War, launched by official Italy, and its democratic wing had deserted it when the conservative wing opposed Giolitti's bill granting universal male suffrage. At the Nationalist Association's second congress, in December 1912 in Rome, Corradini declared: "We finally have the courage to declare ourselves antidemocratic." Thereafter the movement dropped its pose as the bearer of the popular will and its remaining leaders decided to make an open bid for clerical support in the hope of forming a conservative parliamentary party. Thus, unlike the Action Française, the Nationalist Association accepted parliament as a national ideal, though it continued to oppose all parties that supported political and social modernization.

On the eve of the First World War the Nationalist Association's critique of official Italy's liberal leadership received its definitive form in the ideology of Alfredo Rocco, an eminent professor of law. Rocco had two basic goals: to substitute an authoritarian state for the liberal state and to replace the unsupervised conflict of social and economic forces with a hierarchical class structure and with corporations (guilds) for each sector of the economy, which would run their own affairs but would have to submit to the authority of the state. In his 1914 tract *What Is Nationalism and What Do the Nationalists Want?* Rocco said:

> Nationalism is protest and revolt; it is an anathema against the whole secular incrustation of ideas that has deformed and twisted the Italian spirit. Nationalism takes its stand against all the idols of the forum and the piazza, against all the current and dominant ideas in vulgar minds. It attacks democracy, demolishes anticlericalism, fights socialism, and undermines pacifism, humanitarianism, and internationalism. . . . It declares the program of liberalism finished because already enacted.[29]

Despite its small size and lack of connections in high places the Italian Nationalist Association was more influential than any other nationalist movement in Europe in helping to get its country into the First World War. Italy remained neutral until May 1915, when the interventionist campaign reached its climax. There were interventionists from all political groups except the Socialists and Catholics, but the nationalists were the noisiest. By April their street demonstrations attracted many new followers and helped Prime Minister Antonio Salandra to push the declaration of war against Austria-Hungary through parliament. The majority there agreed with Giolitti, now out of office, that intervention was wrong, but they voted for it against their wills when the king threatened to abdicate if they voted against it. On May 5, 1915, eighteen days before the declaration of war, the nationalists swelled the ranks of the almost two hundred thousand people who had come to hear the poet Gabriele D'Annunzio's frenzied oration on the glories of war at Quarto, outside Genoa. Ten days later, in an editorial entitled "Parliament against Italy," the *Idea Nazionale* threatened a rebellion by "the Nation" against "the putrid parliament" that wanted to deny it these glories. Although the direct blame for subverting Italy's principal liberal institution rested with the prime minister and the king, the nationalists and their newly found poet had created the atmosphere that made this subversion possible.

JEWS

The growth of antiliberal, ethnic, and anti-Semitic nationalism made Europe's Jews respond in three ways.[30] Some continued to seek complete assimilation into their respective national societies as individuals. Others, including some former assimilationists, tried to preserve or revive the ethnic identity of the Jews as a separate community within these larger societies. Finally, there were the Zionists, who claimed that the Jews were a true nation, entitled to a territorial homeland of their own

Modernization in the form of the Enlightenment and the French Revolution had led to the legal emancipation of the Jews and the extension of citizenship rights to them. At the end of the eighteenth century this had been done only in France and Holland; by the 1870's it had occurred in all the countries of Western and Central Europe except Spain and Portugal. In Eastern Europe the emancipation of the Jews in Serbia and Bulgaria was imposed by the Congress of Berlin (1878), but the Jews remained unemancipated in Russia until 1917 and in Romania until 1918.

In Western and Central Europe emancipation had different effects in different countries. Toward the end of the eighteenth century there had been Jewish bankers ("Court Jews") with special privileges because they helped finance the activities of their monarchs. But at that time the overwhelming majority of the Jews were still living in ghettos and excluded from most occupations. The philosopher Moses Mendelssohn had tried to introduce the ideas of the Enlightenment to his fellow German Jews, but in the 1780's he had to admit that his own son could become only a physician, a trader, or a beggar—unless he became baptized. One hundred years later many Jews in Germany, the western provinces of Austria, and Hungary could live wherever they wanted to and hold any position except in the military officer corps and the higher ranks of the bureaucracy. Jews achieved a greater pre-eminence in the national cultures of these three countries than in any others. In France and Italy the Jewish population was much smaller* but more fully assimilated into the

* Around 1900 the Jewish population of Europe was distributed approximately as follows. A little over 5 million Jews lived in the Russian Empire,

national society than in Central Europe. The native-born British Jews had also adopted the national way of life, but they were still viewed unofficially as a special group that should be allowed to retain some of its ethnic distinctiveness as long as it did not become too numerous or too powerful. Although no organized anti-Semitic movement appeared in Britain, the influx of Jews from Eastern Europe—which was to increase the size of the Jewish community from fifty thousand in 1883 to two hundred thousand in 1914—seemed sufficiently ominous to warrant restricting immigration through the Alien Act of 1905.[31]

During the course of the nineteenth century most European governments adopted the official policy of granting citizenship rights to those individual Jews who were willing to become assimilated into the national society and culture, while refusing to give legal recognition to the unassimilated ones as an ethnic minority entitled to special dispensations. The cumulative effects of modernization prompted a growing number of middle-class Jews in Western and Central Europe to abandon their traditional culture in order to gain the benefits of this policy, which expressed the growth of national consciousness in all countries. Even in the Russian Empire the government made sporadic efforts to Russify individual Jews until the early 1880's. After that, however, it reaffirmed the inferior status of all Jews and the special restrictions regarding where they could live, what occupations were open to them, and how many of them could attend a university. In Britain and Germany but also in Austria-Hungary and Russia some wealthy and highly educated Jews went so far as to convert to Christianity.

Assimilation and conversion were accompanied by a growing number

---

constituting just under 4 per cent of the total population, but the vast majority of them were still forced to reside in the Pale of Settlement (stretching from the Baltic Sea to the southwestern Ukraine), which had been annexed from the old multinational Kingdom of Poland at the end of the eighteenth century. In Russian Poland almost 15 per cent of the total population was Jewish, in the northwestern provinces a little over 13 per cent, in the southwestern provinces 9 per cent, and in Courland (Latvia) 7.3 per cent. The rest of European Russia had only .34 per cent Jews. Austria had 1.3 million Jews (4.7 per cent of the total population), over half of whom lived in the formerly Polish province of Galicia. Hungary had 850,000 Jews (4.4 per cent); Germany 570,000 (1 per cent); Romania 270,000 (4.5 per cent); the United Kingdom 180,000 (.37 per cent), of whom at least 30,000 were Eastern European Jews soon to move on to North America. France (not counting Algeria) had 86,000 Jews (.22 per cent) and Italy 50,000 (.06 per cent). Bulgaria and Macedonia together had around 25,000 Jews. No other European country had more than 8,000.

of mixed marriages. These marriages produced a peculiarly modern phenomenon, the half-Jew; Marcel Proust and Hugo von Hofmannsthal are two famous examples. On the eve of the war in Berlin and Hamburg one out of three marriages involving Jews were with Gentile partners.

In Germany and the western provinces of Austria, Orthodox religious practices had been deliberately reformed along modern lines and had nearly vanished by the middle of the nineteenth century. In Britain, France, and the rest of Western Europe most Orthodox practices had either never existed or had fallen into disuse without the kind of controversy that Reform Judaism had aroused in Central Europe. In effect, Reform Judaism was an attempt to convince Gentiles that Judaism was *only* a religion—that a German "of the Jewish persuasion" was as German as a Catholic or Protestant. (But Jewish culture was no easier to slough off than Gentile perceptions of the Jewishness of Jewish behavior.) On the other hand, Orthodox Judaism prevailed in Eastern Europe. There the path to assimilation remained barred and traditional Jewish culture was the only consolation in the face of frequent persecution, both official and unofficial.

The Eastern European Jews seemed like a race apart from their coreligionists in Western and Central Europe. Except for a few millionaire industrialists and bankers such as the Günsburgs, Poliakovs, and Brodskis and a small minority of well-to-do merchants and professional men, the majority of the Jews in Russia became poorer than most Russian peasants as that country began to modernize. During the 1860's in some of the increasingly crowded ghettos of the Pale up to 40 per cent of the Jews were *Luftmenschen* (persons without specific skills, occupations, or capital) living on charity and odd jobs. Thereafter industrialization deprived many other Jews of their traditional occupations: Jewish coachmen were put out of work by the railroads; Jews with skills in tailoring, shoemaking, and food processing lost out to mechanized factories.* By the 1890's a growing number of the sons and daughters of these declassed Jews became factory workers themselves.

Although many Russian Jews emigrated, the majority stayed in their ghettos, spoke only Yiddish, and dressed in their traditional garb. They remained mired in poverty and piety and resigned to their ostracism from

* In more highly modernized Germany the number of artisans increased during the 1890's and early 1900's, but many of these artisans provided specialized goods and services for that country's middle-class consumers. In Russia this class was still very small, and most of these goods and services were not provided by Jewish artisans, who were barred from the large cities outside the Pale.

Russian society. The one major exception to this ostracism was that all young men, including Jews, were liable to five years of service in the army. This obligation seemed all the more burdensome to Jews who were otherwise second-class subjects, and some of them fled the country to avoid it.

Worse than their poverty and ostracism were the pogroms (pogrom is the Russian word for devastation) suffered by Eastern European Jews. The 1881 pogroms, along with the new anti-Jewish policies already mentioned, were sparked by the assassination of Tsar Alexander II by a terrorist band that included one Jewish woman. In that year angry mobs in the Ukraine and Russian Poland assaulted their Jewish "oppressors" and looted their shops; usually the authorities tolerated these pogroms for two days before intervening. By the end of the year several hundred Jews had been killed and the material damage in Kiev alone was estimated at 2.5 million rubles (1.3 million dollars). Even more serious than these losses was the feeling of insecurity that this supposedly extinct form of mass persecution gave to Russia's Jews. Yet the 1881 pogroms were merely a prelude to the greater bloodshed in April 1903 in Kishinev and in late October and early November 1905, during which six hundred and sixty Jewish communities were devastated. (In 1899 there was also a pogrom in Jassy, Romania, which prompted a large Jewish emigration from that country.) The chief instigator of the 1905 pogroms was the newly formed League of the Russian People, an antimodernizing nationalist organization of one-hundred-man paramilitary groups known popularly as "the Black Hundreds." They and their followers added subversion to exploitation as their reasons for persecuting the Jews.

This charge of subversion had some truth in it. Although the vast majority of participants in the Revolution of 1905 were not Jews, a number of alienated Jewish university students (many of whom had been forced to study abroad) had become revolutionaries by then. And in 1906 the General Jewish Workers' League—*Bund*—had just been organized by Jewish Socialists. The *Bund* was able to enlist forty thousand members at a time when the Russian Socialist Party had no more than one hundred and fifty thousand and the Polish Socialist Party only twenty-three thousand members. The extreme degradation of Russian Jewry allowed the *Bund* to be the only group in the Second International to combine its Marxist ideology with demands for full emancipation and national-cultural autonomy.

In contrast to Eastern Europe most Western and Central European Jews viewed themselves as culturally assimilated, and many were better off economically than their Gentile compatriots. Around 1900, Jews constituted less than 5 per cent of the total population of Berlin but 15 per cent of those having an annual income of at least 1,500 marks; in Frankfurt they represented over 60 per cent of those earning more than 3,000 marks.[32] In Germany, Britain, France, and western Austria the native-born Jews spoke only the national language (many Hungarian Jews also spoke only Magyar or German) and seemed willing to abandon most external traces of their Jewishness. They had lost their strong sense of community and were divided, like the rest of the population, along class lines. Some of them gave financial help to immigrants fleeing from persecution in Eastern Europe while at the same time worrying lest these obvious foreigners remind their own compatriots how different Jews could be.

Yet these assimilated Jews were well aware of the Gentile prejudices against them, and some of the overzealous ones internalized these prejudices themselves. European literature and drama perpetuated the Shylock and Fagin stereotypes of the unscrupulous Jew who would do anything for money. Gustav Freytag's *Soll und Haben (Debit and Credit)* portrayed the Jewish merchant Ehrenthal as rootless and hateful, impervious to his son Bernard's efforts to convert him to "decency." Freytag's mid-nineteenth-century "liberalism" toward "decent" Jews—those whose behavior measured up to Gentile standards of propriety—"may have helped further the credibility of his Jewish stereotype."[33] Although Émile Zola became one of the most outspoken champions of Alfred Dreyfus in 1898, in his novels he had sometimes made rich Jewish speculators symbols of capitalist exploitation. This stereotype lived on in many cheap French novels aimed at a wider and less educated audience than Zola's: two of many examples were the banker Schwartz in Paul Féval's *Habits noirs* and Baron Isaac Moses in Charles Mérouvel's *Le Roi milliard*.

Upper-middle-class Jews in Central Europe were especially anxious about being considered too "pushy" in Gentile circles. Albert Ballin, owner of the Hamburg-American Line, the largest steamship company in the world, detested the social ambitions of the wives of wealthy Jews who tried to win a place in Society by entertaining lavishly. Even Jews and Gentiles who had done business during the day at the Hamburg stock exchange took their late afternoon coffee at separate tables at the Alster Pavilon.[34] The Viennese novelist Stefan Zweig recalled that his father, a wealthy industrialist, always avoided dining at Sacher's "because of the natural feeling of distance; it would have been distressing or unbecoming to him to sit next to a Prince Schwarzenberg or a Lobkowitz."[35]

Ilsa Barea, another Viennese writer from a similar background, quotes

her father's memoirs to show how his upper-middle-class status had not
protected him from anti-Semitism when he had gone to elementary
school in the early 1880's.

> In my early youth it was still only dumb hate . . . not accepted by
> good society. . . . In nearly every road there was a young hooligan
> who attacked and tormented the little Jew-boys he knew, and . . .
> we were often ambushed by whole gangs. It was not so bad, it meant
> rarely more than some bumps, and it was terribly bad: to meet a
> hatred we couldn't understand, and were unable to combat, neces-
> sarily appeared to us the most violent injustice and evil.[36]

In the 1880's and 1890's this kind of confused and pathetic response made
assimilated Jews even less prepared to face the political anti-Semitism that
began to plague them in Austria, Germany, and France.

Political anti-Semitism could be conservative or radical. The conservative type expressed itself as discrimination against Jews in Society and
in the higher ranks of the public services, on the assumption that only
Christians belonged in these places. In Great Britain practicing Jews were
allowed to sit in parliament beginning in 1858 without taking the Christian oath, and the baptized Jew Benjamin Disraeli became the dominant
political leader and confidant of Queen Victoria during the sixties and
seventies. Yet conservative anti-Semitism persisted in English Society
through the Edwardian period, despite King Edward VII's well-
publicized circle of Jewish friends. In France both conservative and radical anti-Semitism gained unprecedented popularity in connection with
the Dreyfus Affair. In January 1898 Zola's article accusing the army of
injustice against Dreyfus provoked anti-Jewish uprisings in most French
cities. Led by anti-Semitic leagues and urged on by newspapers like
Édouard Drumont's *La Libre Parole*, the mobs attacked Jewish places of
business and worship and assaulted Jews in the streets. Unlike the conservatives, radical anti-Semites like Drumont believed that the Jews were an
alien, enemy race and that neither conversion nor assimilation could
change that "fact." The radical "solution" to the Jewish "problem" was
segregation and, in its extreme version, deportation.

Both types of anti-Semitism were also on the rise in Germany and Austria. Conservative anti-Semites had resisted the emancipation of the Jews
in these two states during the liberal interlude of the late 1860's and they
continued to use their influence on recruitment procedures to bar them
from the upper ranks of the public services right up to 1914. Fear of an-
tagonizing these Conservatives in Germany also prevented the appoint-

ment of Jews to cabinet posts. Not only did these people believe that the state—and hence its highest servants—must be purely Christian and authoritarian, but, as we have seen, they also used the Jews as scapegoats for all the "evils" of modernization: capitalism, urban cosmopolitanism, parliamentary government, democracy, and freedom of the press. Although radical anti-Semites like Schönerer and Drumont favored universal suffrage, others, like Maurras and Stöcker, combined their racial anti-Semitism with a call for a Christian, corporative state.

How did the assimilated Jews of Western and Central Europe respond to these new forms of anti-Semitism? In France not even the attacks against them during the Dreyfus Affair changed most Jews' determination to preserve the assimilationist tradition.

> Having emphasized for so long that they were French, they could scarcely assert with any vigour their right to be Jews. In this, as in everything else they did, they showed themselves truly to be the Frenchmen they claimed to be. And none was more French than Alfred Dreyfus, the Jew who bore his suffering with a firm and undiminished love for the fatherland.[37]

In Germany and Austria some Jewish university students formed their own fraternities as the Gentile ones began to exclude them. And in 1893 some of these students joined other Jews in founding the Central Association of German Citizens of Jewish Faith—a kind of antidefamation league. Its purpose was to "cure" anti-Semitism by means of education and legal protection, and its program was staunchly assimilationist.*

> We are not German Jews but German citizens of the Jewish faith. We are anchored in the ground of our German nationality. We have no more in common with Jews of other countries than have German Catholics or Protestants with Catholics and Protestants of other countries.

* To Eastern European as well as German Jews, Germany seemed a haven of civilized behavior and impartial justice. Many of them clung to this high opinion of Germany and German culture even in the Nazi period. As a result, many Russian and Polish Jews ignored the Soviet authorities' admonition to leave their homes when Hitler invaded Soviet territory; they refused to believe that Germans were capable of bringing on the holocaust that was to engulf all those who did not flee. And to this day some of the surviving German-Jewish intellectuals who did flee in the 1930's refuse to see Nazism as anything more than an aberration from "the gutter"—just as in the 1890's the Central Association viewed political anti-Semitism as a "curable" disease.

The Central Association took a particularly strong stand against Zionism, which was organized by a few former assimilationists who could no longer believe in this kind of program.

Theodor Herzl founded the Zionist Organization in 1897, while he was the Paris correspondent of the Viennese daily *Neue Freie Presse*. He envisioned a Jewish state financed by wealthy Western and Central European Jews. Until his death, in 1904, he spent most of his time and energy seeking financial backing and using diplomacy to win support for his project from the governments of Great Britain, Germany, Russia, and Turkey. Among his principal collaborators were the literary journalist Max Nordau (like Herzl, born in Budapest) and the publicist Bernard Lazare, one of the few Frenchmen in the movement. Following Herzl's death the leadership of the Zionist Organization was dominated by German Jews until 1911 and then by Russian Jews. This shift also represented a change from Herzl's philanthropic and political Zionism, which had failed, to "practical" Zionism, whose goal was to intensify the actual colonization of Turkish-controlled Palestine, particularly by Russian Jews. The events in the early history of Zionism will be omitted here; only the responses of different kinds of European Jews will be discussed.

Zionism was unique among European nationalist movements in several major respects: it had to deal with a Jewish messianic tradition—according to which the world's Jews would have their ultimate confrontation with God in Zion, their homeland; it involved a people that had been exiled from this homeland for almost two thousand years; it was prompted by racial persecution; it had no single government to deal with; it did not even have a common language at first—until 1914 the proceedings of its congresses in Europe were recorded in German, while spoken Hebrew was successfully revived only by the Yiddish- and Russian-speaking colonists in Palestine. Yet Zionism also had many of the features of other nationalist movements of oppressed peoples: it was organized by members of the intelligentsia; it was united by a strong ethnic consciousness; it was divided by clashes of personality and conflicts over ideology and tactics.

Most early Zionists were disillusioned assimilationists. It was the political anti-Semitism sparked by the Dreyfus Affair, not a religious longing for Palestine, that made Herzl, Nordau, and Lazare abandon assimilation for Zionism. Their longing for a Jewish state was purely secular and nationalist. According to Herzl:

> We have sincerely tried everywhere to merge with the national communities in which we live, seeking only to preserve the faith of our

fathers. It is not permitted to us. In vain are we loyal patriots, some-times super-loyal; in vain do we make the same sacrifices of life and property as our fellow citizens; in vain do we strive to enhance the fame of our native land in the arts and sciences, or her wealth by trade and commerce. In our native lands where we have lived for centuries we are still decried as aliens. . . . The majority decides who the "alien" is; this, and all else in the relations between peoples, is a matter of power.[38]

Some of the "practical" Zionists who succeeded Herzl as leaders of the movement were also more natiónalist than religious in orientation. Profes-sor Otto Warburg, the movement's titular head beginning in 1911, was a member of an assimilated Hamburg banking family and a world-renowned botanist. He directed his attention almost solely to colonization and its problems. Chaim Weizmann, a chemist, fled Russia in 1904 and settled permanently in England. He criticized Herzl's diplomatic ap-proach, yet, ironically, it was he who was to obtain the "charter"—the Balfour Declaration in 1917—of which Herzl and Nordau had dreamed, and to become the first president of Israel thirty-one years later.

While still in Russia, Weizmann had been influenced by the "cultural" Zionism of Ahad Ha'am (Asher Ginzberg). Ahad Ha'am had been dis-satisfied with his traditional Jewish education and had studied in Berlin, Vienna, and Brussels. He believed that Palestine could not absorb the Jew-ish masses or become the political or economic base of the Jewish people. Instead he argued that Zion should be their spiritual and cultural center. Like Weizmann, Ahad Ha'am opposed the religious orientation of the Russian Lovers of Zion. These Jews wanted the Palestine colony to be-come a clerical state—a revival on the national scale of the *kahal*, the all-embracing communal organization in each ghetto of the Pale until Tsar Nicholas I had abolished it in 1844.

There was also a Socialist wing in the Zionist movement. This consisted mainly of young Russian Jews whose lower-middle-class parents had become impoverished by the inroads of industrialization and who yearned to become true proletarian workers in a Jewish socialist utopia in Palestine. Between 1904 and 1914 almost forty thousand of them went there, but they soon became disillusioned with the earlier settlers sent by the Lovers of Zion. Not only was the piety of these settlers anathema to these young Marxists, but they also viewed them as their class enemy be-cause they were their employers. Most of the Socialist Zionists either re-turned to Russia or emigrated to America, but those who remained be-came the nucleus of Labor Zionism after the war.

The Zionist movement illustrated the intensification of nationalism everywhere in our period. Except for the Socialist Zionists its strategy was to overcome class and ideological differences through the building of a new nation. Unlike the nationalism of other oppressed peoples, early Zionism was in no position to use strikes, terrorism, or military uprisings to achieve its goals. Only large nation-states could even consider Corradini's ideal of transcending class conflict and finding their redemption in international warfare.

SOCIAL IMPERIALISM

Corradini's ideal came close to the policy of social imperialism, which had advocates in many countries, especially among government leaders.

> Social-imperialism was designed to draw all classes together in defence of the nation and empire and aimed to prove to the least well-to-do class that its interests were inseparable from those of the nation. It aimed at undermining the argument of the socialists and demonstrating that, contrary to the Marxist allegation, the workers *had* more to lose than their chains.[39]

Social imperialism involved giving the franchise and material and social benefits to the masses in order to secure their support for military and economic imperialism. It was thus related to the policy of integrating the workers into a developed system of citizenship rights as a means of stabilizing class differentials in a capitalist society and of maintaining the distinction between the political and economic structures. (See Chapter 4. Introduction.) Both policies tried to use nationalism to counter the class conflicts and protest movements already discussed.

The Boer War (1899–1902) was the first major test of the popularity of military imperialism with the working class. This war originated in a conflict of interests between the British and Afrikaner (Dutch) settlers in South Africa. Not only did the Boer republics in the interior resist demands by the British Cape Colony to form a customs union with them but they also refused to extend citizenship rights to the foreigners (mostly British) who exploited their rich gold and diamond mines. It was Cecil Rhodes, the biggest owner of these mines and the prime minister of the Cape Colony from 1890 to 1896, who tried to link British imperialism in South Africa to the improvement of working-class life at home. In a speech in 1895 he said:

> My cherished idea is a solution for the social problem, i.e., in order to
> save the 40,000,000 inhabitants of the United Kingdom from a bloody
> civil war, we colonial statesmen must acquire new lands to settle the
> surplus population, to provide new markets for the goods produced
> by them in the factories and mines. The Empire . . . is a bread and
> butter question. If you want to avoid civil war, you must become im-
> perialists.

During the Boer War imperialism became popular with many sections of
British society; there were massive street rallies, and tens of thousands of
young men volunteered for the fighting. But a recent study by Richard
Price concludes that "the ethos of imperialism which surrounded the
Boer War had little impact on the working class."[40]

The main reason most British workers were indifferent to imperialism
was that it was too tenuous a concept for them to react to in a clearly
identifiable way. Only when the Boer War touched their own daily lives
did it become a real issue for them. Some young workers volunteered for
the army, but they did so more because of their economic and social circumstances than because of nationalist and imperialist ideals. Price's investigation of workingmen's clubs shows their apathy in contrast to the excitement in all other sectors of society concerning the war. Speakers who
tried to stimulate interest in it at these clubs reported that most questions
from the audience followed the theme of "how much stake in the Empire
has the working man got?" And in the Khaki Election of 1900 most
workers voted for candidates promising social reform rather than imperialist candidates.

Even Joseph Chamberlain, the leading British spokesman for social imperialism, was forced to admit that the Boer War had not captured the
imagination of the working class. This wealthy Birmingham industrialist
had acquired a reputation as a radical social reformer while he was mayor
of that city in the 1870's and early 1880's. In 1885 he shocked the propertied classes by suggesting that they owed a "ransom" to the poor in return for which they would be allowed to retain their wealth. At first he
had made this "ransom" the municipal ownership of the city's utilities
and transportation facilities. As a member of parliament, Chamberlain
moved from his "municipal socialism" toward a state welfare program of
the type sponsored by Bismarck in Germany. He maintained this new interest even after he led a secession from the Liberal Party in opposition to
its support for Irish Home Rule.* According to Chamberlain, the union

* From 1895 to 1903 Chamberlain and other Liberal-Unionists held posts in
the Conservative cabinets that ruled Britain. The electoral victory of the Lib-

with Britain had to be preserved to maintain the Irish market for the manufactured goods of the industrial Midlands. As colonial secretary, Chamberlain also helped to promote the Boer War to keep South Africa within
the British Empire. In 1903, however, he abandoned military imperialism
for economic imperialism as the best means of rallying the workers to the
nation.

Chamberlain became the leader of the Tariff Reform League, whose
goal was to protect British industry from foreign competition. He now
used the "ransom" argument in reverse, telling the British workers that
they had to be prepared to pay higher prices for bread because tariffs
would raise the cost of imported wheat. Then he tried to assure them that
their compensation would be more jobs and good wages because tariffs
would keep out cheap foreign industrial products and would entice foreign manufacturers to move their factories to England.

Social imperialism attracted not only reforming conservatives like
Chamberlain but also George Bernard Shaw, Sidney and Beatrice Webb,
and other members of the Fabian intelligentsia who prided themselves on
being modernizers. Unlike the socialists of the Labour Party and majority
in the Second International, the Fabians wanted to promote the national
and imperial interest rather than a class-oriented politics. Most of them
had favored the Boer War, and Shaw was willing to support Chamberlain's program for tariff protection if its advocates pledged to give the
workers a sliding wage scale to compensate them for price rises caused by
tariffs and not to use tariff revenues to reduce taxes on unearned income. But it soon became clear that Shaw had backed the wrong horse,
for neither the tariff reformers nor the ruling Conservatives were willing
to make these pledges. From 1908 onward it was the Free Trade Liberal-
Imperialists, led by Herbert Asquith and David Lloyd George, who instituted social reforms as a means of breeding an "imperial race," thus preparing the working class for an imperialist war with Germany. And the
majority of the Fabians approved of these reforms, which included old-
age pensions, unemployment and health insurance, and a housing and
town planning act. In her diary Beatrice Webb called the Liberal-Im-
perialists "at once collectivists and imperialists."

Other European statesmen also exploited the appeal of social imperialism. In 1905, Théophile Delcassé, France's foreign minister since 1898,
was forced out of office for provoking a diplomatic crisis with Germany
over control of Morocco, but six years later the angry Chamber of Dep-

---

erals in 1906 drove the Unionists closer to the Conservatives, and they were
soon indistinguishable.

uties overthrew the cabinet for ceding part of the French Congo to Germany during the second Moroccan crisis. Between 1900 and 1903 Chancellor Bernhard von Bülow combined an extension of social insurance with a huge naval building program for Germany. And in the 1907 Reichstag elections Bülow succeeded in inflicting heavy losses on the Center and Socialist parties—which had refused funds for military operations against the Hereros in South West Africa—by rallying many voters to this imperialist cause. But outside of Britain the modernizing government leaders who used social imperialism most successfully were Theodore Roosevelt in the United States and Giovanni Giolitti in Italy.

The case of Giolitti is more problematic than that of Roosevelt. Giolitti started the Libyan War in 1911 because he correctly saw that the current diplomatic crisis between France and Germany over control of Morocco would prevent the major powers from intervening. He did not view this war as an alternative to domestic reforms and, as we have seen, he opposed Italy's intervention in the First World War.[41] Nevertheless, in 1911–12 Giolitti's proposals for universal male suffrage and wide social reform legislation did help to stimulate support for the war in North Africa, at least in the beginning. Although the Italian Socialist Party opposed this war, several of its more independent leaders supported it, just as the Fabians had supported the Boer War and some reformist Socialists in Germany favored a colonialist policy. Many Italian urban workers were also enthusiastic about the war at first. The prospect of getting land in an Italian colony just across the Mediterranean also appealed to alienated southern peasants, and many of them volunteered for the North African army.

It was in Russia that the launching of an imperialist war to counteract domestic unrest took the most dramatic, and tragic, form. In the summer of 1903 V. K. Plehve, the antimodernizing minister of the interior, persuaded Tsar Nicholas II to dismiss Sergei Witte, the prime minister and Russia's leading modernizer, because Witte's policy of conciliation had failed to halt a series of strikes. Plehve then guided an intense campaign of repression not only against the strikers but also against radical and liberal politicians and other "subversives," particularly Jews. But by the beginning of 1904 he became persuaded that repression alone was not working and told the tsar: "In order to hold back the revolution, we need a small victorious war." We have seen that the war with Japan over control of Manchuria was neither small nor victorious and that it led directly to the Revolution of 1905.

In the summer of 1914 some political and military leaders tried to lead their countries into war for the same reason that Plehve had enunciated ten years earlier. The diplomatic and military reasons for the outbreak of the First World War were probably stronger than the need to prevent revolution at home. Yet once the war began, the "sacred unions" invoked in each belligerent state were extremely effective in curbing domestic unrest and in rallying most citizens, including socialists, behind the national war effort. And as hostilities dragged on, most governments promised social reforms in order to maintain popular support for their expanding territorial goals. This was social imperialism—and nationalism—in its most blatant form.

CHAPTER 10

REVOLUTION
IN THE ARTS

The most extreme responses to modernization and its discontents before 1914 were in the arts.[1] Radical nationalists, syndicalists, socialists, and feminists imitated the tactics of a military avant-garde in pursuing their modernizing political goals, but most of them clung to traditional views of reality. The new, self-proclaimed aesthetic avant-garde rejected both the collective goals of the political avant-gardes[2] and their views of reality. These intensely individualistic writers, artists, and composers attacked all artistic forms of expression which assumed these views as deceptive and outmoded façades. The new ways in which they tried to approach the many-sided and often contradictory aspects of contemporary reality varied widely, but they had one thing in common: the creation of new artistic "languages." In this respect the efforts of the aesthetic avant-garde paralleled those of Ludwig Wittgenstein in philosophy, Sigmund Freud in psychology, Max Weber in sociology, and Albert Einstein and Max Planck in physics.

These new artistic languages were more than new styles. Style is a principle of aesthetic coherence; it may modify, echo, or repudiate the historically determined conventions of the medium—or language—of the artist, but it can never completely sever its connections with this medium, no matter how "contemporary" his training and experience may be. But in the early 1900's some artists, writers, and composers tried to invent new languages to express new visions. Like Symbolism since the mid-1880's, Cubism and Abstract art and music represented attempts to go beyond merely stylistic innovations in existing media. The creators of these new languages wanted to use pure form as their means of destroying traditional views of reality and evoking new ones. Even the Expressionists and Futurists, whose works commented more consciously on contemporary emotional and worldly concerns, tried to make their new forms convey new "messages."

Since the Renaissance, despite shifting styles, most artistic creations had represented reality as a coherent totality in which everything had its place: God, nature, society, and man with his thoughts and emotions. By the eighteenth century this structured universe had also incorporated certain values of the first phase of modernization: individualism, personal freedom, and natural law confirmed by reason and ordinary sense perceptions. Marxists call this structured universe "bourgeois-liberal," a useful phrase if we keep in mind the fact that not all bourgeois were liberals and that some nobles were. We should also remember that it meant little to people in the traditional societies of Eastern and Southern Europe, except for their small modernizing elites. Nevertheless it was within this structured universe that the heroes of most European novels and plays worked out their problems and developed their personalities. It was also assumed as given by painters, poets, and composers even when, as in the Baroque and Romantic styles, they stressed the tensions between its different aspects, such as individual pride versus religious longings, or "spontaneous" nature and feelings versus social restrictions.

Both the creative artists and their public assumed that the reality being evoked was objective and unchanging and they accepted certain basic languages—or media—for expressing it: representational painting and sculpture, the diatonic scale, familiar words and metaphors strung together according to standard rules of grammar and syntax. Painting and sculpture, even when allegorical, strove to imitate nature and to portray real individuals with wills of their own. In music from Haydn through Richard Strauss the same basic formal and harmonic guidelines were used to express a wide variety of moods. With rare exceptions, poets continued to combine words in ways that made their literal meaning or their conventional poetic meaning the key to the images and feelings they expressed; this was true for poets with as widely different sensibilities and styles as Pushkin and Baudelaire, Pope and Hölderlin.

Until our period, then (and well into it), the languages or media of all the arts remained rooted in a structured universe that most educated people accepted as given. It was a world in which two plus two made four, in which individual actions were autonomous and purposeful, in which one's relations with institutions and other people were predictable. In this world there were usually clear-cut distinctions between good and evil, prudence and folly, reality and fantasy.

But toward the end of the nineteenth century—the *fin-de-siècle*—modernization was producing large impersonal organizations that sacrificed earlier values for new ones like efficiency, standardization, and unity. Marxists stressed especially the change from a large number of individually or family owned firms to monopolies and trusts. This change certainly occurred, but, as we have seen, there was also a growing trend toward large-scale organization and concentration in the state, in political parties, and in labor unions as well. These developments began to erode many assumptions on which the older bourgeois-liberal world order had been based.

AESTHETICISM AND SOCIAL CONSCIOUSNESS IN THE *fin-de-siècle*

A number of *fin-de-siècle* literary writers who sensed the threat of the emerging new order to the individual tried to transcend it through hedonism and aestheticism. Joris-Karl Huysmans' novel *Against the Grain* (*À rebours*) (1884) served as a breviary of the Decadent movement, which included authors like Paul Verlaine and Oscar Wilde in the late 1880's and the Italian poet-playwright Gabriele D'Annunzio during the next two decades. Huysmans' protagonist, the Duc des Esseintes, is an ultrarefined aesthete living in utter seclusion, socially irresponsible, and nourishing his loveless existence until its very end with perverse and exotic pastimes. The literary Decadents who tried to follow des Esseintes' example believed that they could free themselves from their personal obsessions by giving artistic expression to the evils that haunted them. Some of them eventually renounced their nihilistic self-enchantment for Catholicism, like Huysmans himself; others, like D'Annunzio and Maurice Barrès, turned to nationalism and other secular creeds. In his novels *Under the Eyes of the Barbarians* (*Sous l'oeil des Barbares*) (1888) and

A Free Man (Un Homme libre) (1889) Barrès glorified a completely
self-centered attitude toward life. But shortly thereafter he turned from
anarchic individualism to nativist nationalism as a means of working out
his self-image and his rootlessness in a decadent age.

The German poet Stefan George (1868–1933) illustrates a different
pattern. Before the turn of the century he had been attracted to the aesthetic subjective order that the Symbolists Verlaine and Stéphane
Mallarmé had tried to create. After about 1904, however, George became
one of several German prophets of a new, objective, spiritual order.
Unlike Barrès's populistic nationalism, George's "New Realm" (described
in his volume of poems, *Das neue Reich*, 1908–19) was a kind of Platonic
utopia. Under George's cultural dictatorship it was to be created and imposed by a literary elite that disregarded the social and cultural realities
of the vulgar, materialistic world around it.

Meanwhile, in Vienna as in Paris, the spiritual lassitude of the *fin-de-
siècle* was a response to political and social decadence as well as to the
plight of the egocentric aesthete in the new scientific-technological age,
but in the Austrian capital it lasted until the outbreak of the war. As the
historian Carl Schorske has pointed out, upper-middle-class Austrian liberals sought escape in art and hedonism after losing political power to the
traditional Hapsburg ruling circles by the end of the 1870's. Their
French counterparts, on the other hand, retained their dominant political
role throughout the *belle époque*, despite financial scandals and right-wing
threats. (Indeed in the immediate prewar years they co-opted the extreme
nationalism of the former Boulangists and anti-Dreyfusards and
redirected it toward their own ends.) Their flirtations, duels, and high
living expressed a nervous confidence in their position rather than the self-
pitying irresponsibility of the Austrian upper bourgeoisie. An important
example of this class and the moral-aesthetic culture into which it escaped
was the writer Hugo von Hofmannsthal (1874–1929).

In his youth Hofmannsthal personified the *fin-de-siècle* sensibility. He
began writing poetry at seventeen and until he was twenty-five he
remained an egocentric aesthete—in his own words, "early ripened and
tender and sad." But, as Schorske says, he knew that "the dweller in the
temple of art . . . was condemned to seek the significance of life purely
within his own psyche."[3] By the end of the century Hofmannsthal
sought to free himself from the paralysis of his narcissism and the prison
of his aestheticism through an affirmation of the instinctual as a way of
entering a life of action and social participation. He also wanted to reas-

sert the traditional connection between art and ethics. In his lyrical playlet, *Death and the Fool* (1893) Hofmannsthal had already tried to show the moral consequences of the aesthetic attitude by indicting the des Esseintes-like aristocrat (Fool) who, in pursuit of his refined sensations, ruined his mother, his sweetheart, and his best friend. Death comes to the Fool as a judge to punish his transgression. But instead of materializing as a skeleton, as in a medieval morality play, Death appears as a musician—a Dionysian life force symbolizing the unconscious instincts that an excess of individual self-cultivation had repressed.

In this verse playlet and in his post-1900 dramas and prose works Hofmannsthal criticized the aestheticism and hedonism of his class. Art, he maintained, does not give form to actual experiences but only to the feelings arising out of these experiences. By merely showing us life vicariously art actually separates us from it. And when the devotees of art detach it from other values and view it as a value in itself they become introverted and acquire a sense of being eternal spectators.

Hofmannsthal also tried to redefine the poet's function in modern society in his essay "The Poet and This Age" (1906). Here he argued that the poet must accept the essentially fragmented and pluralistic reality around him and bring unity and cohesion to it through the magic medium of literary language. He must reveal the hidden ties behind the apparent conflict or contradiction that others saw and, through rhythm and sound, develop these ties and bring out their unity. In other words, the poet must become an educator.

Hofmannsthal himself wrote several dramas as libretti for Richard Strauss's operas—*Elektra, Ariadne auf Naxos, Der Rosenkavalier*—in which he tried to express a respect for the fullness of life with all its potentialities for good and evil. But, as in the political life of Austria-Hungary itself, disintegration on the social and psychological levels had proceeded too far. The rifts were too strong to allow Hofmannsthal and other poets to redeem society through the reconciling power of art. "Society could tolerate tragedy or comedy but not redemption through aesthetic harmonization."[4]

Whereas Hofmannsthal, George, and the Decadents generally ignored modern concerns about social justice, a number of writers at the turn of the century dealt with these in the traditions of nineteenth-century Realism and Naturalism.[5] In Germany Gerhart Hauptmann's play *The Weavers* (1892) used a strike of Silesian hand weavers forced out of work by new machines almost half a century earlier as the basis for a Naturalist and socially radical exposé of the plight of the working class in

his own time. Maxim Gorky employed the Realist style in his most popular play, *The Lower Depths* (1902), set in a cavelike night lodginghouse,
to convey a message of hope for better things and of respect for all
human beings, even the most down-and-out. In Italy, which, like Russia,
was still in an early phase of modernization, Giovanni Verga used Naturalist techniques to portray the exploitation and degradation of poor
Sicilian fishermen in his novel *Under the Medlar Tree (I Malavoglia,*
1881). The English Realist Thomas Hardy described the bitterness and
frustration of a sensitive stonemason with aspirations beyond his social
means in the novel *Jude the Obscure* (1896). One of the most notorious
commentators on social issues in the *fin-de-siècle* was the Irish playwright
George Bernard Shaw. At the time, however, two of the most popular
writers of this type were Henrik Ibsen (1828–1906) and Émile Zola
(1840–1902), who had finished their major works somewhat earlier.

Ibsen was best known as what Shaw tried to make of him in his *The
Quintessence of Ibsenism* (1891)—a pedagogue and a reformer; he was
also Europe's greatest dramatist since Shakespeare and Racine. The four
plays that he wrote between 1877 and 1882—*The Pillars of Society, A
Doll's House, Ghosts,* and *An Enemy of the People*—are models of Realism in their attacks on the assumptions of the bourgeois-liberal structured
universe. The "lessons" of the first two plays are that society can strive
toward a truly adult conception of sexual life and that women can and
must be given the same right to self-fulfillment as men. (The fact that
Ibsen himself denied that *A Doll's House* was a feminist play did not alter
its reception as such. See pp. 185–86). The second two plays denounce the
oppressions and hypocrisies hidden behind the façade of middle-class
gentility. They also show us how money interests thwart emotional
fulfillment and intellectual integrity.

More important, however, Ibsen exposes the dangers of self-generated
idealism for various "causes" in the modern world, from which God has
withdrawn and in which all beliefs are precarious. When the idealistic
masks that men and women use to guard against the realities of their lives
are recognized for what they are, Ibsen's characters often choose to die.
In *Rosmersholm* (1886) Rebecca's ideal of emancipation makes her pred-
atory, and her ideal of a pure partnership with Rosmer in his crusade
for nobility drives her to destroy his wife, Beata. When the lovers both
realize that these illusory ideals have made them sin, Rosmer says: "There
is no judge over us; and therefore we must do justice upon ourselves."
Their guilt drives them to drown themselves in the stream of old Rosmersholm. As the critic George Steiner notes, Ibsen's plays are not

tragedies in the Greek and Elizabethan sense, because the most dangerous threats to life and reason come not from without but from the modern consciousness of the contradictory impulses within the individual psyche. In *The Master Builder* (1892) Solness clearly recognizes that he is the agent of his own fate and climbs to the top of the tower he has built and falls. The structure of feeling of Ibsen's characters was shared by many sensitive Europeans in the late nineteenth century. It was his genius in dramatizing their torments, as much as his social philosophy, that made Ibsen one of the most representative writers of his time.

In Zola's novel *Germinal,* whose theme is the almost hopeless struggle for existence of a group of striking French coal miners, he brought the style of Naturalism to its zenith. Although first published in 1885, it went through many later editions and had such obvious appeal to budding socialists that the government tried, unsuccessfully, to block its adaptation for the stage. Zola objectively describes the endless labor of the miners in the stifling pits, the misery of their families, the breakdown of morality, and the violence and destructiveness to which the strikers are driven by pay reductions during an economic crisis. He also shows the varied reactions of different types of mineowners and managers, particularly the small owner who sympathizes with the workers but knows that concessions will prevent him from competing with the more ruthless larger companies. Unlike Gorky in *Enemies,* Zola does not excuse violence or preach revolution. "*Germinal,*" he protested, "is a work of pity and not a work of revolution. . . . Yes, a cry of pity, a cry of justice, I wish no more."[6]

Across the Channel, William Morris (1829–1896), in his utopian novel *News from Nowhere* (1891), foresaw the eventual triumph of socialism through education, in which the arts would play a major role. But, unlike the Marxists, Morris opposed industrialization itself and stated that, in his ideal society, "all work which it is a pleasure to do by hand, machinery is done without." In the late 1880's he was a leading figure in the English Arts and Crafts movement, whose goal was to humanize industrial design and make its products functional. In contrast to overelaborate Victorian furniture, for example, he invented the simple but comfortable Morris chair. Although he insisted (again unlike the Marxists) that artists were obliged to express themselves in a language not understood by the people, Morris believed at the same time that they should teach the people the evils of modern society and prepare them for a better world based on an updated version of the medieval guilds.

Other writers and artists in the 1890's who embraced revolutionary social doctrines experienced the perennial dilemma sidestepped by Morris: how can art serve social ends without losing its artistic integrity? The French painter Camille Pissarro firmly believed in the necessity of bringing anarchist ideas to the masses. But his cover design for Kropotkin's *Les Temps Nouveaux* depicted the same subject (an agricultural worker) and used the same style as his post-Impressionist paintings. On the other hand, the Belgian Symbolist Émile Verhaeren was the first poet of stature to sing of modern life, the pulsation of machines, and the slow rise of the masses. The French critic Rémy de Gourmont found the style of this socialist prophet too harsh but conceded: "What a difference between this poetry and the vulgar 'social poetry' that they try to manufacture for the masses."[7]

Before concentrating on the revolutionary new media in the arts we must note briefly the traditional ones that remained dominant until 1914. We have seen the pervasiveness of cultural lag throughout this study. With the doubtful exception of Art Nouveau, the works of the most popular creative artists continued to ignore the ways in which European civilization was being transformed by organizational, scientific, and technological changes. This negative response was important because it allowed the educated public and even some extreme modernizing leaders to combine cultural conservatism with advanced political and social views. (Lenin's preference for traditional art forms was notorious.) A typical list of late Romantic composers in our period speaks for itself: Elgar, Grieg, Saint-Saëns, Bruckner, Puccini, Rachmaninov, Sibelius, and Richard Strauss, whom many historians and critics view as most representative of the early 1900's. In the novel it was not until the very eve of the war that Kafka and Proust began to use new forms and to present new visions through new media of expression. In painting post-Impressionists like Van Gogh, Gauguin, and Cézanne, along with James Ensor and Edvard Munch, were already moving toward the new languages of the early 1900's. But the dominant forms in the plastic arts were elaborations of earlier styles.

A major cultural event that showed what people at the time thought was new and daring was the first performance of Richard Strauss's opera *Salome,* conducted by Ernst von Schuch at the Dresden Royal Opera House on December 9, 1905. Reporting on this premiere in its December 10 and 11 issues, the daily *Dresdner Nachrichten* said:

> The coarse events in Wilde's text, the triumph over all the perversions of normal feelings which it demands, the loathsomeness of the

Camille Pissarro, *Le Laboreur*, on the cover of Kropotkin's anarchist magazine, *Les Temps Nouveaux*, Paris (1898).

The Stomach Dance, an Aubrey Beardsley drawing illustrating Oscar Wilde's play *Salome*.

material—all this is in part transfigured by the power of the music and is in part brought nearer to the natural instincts as it lets the subject-matter express itself. The high points of the score include the splendid instrumental coloring of the scenes between Salome and Iokanaan [John the Baptist], whose feverish sensuality is brought together with their solemnity and nobleness in fascinating changes of mood. Other high points are the grandiose orchestral piece that mingles the appearance of Herod and the departure of Iokanaan, the masterfully styled "Dance of the Seven Veils," and the final scene depicting Salome's ecstatically mounting transport of love—in which the height of brilliant effect seems to be reached—which touches us deeply and brings about the rousing success of the entire score. In other respects this work is not free from clearly external effects and cunning combinations or from superfluous *longueurs,* miniature painting, and other detracting elements that weaken its impact. But all things considered, Strauss's masterly transfiguration of *Salome* is a work of art. Moreover, the admirable performance, in combination with the magnificently decorative costuming and staging, was sure to give *Salome* a splendid reception. . . . After the final curtain the audience's enthusiastic applause, which lasted for a quarter of an hour, brought the soloists, Strauss, and von Schuch back onto the stage over thirty times. . . . Whoever wants to be conversant with the achievements of the most modern music . . . must see and hear *Salome.*

Because Strauss was considered the most famous and the greatest living composer, many foreign critics and conductors—including Sir Thomas Beecham and Arturo Toscanini—had indeed come to see and hear his new opera. Aside from the music, its exotic Near Eastern sets contrasted with the neoclassical style of the theater (designed in the 1820's by Carl Friedrich Schinkel). And its scandalous subject-matter delayed its performance in other cities for several years. Yet *Salome* was essentially an extension of the Wagnerian medium. The music had a little more dissonance, the text was a little more erotic, the feelings portrayed were a little more decadent than in a typical work of the *fin-de-siècle.* *Salome* was dazzling and exciting but it was not composed in a new artistic language.

In the early 1900's a number of important writers and artists abandoned *fin-de-siècle* aestheticism, hedonism, freethinking, and social protest in a search for spiritual regeneration through a new ethical idealism. Representative of this search were the Christian modernism of Paul Claudel, Shaw's version of Henri Bergson's creative evolution in *Man and Super-*

man, and Tolstoy's ideal of a primitive Christian way of life in the Russian village community, which caused Rainer Maria Rilke to experience a decisive spiritual liberation and which helped German Expressionist writers break away from Nietzsche, the prophet of the anti-Christ and of nihilistic self-exultation. In some instances alterations in the political or social climate may have stimulated this change: the trial of Oscar Wilde in England in 1895, the end of the Dreyfus Affair in France in 1899, the failure of the Revolution of 1905 in Russia. But the main cause seems to have been disillusionment with earlier "revolutionary" ideals as the way to salvation for modern man. A major writer who made this change was the Swedish dramatist August Strindberg (1849–1912) in his *To Damascus*, written between 1898 and 1904. Throughout the three parts of this first Expressionist play the protagonist, a writer called The Stranger and representing Strindberg himself, is conscience-stricken at the sight of unfortunate creatures who owe their wretched plight to his earlier incitements to break with old-fashioned notions of bourgeois morality.

STRINDBERG AND EARLY EXPRESSIONISM AND ABSTRACT ART

Strindberg also exemplified the shift from late nineteenth-century Naturalism to early twentieth-century Expressionism. In the late 1880's he wrote *The Father, Miss Julie*, and *Creditors*—all dealing with plausible characters working out their problems in realistic settings. But, beginning with *To Damascus*, his plays have a dreamlike quality which disregards the empirical laws of causality and relationships and whose single purpose is to express the inner world of the protagonist. Only in *The Dance of Death* (1901) does Strindberg revert to his earlier theme of the battle of the sexes through self-contained, willful characters. In *To Damascus, A Dream Play* (1902), *The Ghost Sonata* (1907), and *The Great Highway* (1909) all the other characters represent aspects of the protagonist's feelings and relationships. Since they are abstractions they have no life of their own and appear at improbable times and places in response to the mood of the protagonist at the moment. The protagonists too are more or less abstract, with generic designations such as "The Stranger" and "The Student." There is no plot or dramatic action in the conventional sense. Rather each play is a statement of the protagonist's pilgrimage "toward a dimly perceived goal of salvation, desperately sought and somewhat tentatively entertained."[8] The scenery reflects the emotional situation of the characters and often changes within a given episode as the psychic forces emanating from them are altered. Thus, space and even time lose their conventional attributes to become functions of expression. In *A Dream Play*, for example, a young officer demonstrates the constancy of his love by aging and turning decrepit before our eyes while waiting for his sweetheart with a bouquet of roses, which also withers. The dreamlike quality of Strindberg's last plays was heightened by new kinds of acting, lighting, and sound effects.

The "message" of *To Damascus*—the protagonist learns the error of his past life through various forms of suffering and in the end understands that these have been imposed by a divine power as punishment for his sins—is hardly novel; what is revolutionary is the new medium through which it is expressed. Strindberg himself described his new medium in his preface to *A Dream Play*:

> As in his previous dream play, *To Damascus*, the author has in *A Dream Play* attempted to reproduce the detached and disunited—although apparently logical—form of dreams. Anything is apt to happen, anything seems possible and probable. Time and space do not exist. On a flimsy foundation of actual happenings, imagination spins and weaves in new patterns: an intermingling of remembrances, experiences, whims, fancies, ideas, fantastic absurdities and improvisations, and original inventions of the mind. The personalities split, take on duality, multiply, vanish, intensify, diffuse and disperse, and are brought into focus. There is, however, one single-minded consciousness that exercises a dominance over the characters: the dreamer's.[9]

In *To Damascus* (I) The Lady embodies The Stranger's links with sexual love and with life itself. Her husband, The Physician, whom The Stranger had once wronged, functions as a reminder of his guilt and as a barometer of his growing repentance and self-awareness. The Beggar, whom The Stranger encounters several times, is the degradation he dreads and the resignation he must still learn—the personification of the kind of existence toward which The Stranger must move. Meanwhile, Caesar, a lunatic living in The Physician's household, angers and frightens The Stranger by functioning as a caricature of his own megalomania and as a foreshadowing of the danger into which his own stubborn pride will lead him. The Mother's initial harshness toward The Stranger mirrors his own hostility and guilt, whereas her later compassion expresses the humility and ability to love which slowly awaken in him toward the end of the play.

Strindberg's exploration of man's most deeply hidden feelings, which

A scene from the Stockholm premiere of Strindberg's *To Damascus*.

paralleled the discoveries of Freud, vividly expresses the self-consciousness of many creative artists concerning the predicament of the individual who has lost his bearings in a world in whose conventions and values he no longer believes. As we have seen, most Europeans before 1914 behaved *as if* these values and conventions still had meaning. Consequently they would have been mystified by the late works of Strindberg and the writings of Kafka and the German Expressionists. Yet the purpose of these writers was not to mystify but rather to bring out through their new languages the true feelings and dilemmas of the individual, which surface relationships and behavior hid even from himself. These writers—and Cubist and Expressionist painters—were also seeking to abstract the essential nature of art by divorcing it from extraneous considerations such as religion, morality, and the imitation of nature, but this purpose is not our concern here. We are primarily interested in their reasons for viewing these things as extraneous.

One reason was surely a loss of faith in traditional religion and morality, which had begun long before our period but which had nevertheless been prompted in part by the influence of modern rationalism and positivism. What was new in Strindberg and the early Expressionists was the view that the natural order itself—the only reality for the positivists— was not only unknowable through observation by the senses but also irrelevant to the individual's search for personal salvation and for a place in a meaningful world. This view, a commonplace today, was a new response to the urban-industrial civilization that was beginning to dominate many people's lives at the turn of the century. Even then, nature—for those city dwellers who had access to it at all—was coming to mean merely recreational areas such as parks and resorts, or something one saw in passing from a train window. (Today we have gone a step further, so that Disney World is more popular than the Grand Canyon.) But avant-garde creative artists and writers of that time saw that a world in which nature was already extraneous needed something else to give people their bearings and that this something else was not being provided by modern civilization. Indeed many of them viewed the bourgeois-liberal establishment that controlled this civilization as hostile not only to art but also to all meaningful feelings and relationships. Their preoccupation with the individual's inner life expressed their rejection of the workaday world and its values and conventions, which they considered meretricious and therefore of no use to them.

The label "Expressionism" was originally used between 1901 and 1910 in France to distinguish Matisse, Derain, Vlaminck, and other "Fauve" (literally wild beast) painters from the Impressionists, but the structure of feeling their new language tried to reveal can be seen in earlier Symbolist painters. Impressionists as diverse in style as Manet, Degas, Renoir, and Monet had shared the radically empirical late nineteenth-century assumption that the informal, unregulated vision of the moment was the only kind of data accessible to analysis. Claude Monet once said in an interview: "Try to forget what objects you have before you. . . . Merely think, here is a little square of blue, here an oblong of pink, here a streak of yellow, and paint it just as it looks to you, the exact color and shape, until it gives your naive impression of the scene . . ."[10] But in the 1880's and 1890's Gauguin, Van Gogh, Ensor, and Munch had already rejected this view and substituted the belief that art is ultimately based upon emotional experience rather than visual analysis. In order to represent experiences that cannot be explained by sense perceptions they searched for new symbols—not the conventional symbols of Classical and

Edvard Munch, *The Shriek* (1896), lithograph, 20⅝ × 15¹³⁄₁₆″.

Romantic art but strange, fantastic, dreamlike, and sometimes primitive images. Vincent Van Gogh's raging nebulae and writhing olive trees give *expression* to the torments of his inner self rather than an *impression* of the landscape. The new trend was particularly clear in the Norwegian painter Edvard Munch's *The Scream*, in which some terrible tension has been released so explosively in the man on the bridge that his emotion visibly agitates the atmosphere and the space around him. In comparison with Van Gogh and Munch the paintings of the Fauves seem superficial, for all their daring splashes of color and disregard for line and perspective.

In 1905, the year of the first Fauvist exhibition in Paris, a group of German painters founded the Bridge (*Die Brücke*) in Dresden under the leadership of Ernst Ludwig Kirchner. The third group of Expressionist painters, the Blue Rider (*Der Blaue Reiter*), began exhibiting together in Munich in 1911; its best-known representatives were Wassily Kandinsky (1866–1944), Franz Marc (1880–1916), and Paul Klee (1879–1940). Although only indirectly related to the two German groups, the Viennese painter and writer Oskar Kokoschka probably did more than anyone else to give Expressionism an international notoriety. Already in 1910 the primal fury of his play *Murder, Hope of Women* and the deliberately horrifying poster that advertised it had made the Viennese press call him a "degenerate artist" and prompted his friend, the architect Adolf Loos, to send him off to Switzerland. By 1910 the Expressionist label was also being applied to new forms of German poetry, drama, and narrative fiction, whose common elements were an intense radicalism of feeling and expression and a pervasive apocalyptic tone—with titles like "Twilight of Mankind," "Day of Judgment," "World's End." Many Expressionists strove to give the same effect of utter horror in print which Munch had achieved on canvas in *The Scream*.

The new Expressionist language showed the extremes to which some artists and writers went in rejecting the conventional material reality of the modern world. As opposed to Naturalism and Impressionism, which deal with what is on the surface, Expressionism brings out what is behind or beneath this surface through two basic approaches. One is surrealistic, subjective, and visionary, as in Strindberg's dream plays, the poetry of Georg Heym, Kafka's stories, and paintings such as Kokoschka's *Bride of the Wind* and Emil Nolde's *Pentecost*. This approach is distinguished from the Surrealism of the 1920's by its seriousness, its consistency, and its primarily spiritual concerns. The other basic Expressionist approach is through abstraction, as in Kandinsky's paintings, the early poetry of

MÖRDER HOFFNUNG DER FRAUEN 1910

Oskar Kokoschka, *Murder, Hope of Women* (1910), poster.

Gottfried Benn, and the plays of Frank Wedekind and Georg Kaiser, in which the characters are not Strindbergian projections of subconscious states but impersonal caricatures of institutions and attitudes or carriers of some ironic turn of the plot.

Although he was associated for a short time with the Bridge group, Emil Nolde (1867–1956) lacked the feeling for humanity that runs through their paintings. Yet perhaps no other painter evoked as forcefully as he the anguish, religious feelings, and intuitive and emotional qualities of Expressionism. The composition of his *Pentecost* dispenses with nonessentials and concentrates its explosive fury on the transcendental significance of the moment he captures. In his reminiscences he says: "I descended once more into the depths of human-divine being. The Pentecost picture was prepared, five of the apostle fishermen were painted in ecstatic supra-sensual reception of the Holy Ghost."[11] The distorted and frightening expressions of their masklike faces have a powerfully grotesque and primitive quality. Their eyes stare as if they see only what lies within; their exaggerated features and blurred contours spring at the viewer with an uncontrolled inner force, intensified by the contrast between the colors of the faces and figures and those of the eyes. Nolde's distortions and color excitement constituted a new artistic language, Expressionist yet intensely individual.

Oskar Kokoschka (b. 1886) had a far more sophisticated and humane outlook than Nolde, and the style of his paintings varied considerably during the six years preceding the outbreak of the First World War. His early portraits, particularly the double one of *Hans and Erica Tietze* (1908–09), expose the throbbing nerves and blood vessels of hypersensitive intellectuals trapped in the dying culture of Freud's Vienna. Kokoschka achieves this image by means of a fragile line nervously threading its way through the flat yellow-gold background of the hands and faces. His *Bride of the Wind* (1914)—also called *The Tempest*—is quite different in conception and style. This painting shows a sleeping woman and wakeful man—recognizable as Alma Mahler and Kokoschka himself—lying side by side in a boatlike cockleshell whirling through infinity. Through various modulations of color (predominantly blue) and swirling movements a vision suddenly materializes of the epic passion of the lovers who ignore the raging tempest around them. In this painting we see the high point of Kokoschka's striving toward a nonnaturalistic expression of inner meaning by mingling the real relationship of the lovers with the surrealistic, unearthly space surrounding them.

In contrast to Nolde and Kokoschka, Kandinsky moved toward an un-

Emil Nolde, *The Lord's Supper* (1909).

compromisingly abstract, nonobjective art in the immediate prewar years. One of the most influential painters then and afterward, Kandinsky, like Picasso and Stravinsky, was a truly international artist. He was also the first major painter to put the goals of nonobjective art into a theory in his book, *Concerning the Spiritual in Art*, written in 1910 and first published in 1912. His own paintings, like Expressionism in general, evoke a mood rather than describing something tangible. But, unlike later forms of nonobjective art, they always retain psychological or spiritual meaning. As Kandinsky says in his book, the starting point is the study of color and its effect on men.

> Generally speaking, color directly influences the soul; color is the keyboard, the eyes are the hammers, the soul is the piano with many strings. The artist is the hand that plays, touching one key or another purposively, to create vibrations in the soul. It is evident therefore that color harmony must rest ultimately on purposive playing upon the human soul; this is one of the guiding principles of internal necessity. . . . Inner necessity is the basis of both small and great problems in paintings. Today we are seeking the road which is to lead us away from the external to the internal basis. The spirit, like the body, can be strengthened and developed by frequent exercises; just as the

body, if neglected, grows weak and finally impotent, so the spirit perishes if untended.[12]

Beginning in 1913, Kandinsky painted numerous abstract compositions in his new medium. Their dominant feature is a spontaneous response to nature or to the painter's mood of the moment. In *Improvisation with Green Center* there are no objects, and subject matter is suggested in a vague, intangible way; the spectator himself must react spontaneously to the emotional stimulus of the color and form. Another painting, *On the White Edge*, evokes feelings of joy and humor through a series of variations on the troika motif.

In drama, as in painting, abstraction became part of the Expressionist medium.

Georg Kaiser, the most outstanding of the Expressionist dramatists, called the writing of a play "a geometric problem."[13] His plays unmask the true character of individual existence and social reality by abstracting and distorting the conditions involved through aphorisms, debates, and parodistic irony. In *The Jewish Widow* (1911), Kaiser reveals his version of the true nature of the heroism of the biblical Judith as the accidental spinoff of sexual frustration. Her real desire was to sleep with the

Wassily Kandinsky, *Study for Painting with White Form* (1913), watercolor, 10⅞ × 15".

Ernst Ludwig Kirchner, *Street, Berlin* (1913), oil on canvas, 47½ × 35⅞″.

Babylonian king because of his renowned sexual potency. When General Holophernes thwarts her desire, she simply kills him, and the leaderless Babylonian army, along with the king, flees in panic, thus liberating the Jewish town it had been besieging. The disappointed Judith is hailed by her people as a heroine and finally satisfied by the sexual prowess of the high priest of Jerusalem. All the characters are mere carriers of the "joke," which is the essence that Kaiser abstracts from the plot.

In his greatest drama, *The Burghers of Calais* (written in 1914 and first performed in 1917), Kaiser transforms heroism into pacifism and self-sacrifice through a series of debates and surprise effects. The setting is another siege, this time of medieval Calais by the English king during the Hundred Years' War. The king offers to spare the city if it will give him six hostages to be put to death as a token of its defeat. In the name of national honor the patriotic leaders inside the city urge a fight to the finish, but the self-sacrificing pacifist Eustache de Saint-Pierre—Kaiser's "new man"—challenges this argument. He offers himself as a hostage, and his example persuades six other burghers to volunteer as well. In one of his typical ironic tricks Kaiser has produced seven hostages where only six were required. They agree to walk together into the enemy camp and to allow the last to arrive to be the one to go free. The six burghers all arrive early, and it looks for a moment as if Eustache has broken his oath. But he is finally carried in on a stretcher, having killed himself in order to give courage to the others and to ensure their regeneration. The same night, the English king celebrates the birth of his son by releasing the six hostages. As the king prays in the cathedral, Eustache's coffin is raised above the altar, so that the king, the hero of the war, is kneeling before the hero of peace.

The Burghers of Calais is a synthesis of the abstractionist medium and the new ethical concerns of many Expressionists by 1914. Kaiser escaped from the "frigidization of self" in the impersonal, hostile world around him into a world of abstract ideas and pure forms. But, along with others, he believed that the "constructive mind" of the writer would help him to spare his fellow men his own agony of self-consciousness and, when properly used, enhance and liberate his own will. Only through his mind, these Expressionists asserted, could the modern "new man" regain his freedom of action and will. Thus, in their own way, some of the abstractionist Expressionist writers—like Kandinsky and the Cubist painters—did try to attune themselves to the new scientific-technological age—an age in which function had replaced substance and the increasing control and transformation of nature were destroying the traditional belief in a given world of nature outside man.

The Expressionists' hostility toward the machine age and their strivings to transcend it were poignantly expressed by the philosopher Martin Buber in describing their vision of a new, humane society: "We say the City—but we do not mean its houses and factories, its goods and its waste matter; what we mean is its millions of . . . individual people, naked under their clothes, blood coursing under their skins, all of those whose exposed heartbeats together would drown out the united voices of its machines."[14] In the immediate prewar years these "exposed heartbeats" were as evident in the paintings of Oskar Kokoschka, Emil Nolde, and Ernst Ludwig Kirchner as they were in the plays of Strindberg and Wedekind (see p. 186). Expressionist painters turned from the desperate psychological situation of modern man to social criticism a few years later than Expressionist writers. This new concern was to reach its peak in the graphic art of George Grosz and Max Beckmann during the 1920's (and in the 1925 film *Metropolis*). But before the war the Expressionists were already developing a new artistic language that would intensify their concrete images of the raw emotions and spiritual longings of people trapped in a hostile, impersonal environment. In spite of their diverse temperaments and styles, all of them eventually became preoccupied with stating the need for a new world community and a new man.

Alternations between inward-looking and outward-looking among writers and artists had occurred before the early 1900's and were to occur again thereafter. So have the more popular and trivialized life styles they have inspired: Ibsen women, lost generations, Existentialism, interest in oriental religions, the political activism of the 1930's and 1960's, the consciousness-raising concerns of the 1970's. The twentieth-century aesthetic avant-garde seems to be caught in an endless cycle of attempting to change things, withdrawal, and renewed activism. But the alternation in the early 1900's was a peculiarly self-conscious rejection of late nineteenth-century modernism in all its forms: positivism, materialism, Impressionism, Art Nouveau, political solutions to social problems, and the social criticism of Ibsen and Zola.

German Expressionism was an early example of a number of twentieth-century efforts to combine the ideal of a new artistic form with the idea of a new man. In this way, the creative artists involved hoped to end their isolation from a society and culture in which their function had been reduced to that of classy entertainers in the case of writers and, in the case of painters, producers of pictures for home decoration or "merchandise" for collectors. But their new artistic language was too difficult and inaccessible to serve as a proselytizing medium. At the same time, the rhetorical directness of some of their efforts to preach to a larger audience compromised their artistic goal of creating new forms unrelated to accepted views of reality.

KAFKA AND THE ISOLATION OF THE CREATIVE ARTIST

Artists and intellectuals had turned away from modern civilization long before our period, and their "alienation" has become a cliché. The critic César Graña says that the overwhelming feature of literary life since the Romantic movement was "the refusal, inconsolable or implacable, to accept the terms, social or symbolic, of Western culture following the political, scientific, and economic events of the first half of the nineteenth century."[15] During the 1850's and 1860's, when France experienced the first major impact of industrialization under Napoleon III, two of that nation's most perceptive writers, Gustave Flaubert and Charles Baudelaire, adopted a new attitude of horror at the vulgarity and philistinism of industrial society in general and of the bourgeois life style in particular. As industrialization and the domination of the bourgeoisie became irresistible, the separation of life from art came to be viewed as complete. After 1870 most European artists and writers were openly hostile to the new, modern order in one way or another. And almost all of them felt that it was unwilling to bow before their accomplishments as a self-appointed elite, as the old order had once bowed before the traditional aristocracy. They were of course responding to their own, not necessarily accurate, images of work, production, and the market. As the German novelist Jakob Wassermann said in 1910:

> The writers . . . sensing their isolation, their alienation, the absence of social coherence and an inner legitimacy based on myth, withdraw into their inner life as into a cave, or proclaim a tyrannical self-sufficiency without finding a bridge to their society and to mankind. On one side a people in feverish activity, all action, all drive, but also wholly without God; on the other side the poet in feverish torment, activated by his dreams, lonely, and deifying himself.[16]

Franz Kafka (1883–1924) personified a certain type of Central European writer in the early twentieth century—a man whose overdeveloped critical intellect ruthlessly dissected the feelings and behavior of others and of himself to the point where he was incapable of gaining his share of the world's love and warmth. He himself blamed this incapability on "introspection, which will suffer no idea to sink tranquilly to rest but must pursue each one into consciousness, only itself to become an idea, in turn to be pursued by renewed introspection. . . . This pursuit, originating in the midst of men, carries one in a direction away from them."[17]

Although Kafka, Strindberg, and a number of early Expressionists typified the "alienated" artist in an unappreciative society that had lost its bearings, they were also struggling with an agonizing moral dilemma within themselves. On the one hand they were ultramodern in their apparent self-sufficiency, intelligence, skepticism, and irony—qualities that equipped them for accepting soberly the visible world as the only and ultimate reality. On the other hand they still believed in divine and hellish powers and in their own damnation. But, according to the critic Walter Sokel, all that was left of their faith was the conviction that their damnation stood out "like a rock in a landscape the softer soil of which has been eroded by the critical intellect. Kafka once said: 'I ought to welcome eternity, but to find it makes me sad.' "[18]

Surely this dilemma was not peculiar to the prewar generation; it had been experienced to some extent by Pascal and Kierkegaard earlier and was to plague the Existentialists later. Nevertheless, in the early 1900's it was felt by men who could no longer make the leap to real faith or accept life as hopelessly absurd. The way the dilemma was experienced at that time, particularly by Kafka, marked a specific stage in the intellectual response to modernization in its broadest sense.

The isolation that Kafka felt was not so much from society as from his image of himself. He was so preoccupied with doubts about what could justify his art or his very existence that he failed to develop the kind of adaptability and practical intelligence which made happiness and success possible in the day-to-day world. In his youth, for example, it never occurred to him that he might have improved his awkward looks with less ill-fitting, badly tailored clothes. His abstract, introspective mind was unable to explain such an obvious connection. Instead he ascribed his ungainly appearance to a special curse by a cruel fate which forbade him to be happy. Yet his spiritual masochism did not prevent him from being wise and humane toward his fellow men. When someone remarked on the stupidity of a common acquaintance, Kafka replied: "To be stupid is human. Many clever people are not wise and therefore in the last resort not even clever. They are merely inhuman out of fear of their own meaningless vulgarity."[19]

Kafka expressed his deep-seated conviction of his own guilt and inferiority most forcefully in his story *The Metamorphosis* (1913). Its protagonist, Gregor Samsa, is caught in a double bind. As the story opens he announces to his parents that he is going to stay in his room instead of leaving for work. By this means he hopes to abdicate his position as breadwinner and head of the household and regain the love of his old father and mother. At the same time he wants to express his resentment toward his family for having parasitically exploited his daily drudgery at his job and to live at home as a free and independent parasite himself. These contradictory impulses flit through his consciousness but are quickly repressed and forgotten. Still, Samsa is haunted by an overwhelming feeling of guilt and self-contempt for harboring them and he yearns for punishment.

Samsa recognizes and at the same time gets out of his predicament by waking up one morning to find that he has turned into a giant cockroach. With this metaphor Kafka expresses the interpenetration and complete simultaneity of Samsa's conflicting emotions in a more intense way than would be possible by normal exposition or a stream-of-consciousness approach. Samsa's metamorphosis accommodates all his repressed ambivalent desires and his guilt feelings for having them; it also provides an immediate punishment through his new state of repulsive helplessness. Kafka treats his metaphor as an actual fact. Thus, by having Samsa's parents inspect the carcass at the end of the story, he assures us that his protagonist is not merely experiencing a hallucination. Through a process of visionary abstraction Kafka condenses the dim prison of Samsa's true existence into an image unconnected with the world outside.

In *The Trial* (1914) Kafka moves from a self-contained vision of personal guilt and inferiority to the quandary of a seemingly guiltless individual in an unjust social order. Unlike Gregor Samsa, Joseph K., the protagonist of *The Trial*, moves about freely in the larger world of the city of Prague. He is the chief clerk in a bank, has an attractive mistress and loving relatives, dines with influential people, and expects others to treat him with the deference due his class and position. One morning, however, his normal routine is interrupted by two warders and an inspector, who tell him that he is accused of some unspecified crime and that he must submit to a series of interrogations preliminary to his eventual trial. For a whole year thereafter K. goes about his business while trying to deal rationally with the unfathomable procedures of his case, at first by himself and then with the help of a lawyer. In his effort to understand these procedures he even listens to the gossip of servant girls, other accused men, sympathetic petty officials, and a disreputable painter who supposedly has connections in the law courts. But he never has a real trial.

Finally, two minor officials in top hats take K. to a deserted quarry out-side the city and stab him in the heart with a butcher knife. K. insists on keeping his intelligence "calm and discriminating to the end." The enor-mity of the injustice inflicted upon him is thus heightened so that it can-not be confused with a bad dream. Also, right up to the end, K. is con-scious of being attractive, particularly to women, because he is an accused man. In presenting his protagonist in this sympathetic light Kafka makes his alleged guilt seem a kind of special privilege to other people who are vaguely aware of the unjust system under which they all live.

In *The Trial,* Joseph K. is caught in what the critic Erich Heller calls "the moral law of a boundlessly deceitful world, and performs in a to-tally incalculable domain, ruled by evil demons, the most precise mathe-matical measurements. . . . It is an excruciatingly familiar world, but reproduced by a creative intelligence which is endowed with the knowl-edge that it is a world damned for ever."[20] It is damned because it is based on lies, total deceit, and evil. As K. says when he first appears before the Examining Magistrate: "What has happened to me . . . is representative of a misguided policy which is being directed against many other people as well."[21] Speaking of the "great organization" that is persecuting him, he says that its significance "consists in this, that innocent persons are ac-cused of guilt, and senseless proceedings are put into motion against them." Almost everyone who tries to help K. is deceitful. One employee in the Law Court says: "Perhaps none of us is hardhearted, we should be glad to help everybody, yet as Law Court officials we easily take on the appearance of being hardhearted and of not wanting to help. That really worries me." (This attitude prophesies that of the "kind-hearted" con-centration-camp guards of a later time.) In the chapter, "The Whipper," K. says of some underlings who were being beaten for having abused him, ". . . in my view they are not guilty. The guilt lies with the organi-zation. It is the high officials who are guilty." In this judiciary system the ranks of officials mounted endlessly; even the initiated could not survey the hierarchy as a whole. Since the proceedings of the courts were usu-ally kept secret from subordinate officials, "they could hardly ever quite follow in their further progress the cases on which they had worked; any particular case thus appeared in their circle of jurisdiction often without their knowing whence it came, and passed from it they knew not whither." After a certain stage the case "was being conducted in remote, inaccessible Courts, where even the accused was beyond the reach of a lawyer."

The judiciary system described in *The Trial* is not that of ordinary state law but is rather a surrealistic symbol of the "totalitarian" structure of the modern world. In this world life has been reduced to a naked power struggle in which man no longer acts according to his own free moral decisions.[22] With clear, unembellished prose and with little drama Kafka sets forth an apocalyptic vision that corresponds to the more exaggerated ones of the prewar Expressionists. K.'s personal apocalypse of estrangement expresses the private and metaphysical correlative of the destruction of human rights in a totalitarian world.

Kafka's novels before and after the First World War (*The Castle* was finished in 1920) were paralleled by other prophecies of doom, such as Robert Musil's *The Man Without Qualities* (1930–33) and Thomas Mann's *The Magic Mountain* (1924). But in a less apocalyptic way Mann's *Buddenbrooks*, published in 1901, already transformed the novel into a medium for cultural criticism. Mann was the first German writer to indicate the disintegration of the traditional bourgeois structured universe. He used the example of a Lübeck family of big merchants to symbolize this disintegration by means of the sickness and death of its leading members at the end of the nineteenth century. For the rest of his life Mann alternated between despair over the new barbarism and efforts to reassert the humanistic values of the age of Goethe. Like many of his prewar contemporaries Mann followed Nietzsche's dictum that art was the last metaphysical activity within the context of European nihilism: the meaninglessness of reason, science, traditional morals and law under the new barbarism. These writers and artists believed that they could no longer concern themselves merely with aesthetic truth—that they must either keep silent or compete with the professional seekers of knowledge, who have been co-opted by the established order. Art must struggle to be the last disinterested form of knowledge. As such it must criticize culture in the broadest sense and expose the totalitarian and inhuman features of the modern world.

HEIGHTENED SELF-CONSCIOUSNESS IN AN AGE OF DISCONTINUITY

While cultural critics like Thomas Mann continued to use conventional language and literary forms, other writers sought to evoke the destructuring of the bourgeois-liberal order as they saw it by transforming poetry and the novel in new ways. Their discontinuous writing expressed their vision of a discontinuous universe. From Rimbaud through Proust and Pirandello the new media themselves were to reveal the real "message."

The French poet Arthur Rimbaud (1854–91) was an extreme prototype of all succeeding creative artists who rejected the conventional aesthetic media of modern civilization. His influence on modern poetry began among his older contemporaries known as Symbolists, particularly Verlaine and Stéphane Mallarmé (1842–98). Like Rimbaud, they tried to strip language of all connecting links—grammar, syntax, accepted meanings of words—that stood in the way of their self-conscious visions. They deliberately cultivated obscurity of expression and invented new symbols for the meanings that could not be expressed in a language contaminated by modern rhetoric.

Mallarmé proclaimed that poems are made of words, not ideas, and he tried to strip words of their civilized connotations and give them back their original, primitive sense. Along with the other Symbolists, Mallarmé tried to create a form of speech that revealed our inner powers and that had its own value as pure sound. His ambition to write poetry that would live by and for itself was a form of exile comparable to Rimbaud's physical exile in Africa and to the Symbolist painter Paul Gauguin's flight to Tahiti. In order to achieve this kind of poetry the Symbolists combined words so that neither their literal meaning nor their conventional poetic meaning were any longer the key to the images and feelings they evoked. In his sonnet *La Vierge, le vivace et le bel aujourd'hui*, Mallarmé often used the same word to symbolize two different things at the same time. This sonnet describes a swan whose wings are caught in a frozen lake, but Mallarmé uses the swan to symbolize the sensitive poet prevented from developing his genius fully in the crass, complacent bourgeois order of the late nineteenth century.

Just as the destruction of conventional language by Rimbaud, Mallarmé, and the twentieth-century Symbolist poets in Europe and America expressed the disintegration of bourgeois consciousness and social discourse, so the destructuring of the bourgeois novel expressed the destructuring of the bourgeois-liberal order itself. In the novels of the nineteenth century the autonomous individual was presumed to be able to find his way by his own efforts in a familiar structured universe. But in the early twentieth century the forms of this medium began to break down in certain avant-garde works as the world in which their protagonists operated became increasingly impersonal and unfamiliar. In the immediate prewar years the novels of Kafka, Proust, and Pirandello dealt with nonheroes desperately trying to reassure themselves that they had any individual identity at all in a world where individualist values were contradicted or ignored in practice. The destruction of conventional plot and character development as a means of portraying the deterioration of the individual personality in a disoriented world was to be intensified in the postwar works of these authors.

This kind of deterioration was already highlighted in the Expressionist first novel of Kafka's friend Max Brod, *Nornepygge Castle: The Novel of the Indifferent One* (1908). Its protagonist, Walder Nornepygge, envies ordinary people because they automatically accept the fool's paradise in which they live. Their life style gives them their identity.

> They are fenced in by certain habits, hobbies, instincts, prejudices; they live happily; they operate a firmly defined individuality. And it surrounds them like a wall, gives them strength and courage, helps them across contradictions, dims their consciousness so that they never learn of their lack of freedom. Style hides for them the strings on which necessity pulls them. . . . They live . . . But I . . . alas, am weary, my logic is prompt and neat. . . . I am nothing but consciousness.[23]

Walder's overdeveloped self-consciousness prevents the changing roles he assigns himself—Don Juan, devoted husband, decadent hedonist, political revolutionary—from becoming his real self. This precursor of The Man Without Qualities already knows that his innermost personality is lack of personality. "I float along with the wind, I am transparent, I am nothing at all but a warm breeze, a questioning intonation, an unaspirated H."

The metaphoric visualizations that Kafka himself used in *The Metamorphosis*, *The Trial*, and *The Castle* seemed particularly appropriate for the modern age, according to the Abstract Expressionist painter Kandinsky. He claimed that the aesthetic media of earlier times no longer sufficed in an age of multifaceted and ambiguous personalities. The truly modern sensibility demands to experience in art the mysteries of the human soul rather than realistic portrayals of daily living. The kinds of abstract characters and dreamlike scenes that Kafka, the later Strindberg, and many Expressionist writers used allowed them to "pack a very great emotional complexity and extensive meaning into a very small space with the resultant heightening of concentration and pungency."[24]

Marcel Proust (1872–1922) used the new medium of the *roman-fleuve* to carry the destructuring of the novel even further than the Expressionists in his *Remembrance of Things Past (À la recherche du temps perdu)*, the first volume of which was published in 1913. In this vast work the author-protagonist abandons conventional forms of plot and sequence, which hide the discontinuities in the world and in individuals' experiences. Instead he tries to

> describe men—even should that give them the semblance of monstrous creatures—as occupying in Time a place far more considerable than the so restricted one allotted them in space, a place, on the contrary, extending boundlessly since, giant-like, reaching far back into the years, they touch simultaneously epochs of their lives—with countless intervening days between—so widely separated from one another in Time.[25]

To accomplish this task Proust shuts himself away from the world and, through memory, re-creates impressions that he plumbs to their depths, brings into the light, and transforms into intellectual equivalents. He takes as a landmark in the enormous dimension of time the tinkling of a little bell which he had heard in his childhood at Combray.

> When the bell tinkled, I was already in existence, and, since that night, for me to have been able to hear the sound again, there must have been no break of continuity, not a moment of rest for me, no cessation of existence, of thought, of consciousness of myself, since this distant moment still clung to me and I could recapture it, go back to it, merely by descending more deeply within myself. It was this conception of time as incarnate, of past years as still close held within us, which I was now determined to bring out into such bold relief in my book. . . . This dimension of Time . . . I would try to make continually perceptible in a transcription of human life necessarily very different from that conveyed to us by our deceptive senses.

The form of this novel expresses the author-protagonist's growing awareness of a discontinuous universe. Since Proust felt that it was hopeless to seek his true reality in his ever-changing private existence and the continual transformation of the world, he looked within himself. What he found in this search he tried to preserve in a work of art: "Great works of art are less disappointing than life, for they do not begin by giving us the best of themselves." Out of the flux of his memories Proust eventually found a kind of reward in the continuous movement between his analytic intelligence and the pathos of temporal existence. In his book he tries to recapture the unique events in his life in a gigantic dense mesh of complicated relations with innumerable cross-references between different groups of characters. Among the major topics he weaves into his rambling narrative are art, politics, social ambition, and the elusiveness of physical reality. He is especially concerned with the foibles of love.

The Narrator and all the characters in *Remembrance of Things Past* suffer from some kind of unsatisfied longing or disappointed hope. The lovers who fix their aspirations upon other human beings are frustrated, because love, according to Proust, is a fatal drama leading to inevitable catastrophe. It is played by people who seek each other out, establish momentary relationships, wound and irritate their partners, separate, and forget them. Love cannot last, not only because time destroys it, but also because each person is imprisoned in his own world, which is isolated and impenetrable.

Love is a spell, as in a fairy tale. The initial physical attraction is fortuitous. Love really takes hold only as the result of an internal crisis caused by the fear of losing the person who interests us. Thus, Swann does not fall in love with Odette until the evening she fails to appear at a rendezvous, and he, distraught with anxiety, searches for her in the cafes and streets of Paris. The Narrator too does not totally suspend his normal activities in order to devote himself to Albertine until he learns of her attachment for Mademoiselle Vinteuil.

Eventually the causes of the enchantment lose their force, and habit sets in. Then jealousy appears, and it revives the anxiety over losing the loved one. Here the pathological side of love is most evident. Speaking of Swann's feelings toward Odette in later years, Proust says: "Regrets over a mistress and persistent jealousy are physical diseases like tuberculosis or leukemia." No individual can satisfy the emotional needs of another. Even those characters who pursue evil and perversity for their own sake, like Baron de Charlus near the end of Proust's novel, are disappointed when their satisfaction depends upon others.

Concerned with the age-old drama of appearance versus reality, Proust's contemporary Luigi Pirandello (1867–1936) sought to shock modern Europeans into realizing how they duped themselves into believing they knew who and what they were. During the early 1920's he was to find the medium for expressing this drama in plays like *Six Characters in Search of an Author*, *Henry IV*, and *Naked*, but before the war he was already developing it in his short stories and his early novel *The Late Mattia Pascal* (1904). Like James Joyce's *Portrait of the Artist as a Young Man* and Thomas Mann's *Tonio Kröger* this novel marks the artist's sublimation of his alienation into heightened self-consciousness. Thereafter his whole literary and dramatic oeuvre is an exploration of consciousness. But by exploding the notion of a fixed personal identity Pirandello does not necessarily imply the moral annihilation of the individual self. Like Kafka, Brod, and Proust, he seems rather to be trying to dissuade human beings from taking one another and even themselves for granted. In Pirandello's fictional world the elusive reality of personal existence is intensified by his depiction of the predominantly petty-bourgeois structured universe of his characters as coming apart at the seams.

The plot of *The Late Mattia Pascal* concerns a young librarian who, while returning from a gambling spree at Monte Carlo sparked by his suffering over the death of his mother and daughter, reads in a newspaper that a corpse in a stream near his home town has been pronounced a suicide and identified as his own by his wife. After his initial bewilderment Mattia leaps at the chance to live a new life. "I was dead! And a dead man has no debts! A dead man has no wife! A dead man has no mother-in-law! What more could a fellow ask for? I was free, free, free!" Refusing conventions and the lie of the hated mask he had been forced to wear, he resolves to live in a new dimension of pure consciousness, "free of the complicating coils that had been strangling me." After traveling from town to town under the name of Adriano Meis, Mattia decides to live frugally on the remainder of his winnings at Monte Carlo and he moves into a boardinghouse in Rome. There he soon realizes that his fictional existence as Adriano makes his relations with other people even more intolerable than those of his former life as Mattia. He cannot marry the girl he has fallen in love with (who has the female version of his name—Adriana) because he has no papers to prove that he is Adriano and because as Mattia he is legally married already. Finally his position in Rome is made impossible by an almost farcical episode in which he is challenged to a duel and cannot find anyone to be his seconds. So he stages a second "suicide," this time of Adriano, and decides to return to his home town. There he finds his wife married to his best friend and nursing a one-year-old child. Mattia is almost as much an outsider here as he had been as Adriano in Rome.

As in so many of Pirandello's plays, the story of Mattia Pascal ends ambiguously. A priest tells Mattia, who has gone to live with an aunt, that "outside the law of the land, and apart from those little happenings . . . that make us each what we are, life . . . is impossible." Mattia replies that he fails to see how that can be, for he has not regularized either his legal or his private life. "My wife is the wife of Pomino, and I'm not quite sure who I am myself!"[26] From time to time Mattia visits the grave of the unknown suicide whose tombstone bears his name. When somebody asks him who he really is, he answers: "Why, what can I say? . . . I guess I'm the late Mattia Pascal!"

Georges Braque, *Still Life with Violin and Pitcher* (1910).

In this novel Pirandello was already grappling with the new medium that would convey his "message" in his postwar plays. His objective and realistic portrayal of grotesque situations and the crisis of ordinary human relationships is in sharp contrast to the rhetorical and theatrical conventions of Classical and Romantic drama. The inhabitants of the Roman boardinghouse seem like puppets with their petty concerns and their ignorance of the artificiality of their structured universe. This point is made explicit in a conversation betweeen Mattia and Anselmo Paleari, an elderly gentleman who lives there. Anselmo has just invited Mattia to see a puppet-theater version of Sophocles' *Elektra* and says:

> I've just thought of something. Suppose that, just at the climax, when the puppet representing Orestes is about to avenge his father's death on Aegisthus and his mother, someone should suddenly tear a hole in the paper ceiling over the stage. . . . Orestes would be quite flabbergasted by that hole in the sky. . . . The whole difference between ancient and modern tragedy consists of that—a hole in the paper sky.

Sighing, Mattia replies:

> How lucky the puppets are! The make-believe heaven over their heads is rarely torn apart; and if it is, it can be glued together again. They can just sit still, enjoying their comedy, loving, respecting, admiring each other, never getting flustered, never losing their heads; because their characters and their actions are all proportioned to the blue roof that covers them. And the prototype of these puppets, my dear Mr. Anselmo, you have right here in your own house in the person of that precious son-in-law of yours.

It is Mattia's consciousness that forces these unsettling perceptions on him. By reducing the proportion of the human drama to that of self-deceived puppets Pirandello is able to tear a hole in the paper sky that symbolizes the false version of the world in which it takes place. Through Mattia he shows the awful loneliness in the consciousness of a fractured ordinary man who fails in his anarchic attempt to free himself from convention and discovers the impossibility of any escape from the formless flux of experience. Pirandello was too positivistic and skeptical to push this discovery to the position adopted by the Existentialists: a constructive quest for self-awareness in that flux. For him, as for Proust and the Symbolist poets, the only deliverance from life in a discontinuous universe was through art.

Pablo Picasso, *Nude* (1910), charcoal.

CUBISM, FUTURISM, AND THE BEGINNINGS OF MODERN ARCHITECTURE

Cubism is probably the best-known and certainly the most extreme ex-ample before 1914 of an attempt to approach the many-sided and often contradictory aspects of modern reality through a new artistic language. Georges Braque (1882–1963), Juan Gris (José Victoriano Gonzalez, 1887–1927), and Pablo Ruiz Picasso (1881–1973) in his Cubist period, painted in a deliberately ambiguous language for a century that ques-tioned the very possibility of absolute truth or value. The sensitive viewer of a Cubist work of art soon understood that there could be no single, complete interpretation of the fluctuating shapes, spaces, textures, and objects before him. It offered him a visual equivalent of the twen-tieth-century awareness of the problematic character of reality and the need for describing it in multiple and paradoxical ways.

Braque and Picasso produced their first Cubist paintings in 1908, and, al-though Braque, Gris, and others remained Cubists after the war, the movement's heyday was between 1910 and 1914. The cubelike forms in Braque's 1908 painting *Maison à l'Estaque* prompted one critic to invent the term "Cubist," but the medium itself soon became more two-dimen-sional and, by 1912, included bits of pasted papers (*papiers collés*) and other materials glued to the painted canvas (*collages*). The complexity and variety of Cubist works of art have sparked all sorts of inter-pretations regarding their origins and meaning. But almost all the critics agree that what distinguishes Cubism from all previous art, at least in Europe, is its basic assumption that art and conventional perceptions of nature have nothing in common.

Whatever its subject matter, a Cubist painting represents nothing but itself. The Cubists assumed that a painting is only a painting and that it should look no more like a segment of real space than a building ought to resemble a football. For the first time in history they divorced the means of representation from anything represented. In principle, it did not mat-ter what they painted, though most often they chose still-life objects from their own bohemian surroundings: drinking glasses, musical instru-ments, pipes, newspapers, and even nudes. But, whatever the objects ren-dered by the artist, his sole concern was the object created by him, that is the picture itself.

In a Cubist picture form is not a fixed or finite characteristic of objects. According to Picasso, there are no concrete or abstract forms in art "but only forms which are more or less convincing lies."

Art is a lie that makes us realize truth, at least the truth that is given to us to understand. The artist must know how to convince others of the truthfulness of his lies. . . . Through art we express our conception of what nature is not. . . . That those lies are necessary to our mental selves is beyond any doubt, as it is through them that we form our aesthetic view of life.[27]

Although Picasso also insisted that Cubism was no different from any other school of painting in its goals, no other school had ever been so exclusively concerned with purely aesthetic considerations and none had broken so completely with conventional visions of the forms of real objects.

Braque's *Still Life with Violin and Pitcher* (1910) illustrates what the new artistic language of Cubism was trying to express. It exudes visual and intellectual paradoxes. The pitcher, presumably made of glass, appears more opaque than the violin, whose wooden substance seems to dissolve into transparent fragments. The sharp cut of the triple molding and wall at the right give an illusion of depth that is belied in the rest of the picture by the oscillating planes that seem to have fluttered in from the air and got stuck on the surface of the canvas. In this painting space has acquired an ambiguous pliancy, warped, hollowed, and steam-rollered, but always striving to define itself. The viewer has so much difficulty "locating" himself in this and other Cubist canvases because of his preconception that depth is continuously perceptible in space. The crowning paradox is the *trompe-l'oeil* nail that seems to project outward from the top of this picture and cast a shadow on its flat surface. Conceived as external reality, this nail is just as false as the apparently unreal Cubist still life under it but is just as true when conceived as art.

The Cubists were trying to give us a new conception of space, somewhat as Proust did with time. Neither he nor they were aware of Einstein's Theory of Relativity, and their new languages were as different from his as all art is from science. Yet in their own way they too were expressing new ideas of nature as formless and indeterminate and trying to show that space and time are relative to the relationships we conceive within them. Proust's novel encompasses the principle of "intermittence," according to which the temporal aspect of our humanity makes it impossible to resolve the different and often conflicting aspects of the reality we perceive into a unitive point of view. In his search for lost time even the Narrator finds "not oneself, but a succession of selves." Picasso said: "I paint objects as I think them, not as I see them." And, according to Braque, "the relationship between things is more important than the things themselves." The Cubist painters wanted to impose a purely aesthetic, multifaceted order on the discontinuous dimensions of the universe.

The purity that the Cubist language had achieved by 1910 can be seen especially clearly in Picasso's charcoal *Nude*. As the art historian Robert Rosenblum says of it:

> The impulse toward fragmentation of surfaces into component planes is now so strong that the very core of matter seems finally to be disclosed as a delicately open structure of interlocking arcs and angles. Yet paradoxically, if this form appears to dissolve outward into the openness of the surrounding void, it also appears to coalesce inward into a strangely crystalline substance.[28]

By 1911 the Cubist syntax had grown so complicated that it threatened to obscure the relationships of the "real" elements the artists were trying to fuse into an autonomous whole.

In 1912 Picasso and Braque revitalized their effort to show the paradoxical relationships between reality and art by introducing *papiers collés* and *collages* into their paintings. With this surprising but logical extension of their basic vocabulary their paintings lost their small, broken, shadowy transitions and emphasized prominent, self-contained contrasts. The connections and disconnections are now self-evident. No longer does the viewer's eye have to make countless tiny scans. Maximum visual impact is achieved by simplifying the patterns and reducing the armature and the number of superimpositions. Thus the viewer can quickly move on to seeing the basic conception behind the work.

Picasso first used a *collage* (which in French slang connotes two people living together) by gluing a piece of oilcloth with a chair-caning pattern onto his canvas in *Still Life with Chair-Caning* (1912). Here the paradox between art and reality, between true and false, is more explicit than in earlier Cubist works. Since the oilcloth is a machine-made product from the outside world, it is in one sense more real than the illusory Cubist still-life objects created by Picasso. Yet, since it is only an imitation of chair caning, it is as false as the fictional objects painted around and over it. Indeed, some of these objects, particularly the pipestem, convey a feeling of true depth that contrasts vividly with the flatness of the chair caning. Picasso creates another contrast by surrounding his canvas with a real rope, which functions as a conventional picture frame but contradicts this function by seeming to be decorative woodcarving on a flat surface from which the illusory objects within the picture project outward.

The "message" of Cubist *collages* is that no single medium, such as oil on canvas, can give us a credible pictorial view of reality in the twentieth century. Sensitive people have become too conscious of discontinuities in the world around them and of the disconnectedness of all sensation. The Cubists believed—and here they unwittingly paralleled much contemporary thought—that there are only propositions about reality. And one of these propositions is that things are related to one another on different levels. Thus the artist must not only synthesize traditional and commercial media but he must also play on the spatial and tactile discrepancies among them. The different materials he uses determine the subject matter as well as the form of the painting. In this sense each of the diverse media provides its own reality, and their juxtaposition conveys its own message.

Collages and *papiers collés* helped the language of Cubism develop toward a simpler, clearer kind of painting that could mix sensual and mechanical elements. Picasso's *Woman in an Armchair* (1913) has been called "a deft misalliance of 'living' geometry and creaturely objects." This Cubist version of a boudoir sex object has her disemboweled, with her hair moistly streaming and her underwear crumpled. The fragments of her body are immersed in or propped up by Cubist versions of machine-like forms. Yet her sensuality comes through in the tawny hues of her flesh and the large sinuous curves that frame her. Marcel Duchamp's mechanical nudes, especially his famous *Nude Descending a Staircase* (1913), carried the simile of the body as an inorganic assembly of moving parts much further than Picasso. In Duchamp's mind, machines were even capable of reproducing themselves through a mating process of their own. And the human figures in the paintings of Fernand Léger look frankly like robots. This merging of human and mechanical imagery was perhaps the most immediately accessible Cubist response to the impact of modernization.

Unlike the Cubists, the Futurists set out to change life as well as art. Both groups were in some sense responding to the ways in which industrialization was destroying art's traditional vision of nature as a system of imaginary relations among a multitude of single objects each having a unique location and replacing it with repeated series of identical objects; both groups subverted conventional conceptions of space in order to show the multiple relations that were possible among objects. But the Futurists carried these experiments beyond pure aesthetics into revolutionary acts. The Cubists—except for a peripheral one like Léger—expressed no enthusiasm for the symbolic values associated with the machine age. But the Futurists glorified man-made energy and machinery and wanted to use their speed, power, and violence to force revolutionary changes in society and politics as well as in all fields of culture. In 1909, in his first manifesto, their major spokesman and impresario, the wealthy Italian poet Filippo Tommaso Marinetti, proclaimed: "A roaring motor car is more beautiful than the Victory of Samothrace" (the well-known Greek statue *Winged Victory* in the Louvre Museum in Paris).

Exactly contemporary with Cubism, Futurism included the painter-sculptor Umberto Boccioni (1882–1916) and the painters Giacomo Balla (1871–1958), Carlo Carrà (1881–1966), Luigi Russolo (1885–1947), and Gino Severini (1883–1966). Between 1909 and 1914 the Italian Futurists issued over thirty manifestoes in Paris, Madrid, Berlin, and London as well as in Milan, Florence, and Rome. Offshoots of Futurism were also flourishing in Moscow when Marinetti finally got there. No other avant-garde movement had such a pervasive and long-lasting influence or matched its hostility for the past and its mania for the new. For the Futurists all experience was provisional. They therefore wanted to set up an art of the becoming, the perishable, the transitory, and the expendable. Some of these goals were to be taken up by the Dadaists and Surrealists immediately after the First World War and by the creators of "happenings" in the 1950's and 1960's. But from the historian's point of view the Futurists' works of art as well as their manifestoes remain startling documents of the most optimistic response to modernization in the twentieth century.

The Futurists were fascinated with speed and the dynamic qualities of electric light. In his *The Street Light—Study of Light* (1909) Balla immerses the viewer in a glittering network of electrical and magnetic charges whose multiple stresses suggest invisible forces under man's control. Balla's *Speeding Automobile* (1912) conveys the kinetic activity of this ultracontemporary subject in a bursting web of transparent, overlapping planes. Because its great speed cannot be located in a single, static position, the image of the dynamic metal machine is broken down into multiple and partial views. And Balla suggests the sudden, dazzling play of the headlights on the metal body with intersecting beams and arcs. Whereas Balla captures the perception of a swiftly moving motorcar by disintegrating its mass, Russolo, in his *Dynamism of an Automobile* (1912), transforms the same subject into a convoluted, bullet-like mass bending the intervals of space through which it hurtles.

Futurist painters also exalted the dynamism of the modern city. Unlike the Impressionists, whose images of it were basically static, they por-

Giacomo Balla, *Street Light* (1909), oil on canvas, 68¾ × 45¼″.

trayed it as perpetual movement and excitement, as in Boccioni's drawing, *Street Forces* (1911). Carrà and Severini evoked the bustle of Parisian buses, streetcars, and railroad stations in several studies. And no one in this period surpassed Carrà's depiction of the emotion of an urban riot in his *Funeral of the Anarchist Galli.* (1911).

In 1912 and 1913 Balla tried to paint images of movement through time. His *Iridescent Transparencies*—one of which is called *Today Is Tomorrow*—are series of repeated abstractions. In *Girl Running on a Balcony* he uses a series of recognizable physical gestures. Seen from a distance, this painting gives the effect of motion-picture frames, in which everything occurs simultaneously and there are no distinctions between the beginning and the end of the action. Viewed close up the palpitating colored blocks out of which the painting is constructed appear as a loosely set mosaic. But finally we grasp Balla's conception of space as a visual substitute for time.

The most famous example of Futurist sculpture, Boccioni's *Unique Forms of Continuity in Space* (1913), seems at first glance like a defiant twentieth-century answer to the *Victory of Samothrace*, which Marinetti had specifically condemned in his first manifesto. But one soon sees that it is not a "statue" at all. Boccioni has abandoned the organic and individualized suggestion of movement in past sculpture and substituted a metaphor of abstract growth intimated by qualities of ruthless, mechanistic will. As he wrote while exhibiting this work in Paris: "My spiral, architectonic construction . . . creates before the spectator a continuity of form-force released by the *real* form, a new, close line, delineating the body in its material movements. The form-force, with its centrifugal direction, is the potentiality of the real form."[29] The bursting energy "released" in this striding, gladiator-like figure dissects the flesh and muscles into fragments that seem to bend and lacerate the space around them in an almost palpable way. This compelling masterpiece expresses the infinite possibilities of transforming matter and energy into one another and destroys the notion that matter occupies space in fixed forms. It makes us feel in our own bodies the power and dynamism unleashed by modern civilization.

The Futurists did not always unite art and life in their works the way Boccioni's sculpture did, but this was the supreme goal they proclaimed in their manifestoes. Although they had little patience with ideological or philosophical systems, some of them felt that their art was an example of Bergson's Creative Evolution. In the August 1, 1913, issue of the Florentine review *Lacerba*, Boccioni said that "the Futurist painters can bring

Umberto Boccioni, *Unique Forms of Continuity in Space* (1913), bronze, 43⅞ × 34⅞ × 15¾".

about the great dynamic realization of evolution." Their surging creative consciousness would unite with a new consciousness of life. In order to achieve this union, however, Marinetti insisted that "art can only be violence, cruelty, injustice." Futurist art, according to Boccioni, would inflame the industrial workers with "the uproar, the scientific division of work in the factories . . . anxiety!, rapidity!, precision! . . . the screaming of the siren . . . the pulsation of the motors." (Needless to say, this euphoric vision was not shared by real factory workers.) The Futurists also tried to glorify the English music hall, which they mistakenly took for a new popular medium, as a means of giving the working classes a new sensibility when combined with motion-picture images of battles, riots, races, and speeding autombiles and airplanes.[30] In Italy, where resistance to modernization was particularly strong, they tried to shake the country out of its rut with sensational posters and spectacles urging its intervention in the First World War. After the war had failed to accomplish this purpose some of the Futurists were to see in Fascism the revolutionary agency that would finally bring about the combined revolution in art and life which they were seeking. But unlike the postwar German Expressionists, who saw similar hope in revolutionary socialism, these Futurists remained elitists. For them, "the people" were simply another "mass" to be plastically orchestrated.

The revolutionary cultural atmosphere created by Expressionism, Cubism, Futurism, and Abstract Art helped launch the modern movement in architecture through the Deutscher Werkbund (German Arts and Crafts Society) and the influence of Peter Behrens (1868–1940). In 1907, the year in which this meeting place of progressive industrialists, architects, and designers was founded, Behrens joined the Allgemeine Elektrizitäts-Gesellschaft (General Electric Company) of Berlin and took charge of designing its new buildings, its products, its packaging, and even its stationery. His pupil-assistants included Walter Gropius (1883–1969), Ludwig Miës van der Rohe (1886–1969), and Le Corbusier (Édouard Jeanneret-Gris, 1887–1965). Both Behrens and the architects in the Werkbund insisted that aesthetics could be independent of material quality, that standardization could be a virtue, and that product design could be based on abstract form. In 1909 Behrens' Turbine Factory proclaimed a new, monumental dignity for industrial architecture. Two years later Gropius and Adolf Meyer began building the Fagus Works at Alfeld, near Hanover. Like much pre-1914 avant-grade art, the new "language" of this structure has become a cliché, but at the time it was truly

Traditional public architecture: Brussels Palace of Justice.

Bruno Taut, Glass Pavilion, at the Werkbund exhibition in Cologne, 1914.

revolutionary, with the stark rhythms of its main block, the glazing continuing around the rounded corners, the flat roof with no cornice, and the horizontal banding of the porch.

In 1914 the Werkbund exhibition at Cologne summarized the ways in which modern architecture would develop, particularly in Henri van de Velde's Model Theatre, Gropius' and Meyer's office and factory building, and the pavilion for the German glass industry of Bruno Taut (1880–1938). In his Model Theatre van de Velde completely dissociated himself from the Art Nouveau type of decoration and found purely architectural solutions to the solidity and sculptural form of the building. He also stressed its plasticity by contrasting the molded forms of its exterior with its classically organized plan. Taut's pavilion was more visionary, with its effort to extend the interior outward by means of glass, color, and light. In his experiments with the architectural potential of glass, concrete, and steel, Taut was already developing new ideas for the prefabrication of building elements.[31] Although Gropius' factory appears clumsy compared to van de Velde's and Taut's structures, the future lay with him and those architects who felt as he did. What they still lacked was an aesthetic principle with which to make sense of their cantilevers, transparencies, glass walling, and other technical innovations.[32] Only after the war was the movement toward Abstract Art to inspire Gropius and his associates to invent the principle of Functionalism for architecture.

If Functionalism means making style the servant of use, then much of what passes for modern architecture does not measure up to this standard. The familiar concrete-and-glass shoe boxes or slabs that were constructed from the late 1920's on have generalized, multipurpose structural designs that can lend themselves to any function. This so-called International Style is an anonymous, stylized structuralism. It is so unrelated to any particular time or place that it can house a book publisher in New York, a trade-union headquarters in Hamburg, a bank in Tokyo, a theater in Sydney, or an airport in Mexico City. Before 1914 the prophet of an architecture that would adapt every design to its own specific use was the Viennese Adolf Loos (1870–1933).

Loos did not consider himself a revolutionary; like the prophets of the

Adolf Loos, Steiner House, Vienna (1910).

Old Testament he condemned everything he saw as bad in his own society and culture but, unlike most revolutionaries, he held no final vision of what was good. He believed that each time must create its own style. In the early 1900's he saw his task as eliminating all meaningless detail and decoration from the buildings he designed. He wanted to achieve his effects only with immediately available construction materials.

For Loos ornamentation of any kind was synonymous with poor quality goods and corrupted, snobbish feelings. He viewed even the most solid and expensive public buildings in imperial Vienna as empty symbols of bygone majesty. And he condemned as *Kitsch* (artistic rubbish) the bric-a-brac with which the Viennese bourgeoisie cluttered their homes. "New aspects of our civilization (railroad cars, telephones, typewriters, etc.) must be resolved without conscious echoes of stylistic forms already outdated."[33] Loos also believed that modern architects had to meet the needs of people forced to live in constricted environments. Even the furniture must be part of the walls as much as possible, such as built-in tables, beds, desks, and wardrobes.

The 1910 building in the Michaelerplatz (see illustration on page 105) was a famous example of Loos's notion of spatial economy. This combination private dwelling and store had a completely smooth front; even its windows had no decorative frames or "eyebrows." Inside no space was wasted by useless dividing walls, lowered ceilings, or stairwells. Around the reception room, with its high ceiling, raised office areas were partially enclosed by low, open dividers. Below these office areas were fitting rooms, reached by an open staircase. The split-level suburban homes of the 1950's stemmed from Loos's 1910 innovation.

According to Loos, the architect must think like an engineer and concentrate on the "functional necessities" of everything he designs. "If you want to understand the significance of, for example, the system of water piping in a house, look at the *use* to which that system is put."[34] During his three-year stay in the United States in the mid-1890's Loos acquired a permanent awareness of the contrast between the modern, democratic life style he perceived there and the old-fashioned, class-ridden culture of his native Austria. For the rest of his life he was the outstanding pioneer for unadorned mass-produced goods of good quality for all social classes. He wanted houses, furniture, and even clothes to be as simple and functional as possible so that all people could devote themselves to the noblest activities of life.

Before 1914 only two architects, Tony Garnier (1869–1948) and Antonio Sant'Elia (1888–1916), tried to deal with the physical problems of

Antonio Sant'Elia, *Città Nuova:* sketch of a building with exterior elevator.

city living by designing new urban complexes. Garnier's plan for an ideal Industrial City (Cité Industrielle) was first exhibited in 1904. It located factories, public buildings, and private housing to suit the convenience and comfort of the people who used them rather than the greed of real estate promoters. All the buildings in Garnier's plan were to use reinforced concrete, the private ones being severely cubic, the public ones with cantilevering canopies whose boldness matched those of Frank Lloyd Wright's houses. Sant'Elia's designs for his New City (Città Nuova) were not co-ordinated like Garnier's, but the individual structures were even more revolutionary. For Sant'Elia was a Futurist.

Sant'Elia's numerous imaginative drawings of buildings and town-planning ideas were first exhibited in May 1914, and on July 11 a manifesto of Futurist architecture (reworked by Marinetti) appeared over his name. According to this manifesto, Futurist architects must start from scratch in constructing their buildings

> with all the resources of science and technology. They must take ample account of all the demands of our habits and our dispositions, rejecting everything that goes against our spirit—tradition, style, aesthetics, proportion—and create completely new forms and lines . . . in an architecture whose reasons for existence are derived strictly from the special conditions of modern life.

In the completely new Futurist city:

> Elevators must no longer insinuate themselves like solitary worms in the stairwells. Instead, the stairs, now useless, must disappear whereas the elevators must climb up the outer surface of the buildings like snakes of iron and glass. . . . The houses of concrete, glass, and iron . . . must soar up from the brink of a tumultuous abyss: the street. This street will no longer be a pavement spread out at the level of the ground-floor entrances but will be sunk several stories into the ground, where it will gather up the traffic of the metropolis, with necessary transfers provided by metal cat-walks and high-speed conveyor belts.[35]

Except in a few cities in South America, many of Sant'Elia's ideas are still futuristic today.

MUSIC

Cultural lag in accepting revolutionary changes in music has persisted longer than in the plastic arts, literature, or drama. Even today people who decorate their homes with the most abstruse contemporary paintings and sculpture and who stand in line to see the latest films of Michelangelo Antonioni or Stanley Kubrick still wince at compositions of Anton Webern written over sixty years ago. It is difficult—particularly when one is trapped in a concert hall or an opera house—to abandon the traditional post-Renaissance attitude that music is supposed to *express* something about individual will and feelings and communicate this to an audience. But a major goal of modern music, from Debussy through Stravinsky, Schoenberg, Webern, and Boulez, has been to *reveal* the unconscious as well as preliterate levels of experience usually associated with religion, mysticism, and magic. Intuitively these composers grasped the radical changes that science and technology were forcing sensitive people to make in their conceptions of time and space and the discontinuities within them. These changes are now also recasting our ordinary perceptions and habits of behavior in ways that we find both painful and chaotic because of our post-Gutenberg heritage of rational, linear thinking. Thus many people still cling to familiar forms of musical expression as an escape from their other perplexities. They want relaxation, not revelation.

The avant-garde composers of the early 1900's rejected the structure of feeling of traditional music lovers and the media that had catered to them. Like their counterparts in the plastic arts, literature, and drama, they broke through the façade of order and unity that this structure assumed and saw that it hid more than it revealed about the modern world and the human predicament in it. They also viewed the musical language of the late nineteenth century—with its heavy chromaticism, overblown rhetoric, and interminable repetitions—as incapable of further development for any purpose, let alone theirs of creating a new aesthetic sensibility for their own time and the future. In order to achieve this purpose different composers attacked this language in a variety of ways: Debussy dissolved the harmonic sensuality of Wagner into quasi-Eastern arabesque; Schoenberg and Webern continued the Wagnerian disintegration of harmony into line and moved toward atonal serial structures; Stravinsky exposed man's most violent urges with his unprecedented use of archetypal primitive rhythms in *The Rite of Spring* (1913).

In his opera *Pelléas and Mélisande* (1902) Claude Debussy (1862–1918) used the same scenario that Wagner had in *Tristan and Isolde*—a fatal adulterous love affair involving legendary royalty—but he treated it quite differently. In Wagner's late Romantic opera, when the heroic Tristan knows that he must die he does so by his own will, believing in the ultimate triumph of his consuming passion. Debussy's work, in contrast, dethrones the hero and is naturalistic in expression. For Pelléas and Mélisande the only happiness lies in submitting to a dark emptiness, a destiny they accept will-lessly but without terror. Every aspect of Debussy's music conveys this "message." Its texture is softer and more delicate than Wagner's but it envelops us even more. By avoiding the Wagnerian desire to show how the composer shapes the themes and molds the sonority Debussy gives us a feeling of release among the mists of the unknown with which his music engulfs us. The sonority itself creates a pervasive atmosphere that mutes our conscious passions and makes us respond to those of the performers with an almost oriental passivity—or like a seismograph recording unpredictable tremors.

Until the end of the Second World War, Debussy continued to be viewed as an Impressionist and "soft-focus painter"; only since then have we come to see him as a pioneer comparable to Van Gogh, Cézanne, Rimbaud, and Mallarmé. Some musicologists now consider him the composer who invented the contemporary approach to form, destroyed rhetoric, and reinstated the aesthetic power of pure sound. His own works also carried deep within them the means of transcending the symphony and other large-scale forms to which the Classical and Romantic masters were addicted.

The Viennese composer Arnold Schoenberg (1874–1951) went much further than Debussy in inventing a new musical language. But whereas Debussy developed his language of pure sound with no abrupt break at any point, Schoenberg began in the tradition of late Romanticism, extending elements of the language of Wagner in his early compositions. His youthful enthusiasm for Wagner and Mahler is evident in the morbid ecstasy of his string sextet *Transfigured Night* (1899) and the bombast of his enormous cantata *Gurrelieder*, composed around 1900. But beginning with his *Chamber Symphony*, Opus 9 (1907) and *Five Pieces for Orchestra*, Opus 16 (1909) he moved increasingly toward atonality. Both the atonality and the large intervals of his melodic style created a steady high tension that destroyed the traditional notion of alternating tension and relaxation. For the rest of his life Schoenberg was to develop his concern with the logical articulation of musical ideas.

Schoenberg's emphasis on developing musical ideas versus "pleasant sounds" paralleled the concerns of a number of avant-garde writers and artists of the years before 1914. In Vienna we have already (see pp. 246 and 356–57) noted how Karl Kraus and Hugo von Hofmannsthal rejected the amateur refinements of *fin-de-siècle* bourgeois aestheticism. They sought a purer, more serious literary language, just as Ludwig Wittgenstein wanted to purify philosophical language and analyze it in a strictly professional way and as Adolf Loos sought a no-nonsense architectural language based on functional necessities. In Paris the Cubists also emphasized aesthetic ideas instead of pleasant images in their paintings. But unlike the Futurists and some Expressionists, these artists and writers did not see themselves as revolutionaries. Rather they believed that they were getting back to the basic problems of artistic expression.

In his masterpiece, *Pierrot Lunaire* (1912), Schoenberg fills a series of traditional formal shapes with a totally new world of sound. Formally it is a combination of spoken verse accompanied by a small chamber ensemble; in each of the twenty-one short "songs" the vocalist "speaks" the melody, giving the notated pitch but immediately leaving it to fall or rise. Sometimes the instrumental accompaniment reinforces the vocalist, sometimes it seems to go its own way. The music itself is completely atonal. Each "song" has a style appropriate to the mood being evoked, yet the whole work melts into sound the feelings of the moon-struck Pierrot (a white clown character from the Italian *commedia dell' arte*). The first number describes the rapture of the moon-drunk poet who "swallows the wine from the moon, which only eyes may drink." In the third, Pierrot the Dandy shoves aside rouge and oriental green and makes up his face with moonbeams. Number 15 evokes Pierrot's sweetly plaintive homesickness. Some of the numbers, like the "Gallow's Song" (Number 12) are aphoristic, ghostly, and fleeting; others are dense and fully developed, like "A Chopin Waltz" (5) and "Night" (8). Although Schoenberg claimed to be unconcerned with the texts of these poems aside from their basic moods, his music transforms their *fin-de-siècle* aestheticism into an eerie, expressionistic evocation of strange emanations from outer space.

It was to take Schoenberg over ten years after the composition of *Pierrot Lunaire* to reintegrate atonality into a logical structure by means of the twelve-tone-row principle, but "Night," the eighth piece in this work, already marks the transition to tone-row, or serial, music. Here we already sense the uncompromising responsibility of every single note, which Schoenberg was to insist on increasingly in his serial compositions. Written in the form of a passacaglia, "Night" is built entirely on a three-note motif, which appears in numerous complex variations, sometimes transposed, inverted, or retrograded, sometimes written out as a melody or compressed into chords. Yet it is the extraordinary sounds, with their ritualistic and even magical undertones, rather than the logical structure of the form, which strike the listener. And these sounds are expressionistic. They are consistent with Schoenberg's aesthetic concepts at that time, which were also revealed in his paintings and in the essays and drawings he contributed to Expressionist periodicals in Germany. (The most thoroughly Expressionist achievement in music is the opera *Wozzeck*, composed by Schoenberg's pupil Alban Berg between 1917 and 1921.) Meanwhile it was Schoenberg's pupil Webern who was creating the new musical language that, after the Second World War, was to inspire a new avant-garde whose best-known representatives were Olivier Messiaen (b. 1908), Pierre Boulez (b. 1925), and Karlheinz Stockhausen (b. 1928).

Anton Webern (1883–1945) was even more of a purist than his teacher. The early influence of Wagner and Mahler on him soon disappeared and he had little affinity for Expressionism. He received a strict education in the style of Schoenberg's middle period and later deduced the most radical inferences from it. His exclusive preoccupation with musical ideas convinced him early in his career that an athematic, seemingly discontinuous and fragmented but highly concentrated approach to music was necessary in order to create a new sensibility and to foster the rigorous elaboration of free forms. Like the most hermetic Symbolist poets and like Mondrian, Kandinsky, and other abstract painters, Webern sought to create an artistic language that would exist by and for itself, uncontaminated by emotional or worldly concerns.

Before 1914 Webern already challenged traditional notions of theme and accompanied melodic line and introduced compositional techniques that anticipated his later twelve-tone works. His *Five Movements for String Quartet*, Opus 5 (1909), are musical thoughts that strike the listener as vibrations on the innermost world of his own mind. The brief, slow numbers in Webern's *Six Pieces for Orchestra*, Opus 6 (1910), use tiny, evocative melodic phrases that whimper into silence over repeated chords (in the same pitch and voice) on muted brass, or repeated static figures on harp, celesta, or string harmonics. In this work timbre is as important as pitch, and Webern stressed timbre differences in a melodic line more than any other composer before him. Like Debussy, he made the individual chord an end in itself, but his isolated sounds or tone colors have become discontinuous events as well.

In his compositions of the 1920's and 1930's Webern was to perfect the organization of his microcosmic musical world into highly canonic, strict serial constructions. When Schoenberg was developing his twelve-tone-row principle, he thought of the row as derived from the themes, which crystallized melodic utterances. But Webern was to make the row into a form-generating structure, the only medium within which musical creation could occur. He himself said that the row was not only "the highest reality" but also a revelation and that "a primal blessing shall come to bestow greater blessings." Thus, by transcending the tonal system and by distilling beauty into form alone Webern was to create a kind of purely abstract music hitherto unknown in the Western world.

The concentrated form of Webern's musical language was a complete rejection of the diffuse, repetitive, rhetorical language of late Romanticism. The listener too must concentrate more intensely than ever before in order to apprehend every sound, every change in register and volume, and every silence as part of Webern's microcosm of the whole range of purely musical expression, without ornament and with no reference to anything but itself. Schoenberg said in his Preface to the published score of Webern's *Six Bagatelles for String Quartet,* Opus 9 (1913): "These pieces will only be understood by those who share the faith that music can say things that can only be expressed by music." To be sure, we must retrain our ears and our sensibility in order to have the aesthetic experience that Webern's miniaturistic compositions offer. But this kind of retraining is typical of the modern world—from the first factory workers who had to adapt their reflexes to the rhythm of machines to today's office clerks who have to "think" like computers.

While the music of Webern had almost no repercussions until after his death in 1945, his contemporary Igor Stravinsky (1882–1971) was making musical history before the First World War with three consecutive works—*The Firebird, Petrushka,* and *The Rite of Spring*—all written for Paris performances of the Russian Ballet in 1911, 1912, and 1913 respectively. Indeed, like Picasso in painting, Stravinsky was the most famous and probably the most representative, though hardly the most advanced, figure in twentieth-century music. And like Picasso he went through many different media and had an extremely long and prolific career. In these respects too he differed from Webern, who spent most of his life in isolation elaborating one language in a limited number of incredibly short pieces (some of which take less than a minute to perform). But in his greatest masterpiece, *The Rite of Spring,* Stravinsky made all the revolutionary changes that released the violence and potency of primitive communal passions.

Unlike the single line of development from post-1909 Schoenberg and Webern, Stravinksy's *The Rite of Spring* incorporated many diverse innovations of the decade preceding it. These innovations all involved either consciously analytical efforts to rejuvenate traditional and humanistic forms of musical expression or intuitive attempts to evoke archetypal primitive feelings. At various points in their careers certain composers tried to combine these two approaches, such as Bartók in his *Allegro Barbaro* (1910–11) and Prokofiev in his *Scythian Suite* (1914). Some moved tentatively in this direction—like Richard Strauss in *Salome* and especially *Elektra*—and then relapsed into a baroque-like neo-Romanticism. Others rejected the excessive tonal tensions of Wagner and Strauss and tried to smother primitive passion by using new forms of musical logic and equilibrium to reassert the values of the humanistic tradition. This effort was carried furthest in some of the works of the leading French composers: Ravel, Fauré, Roussel, d'Indy at times, and Debussy himself in an equivocal way. Another group filtered barbaric urges through the tamer feelings expressed in the traditional music of their national folklore. But after passing through this phase Falla, Bartók, and Kodály developed a new musical language that reached back to the sources of the folk music of Spain and Hungary. Stravinsky used early Russian folk music in parts of *Petrushka* but tried to delve even further into man's past in *The Rite of Spring*.

During the early years of this century a number of avant-garde composers became preoccupied with the wild, primitive urge lurking in most civilized men. Many metaphors and theories have been proposed to explain this phenomenon: Caliban, Dionysus, the id, an elemental life-force, the aggressive violence latent in all of us. Since prehistoric times this savage urge had been satiated in religious sacrifices or sublimated through art. But by the beginning of the twentieth century religion and art had lost their capacity to deal with it and science no longer assumed that it simply did not exist. At the same time, the impersonal forces of modernization were undermining the traditional cultural norms that had controlled it in ordinary people.

As we saw earlier, avant-garde writers and painters beginning with Rimbaud and Van Gogh had confronted the savage urge, sometimes in extreme ways. The Expressionists were also particularly concerned with exposing it. Those composers who felt its presence tried to come to terms with it through the new forms of musical expression already mentioned, but no one went as far as Stravinsky in *The Rite of Spring*.

The opening bars of this work immediately plunge us into a timeless world of prehistoric myth. Stravinsky resurrects a primitive collective unconscious that five thousand years of civilization had supposedly obliterated. Although the myth and the ritual dances of the ballet itself have to do with sexual fertility and the renewal of the soil, Stravinsky's music also evokes the more basic myth of the founding of the first human communities. The final section confronts us implacably with the chaos out of which these communities sprang and which they could fall back into unless they expelled the instinctual violence that this chaos unleashed in them. And they could only do this through sacrificial rites that bound each and every member of the tribe together. These bloody sacrifices were acts of decontamination. They worked only so long as their violence was experienced in this way by the entire group; otherwise its urge toward unrestrained, impure violence would become contagious and engulf it in chaos once again.

Stravinsky succeeds in reproducing this primitive structure of feeling by using rhythm—the most elemental aspect of music—in audacious new ways. In some sections he has the pounding rhythms of the accompaniment seem to work against the shattering dissonance of the melodic line, thus making our blood boil and chilling our bones at the same time. Elsewhere he conveys feelings of ritualized violence by setting up conflicts between simple rhythms and rhythmic structures. Contrary to the symmetry expected by the Western ear, Stravinsky's rhythmic language in *The Rite of Spring* is based on a notion of asymmetrical balance. New techniques such as these give this work its revolutionary importance in musical history. But even the most casual listener cannot avoid responding to the insistent primitive beats of the bass drums which punctuate the score.

The uproar provoked by the first performance of *The Rite of Spring*, on May 28, 1913, was almost as instinctual as the feelings expressed in the music itself. Since Stravinsky was seeking new values outside the range of civilized emotional expression, he tried in a concrete way to evoke magical occurrences and ecstatic incantations through his new rhythmic language. His music revealed the primordial experience of early humans who surrendered their egoism in communal rites of death and creation. It also emphasized the primitive heritage in our own genes more than any music modern Europeans had ever heard. Many people at the premiere recoiled at its uncompromisingly barbaric effects, and some were scared to the point of hysteria by its revelation of the savage urge in man's collective unconscious. Saint-Saëns left the theater indignantly, but Ravel cried: "Genius!" Enthusiasts for Stravinsky's music responded to the howls and catcalls of its opponents by trying to shout them down and sometimes hitting them. One young man was so caught up in it that he began to beat out its rhythms on the head of the man in front of him,

whose own excitement was so great that he later claimed not to have felt
the blows at first. Like most works of the pre-1914 avant-garde, *The Rite
of Spring* was soon to be accepted as a revolutionary call to turn our
backs on most of the values and assumptions that prevent us from coming
to terms with the twentieth century. But its initial reception in Paris, the
most sophisticated capital in the world, showed how instinctual our resistance can be to this call.

On the eve of the Great War the revolution in the arts was the most
uncompromising cultural response to modernization. Freud, Durkheim,
and Weber brilliantly explained the discontents of their time but gave little hope for overcoming them. And most philosophers continued the
effort, dating back to Descartes and Kant, "to delimit that which may be
saved" from the destruction wrought by modern science on "our old vision and our very identity."[36] (By the 1930's Wittgenstein himself was to
abandon his earlier restrictions on what propositions could say and to
argue that all cultural "forms of life"—including those embodying various religions—are valid in their own terms.) In contrast, the pre-1914 aesthetic avant-garde accepted this destruction and sought to transcend it
through new visions.

The revolution in the arts was more successful in destroying traditional
views of reality than in creating new ones. Avant-garde artists, writers,
and composers sensed the many-sided and often contradictory aspects of
the discontinuous universe in which they found themselves and tried to
invent new languages capable of evoking its complexities and paradoxes.
But modern art has not been able to supply the values that could make
life meaningful in this universe. Proust, Kafka, and Pirandello have become overfamiliar prophets, their languages emptied of meaning by films
and television. The pure forms of Cubism, abstract art and music, and
functional architecture have also lost much of their original power to
summon up new visions. It has been some time since a Mark Rothko at
his best succeeded in making the observer a participant in the release
from physical reality into the realm of the spiritual, which abstract painting represented for Kandinsky in his treatise of 1910. An example of the
musical avant-garde of the 1970's was the *Spectral Continuum for Piano*
of Charlemagne Palestine (b. 1947). In this improvisational piece, which
can last from two and a half to four hours, both performer and audience
are meant to achieve a "somnambulistic state," according to Mr. Palestine.[37]

Initiated at the turn of the century, this kind of novelty has become an ongoing feature of contemporary artistic life. Even the French poet Jean Cocteau, who contributed his share of aesthetic experiments, observed: "The avant-garde has become the classicism of the twentieth century." It has been co-opted by the sophisticated public, the academies, the foundations, and state arts councils. Thus domesticated, it has lost its original goal of fusing art and life. Like all classicisms, today's avant-garde has become culture with a capital C; its media are viewed and commented on as ends in themselves. Marxists call this kind of culture a typical product of late capitalism. For them this "bourgeois formalism" is a hindrance to the promotion of the masses, which they see as the true end of modernization.

But as this book has tried to show, modernization provides no permanent solutions to the discontents it provokes. Communist dictatorships can force outward conformity to their own standards, but in other modern societies people have resisted the domination of one moral orientation over others. As the pace of modernization accelerated at the turn of the century, Europeans torn away from their familiar worlds became increasingly secular, materialistic, and self-centered. The popular culture of the time merely reflected this outlook without providing adequate justifications for the new economic, political, social, and educational systems in which people had to function. While philosophers and social scientists stressed the importance of the irrational and the unconscious in human affairs, ordinary Europeans became more self-conscious about their occupational, sexual, and class status, their nationality, and their place in the power structure. The First World War intensified these responses and sparked ever-growing demands for scarce resources and consumable values. So far these have been the main compensations that modernization has substituted for the meaning that people miss in their lives.

APPENDIX ON MODERNIZATION

Modernization is a process involving all human affairs. Its specific manifestations are as real as breathing, digestion, and sexual reproduction. Just as these processes are part of the life-cycle of individuals, so modernization includes the processes of secularization, rationalization, bureaucratization, industrialization, urbanization, structural differentiation, consolidation of policy-making, and the elimination of political and social inequalities. The inherited structure of the human body precludes any basic changes in the life-cycle. Modernization, however, forces the inherited or traditional structures of human societies to change the functions they must perform. When they are unable to do this they are eventually replaced with new structures.

Unlike the life-cycle of individuals or the presumed rise and fall of earlier civilizations, modernization is a continuing process with no fixed beginning or end. There are pendulum swings and oscillations in many areas of human activity: political revolutions are often followed by periods of reaction; economies alternate between prosperity and depression; people fall in and out of love. Ancient civilizations were transformed by irrigation, new techniques of warfare, and alien religions without losing their basic structures. Even today the recent structural changes in American race relations have not completely destroyed older attitudes and cultural patterns among whites. But in the long run modernization makes everything change. Innovations in one sector of activity modify ways of doing things in others through various feedback processes. These different sectors seem to be continuously out of phase with one another, and there is no stability in sight.

The current erosion of the representative institutions that mediate between individuals and authority in Western Europe and North America shows that economic and social modernization do not necessarily bring political modernization.[1] In the early years of this century this deficiency was a serious problem in Germany, Austria-Hungary, and Russia, but it did not seem significant in England, France, and the United States. Liberals everywhere viewed the political institutions of these three countries as classic models of adaptation to economic and social modernization. These institutions provided some of the social means, particularly schools, for people to develop the new capabilities demanded by a modern economy. And, by fostering integration, negotiation, and continuity, they aided the process of social mobilization—whereby "major clusters of old social, economic, and psychological commitments are eroded or broken and people become available for new patterns of socialization and behavior."[2] Thus in the 1890's and early 1900's the politically stable Western democracies helped their citizens adapt their attitudes, values, and aspirations to the requirements of a modern society. Yet economic and social modernization had already provoked political crises in England in the 1830's, in the United States in the 1860's, and in France during much of the nineteenth century. In the 1970's cultural innovation and social conflict may become the only effective means for revealing the struggles and contradictions in the most highly modernized countries and for stimulating their future development.[3]

Although modernity has no upper limit, it does have a lower one. Tradition and modernity are abstract terms designating clusters of perceived choices which serve to legitimate action. Modernizing and traditional systems of thought and action exclude one another in theory but often interpenetrate in practice. Many political and economic modernizers have been traditionalists in their social and cultural attitudes. Tradition and modernity can also interpenetrate in a single sector of activity: like many European industrialists after him Henry Ford combined the latest assembly-line techniques with a paternalistic policy toward his employees. But once a certain level of modernization is generally accepted as a standard, people refuse to give it up and go back to a traditional standard. People brought up on the assumptions of scientific inquiry can no longer believe in magic; people accustomed to the freedom of the city will not readily exchange it for the restrictions of village life; people led to expect the state to look out for their welfare assume that it must do so. What was once an innovation becomes a standard and then a "floor."

New knowledge accumulated over many centuries was the original stimulus for modernization in Europe. The civilizations of the world had remained relatively static as long as they were ordered by beliefs whose only criterion for acceptance was that they had been believed before. These traditional beliefs, incorporated into particular structures, provided a consensus through time. European civilization changed very slowly during the Middle Ages, but a few late medieval thinkers began to prepare the way for modern scientific knowledge by questioning the picture of nature offered by Aristotelian philosophy and Christian theology. The first revolutionary theories of modern science were set forth by Copernicus in the sixteenth century and by Galileo and Newton in the seventeenth. Meanwhile, technological innovations such as gunpowder, printing, double-entry bookkeeping, and ocean-going sailing ships had also begun to alter European civilization.

New scientific and technological knowledge permitted increasing control over man's environment, thereby imposing new functions on traditional structures. It made possible the "discoveries" of Columbus and Cortez, which enabled the kings of Spain to adapt that country's political structure to the functions of a world empire. From the end of the seventeenth to the end of the nineteenth centuries scientists proclaimed the idea of a mechanistic, rationally ordered universe. God was still given a place in this universe, but the judicial structures of Europe banished the devil and witches to the realm of superstition. Fear of the unknown gradually gave way to curiosity about strange phenomena and faraway places, a curiosity fed in the eighteenth century by scientific and pseudo-scientific public demonstrations and an abundant travel literature. In that age of Enlightenment philosophers and publicists spread the idea that political, social, and economic relations were as subject to natural laws as nature itself and urged that the structures governing these relations be reformed accordingly.

The second phase of modernization was launched by modernizing political leaders. During the English Revolution of 1688 and the French Revolution of 1789 these leaders replaced the last vestiges of relations based on traditional status and arrangements with new legal relations based on property and voluntary contracts. These changes did not reach Eastern and Southern Europe until much later and they did not completely destroy the traditional social structure anywhere. But they were necessary prerequisites for modernization, and modernizing political leaders tried to make them prevail throughout Europe in the years 1890 to 1914.

Like all aspects of modernization the growth of large impersonal organizations sponsored by modernizing political leaders was a long-term development. State bureaucracies were already being set up in the eighteenth century in Prussia, Austria, and Russia. In France at the beginning of the nineteenth century Napoleon I created Europe's first modern civil administration recruited on the basis of talent rather than social origins, along with the first centralized system of secondary and higher education. These innovations were copied in the newly united Kingdom of Italy in the 1860's. The Prussian system of universal military training in mass armies, devised in the early nineteenth century, was adopted in most continental countries in the 1870's. Great Britain shunned universal military training until the First World War but had already created the first modern police force in the 1840's and a professional civil service and a national system of compulsory elementary education in the 1870's.

By then the third phase of modernization, the transformation of the economic and social structures, was under way. An increasing proportion of the total population was moving out of agriculture into industry and from the countryside to the cities. For some time population growth had been producing more people than the agricultural economic structure could support. In Germany particularly, rapid industrialization and urbanization were able to absorb the rural population surplus whose poverty-stricken and propertyless members threatened the stability of agrarian society at its foundations. This process of disintegration in the agrarian social structure was in turn checked by the new capacity of the towns, factories, and mines to provide places for these people. Not only could they move from the country to the city and from one town to another but they could also rise (or fall) more easily in the more differentiated structures of urban industrial society.

Dramatic as these transformations were, they depended to a great extent on the continuing growth in knowledge and the ability of modernizing political leaders to mobilize resources. All these aspects of the process of modernization encouraged governments to undertake the systematic regulation of society. It was easier to control working conditions in cities and large factories than in isolated rural areas and workshops; it was also more practicable to insist on sanitation, water, roads, and hospitals. Besides, the enforcement of minimum public health regulations became a matter of public efficiency and political necessity in conditions of mass living and mass working. Crime prevention and detection were improved with the spread of identity cards, police control of hotel registration, and new ways of identifying criminals through their fingerprints and handwriting. The threat of socialist-inspired labor unrest prompted governments to initiate the first social insurance plans in history. Concerned with "reliable" manpower resources in the future, they not only instituted compulsory elementary education but they also passed laws limiting child labor, and, at the beginning of the twentieth century, they created courts to take preschool children away from "unfit" parents.

None of these changes can be understood in isolation. Not only did each of them have its own side effects and unanticipated consequences but each was also influenced by transformations in other sectors of activity. For example, developments in the wood products industry in Sweden had "backward linkage effects" in the forestry sector. Thus in discussing the development of this specific industry one cannot speak only of the forty thousand workers in the sawmills and plants making lumber, paper, and matches. One must also link their activities with those of the men who felled the trees and transported wood products. The number of workers in agriculture, forestry, and fishing declined with industrialization, but those who remained in these activities became more specialized.

The sixfold to eightfold growth of city size in nineteenth-century Europe is often attributed to the migration of labor to the factories, but it was also part of a larger process. We have already noted the acceleration of education and specialization and improvements in transportation, in organization, and in public health necessary to maintain large numbers of people in one place. But urbanization on such a scale would have been impossible without the chemicalization and mechanization of agriculture as well. These changes allowed fewer people to work the land while ensuring adequate food supplies for the sprawling new urban centers. All these "phased-in" developments were part of the process of modernization.

The fourth, and final, phase of modernization is supposed to be the integration of society on a centralized, participatory, functional basis. As the individual's ties with the village, the family workshop, and local traditions disappear, his ties with the urban, industrial, national network of structures are strengthened. In its ultimate form modern society will have abolished all social conditions of traditional authoritarianism and liberated all men and women from unwanted fetters of heritage and customs. But such a society still seems utopian. We already know that modernization also brings about feelings of alienation, isolation, insecurity, and fear of the very freedom it is organized to guarantee. And during the past fifty years we have seen how this fear can stimulate defense mechanisms such as authoritarianism, destructiveness, and automaton conformity. Still, as part of the model of modernization, the trend toward the integration of society helps us to understand much that was happening in Europe in the period 1890–1914.

Modernization has varied from one society to another, and European models have been radically altered in other parts of the world. There has never been a single pattern of the transition from traditional to modern. Responses to it arise from the whole society and culture. These include "the systems of power, property-relations, religious institutions, etc., inattention to which merely flattens phenomena and trivializes analysis."[4]

In Europe itself the pattern varied from one country to another and among different regions in the same country during the same time span. Between 1890 and 1914 there were many similarities in the economic, social, and cultural life of Europe's great cities. London, Paris, Vienna, Berlin, St. Petersburg, Milan, Budapest, Warsaw, Madrid, and Copenhagen all had the same kinds of government buildings, offices, shops, theaters, and municipal services; all had comparable social classes; all had writers and artists involved in similar intellectual and aesthetic movements. But each country as a whole presented a different picture from that of its capital. The further east and south one went in Europe the greater was the proportion of people living in relatively closed peasant social structures, which were markedly different from the relatively open and highly differentiated structures of these cities. Many countries also had a dual economic structure, part traditional and part modern. Those with the largest modern sectors were Great Britain, Germany, and Belgium; those with a larger traditional sector included Italy, Spain, and Russia. The greatest extremes in degree of modernization among the major countries were Great Britain and Russia. And these differences were to show up in their experiences during and immediately after the First World War, in their efficiency in mobilizing resources and in their responses to revolution.

By and large, in the generation preceding the war, many regions of northwestern and Central Europe had reached a stage of economic and social transformation which allowed the majority of their inhabitants to feel relatively content, whereas Southern and Eastern Europe were experiencing the hardships and discontent that had accompanied the beginnings of this transformation in northwestern Europe during the first two thirds of the nineteenth century.

NOTES

INTRODUCTION

1. Raymond Williams, *Drama from Ibsen to Brecht* (London: Chatto & Windus, 1968), p. 18.
2. Fred Weinstein and Gerald M. Platt, "The Coming Crisis in Psychohistory," *Journal of Modern History*, 47 (June 1975), 221–22.

CHAPTER 1

1. See David S. Landes, *The Unbound Prometheus. Technological Change and Industrial Development in Western Europe from 1750 to the Present* (London: Cambridge University Press, 1969).
2. Michael Tracy, *Agriculture in Western Europe* (New York: Praeger, 1964), p. 114.
3. Holger Begtrup, *The Folk High Schools of Denmark and the Development of a Farming Community* (London: Oxford University Press, 1936), p. 21.
4. Adna Ferrin Weber, *The Growth of Cities in the Nineteenth Century: A Study in Statistics* (New York: Macmillan, 1899), p. 346.
5. Edward Shorter, "Female Emancipation, Birth Control, and Fertility in European History," *American Historical Review*, 78 (June 1973), 631. Shorter's thesis in this article has been challenged by Louise A. Tilly, Joan W. Scott, and Miriam Cohen in "Women's Work and European Fertility Patterns," *The Journal of Interdisciplinary History*, 6 (Winter 1976), 447–476.
6. Joseph Lee, *The Modernisation of Irish Society, 1848–1919* (Dublin: Gill and Macmillan, 1973), pp. 4 and 10.
7. Edward Anthony Wrigley, *Industrial Growth and Population Change, a Regional Study of the Coalfield Areas of North-West Europe in the Later Nineteenth Century* (London: Cambridge University Press, 1961), p. 169.
8. Lee, op. cit., p. 8.
9. Wilhelm von Polenz, *Der Grabenhäger*, 3rd ed., 2 vols. (Berlin, 1903), II, p. 22; quoted in Frieda Wunderlich, *Farm Labor in Germany, 1810–1945* (Princeton, N.J.: Princeton University Press, 1961), p. 23n.
10. Wolfgang Köllmann, "The Process of Urbanization in Germany at the Height of the Industrialization Period," *Journal of Contemporary History*, 4 (July 1969), 69.

11. Harold James Dyos and Michael Wolff, eds., *The Victorian City. Images and Realities*, 2 vols. (London: Routledge & Kegan Paul, 1973), 2, p. 904.

12. Köllmann, loc. cit., pp. 72–73.

13. Franz Rehbein, *Das Leben eines Landarbeiters* (Jena: E. Diederichs, 1911), p. 65.

14. T. H. S. Escott, *England: Its People, Polity and Pursuits* (1885 ed.), p. 56. Quoted in Donald Read, *The English Provinces c. 1760–1960: a Study in Influence* (New York: St. Martin's Press, 1964), p. 246.

15. Lee, op. cit., p. 13.

16. Theodore Zeldin, *France 1848–1945*, Vol. I, *Ambition, Love and Politics* (Oxford: Clarendon Press, 1973), pp. 377–80.

17. Julie Sevrette, *La Jeune ménagère* (Paris: Librairie Larousse, 1904), p. 181.

18. Luc Boltanski, *Prime éducation et morale de classe* (Paris–The Hague: Mouton, 1969), pp. 131–32.

19. Quoted in Richard J. W. Selleck, *The New Education, 1870–1914* (London: Pitman, 1968), p. 62.

20. John Gill, *Introductory Textbook to School Education, Method and School Management* (London: Longmans, Green, 1883), p. 127.

21. Franck Alengry, *Psychologie et éducation*, Vol. 3, *Psychologie et morale* (Paris: Librairie d'Éducation Nationale, 1907), p. 150.

22. Selleck, op. cit., pp. 329–38.

23. James M. Olson, "The Prussian *Volksschule*, 1890–1914: A Study of the Social Implications of the Extension of Elementary Education," unpublished Ph.D. dissertation, New York University, 1971, pp. 254–56.

24. *Paedogogische Zeitung*, 40 (1911), 1.

25. Carlo M. Cipolla, *Literacy and Development in the West* (Baltimore: Pelican, 1969), pp. 115 and 127–28.

26. Gregory Grossman, "The Industrialisation of Russia and the Soviet Union," in Carlo M. Cipolla, ed., *The Fontana Economic History of Europe. The Emergence of Industrial Societies*, 2 vols. (London: Collins/Fontana Books, 1973), II, p. 490.

27. Robert Wohl, Introduction to Harvey Mitchell and Peter N. Stearns, *Workers and Protest: The European Labor Movement, the Working Classes and the Origins of Social Democracy, 1890–1914* (Itasca, Ill.: Peacock, 1971), pp. 7–8.

CHAPTER 2

1. *Years of Plenty* (New York: Jonathan Cape & Harrison Smith, 1931), pp. 92–93.

2. Ibid., pp. 97–98.

3. C. K. Yearley, "The Provincial Party and the Megalopolises: London, Paris, and New York," *Comparative Studies in Society and History*, 15 (January 1973), 56. Karl Lueger, the mayor of Vienna in the early 1900's, was a leader of the Christian Social party, which derived much of its support from rural interests.

4. The information in this paragraph comes from Hans Rosenberg, "Die

Pseudodemokratisierung der Rittersgutsbesitzerklasse," in Hans-Ulrich Wehler, ed., *Moderne deutsche Sozialgeschichte* (Cologne-Berlin: Kiepenheuer & Witsch, 1966), pp. 302–3, James J. Sheehan, "Conflict and Cohesion among German Elites in the Nineteenth Century," in Robert J. Bezucha, ed., *Modern European Social History* (Lexington, Mass.: D. C. Heath, 1972), pp. 13–14, and Holger H. Herwig, *The German Naval Officer Corps: A Social and Political History 1890–1918* (London: Oxford University Press, 1974), passim.

5. Raymond L. Gartoff, "The Military as a Social Force," in Cyril E. Black, ed., *The Transformation of Russian Society: Aspects of Change Since 1861* (Cambridge, Mass.: Harvard University Press, 1967), pp. 326–27.

6. Ralph E. Pumphrey, "The Introduction of Industrialists into the British Peerage: A Study in Adaptation of a Social Institution," *American Historical Review*, 65 (October 1959), 11.

7. F. M. L. Thompson, *English Landed Society in the Nineteenth Century* (London: Routledge & Kegan Paul, 1963), p. 326.

8. Alcime-Armand-Pierre-Henri Gouraud, *Instruction pastorale* (Vannes: Imprimerie de Galles, 1911), p. 5.

9. Pierre-Célestin Cézérac, *Lettre pastorale* (Cahors, 1914), p. 152.

10. *Three Months in a Workshop. A Practical Study* (New York: Scribner, 1895), p. 151.

11. Rev. Charles Haddon Spurgeon, *Messages to the Multitude* (London: Sampson, Low, & Marston, 1892), pp. 253 and 259.

12. Warren Sylvester Smith, *The London Heretics, 1870–1914* (London: Constable, 1967), p. 223.

13. *The Six Lambeth Conferences, 1867–1927* (London: Society for Promoting Christian Knowledge, 1929), pp. 267–68 and 414.

14. François-Virgile Dubillard, *Lettre pastorale* (Chambéry: Imprimerie générale savoisienne, 1912), p. 310.

15. *Reflections of a Russian Statesman* (Ann Arbor: University of Michigan Press, 1965), pp. 90–93.

16. Louis Dimier, *Vingt ans de l'Action Française et d'autres souvenirs* (Paris: Nouvelle Librairie Nationale, 1926), pp. 29–30.

17. *The Beautiful in Music* (Indianapolis: Bobbs-Merrill, 1957), p. 51.

18. *Hans Makart* (Vienna: Bergenland Verlag, 1954), p. 29.

19. Sheldon Rothblatt, *The Revolution of the Dons: Cambridge and Society in Victorian England* (New York: Basic Books, 1968), p. 228ff.

20. Henry Jackson, "Cambridge Fifty Years Ago," cited in ibid., p. 228.

21. Paul Gerbod, *La Condition universitaire en France au XIXe siècle* (Paris: Presses Universitaires de France, 1965), p. 634.

22. Fritz K. Ringer, *The Decline and Fall of the Mandarins: The German Academic Community, 1890–1933* (Cambridge, Mass.: Harvard University Press, 1970), pp. 11–13.

23. *My Life as a Rebel* (Bloomington, Ind.: Indiana University Press, 1973), p. 21.

24. Friedrich Paulsen, *An Autobiography* (New York: Columbia University Press, 1938), p. 385.

25. Ringer, op. cit., p. 129.

26. See Folke Dovring's review article "Peasantry, Land Use, and Change," *Comparative Studies in Society and History*, 4 (April 1962), 364–74. French historians and geographers have excelled in producing regional studies using quantitative methods for long periods of time. See Emmanuel Le Roy Ladurie, *Les Paysans de Languedoc*, 2 vols. (Paris: S.E.V.P.E.N., 1966); Paul Bois, *Paysans de l'ouest* (Ryswijk, Netherlands: Mouton, 1960); Étienne Juillard, *La Vie rurale dans la plaine de Basse-Alsace. Essai de géographie sociale* (Paris: Société d'Éditions: Les Belles Lettres, 1953); Philippe Pinchemel, *Structures sociales et dépopulation rurale dans les campagnes picardes de 1836 à 1936* (Paris: A. Colin, 1957); and Daniel Faucher, *L'Homme et le Rhône* (Paris: Gallimard, 1968). For the views of an outstanding rural sociologist see Henri Mendras, *The Vanishing Peasant: Innovation and Change in French Agriculture* (Cambridge, Mass.: M.I.T. Press, 1970).

27. Émile Guillaumin, *La Vie d'un simple* (Paris: Stock, 1943), p. 146. The original edition of this unique biography of a peasant by a man who remained a peasant himself appeared in 1904.

28. Emilio Willems, "Peasantry and City: Cultural Persistence and Change in Historical Perspective. A European Case," *American Anthropologist*, 72 (1970), 542.

29. Ibid., p. 536.

30. Pierre Barral, *Les Agrariens français de Méline à Pisani* (Paris: A. Colin, 1964), pp. 105–75, passim.

31. Henri Mendras, "Un Schéma d'analyse de la paysannerie occidentale," *Peasant Studies Newsletter*, 1 (1972), No. 3, 79–88, and No. 4, 126–38. Many of the generalizations in the following pages were suggested by this two-part article.

32. Edit Fél and Tamós Hofer, *Proper Peasants: Traditional Life in a Hungarian Village* (Chicago: Aldine, 1969), p. 75.

33. Leonard W. Moss, "The Passing of Traditional Peasant Society in the South," in Edward R. Tannenbaum and Emiliana P. Noether, eds., *Modern Italy: A Topical History Since 1861* (New York: New York University Press, 1974), p. 159.

34. Teodor Shanin, *The Awkward Class* (Oxford: The Clarendon Press, 1972), p. 41. See also Peter Czap, Jr., "Peasant-Class Courts and Peasant Customary Justice in Russia, 1861–1912," *Journal of Social History*, 1 (Winter 1967), 149–178.

35. Lee, op. cit., p. 3.

36. Maurice O'Sullivan, *Twenty Years A-Growing*, translated from the Irish (New York: Viking, 1933), p. 55.

37. Marcelle Bouteiller, *Médécine populaire d'hier et d'aujourdhui* (Paris: Éditions G.-P. Maisonneuve et Larose, 1966), passim. Even in parts of England as late as the 1880's midwives not only delivered babies but were also called upon for their "skill in the use of herbs and the care of the sick," according to *The Hard Way Up: The Autobiography of Hannah Mitchell* (London: Faber and Faber, 1968), p. 46.

38. Franz Rehbein, op. cit., p. 23.

39. Ernest Henry Phelps Brown, *The Growth of British Industrial Relations; a Study from the Standpoint of 1906–1914* (London: Macmillan, 1959), p. 91. See also Jürgen Kocka, *Unternehmensverwaltung und Angestelltenschaft am Beispiel Siemens 1847–1914* (Stuttgart: Ernst Klett Verlag, 1969), pp. 124–27, and Joan Wallach Scott, *The Glassworkers of Carmaux* (Cambridge, Mass.: Harvard University Press, 1974), passim.

40. Standish Meacham, " 'The Sense of an Impending Clash': English Working-Class Unrest Before the First World War," *American Historical Review*, 77 (December 1972), 1359.

41. Adolf Levenstein, *Die Arbeiterfrage* (Munich: E. Reinhardt, 1912), pp. 115, 123, 130, 223, 232, 242.

42. Henry Pelling, *Popular Politics and Society in Late Victorian Britain* (London: Macmillan, 1968), p. 18.

CHAPTER 3

1. Stephan Thernstrom, *The Other Bostonians: Poverty and Progress in the American Metropolis, 1880–1970* (Cambridge, Mass.: Harvard University Press, 1973), pp. 259–60.

2. Frank Thistlethwaite, "Migration from Europe Overseas in the Nineteenth and Twentieth Centuries," International Congress of Historical Sciences. Stockholm, 1960, *Rapports*, V, *Histoire Contemporaine* (Göteborg-Stockholm-Uppsala: Almquist & Wiksell, 1960), p. 52.

3. Ibid., p. 53. See also Kristian Hvidt, *Flight to America. The Social Background of 300,000 Danish Emigrants* (New York: Academic Press, 1975), passim.

4. Italy. Direzione Generale della Statistica. *Statistica della Emigrazione Italiana per l'estero negli anni 1908–1909* (Rome: Tipografia Nazionale di G. Bertero, 1910), p. xxiv, and ibid., *1912–1913* (Rome: Tipografia Ditta Ludovico Cecchini, 1915), p. xxiii.

5. Quoted in Ronald Blythe, *Akenfield: Portrait of an English Village* (New York: Pantheon, 1969), pp. 37–38.

6. Quoted in Arnold Schrier, *Ireland and the American Emigration 1850–1900* (Minneapolis: University of Minnesota Press, 1958), p. 38.

7. Eric J. Hobsbawm, "The Tramping Artisan," in his *Labouring Men. Studies in the History of Labour* (New York: Basic Books, 1964), p. 46.

8. Cited in Rolande Trempé, *Les Mineurs de Carmaux, 1848–1914,* 2 vols. (Paris: Les Éditions ouvrières, 1971), I, 184–85.

9. Fél and Hofer, op. cit., p. 270n.

10. William Isaac Thomas and Florian Znaniecki, *The Polish Peasant in Europe and America,* 2 vols. (New York: Dover, 1958), II, 1503.

11. Jean-Alain Lesourd, "Paysans de Lorraine au XIXe et XXe siècles: esquisse d'une évolution," *Paysans d'Alsace* (Strasbourg: F. X. Le Roux, 1959), p. 592.

12. Schrier, op. cit., pp. 110 and 118.

13. Jacques Ozouf, "Les instituteurs de la Manche et leurs associations au début du XXe siècle," *Revue d'Histoire Moderne et Contemporaine*, 13 (January–March, 1966), 85.

14. Thistlethwaite, loc. cit.

15. Brinley Thomas, *Migration and Economic Growth. A Study of Great Britain and the Atlantic Economy*, 2nd ed. (London: Cambridge University Press, 1973), p. 64.

16. Ibid., p. 57.

17. This summary of Pasquale's emigrant years is based on personal recollections of the old man and three of his children during conversations with me in the late 1960's.

18. Wladek's autobiography appears in Thomas and Znaniecki, op. cit., II, pp. 1831–2226.

19. Ibid., pp. 2203–4.

20. Ibid., p. 2226.

21. Juan F. Marsal, *Hacer la América. Autobiografía de un inmigrante español en la Argentina* (Buenos Aires: Editorial del Instituto, 1969), p. 34.

22. Ibid., p. 118.

23. A. K. Cairncross, "Internal Migration in Victorian England," *The Manchester School*, 17 (January 1949), 79.

24. Raymond Dugrand, *Villes et campagnes en Bas-Languedoc. Le Réseau urbain du Bas-Languedoc méditerranéen* (Paris: Presses Universitaires de France, 1963), pp. 463–64.

25. Jorge Nadal, *La Población española. Siglos XVI a XX* (Barcelona: Ediciones Ariel, 1966), p. 171.

26. Dorothy Swaine Thomas, *Social and Economic Aspects of Swedish Population Movements, 1750–1933* (New York: Macmillan, 1941), p. 326.

27. Wrigley, op. cit., pp. 162–63.

28. Köllmann, loc. cit., p. 68.

29. See Paul Hohenberg, "Migrations et fluctuations démographiques dans la France rurale, 1836–1901," *Annales: Économies, Sociétés, Civilisations*, 29 (March–April 1974), 461–97.

30. Köllmann, loc. cit., p. 69.

31. Thernstrom, op. cit., pp. 221–24.

32. Edward E. Malefakis, *Agrarian Reform and Peasant Revolution in Spain: Origins of the Civil War* (New Haven: Yale University Press, 1970), pp. 104–6; J. C. Macdonald, "Agricultural Organisation, Migration and Labour Militancy in Rural Italy," *The Economic History Review*, Second Series, 16 (August 1963), 74–75; Joso Tomasevich, *Peasants, Politics, and Economic Change in Yugoslavia* (Stanford, Cal.: Stanford University Press, 1955), p. 197; Teodor Shanin, op. cit., pp. 92–95.

33. Köllmann, loc. cit., pp. 73–76.

34. William L. Blackwell, "Modernization and Urbanization in Russia: A Comparative View," in Michael F. Hamm, ed., *The City in Russian History* (Lexington: University of Kentucky Press, 1976), pp. 309–10.

35. Local Government Board, *Report on the Methods of Administering Poor Relief in Certain Large Town Parishes in Scotland* (Glasgow: H.M. Stationery Office, 1905), p. iii; *Statistical Abstract for the United Kingdom*, No. 56 (1909), p. 388.

36. This approximation was arrived at by dividing the number of people

(1639) on out-relief in the English city of York (*not* including those from other districts) in 1901 into the total amount ($£5950$) given to them in that year. Thus the average for each person was $£3.02$, or $15, in 1901 currency. Multiplying this $15 by 12 for today's equivalent we get $180, which is about the average *monthly* payment to a single person "on welfare" in a large American city. Figures for York are from B. Seebohm Rowntree, *Poverty. A Study of Town Life,* new ed. (London: Longmans, Green, 1922), pp. 425 and 435.

37. Kellow Chesney, *The Anti-Society; an Account of the Victorian Underworld* (Boston: Gambit, 1970), p. 367.

38. Ibid., p. 368.

39. *Schriften der Centralstelle für Arbeiter-Wohlfahrtseinrichtungen,* No. 26, "Schlaftstellenwesen und Ledigenheime" (Berlin: Carl Heymanns Verlag, 1904), p. 48.

40. Charles O. Hardy, *The Housing Program of the City of Vienna* (Washington, D.C.: The Brookings Institution, 1934), p. 19.

41. Ilsa Barea, *Vienna* (New York: Knopf, 1966), p. 336.

42. Theodore H. Von Laue, "Russian Peasants in the Factory, 1892–1904," *Journal of Economic History,* 21 (March 1961), 66; Von Laue cites statistics from the 1897 census.

43. Gyula Illyés, *People of the Puszta* (Budapest: Corvina, 1967), p. 285.

44. *The Portable Chekhov,* ed., Avrahm Yarmolinsky (New York: Viking, 1947), p. 320.

45. J. A. Banks, "The Contagion of Numbers," in Dyos and Wolff, op. cit., pp. 117–18.

46. George Ewart Evans, *Where Beards Wag All. The Relevance of the Oral Tradition* (London: Faber and Faber, 1970), pp. 263–67.

47. Daniel Faucher, *La Vie rurale vue par un géographe* (Toulouse: Institut de Géographie de la Faculté des Lettres et Sciences Humaines, 1962), pp. 193–94.

48. Else Hofmann, "Sprachsoziologische Untersuchung über den Einfluss der Stadtsprache auf mundartsprechende Arbeiter," *Marburger Universitätsbund,* Jahrbuch 1963, 2, 211.

49. "The Nature of Abstract Art," *Marxist Quarterly,* 1 (January–March, 1937), 83.

50. "Tradition and Modernity Reconsidered," *Comparative Studies in Society and History,* 9 (April 1967), 321.

51. *Grosstadt und Religion,* 2 vols. in 1 (Hamburg: C. Goysen, 1913–19), I, p. 8.

52. Raymond Williams, *The Country and the City* (London: Oxford University Press, 1973), p. 200.

53. Steven Marcus, "Reading the Illegible," in Dyos and Wolff, op. cit., p. 261.

54. H. J. Dyos and D. A. Reeder, "Slums and Suburbs," in ibid., pp. 370–71.

55. *Wage Earning Mothers,* Mrs. J. R. MacDonald and others (The Women's Labour League, undated), quoted in Phelps Brown, op. cit., p. 68.

56. Marghanita Laski, "Domestic Life," in Simon Nowell-Smith, ed., *Ed-*

wardian England, 1901–1914 (London: Oxford University Press, 1964), p. 205.

57. Richard Woldt, *Das grossindustrielle Beamtentum. Eine gewerkschaftliche Studie* (Stuttgart: Dietz, 1911), p. 12ff.

58. Marghanita Laski, loc. cit., p. 187.

59. Otto von Leixner, *1888 bis 1891; Soziale Briefe aus Berlin 1888–1891* (Berlin: F. Pfeilstücker, 1891), p. 8off.

60. Marghanita Laski, loc. cit., p. 200.

61. Edward Shorter, John Knodel, Etienne van de Walle, "The Decline of Non-Marital Fertility in Europe, 1880–1940," *Population Studies,* 25 (November 1971), 378.

62. Wrigley, op. cit., pp. 152–53.

63. France. Statistique Générale de la France. *Annuaire statistique,* 3 (1880), p. 186; 26 (1906), p. 80; 33 (1913), p. 67.

64. Great Britain. *Parliamentary Papers,* 25 (1901), *Reports, Commissioners* (17), pp. lii–liii; ibid., 31 (1913), pp. xliv–xlvi; Tom Percival, *Poor Law Children* (London: Shaw & Sons, 1911), pp. 334–55.

65. James Samuelson, *The Children of Our Slums* (Liverpool: The Liverpool Booksellers, 1911), pp. 87–88.

66. Germany. Statistisches Amt. *Statistisches Jahrbuch für das Deutsches Reich, 1911* (Berlin: Puttkamer & Mühlbrecht, 1911), p. 17.

67. *Manuel des oeuvres, institutions religieuses et charitables de Paris et principaux établissements des départements pouvant recevoir des orphelins, des indigents et des malades de Paris,* 11th ed. (Paris: J. de Gigord, 1912), p. 79.

68. Charles E. B. Russell, *Manchester Boys. Sketches of Manchester Lads at Work and Play* (Manchester: The University Press, 1913), p. 126.

69. Henriette Arendt, *Kleine weisse Sklaven* (Berlin-Charlottenburg: Vita Deutsches Verlaghaus, 1911), p. 23.

CHAPTER 4

1. Anthony Giddens, *The Class Structure of the Advanced Societies* (New York: Barnes and Noble, 1973), pp. 134–35. Much of my analysis of classes and class consciousness is based on this important book, which also discusses the class theories of Karl Marx, Max Weber, Stanislaw Ossowski, Ralf Dahrendorf, and Alain Touraine.

2. According to John Kenneth Galbraith, in *The New Industrial State* (Boston: Houghton Mifflin, 1971), effective power of decision has now passed from the managers to those members of the staff whose specialized mastery of technical and scientific information makes them indispensable. But, as Giddens points out, "this confuses indispensability and power . . . if being indispensable necessarily confers power, then in a slave economy the slaves would be dominant" (op. cit., p. 173).

3. Giddens, op. cit., p. 109.

4. The definitions in this paragraph are from Giddens, pp. 111–13.

5. Roger Thabault, *Education and Change in a Village Community. Mazières-en-Gâtine, 1848–1914* (London: Routledge & Kegan Paul, 1971), p. 178.

6. Quoted in Andreas Kazamias, *Politics, Society and Secondary Education in England* (Philadelphia: University of Pennsylvania Press, 1966), p. 144.

7. Quoted in J. C. G. Röhl, "Higher Civil Servants in Germany, 1890–1900," *Journal of Contemporary History*, 2 (July 1967), 113. This entire issue is devoted to the subject of education and social structure.

8. Op. cit., pp. 340–41.

9. France. Assemblée Nationale, Annales de la Chambre des Députés, *Documents Parlementaires*, 1899, Introduction to an Enquête sur l'enseignement secondaire, November 16, 1899, p. 415.

10. Manfred Studier, *Der Corpsstudent als Idealbild der Wilhelminischen Ära, Untersuchungen zum Zeitgeist 1888 bis 1914* (Dissertation, University of Erlangen-Nürnberg, 1965), pp. 46–48.

11. *Gesammelte politische Schriften*, 2nd ed. (Tübingen: Mohr, 1958), pp. 235–36, quoted in Fritz K. Ringer, "Higher Education in Germany in the Nineteenth Century," *Journal of Contemporary History*, 2 (July 1967), 138.

12. Quoted in Ilsa Barea, op. cit., p. 283.

13. Theodore Zeldin, "Higher Education in France, 1848–1940," *Journal of Contemporary History*, 2 (July 1967), 79.

14. Ringer, loc. cit., pp. 136–37.

15. Alex Inkeles, "Summary and Review: Social Stratification and Modernization in Russia," in C. E. Black, op. cit., pp. 344–45.

16. Letter to a friend, October 3, 1893, quoted in Georg Kotowski, Werner Pöls, and Gerhard Ritter, eds., *Das wilhelminische Deutschland* (Frankfurt: Fischer Bucherei, 1965), p. 76.

17. William Joseph Reader, *Professional Men: The Rise of the Professional Classes in Nineteenth-Century England* (London: Weidenfeld & Nicolson, 1966), p. 203.

18. Zeldin, *France: 1848–1945*, Vol. I, p. 42.

19. Reader, op. cit., p. 197.

20. John P. Cullity, "The Growth of Governmental Employment in Germany, 1882–1950," *Zeitschrift für die gesamte Staatswissenschaft*, 123 (1967), 211.

21. Röhl, loc. cit., p. 103n.

22. Reader, op. cit., p. 95.

23. Samuel Hynes, *The Edwardian Turn of Mind* (Princeton, N.J.: Princeton University Press, 1968), p. 71.

24. Hobsbawm, op. cit., p. 266.

25. *Tono-Bungay* (New York: The Modern Library, 1935—originally published in 1909), p. 249.

26. Letter to Martha Fontane, April 18, 1884, in Theodor Fontane's *Briefe an seine Familie*, 2 vols. (Berlin: F. Fontane Co., 1905), II, 90–91; quoted in Joachim Remack, *The Gentle Critic; Theodor Fontane and German Politics, 1848–1898* (Syracuse, N.Y.: Syracuse University Press, 1964), p. 40.

27. Jürgen Kocka, op. cit., pp. 225 and 346.

28. Ibid., pp. 309–11, 510–11. See also David Lockwood, *The Black Coated Worker; a Study in Class Consciousness* (London: Allen & Unwin, 1958), pp. 29–30.

29. Eda Sagarra, *Tradition and Revolution: German Literature and Society, 1830–1890* (New York: Basic Books, 1971), p. 287.

30. Robert Gellately, *The Politics of Economic Despair: Shopkeepers and German Politics, 1890–1914* (Beverly Hills, Cal.: Sage Publications, 1975), and Jürgen Kocka, "The First World War and the 'Mittelstand': German Artisans and White-Collar Workers," *Journal of Contemporary History*, 8 (January 1973), especially pp. 101–7.

31. Kocka, loc. cit., p. 106–7.

32. *The Listener*, December 28, 1961. See also Arno J. Mayer, "The Lower Middle Class as a Historical Problem," *Journal of Modern History*, 47 (September 1975), 409–36.

33. See Pelling, *Popular Politics*, pp. 62–81.

34. See, for example, José Harris, *Unemployment and Politics: A Study in English Social Policy, 1886–1914* (London: Oxford University Press, 1973), passim.

35. Hannah Arendt, "Lawlessness Is Inherent in the Uprooted," *New York Times Magazine*, April 28, 1968, pp. 24–25. Arendt was just as wrong in saying that more urban crimes were committed by blacks recently arrived from the South than by those born in the urban ghettos as the German sociologists seventy years ago had been who claimed that immigrant Polish workers in the Ruhr coal districts were more lawless than native-born workers.

36. Hans Staudinger, "Das Kulturproblem und die Arbeiterpsyche," *Die Tat*, 5 (January 1914), 990–1002.

37. Robert Roberts, *The Classic Slum. Salford Life in the First Quarter of the Century* (Manchester: Manchester University Press, 1971), p. 109.

38. Peter N. Stearns, *Lives of Labor: Work in a Maturing Industrial Society* (New York: Holmes & Meier, 1975), p. 13. Much of my analysis here is based on this important book.

39. Ibid., p. 21.

40. Ibid., p. 353.

41. Standish Meacham, loc. cit., pp. 1363–64.

42. Jules Huret, *Enquête sur la question sociale en Europe* (Paris: Perrin, 1897), pp. 39–43. This work is based on a series of interviews conducted in 1892 by the author, a reporter for the Parisian daily *Le Figaro*.

43. Quoted by Eric E. Lampard, "The Urbanizing World," in Dyos and Wolff, *The Victorian City*, p. 29.

44. Göhre, op. cit., p. 28.

45. Roberts, op. cit., p. 23.

46. Wilhelm Brepohl, *Industrievolk im Wandel von der Agraren zur industriellen Daseinsform, dargestellt am Ruhrgebiet* (Tübingen: Mohr, 1957), p. 129.

47. John Foster, "Nineteenth-Century Towns—A Class Dimension," in H. J. Dyos, ed., *The Study of Urban History* (New York: St. Martin's, 1968), p. 283. On the miners in the Ruhr town of Bochum see David Crew, "Definitions of Modernity: Social Mobility in a German Town, 1880–1901," *Journal of Social History*, 7 (Fall 1973), 68. Crew argues that "Occupational group identity

may have been Germany's alternative to class; an alternative form of modernity, not just the persistence of traditionalism" (p. 74, n. 50).

48. See Guenther Roth, *Social Democrats in Imperial Germany* (Totowa, N.J.: Bedminster Press, 1963), passim.

49. Brian Simon, *Education and the Labour Movement, 1870–1920* (London: Lawrence & Wishart, 1965), p. 174.

50. Mona Ozouf, *L'Ecole, L'Eglise et la République, 1871–1914* (Paris: A. Colin, 1963), pp. 239–41. Within the French labor movement some revolutionary syndicalists (see Chapter 8) charged that the techniques for indoctrinating children in Socialist "nurseries" were as manipulative as those of the state schools. See Léon Clément and Maurice Bouchor, *Les Groupes de pupilles. L'éducation de l'enfant dans les milieux ouvriers* (Paris: Éditions de "La Vie ouvreière," 1913), p. 16.

51. *Studies of Boy Life in Our Cities* (London: J. M. Dent, 1904), pp. 57–60.

52. Charles E. B. Russell, op. cit., pp. 48–49.

53. Roberts, op. cit., p. 129.

54. Quoted in Thomas and Znaniecki, op. cit., p. 1218.

55. Illyés, *People of the Puszta*, p. 144.

56. Blythe, op. cit., p. 36.

57. Stearns, op. cit., p. 285.

58. Giddens, op. cit., p. 222.

CHAPTER 5

1. Fred Weinstein and Gerald M. Platt, *The Wish to Be Free: Society, Psyche, and Value Change* (Berkeley: University of California Press, 1969), p. 219.

2. The quotations in this paragraph are from John Milton Yinger, *The Scientific Study of Religion* (New York: Macmillan, 1970), p. 7.

3. *Wandlungen der deutschen Familie in der Gegenwart* (Stuttgart: F. Enke, 1954), p. 270.

4. Annemarie Burger, *Religionszugehörigkeit und soziales Verhalten. Untersuchungen und Statistiken der neuren Zeit in Deutschland* (Göttingen: Vandenhoeck & Ruprecht, 1964), pp. 358–59.

5. On French religious practice see Gabriel Le Bras, *Études de sociologie religieuse*, 2 vols. (Paris: Presses Universitaires de France, 1955–56). The journal *Archives de Sociologie des Religions* is also indispensable for this topic.

6. The figures in this paragraph are from Burger, op. cit.

7. John Wordsworth, *The National Church of Sweden* (London: A. B. Mowbray, 1911), p. 425.

8. *The Condition of England* (London: Methuen, 1909), pp. 14 and 268.

9. Pelling, op. cit., p. 35.

10. A. A. Maclaren, "Presbyterianism and the Working Class in a Mid-nineteenth Century City," *Scottish Historical Review*, 46 (1967), 134.

11. See Anatole Leroy-Beaulieu, *L'Empire des Tsars*, 3 vols. (Paris: Hachette, 1898), III, *La religion;* Harold Williams, *Russia of the Russians*

(New York: Scribner, 1914); Maurice Baring, *What I Saw in Russia* (New York: T. Nelson, 1913). Donald Treadgold, in his chapter "The Peasant and Religion," in Wayne Vucinich, ed., *The Peasant in Nineteenth Century Russia* (Stanford, Cal.: Stanford University Press, 1968), pp. 102–3, quotes the Soviet historian Vladimir Bonch-Bruevich on the revival of religious fervor among the Orthodox and schismatic peasants.

12. Kenneth Scott Latourette, *Christianity in a Revolutionary Age. A History of Christianity in the Nineteenth and Twentieth Centuries,* 5 vols. (Westport, Conn.: Greenwood Press, 1973), I, 356.

13. Ibid., p. 467.

14. *D'Amour et d'anarchie. Récit de la vie d'une femme de militant,* as told to Claire Sainte-Soline (Paris: Grasset, 1955), pp. 48–49.

15. René Rémond, "Présentation," *Le Mouvement Social,* 57 (October–December 1966), 12. This entire issue is devoted to the Church and the French working classes during the nineteenth and twentieth centuries. See also François André Isambert, *Christianisme et classe ouvrière* (Paris: Casterman, 1961), passim.

16. Göhre, op. cit., pp. 144–53.

17. Quoted in Kenneth Stanley Inglis, *Churches and the Working Classes in Victorian England* (London: Routledge & Kegan Paul, 1963), p. 60.

18. Joseph Arch, *The Story of His Life, Told by Himself* (London: Hutchinson, 1898), pp. 8, 18, and 21.

19. *La Vie Ouvrière,* September 20, 1910.

20. Stephen Reynolds, *A Poor Man's House* (London: John Lane, 1911), p. 104.

21. *The Living Message of the Church for Today* (London: National Council of Evangelical Free Churches, n.d.), p. 444.

22. Frederick St. George de Latour Booth-Tucker, *The Life of Catherine Booth, the Mother of the Salvation Army,* 2 vols. (New York: Fleming H. Revell, 1892), II, p. 234.

23. Arch R. Wiggins, *The History of the Salvation Army,* 5 vols. (London: T. Nelson, 1964), IV, pp. 268–79.

24. See note 21, loc. cit.

25. *Christianity and the Social Order* (London: Chapman and Hall, 1907), p. 18.

26. Peter d'A. Jones, *The Christian Socialist Revival, 1877–1914. Religion, Class, and Social Conscience in Late-Victorian England* (Princeton, N.J.: Princeton University Press, 1968), p. 458.

27. See Charles Molette, *L'Association Catholique de la Jeunesse Française, 1886–1907* (Paris: A. Colin, 1968), and Henri Rollet, *L'Action sociale des catholiques en France, 1871–1914,* 2 vols. (Bruges: Desclée de Brouwer, 1958). On Social Catholicism in Belgium see Rudolf Rezsohazy, *Les Origines et la formation du catholicisme social en Belgique, 1842–1909* (Louvain: Bibliothèque de l'Université, 1958).

28. See Gabriele De Rosa, *Storia politica dell'azione cattolica in Italia,* 2 vols. (Bari: Laterza, 1953–54).

29. Quoted in Edward Shorter, "Towards a History of *La Vie Intime:* The

Evidence of Cultural Criticism in Nineteenth-Century Bavaria," in Michael R. Marrus, ed., *The Emergence of Leisure* (New York: Harper & Row, 1974), p. 48.

30. The quotations in this paragraph are from Weinstein and Platt, op. cit., pp. 221–23.

31. See Philippe Ariès, *Centuries of Childhood: A Social History of Family Life* (New York: Vintage, 1965); John R. Gillis, *Youth and History: Tradition and Change in European Age Relations 1770–Present* (New York: Academic Press, 1974); and Edward Shorter, *The Making of the Modern Family* (New York: Basic Books, 1975).

32. Frank Musgrove, "Population Changes and the Status of the Young in England since the 18th Century," *Sociological Review*, 11 (1963), 80.

33. Walther Jantzen, "Die soziologische Herkunft der Führungsschicht der deutschen Jugendbewegung, 1900–33," in *Führungsschicht und Eliteproblem* (Frankfurt: Diesterweg, 1957), p. 130.

34. Walter Laqueur, *Young Germany: A History of the German Youth Movement* (New York: Basic Books, 1962), p. 44.

35. Ibid., p. 57. See also Harry Pross, *Jugend, Eros, Politik; die Geschichte der deutschen Jugendverbände* (Bern: Scherz, 1964).

36. Edward Shorter, "Illegitimacy, Sexual Revolution, and Social Change in Modern Europe," *Journal of Interdisciplinary History*, 2 (1971), 254.

37. Ibid., pp. 252–53, 256.

38. Göhre, op. cit., pp. 202–3.

39. Abraham Flexner, *Prostitution in Europe* (New York: Century, 1914), pp. 43–45.

40. Sigmund Freud, "Contributions to the Psychology of Love," in *Collected Papers*, 5 vols. (London: Hogarth Press, 1950–56), IV, p. 210.

41. Germany. Reichstag, *Stenographische Berichte über die Verhandlungen*, 9th Legislative Session, 1897–98, I, p. 410. See also James D. Steakley, *The Homosexual Emancipation Movement in Germany* (New York: Arno Press, 1975).

42. Max Nordau, *Degeneration* (New York and London: D. Appleton, 1912), p. 5.

43. Ibid., p. 261.

44. Ibid., p. 461.

CHAPTER 6

1. Emile Cheysson, "Les Réformes de la statistique de la criminalité en France," report made at the Société Générale des Prisons, November 10, 1909, and published in the *Revue Pénitentiaire et de Droit Pénal* (November–December 1909); Donald Read, op. cit., p. 51.

2. Asa Briggs, "Work and Leisure in Industrial Society," *Past and Present*, No. 30 (April 1965), 98; Michael R. Marrus, "Social Drinking in the Belle Epoque," *Journal of Social History*, 7 (Winter 1974), 132–33.

3. Walter Kiaulehn, *Berlin Schicksal einer Weltstadt* (Munich, Berlin: Biederstein, 1958), p. 389.

4. Ibid., p. 393.

5. Charles E. B. Russell, op. cit., p. 87; see also Charles E. B. Russell and E. T. Campagnac, "Poor People's Music-Halls in Lancashire," *Economic Review*, 10 (1900), 389–98. Two recent surveys are: Laurence Senelick, "A Brief Life and Times of the Victorian Music-Hall," *Harvard Library Bulletin*, 19 (1971), 375–98, and Martha Vicinus, *The Industrial Muse: A Study of Nineteenth-Century Working-Class Literature* (London: Croom Helm, 1974), Chapter 6, "The Music Hall," pp. 238–85.

6. Barea, op. cit., p. 320.

7. John Maynard Keynes, *The Economic Consequences of the Peace* (London: Macmillan, 1919), p. 10.

8. Roberts, *The Classic Slum*, p. 130.

9. Charles E. B. Russell, op. cit., p. 52.

10. Ibid., p. 75f.

11. See Eugen Weber, "Gymnastics and Sports in *Fin-de-Siècle* France: Opium of the Classes?," *American Historical Review*, 76 (February 1970), 85.

12. Ibid., p. 92.

13. Op. cit., p. 325.

14. John Arlot, "Sport," in Nowell-Smith, op. cit., p. 471.

15. Op. cit., pp. 127–28.

16. Ernest A. Baker, *The Library Association Record*, Vol. 9, cited by Derek Hudson, "Reading," in Nowell-Smith, op. cit., p. 310.

17. My information about Courths-Mahler was derived from the following studies: Walter Krieg, *"Unser Weg ging hinauf," Hedwig Courths-Mahler und ihre Töchter als literarisches Phänomen* (Vienna: H. Stubenrauch, 1954); Gertrud Willemborg, "Adel und Authorität zu den Romanen der Courths-Mahler," in *Trivialliteratur. Aufsätze* (Berlin: Literarisches Colloquium, 1964), pp. 192–217; Gustav Sichelschmidt, *Hedwig Courths-Mahler, Deutschlands erfolgreichste Autorin; eines literatursoziologische Studie* (Bonn: H. Bouvier, 1967). I owe a special debt to my friend Ella Anderson for describing to me in detail the Courths-Mahler novels she had read fifty years ago while she was a student in the *Gymnasium*.

18. Noël Arnand, Francis Lacassin, and Jean Tortel, eds., *Entretiens sur la paralittérature* (Paris: Plon, 1970), p. 103.

19. Ibid., p. 86.

20. Roberts, op. cit., p. 142n.

21. Claude Bellanger, Jacques Godechot, Pierre Guiral, and Fernand Terrou, *Histoire générale de la presse française*, 3 vols. (Paris: Presses Universitaires de France, 1969–72), III, p. 297.

22. In 1885 the total population of Bremen was 118,000 and the total number of local papers sold each day was 23,600; in 1914 the figures were 247,000 and 86,000. See Rolf Engelsing, *Massenpublikum und Journalistentum im 19. Jahrhundert in Nordwestdeutschland* (Berlin: Duncker & Humblot, 1966), p. 285.

23. Francis Williams, *The Right to Know. The Rise of the World Press* (London: Longmans, 1969), p. 65.

24. Engelsing, op. cit., pp. 277–78.

25. See Francine Amaury, *Histoire du plus grand quotidien de la IIIe République. Le Petit Parisien, 1876–1944,* 2 vols. (Paris: Presses Universitaires de France, 1972).

26. The quotations of Harmsworth in this paragraph are taken from Reginald Pound and Geoffrey Harmsworth, *Northcliffe* (London: Cassell, 1959). Most of my observations are based on my own perusal of pre-1914 issues of the *Daily Mail* in the British Museum Newspaper Library.

27. Williams, op. cit., p. 75.

28. Ibid., p. 68.

29. See *Facsimile Querschnitt durch die Gartenlaube* (Bern-Stuttgart-Vienna: Scherz, 1963).

30. See Ernest K. Bramsted, *Aristocracy and the Middle-Classes in Germany: Social Types in German Literature 1830–1900,* rev. ed. (Chicago: University of Chicago Press, 1964), pp. 209–15, and Ruth Horovitz, *Vom Roman des Junge Deutschland zum Roman der Gartenlaube; ein Beitrag zur Geschichte des deutschen Liberalismus* (Breslau: M. & H. Marcus, 1937).

CHAPTER 7

1. *Pragmatisme et sociologie* (1955), pp. 142–43, quoted in Anthony Giddens, ed., *Émile Durkheim: Selected Writings* (London: Cambridge University Press, 1972), p. 252.

2. See Walter Kaufmann's more accurate edition of Friedrich Nietzsche, *The Will to Power* (London: Weidenfeld & Nicolson, 1969). The interpretations in the following paragraphs come from Kaufmann's *Nietzsche, Philosopher, Psychologist, Antichrist,* 3rd ed. (New York: Vintage Books, 1968).

3. For a recent study of this aspect of the Bayreuth festivals see Winfried Schüler, *Der Bayreuther Kreis von seiner Entstehung bis zum Ausgang der Wilheminischen Ära: Wagnerkult und Kulturreform im Geiste Völkischer Weltanschauung* (Münster: Verlag Aschendorff, 1971).

4. Quoted in Kaufmann, ed., *The Will to Power,* p. 86.

5. See, for example, Geneviève Bianquis, *Nietzsche en France* (Paris: F. Alcan, 1929) and David S. Thatcher, *Nietzsche in England 1890–1914* (Toronto: University of Toronto Press, 1970).

6. Quoted in Gerhard Masur, *Imperial Berlin* (New York: Basic Books, 1970), p. 199.

7. *History as the Story of Liberty* (London: George Allen & Unwin, 1941), pp. 32–33. This work was a continuation of Croce's *Theory and History of the Writing of History,* written in 1912–13.

8. See Wilma Abeles Iggers, *Karl Kraus: A Viennese Critic of the Twentieth Century* (The Hague: Nijhoff, 1967).

9. "Politics and the Psyche in *fin-de-siècle* Vienna: Schnitzler and Hofmannsthal," *American Historical Review,* 66 (July 1961), 935.

10. Allan Janik and Stephen Toulmin, *Wittgenstein's Vienna* (New York: Simon and Schuster, 1973), pp. 75–80.

11. Ibid., p. 198.

12. Ludwig Wittgenstein, *Tractatus Logico-Philosophicus* (New York: Harcourt, Brace, 1922), 3.3.

13. Janik and Toulmin, op. cit., pp. 186–87.

14. *Tractatus*, 6.54.

15. See Henri F. Ellenberger, *The Discovery of the Unconscious. The History and Evolution of Dynamic Psychiatry* (New York: Basic Books, 1970).

16. Richard Wollheim, *Sigmund Freud* (New York: Viking, 1971), p. ix.

17. Quoted in ibid., p. 27.

18. *The Standard Edition of the Complete Psychological Works of Sigmund Freud*, edited by James Strachey, 23 vols. (London: Hogarth Press, 1953–64), V, 608. Quotations from this edition will be noted with the volume and page numbers only.

19. Ibid., XV, 216.

20. Ibid., XV, 83.

21. Ibid., XV, 72.

22. Ibid., VI, 80.

23. Ibid., XVI, 314.

24. Ibid., X, 241.

25. *The Coming Crisis of Western Sociology* (New York: Basic Books, 1970), p. 116.

26. H. Stuart Hughes, *Consciousness and Society. The Reorientation of European Social Thought, 1890–1930* (New York: Knopf, 1961), p. 16.

27. See Talcott Parsons, *The Structure of Social Action. A Study in Social Theory with Special Reference to a Group of Recent European Writers* (New York: The Free Press, 1949). The most recent sociological theory tends to reject Parsons' effort to link Pareto, Durkheim, and Weber through his concept of "the structure of social action."

28. *The Mind and Society. A Treatise on General Sociology*, 4 vols. bound as 2 (New York: Dover, 1963), III, 1915.

29. Ibid., p. 1202.

30. Ibid., p. 1214.

31. Ibid., p. 1432.

32. Ibid., p. 1217.

33. *Suicide* (New York: The Free Press, 1951), p. 253. The best recent treatment of Durkheim is Steven Lukes, *Émile Durkheim. His Life and Work, a Historical and Critical Study* (London: Allen Lane, 1973).

34. *Suicide*, p. 391.

35. *The Elementary Forms of the Religious Life* (London: George Allen & Unwin, 1915), p. 94.

36. *De la division du travail social*, 7th ed. (1960), p. 182, quoted in Anthony Giddens, op. cit., p. 12.

37. See Peter L. Berger and Thomas Luckmann, *The Social Construction of Reality. A Treatise in the Sociology of Knowledge* (Garden City, N.Y.: Anchor, 1967).

38. *Elementary Forms*, p. 444.

39. Ibid.

40. In an article entitled "Individual and Collective Representations," published in 1898 in the *Revue de Métaphysique et de Morale*, translated and

republished in *Sociology and Philosophy* (New York: The Free Press, 1953), p. 34.

41. *Economy and Society. An Outline of Interpretive Sociology*, edited by Guenther Roth and Claus Wittich, 3 vols. (New York: Bedminster Press, 1968), I, 4. Weber conceived this major work in 1914, and it includes sections written before then. But he died before finishing it, and much of it has been edited from first drafts.

42. Ibid., p. 58.

43. Ibid., p. 12.

44. " 'Objectivity' in the Social Sciences and Social Policy" (originally published in 1904), in *The Methodology of the Social Sciences*, translated and edited by Edward A. Shils and Henry A. Finch (New York: The Free Press, 1949), pp. 89–90.

45. Ibid., pp. 110–11.

46. *Economy and Society*, III, 983.

47. See for example his remarks at the 1909 convention of the *Verein für Sozialpolitik* as quoted by Reinhard Bendix, *Max Weber: An Intellectual Portrait* (Garden City, N.Y.: Doubleday, 1960), pp. 455–56.

48. *Economy and Society*, III, 1002.

49. Michel Crozier, *The Bureaucratic Phenomenon* (Chicago: The University of Chicago Press, 1964), p. 177.

50. See Herbert Spencer, *Principles of Sociology*, 1876–96, and *Man Versus the State*, 1884.

51. Berger and Luckmann, op. cit., p. 18.

52. Ibid., p. 61.

53. On the theory of ego-oriented integrative behavior as a corrective to Freud's emphasis on drives and defenses, see Fred Weinstein and Gerald M. Platt, "The Coming Crisis in Psychohistory," *Journal of Modern History*, 47 (June 1975), 202–28.

CHAPTER 8

1. Jules Huret, *Enquête sur la question sociale en Europe* (Paris: Perrin, 1897), p. 248.

2. See Harvey Mitchell and Peter N. Stearns, *Workers and Protest: The European Labor Movement, the Working Classes and the Origins of Social Democracy 1890–1914* (Itasca, Ill.: Peacock, 1971).

3. The theoretical literature on protest movements is cogently discussed in Charles Tilly, Louise Tilly, and Richard Tilly, *The Rebellious Century, 1830–1930* (Cambridge, Mass.: Harvard University Press, 1975), an important attempt to formulate a new theory and typology based on the experiences of France, Germany, and Italy.

4. This section is based mainly on the following works: *Anarchici e anarchia nel mondo contemporaneo*, Atti del Convegno promosso dalla Fondazione Luigi Einaudi, Turin, December 5–7, 1969 (Turin: Fondazione Luigi Einaudi, 1971); Eduardo Colomer Comín, *Historia del anarquismo español* (Madrid: Editorial R.A.D.A.R., 1948); Jean Maitron, *Histoire du mouvement*

anarchiste en France, 1880–1914 (Paris: Société Universitaire d'Éditions et de Librairie, 1955); James Joll, *The Anarchists* (New York: Grosset & Dunlap, 1966); George Woodcock, *Anarchism* (Cleveland: World Publishing Co.-Meridian Books, 1962); and Paul Avrich, *The Russian Anarchists* (Princeton, N.J.: Princeton University Press, 1967).

5. J. Romero Maura, "Terrorism in Barcelona and Its Impact on Spanish Politics, 1904–1909," *Past and Present*, No. 41 (December 1968), 156.

6. See Georges Lefranc, *Le Mouvement syndical sous la troisième République* (Paris: Payot, 1967); Frederick F. Ridley, *Revolutionary Syndicalism in France: The Direct Action of Its Time* (London: Cambridge University Press, 1970); Peter N. Stearns, *Revolutionary Syndicalism and French Labor: A Cause Without Rebels* (New Brunswick, N.J.: Rutgers University Press, 1971); and Jacques Julliard, *Fernand Pelloutier et les origines du syndicalisme d'action directe* (Paris: Éditions du Seuil, 1971). Julliard's full-scale study of revolutionary syndicalism is in press at the time of this writing.

7. Julliard, op. cit., p. 259.

8. Appeal of March 15, 1895, of the Fédération Nationale des Bourses du Travail to the craft and industrial unions to set up local Bourses; cited in ibid., p. 235.

9. *Action directe*, April 23, 1908.

10. *La Bataille syndicaliste*, July 15, 1913.

11. See Carl Landauer, *European Socialism: A History of Ideas and Movements*, 2 vols. (Berkeley: University of California Press, 1959); Jacques Droz, *Le Socialisme démocratique, 1864–1960* (Paris: A. Colin, 1966); George Lichtheim, *A Short History of Socialism* (New York: Praeger, 1970); Leslie Derfler, *Socialism Since Marx. A Century of the European Left* (New York: St. Martin's, 1973); and Julius Braunthal, *The International*, I, *1864–1914* (New York: Praeger, 1968).

12. J. Peter Nettl, *Rosa Luxemburg* (London: Oxford University Press, 1966), pp. 12–13.

13. Robert Wohl, Introduction to Mitchell and Stearns, op. cit., p. 7.

14. On pages 318–34 of their book *Strikes in France, 1830–1968* (London: Cambridge University Press, 1974) Edward Shorter and Charles Tilly find a remarkable similarity in the level of strike activity from 1900 to 1929 in France, Germany, Belgium, Italy, and Spain. In all five countries the duration of strikes was in the 10–20 day range, the number of workers per strike was in the 300–400 range, and the annual rate of strikes per 100,000 workers was in the 6–12 range. Britain's strike profile during the same period was quite different: longer but fewer strikes with almost three times the average number of participants. Shorter and Tilly suggest that the difference in the British level of strike activity had something to do with "a reformist union tradition within the context of great industrial concentration." It may also have been related to the earlier achievement of political representation and citizenship rights by British workers, in comparison with those in the five Continental countries. In any case, during the immediate prewar years Britain experienced a wave of industrial action for political ends. See Henry Pelling, *Popular Politics and Society in Late Victorian Britain* (London: Macmillan, 1968), Chap-

ter 9, "The Labour Unrest, 1911–14"; Standish Meacham, "'The Sense of Impending Clash': English Working-Class Unrest Before the First World War," *American Historical Review*, 77 (December 1972), 1343–64; Ernest Henry Phelps Brown, *The Growth of British Industrial Relations* (London: Macmillan, 1959), Chapter 7, "Strife, 1906–1914."

15. Peter N. Stearns, in Mitchell and Stearns, op. cit., pp. 141–45.

16. See H. Llewellyn Smith and Vaughn Nash, *The Story of the Dockers' Strike, Told by Two East Londoners* (London: Unwin, 1890), and Max Jürgen Koch, *Die Bergarbeiterbewegung im Ruhrgebiet zur Zeit Wilhelms II, 1889–1914* (Düsseldorf: Droste-Verlag, 1959).

17. Robert Arthur Leeson, *Strike. A Live History, 1887–1971* (London: Allen & Unwin, 1973), p. 41.

18. Carl E. Schorske, *German Social Democracy, 1905–1917* (New York: Wiley, 1965), p. 52.

19. Unofficial Reform Committee, S.W.M.F., *The Miners' Next Step* (Tonypandy, 1912), p. 30, quoted in Pelling, op. cit., p. 157.

20. Pelling, op. cit., p. 160.

21. Joan Wallach Scott, op. cit., pp. 139–59; the quotations are from pp. 142–43 and 159.

22. K. Oldenberg, "Der Berliner Bierboykott im Jahre 1894," *Schmollers Jahrbuch*, 20-(1896), 261–93.

23. Louise Tilly, "*I Fatti di Maggio:* The Working Class of Milan and the Rebellion of 1898," in Robert J. Bezucha, ed., *Modern European Social History* (Lexington, Mass.: D. C. Heath, 1972), p. 148.

24. See Joan Connelly Ullman, *The Tragic Week. A Study of Anticlericalism in Spain, 1875–1912* (Cambridge, Mass.: Harvard University Press, 1968).

25. See pp. 294–96 and 321–22. The best over-all study is Sidney Harcave, *First Blood: The Russian Revolution of 1905* (New York: Macmillan, 1964).

26. Barrington Moore, Jr., *Social Origins of Dictatorship and Democracy. Lord and Peasant in the Making of the Modern World* (Boston: Beacon Press, 1966), p. 477; see also Eric Wolf, *Peasant Wars of the Twentieth Century* (New York: Harper & Row, 1969); and Eric J. Hobsbawm, *Primitive Rebels: Studies in Archaic Forms of Social Movement in the 19th and 20th Centuries* (New York: Norton, 1965). My main authorities for the uprisings described in this section are: Salvatore Francesco Romano, *Storia dei fasci siciliani* (Bari: Laterza, 1959); Philip Gabriel Eidelberg, *The Great Rumanian Peasant Revolt of 1907. Origins of a Modern Jacquerie* (Leiden: Brill, 1974); Henry L. Roberts, *Rumania: Political Problems of an Agrarian State* (Hamden, Conn.: Archon Books, 1969), pp. 3–21; and Harcave, op. cit.

27. Quoted in Romano, op. cit., p. 234.

28. Maureen Perrie, "The Russian Peasant Movement of 1905–1907: Its Social Composition and Revolutionary Significance," *Past and Present*, No. 57 (November 1972), 124.

29. Harcave, op. cit., p. 218.

30. Quoted in ibid., pp. 268–73.

31. Quoted in Henry L. Roberts, op. cit., p. 5.

32. *Feminism in Germany and Scandinavia* (New York: Holt, 1916), pp. 230–31.

33. Much of the information in this paragraph comes from the *Report of the International Congress of Women*, Toronto, June 24–30, 1909, 2 vols. (Toronto: George Parker & Sons, 1910); Susanne C. Engelmann, *German Education and Re-education* (New York: International Universities Press, 1945); Edmée Charrier, *L'Évolution intellectuelle féminine* (Paris: A. Mechelinck, 1931); and *The Woman's Movement in the Netherlands* (Pamphlet, Leiden, n.d.–c. 1915). On the struggle of English women to enter the professions see William Joseph Reader, *Professional Men: The Rise of the Professional Classes in Nineteenth-Century England* (London: Weidenfeld & Nicolson, 1966). On changing ideas and social attitudes toward higher education for English women see Elaine Kay, *A History of Queen's College, London, 1848–1972* (London: Chatto & Windus, 1972).

34. *The Renaissance of Motherhood* (New York: G. P. Putnam's Sons, 1914), p. 89.

35. Quoted in Anthony, op. cit., p. 7.

36. The material in this paragraph is based on Gabriele Swecker, *Hundert Jahre Frauenbewegung in Deutschland* (Pamphlet, printed by the Wiesbadener Graphische Betriebe, Wiesbaden, 1951); *Alice Salomon, Die Begründerin des sozialen Frauenberufs in Deutschland. Ihr Leben und ihr Werk* (Cologne: Carl Heymanns, 1958); and Anthony, op. cit.

37. In addition to the titles already cited, the following works on individual countries were helpful to me: on Belgium, Louise van den Plas, *Féminisme. Souvenirs de vingt ans d'efforts* (Pamphlet, printed by the Librairie Albert Dewit, Brussels, 1922); Maria de los Laffitte y Pérez del Pulgar, *La Mujer en España. Cien años de la historia, 1860–1960* (Madrid: Aguilar, 1964); Marie Thérèse Renard, *La Participation des femmes à la vie civique* (Paris: Les Éditions Ouvrières, 1965); and Franca Pieroni Bortolotti, *Socialismo e questione femminile in Italia, 1892–1922* (Milan: Gabriele Mazzotta, 1974).

38. See Adelheid Dwořak-Popp, *Der Weg zur Höhe; die sozialdemokratische Frauenbewegung Österreichs; ihr Aufbau and ihr Aufstieg* (Vienna: Frauenzentralkomitee der Sozialdemokratischen Arbeiterpartei Deutschösterreichs, 1930), especially pp. 31–33.

39. *Les Droits de la femme* (Paris: Marcel Rivière, 1912), p. 126.

40. Quoted in E. Sylvia Pankhurst, *The Suffragette* (New York: Sturgis & Walton, 1911), p. 22.

41. Théodore Joran, *Autour du feminisme* (Paris: Plon-Nourrit, 1906) and Émile Faguet, *Le Féminisme* (Paris: Société Française d'Imprimerie et de Librairie, 1910).

42. *The Fraud of Feminism* (London: Grant Richards, 1913), pp. 66–75 and 163.

43. *Revolted Women: Past, Present, and to Come* (London: Elkin Matthews, 1894), p. xi.

44. "Woman Suffrage," *Quarterly Review*, January 1909, 303.

45. United Kingdom. *The Parliamentary Debates (Official Report)*, Fifth Series, Vol. 25, p. 764.

46. *An Englishwoman's Home* (London: Sampson Low, Marston, 1909), p. 154.

47. *Woman, or,—Suffragette?* (Pamphlet, printed by Horace Cox. London, 1907), pp. 14–15.

48. London *Times*, July 22, 1908.

49. Miss Gladys Post at a newly formed branch of the National League for Opposing Woman Suffrage, quoted in the *Manchester Guardian*, October 21, 1911.

50. This exchange took place in *The Standard* in 1912 or 1913. The press clippings I read in the Fawcett Library in London are undated.

51. Rosa Mayreder, *A Survey of the Woman Problem* (New York: G. H. Doran, 1913), p. 89.

52. Constance Rover, *Love, Morals and the Feminists* (London: Routledge & Kegan Paul, 1970), p. 145.

53. Much of my material on the WSPU comes from the excellent monograph by Andrew Rosen: *Rise Up, Women! The Militant Campaign of the Women's Social and Political Union, 1903–1914* (London: Routledge & Kegan Paul, 1974).

54. Quoted in ibid., p. 77n.

55. Rosen, op. cit., pp. 138–39.

56. Ibid., p. 242.

CHAPTER 9

1. Nationalism, like modernization, has taken diverse forms at various times and in different parts of the world. The definitions given here are derived from the European experience in the late nineteenth and early twentieth centuries and are offered only to elucidate that experience. For an analysis of those definitions and typologies that try to relate nationalism to modernization in all parts of the world through the 1960's see Anthony D. Smith, *Theories of Nationalism* (New York: Harper & Row, 1971).

2. Hans Kohn, *The Idea of Nationalism* (New York: Macmillan, 1944, 1967), p. 16.

3. Smith, op. cit., p. 171. The "core doctrine" that follows is from Smith, p. 21.

4. Boyd C. Shafer, *Faces of Nationalism: New Realities and Old Myths* (New York: Harcourt Brace Jovanovich, 1972), p. 13. The literature on nationalism is enormous. See the bibliography in Shafer's book and Karl W. Deutsch and Richard L. Merritt, *Nationalism and National Development; an Indisciplinary Bibliography* (Cambridge, Mass.: MIT Press, 1970).

5. Smith, op. cit., p. 107. An excellent study of some positive effects of nationalism in France is Eugen Weber's forthcoming *Peasants into Frenchmen: The Modernization of Rural France, 1870–1914.*

6. Ernst Schürch, *Sprachpolitische Erinnerungen* (Bern: Paul Haupt Verlag, 1943), pp. 36–37.

7. Christian Spielmann, *Deutsche Geschichte vom Ende des grossen Krieges bis zum des zwanzigsten Jahrhunderts* (Halle: Gesenius, 1908), p. 612.

8. This section is based on J. O. Springhall, "The Boy Scouts, Class and Militarism in Relation to British Youth Movements, 1908–1930," *International Review of Social History*, 16 (1971), 125–58. See also Paul Wilkinson, "English Youth Movements, 1908–1930," *Journal of Contemporary History*, 4 (April 1969), 3–23.

9. E.g., *Le Devoir militaire. Manuel d'éducation militaire* by H. B. (Paris: Libraire Militaire R. Chapelot, 1909).

10. Amaury, op. cit., I, p. 270n.

11. See Raymond Lindgren, *Norway-Sweden: Union, Disunion, Reunion* (Princeton: Princeton University Press, 1959), and Karl W. Deutsch, *et al.*, *Political Community and the North Atlantic Area* (Princeton, N.J.: Princeton University Press, 1957).

12. See Harcave, op. cit.

13. Alberto Aquarone, "A Concluding Commentary," in Edward R. Tannenbaum and Emiliana P. Noether, op. cit., p. 365.

14. Christ Anastasoff, *The Tragic Peninsula: A History of the Macedonian Movement for Independence Since 1878* (St. Louis: Blackwell Wielandy, 1938), p. 90n.

15. The most balanced and up-to-date accounts of modern Irish nationalism are F. S. L. Lyons, *Ireland Since the Famine* (London: Collins/Fontana, 1973); J. C. Becket, *The Making of Modern Ireland* (New York: Knopf, 1966); Nicholas Mansergh, *The Irish Question: A Commentary on Anglo-Irish Relations and on Social and Political Forces in the Age of Reform and Revolution* (London: Allen & Unwin, 1965); Owen Dudley Edwards, *et al.*, *Celtic Nationalism* (London: Routledge & Kegan Paul, 1968); Lawrence McCaffrey, *The Irish Question, 1800–1922* (Lexington: University of Kentucky Press, 1968); and Joseph Lee, *The Modernization of Irish Society* (Dublin: Gill & Macmillan, 1973).

16. Edwards, op. cit., pp. 88–89.

17. Lyons, op. cit., p. 168.

18. Lee, op. cit., p. 150.

19. Ibid., p. 52.

20. Sybil E. Baker, "Orange and Green," in Dyos and Wolff, op. cit., p. 809.

21. See Edward R. Tannenbaum, *The Action Française: Die-hard Reactionaries in Twentieth-Century France* (New York: Wiley, 1962), and Eugen Weber, *Action Française* (Stanford, Cal.: Stanford University Press, 1962).

22. See Eugen Weber, *The Nationalist Revival in France, 1905–1914* (Berkeley: University of California Press, 1959).

23. See Fritz Stern, *The Politics of Cultural Despair* (Berkeley: University of California Press, 1961), and George L. Mosse, *The Crisis of German Ideology* (New York: Grosset & Dunlap, 1964).

24. Peter G. J. Pulzer, *The Rise of Political Anti-Semitism in Germany and Austria* (New York: Wiley, 1964), pp. 145–60. See also Andrew G. Whiteside, *The Socialism of Fools: Georg Ritter von Schönerer and Austrian Pan-Germanism* (Berkeley: University of California Press, 1975).

25. Mildred Salz Wertheimer, *The Pan-German League, 1890–1914* (New York: Columbia University Studies in History, Economics, and Public Law,

1924), p. 65, and Alfred Kruck, *Geschichte des Alldeutscher Verbandes* (Wiesbaden: F. Steiner, 1954), p. 18.

26. See Franco Gaeta, *Nazionalismo italiano* (Naples: Edizioni Scientifiche Italiane, 1965), pp. 71–125, and John A. Thayer, *Italy and the Great War: Politics and Culture, 1870–1915* (Madison: University of Wisconsin Press, 1964), pp. 191–229.

27. *Classi proletarie: socialismo, nazioni proletarie, nazionalismo,* in *Il nazionalismo italiano. Atti del congresso di Firenze* (Florence: 1911), pp. 22–35, cited in Gaeta, op. cit., p. 85. See also Corradini's "Le nazioni proletari e il nazionalismo," in *Discorsi politici, 1902–1923* (Florence: Vallecchi, 1923), p. 13.

28. Gaeta, op. cit., pp. 94–95.

29. "Che cosa è il nazionalismo e che cosa vogliono i nazionalisti," in *Scritti e discorsi politici,* 3 vols. (Milan: A. Giuffrè, 1938), I, 89.

30. The material in this section is based on the following works: Salo W. Baron, *The Russian Jew Under Tsars and Soviets* (New York: Macmillan, 1964); Norman Bentwich, "The Social Transformation of Anglo-Jewry, 1883–1960," *Jewish Journal of Sociology,* 1 (April 1960), 94–112; Michael R. Marrus, *The Politics of Assimilation: a Study of the French Jewish Community at the Time of the Dreyfus Affair* (Oxford: Clarendon Press, 1971); H. G. Adler, *The Jews in Germany; from the Enlightenment to National Socialism* (Notre Dame, Ind.: University of Notre Dame Press, 1969); Ismar Schorsch, *Jewish Reactions to German Anti-Semitism, 1870–1914* (New York: Columbia University Press, 1972); Peter G. J. Pulzer, op. cit.; Uriel Tal, *Christians and Jews in Germany. Religion, Politics, and Ideology in the Second Reich, 1870–1914* (Ithaca, N.Y.: Cornell University Press, 1975); Jehuda Reinharz, *Fatherland or Promised Land: The Dilemma of the German Jew, 1893–1914* (Ann Arbor: University of Michigan Press, 1975); Mark Wischnitzer, *To Dwell in Safety: the Story of Jewish Migration Since 1800* (Philadelphia: Jewish Publication Society of America, 1948); Walter Laqueur, *A History of Zionism* (New York: Holt, Rinehart & Winston, 1972); Arthur Hertzberg, ed., *The Zionist Idea: a Historical Analysis and Reader* (Garden City, N.Y.: Doubleday, 1959).

31. See Bernard Gainer, *The Alien Invasion. The Origins of the Alien Act of 1905* (London: Heinemann Educational, 1972), and Lloyd P. Gartner, *The Jewish Immigrant in England* (London: Simon Publications, 1973).

32. Schorsch, op. cit., p. 16.

33. George L. Mosse, "The Image of the Jew in German Popular Culture," in Leo Baeck Institute for Jews from Germany, *Year Book,* 2 (1957), p. 226.

34. Lamar Cecil, *Albert Ballin: Business and Politics in Imperial Germany, 1888–1918* (Princeton, N.J.: Princeton University Press, 1967), pp. 37 and 109.

35. *The World of Yesterday* (New York: Viking, 1943), pp. 21–22.

36. Op. cit., p. 305.

37. Marrus, op. cit., p. 284.

38. From *Der Judenstaat* (1896), quoted in Hertzberg, op. cit., p. 209.

39. Bernard Semmel, *Imperialism and Social Reform: English Social-Imperial Thought, 1895–1914* (Garden City, N.Y.: Anchor, 1968), p. 12.

40. Richard Price, *An Imperial War and the British Working Class* (London: Routledge & Kegan Paul, 1972), p. 241. On the development of British social imperialism after 1900 see Robert J. Scally, *The Origins of the Lloyd George Coalition: The Politics of Social Imperialism 1900–1918* (Princeton, N.J.: Princeton University Press, 1975).

41. In Italy an important group of northern industrialists supported the National Association's version of social imperialism. See Richard A. Webster, *L'imperialismo industriale italiano, 1908–1915* (Turin: G. Einaudi, 1974), p. 355. This work has been published in English under the title *Industrial Imperialism in Italy, 1908–1915* (Berkeley: University of California Press, 1975).

CHAPTER 10

1. In addition to the works cited in the succeeding footnotes the following were particularly useful to me: Roger Shattuck, *The Banquet Years: The Arts in France, 1885–1918* (Garden City, N.Y.: Anchor, 1961); L. Brion-Guerry, ed., *L'Année 1913: Les formes esthétiques de l'oeuvre d'art à la veille de la première guerre mondiale,* 2 vols. (Paris: Klincksieck, 1971); George Heard Hamilton, *Painting and Sculpture in Europe 1880–1914* (Baltimore: Penguin, 1972); Gerhard Masur, *Prophets of Yesterday: Studies in European Culture, 1890–1914* (New York: Harper & Row, 1961); Michael Hamburger, *From Prophecy to Exorcism: The Premises of Modern German Literature* (London: Longmans, 1965); Raymond Williams, *Drama from Ibsen to Brecht* (London: Chatto & Windus, 1968); Wilfrid Mellers, *Caliban Reborn: Renewal in Twentieth-Century Music* (New York: Harper & Row, 1967).

2. Robert Estivals, Jean-Charles Gaudy, and Gabrielle Vergez, *"L'avant-garde": Étude historique et sociologique des publications périodiques ayant pour titre "L'avant-garde"* (Paris: Bibliothèque Nationale, 1968), p. 109.

3. "Politics and the Psyche in *fin-de-siècle* Vienna," *American Historical Review,* 65 (July 1961), 941.

4. Carl Schorske, "The Transformation of the Garden: Ideal and Society in Austrian Literature," *American Historical Review,* 72 (July 1967), 1317.

5. Joseph Peter Stern, in *Re-interpretations: Seven Studies in Nineteenth-Century German Literature* (New York: Basic Books, 1964), p. 298, makes the following distinction between Realism and Naturalism: "Realism . . . I have taken to mean no more than the fulfilment of an expectation which we carry from the social world into the work of art. It is distinct from . . . naturalism by the nature of the expectation it elicits in us; our expectation is not statically fixed by the facts of the social world but constantly modified, enriched and refined, by the work of art: by the art at work on our sensibility. That is, instead of being merely told what we know anyhow, we are shown what, but for the realism of the work, we should know less clearly, less meaningfully."

6. Quoted in Eugenia W. Herbert, *The Artist and Social Reform: France and Belgium, 1885–1898* (New Haven: Yale University Press, 1961), p. 165.

7. *Promenades littéraires,* Series I, 7th ed. (Paris: Mercure de France, 1916), p. 225.

8. *Eight Expressionist Plays by August Strindberg*, Introduction by John Gassner (New York: New York University Press, 1972), p. 9.

9. Ibid., p. 343.

10. Quoted by Lilla Cabot Perry in "An Interview with Monet," *The American Magazine of Art*, 18 (March 1927), 120.

11. *Jahre der Kämpfe* (Berlin: Rembrandt Verlag, 1934), p. 105.

12. *Concerning the Spiritual in Art* (New York: George Wittenborn, 1947), pp. 45 and 54.

13. Quoted in Eric A. Fivian, *Georg Kaiser und seine Stellung im Expressionismus* (Munich: Kurt Desch, 1946), p. 225.

14. Quoted in Bernard S. Myers, *The German Expressionists. A Generation in Revolt* (New York: Praeger, 1957), pp. 13–14.

15. *Fact and Symbol. Essays in the Sociology of Art and Literature* (London: Oxford University Press, 1971), p. xii.

16. "Offener Brief," *Neue Rundschau*, 21 (July 1910), 999.

17. *The Diaries of Franz Kafka, 1914–1923*, ed., Max Brod (New York: Schocken Books, 1949), p. 202.

18. Walter Sokel, *The Writer in Extremis* (Stanford, Cal.: Stanford University Press, 1959), p. 207.

19. Quoted in Gustav Janouch, *Conversations with Kafka* (New York: Praeger, 1953), pp. 99–100.

20. *The Disinherited Mind* (3rd ed., New York: Barnes & Noble, 1971), pp. 202 and 205.

21. All quotations in this paragraph are from the 1965 edition published by Alfred Knopf.

22. Wolfgang Rothe, *Schriftsteller und Totalitäre Welt* (Bern: A. Francke, 1966), p. 208.

23. The quotations in this paragraph are translated from Max Brod, *Schloss Nornepygge. Der Roman des Indifferenten* (Leipzig: Kurt Wolff Verlag, 1918), pp. 463–68.

24. Quoted in Sokel, op. cit., p. 48.

25. The quotations in this paragraph are from the 1927 Random House edition. Vol. 2, pp. 1121–24.

26. The quotations in this and the following paragraphs are translated from *Il fu Mattia Pascal*, in *Tutti i romanzi* (Milan: Mondadori, 1941).

27. Quoted in Max Kozloff, *Cubism/Futurism* (New York: Charterhouse, 1973), p. 12.

28. *Cubism and Twentieth-Century Art* (New York: Abrams, 1960), p. 60.

29. Quoted in Kozloff, op. cit., p. 201.

30. "Futurism Glorifies the Music-Hall," *Daily Mail*, November 21, 1913.

31. Dennis Sharp, *Modern Architecture and Expressionism* (New York: Braziller, 1966), p. 85.

32. Reyner Banham, *Theory and Design in the First Machine Age* (London: The Architectural Press, 1960), p. 87.

33. Quoted in Ludwig Münz, *Adolf Loos* (Milan: Il Balcone, 1956), p. 13.

34. Quoted in Allen Janik and Stephen Toulmin, op. cit., p. 252.

35. Adapted from the French translation in the catalogue of the Futurist ret-

rospective exhibition at the National Museum of Modern Art in Paris, September 19–November 19, 1973, pp. 128–31.

36. Ernest Gellner, *Legitimation of Belief* (London: Cambridge University Press, 1974), p. 107.

37. New York *Times*, January 29, 1974, p. 29.

APPENDIX

1. See Samuel P. Huntington, *Political Order in Changing Societies* (New Haven: Yale University Press, 1968).

2. Karl W. Deustch, "Social Mobilization and Political Development," *American Political Science Review*, 55 (September 1961), 494.

3. Alain Touraine, "It's All About to Come Tumbling Down," New York *Times*, December 27, 1974, p. 31.

4. Edward P. Thompson, "Time, Work-Discipline, and Industrial Capitalism," *Past and Present*, No. 38 (December 1967), 80. A good analysis of the usefulness of modernization theory for historians, along with an up-to-date bibliography, is to be found in Hans-Ulrich Wehler, *Modernisierungstheorie und Geschichte* (Göttingen: Vandenhoeck & Ruprecht, 1975). See also S. N. Eisenstadt, "Studies of Modernization and Sociological Theory," *History and Theory*, 13 (1974), 225–52.

INDEX

About the Author

Edward R. Tannenbaum received his B.A. and Ph.D. degrees from the University of Chicago and also studied abroad at the Universities of Paris and Grenoble. He has been awarded many grants, including ones from the Ford Foundation and the National Endowment for the Humanities, and has taught at Colorado State University and Rutgers University. He is currently professor of history at New York University and president of the Society for Italian Historical Studies.

Professor Tannenbaum's interest in European cultural history dates back to 1961 and the publication of his first book, *The New France*. His book *The Fascist Experience* was awarded the Howard Marraro Prize of the American Historical Association in 1973.

Please remember that this is a library book, and that it belongs only temporarily to each person who uses it. Be considerate. Do not write in this, or any, library book.